On the Preparation
and Delivery of Sermons

❖

ON THE PREPARATION

AND DELIVERY

OF SERMONS

BY

JOHN A. BROADUS

New and Revised Edition by

JESSE BURTON WEATHERSPOON, TH.D., D.D.

HARPER & ROW, PUBLISHERS

New York 18 17 and Evanston

PREFACE
to the New and Revised Edition

<hr>

THE first edition of Broadus' *Preparation and Delivery of Sermons* was published in 1870. In 1897 it was revised by Dr. E. C. Dargan, student of Dr. Broadus and his successor as professor in the Department of Homiletics at Louisville. That revision was made largely on the basis of Dr. Broadus' own notes and suggestions made in numerous conversations with the reviser. In 1926 Dr. C. S. Gardner, successor to Dr. Dargan, revised the bibliography, classifying and appraising the principal works on preaching. That the book has been in constant and increasing use since its first appearance and after three quarters of a century remains the outstanding text-book of Homiletics is full justification for its continuance.

At the request of the publishers, and with the consent and generous co-operation of Mrs. Ella Broadus Robertson, daughter of Dr. Broadus, the task of making such further revision as the passing years require is now undertaken by still another professor in the department where the book was born. He accepts the task with humble appreciation of the honor of standing in so noble a succession as Broadus, Dargan, and Gardner, and in the belief that a revised Broadus will have greater worth for the next generation of preachers than a new book. Few if any books on Homiletics have been able to achieve the comprehensiveness, the timelessness, and, withal, the simplicity of Broadus. Refusing to yield to the temptation to impose on the student his own favorite methods, he gave steadfast attention to principles and tested procedures, bringing to his aid the classical works of the centuries which bore upon the art of preaching. For that reason the book still lives and even now needs revision only in secondary matters.

In the present edition the purpose has been to retain the essential character of the work of Dr. Broadus. Teachers, however, will find numerous changes—condensations, expansions, restatements, omissions, insertions—which cannot be explained in a preface. It is hoped that they will commend themselves as being wholly in the interest of present-day students.

Perhaps the most obvious changes will be observed in the plan of the book. In former editions all the material elements of the sermon were included in Part I. This has been divided into two parts: the one, Foundations of the Sermon, including chapters on the Text, Interpretation of Texts, the Subject (a new chapter), Classification of Subjects, and the General Materials of the Sermon; the other, Functional Elements of the Sermon, including chapters on Explanation, Argument, Illustration, and Application. Between these two, Part II of earlier editions is inserted as the Formal Elements of the Sermon, in keeping with teaching practice as followed by most teachers, including Dr. Broadus himself. The remaining parts of the book follow the order of previous editions. Part V, dealing with methods of preparation and delivery presents a rearrangement of material, with an enlargement of the discussion of methods of preparation, bringing to the student the advantages of the practice of outstanding modern preachers.

Other changes are based on the observed needs of students over a period of years. The chapter on Interpretation of Texts has been somewhat reduced, but with the hope that its value will not be impaired for students who have not had separate courses in Interpretation. The chapter on Argument also has been reduced and rearranged. Literary references and footnotes have been revised by eliminating such as are of no great value to the modern student and by inserting references to selected modern authors. The excellent bibliographical work of Dr. C. S. Gardner has been retained with the addition of a supplementary book list.

The kindness of the various publishers in permitting the use of quotations from the books that have been of so great value is most gratefully acknowledged, as are also the many helpful suggestions made by my students and colleagues.

J. B. WEATHERSPOON

Southern Baptist Theological Seminary
November, 1943

PREFACE
to the Revised Edition

◇◇◇

THE first edition of this work was published in the summer of 1870. Immediately after getting it through the press the author went abroad for some months, and did not expect to teach Homiletics again after his return. But circumstances made it necessary that he should resume his work in that department—always a favorite subject with him. The book was a great success. It became the most popular and widely-read text-book on Homiletics in this country, and has passed through twenty-two editions, thousands of copies having been sold. It has been adopted in many theological seminaries of different denominations as the text-book, and in many where no text-book is used it is highly commended for study and reference. Besides this, it has had a wide and useful circulation among the ministry in general. Two separate editions were published in England; the book was used in the mission schools in Japan, in its English form, and was translated for similar use in the Chinese missions. A translation into Portuguese for the Protestant missions in Brazil has been prepared, and only waits for funds to be published.

The following several things call for a revised edition at this time: The copyright will have to be renewed in 1898, and this affords good opportunity to bring out a new edition; the original stereotype plates have become greatly worn; the correction of a few minor errors, and some additions and alterations, made desirable by the author's larger experience in studying and teaching the subject, are called for; there have been great contributions to the literature of Homiletics since the work was first published, and the author always kept abreast of progress; and, most of all, the continued demand for the book after twenty-seven years of useful service requires response in the way of bringing the work up with the times.

The present writer's connection with this revision is easily explained. In the fall of 1892 I became associate professor of Homiletics with Dr. Broadus in the Southern Baptist Theological Seminary, and had the privilege of teaching the subject with him up to the time of his lamented death in March, 1895. We divided the work of teaching under his direction, and as the state of his health permitted. It fell to my lot to do more and more of the work as his health declined.

During these years we had frequent conversations in regard to the revision of this volume. It was one of his cherished plans to bring out a revised edition before his death. With that end in view he had accumulated a good deal of material, mostly in the shape of notes, some in various note-books, and some written on the margins and fly-leaves of the book which he had used in the class-room for a number of years. In addition to these notes there were many points which he had discussed in conversation with me in regard to changes and improvements in the work. At the opening of the session of 1894-95 he gave me an interleaved copy of the book to use in the class-room, with the request that I should note on the blank pages every suggestion which occurred to me, looking toward the proposed revision. In the latter part of February, 1895, I took him the book and talked to him about the revision; but alas! in less than three weeks he was in his grave.

As the revision seemed absolutely imperative, with the full approbation of Dr. Brodus' family, I have felt it a sacred duty and privilege to undertake the task. How well or how ill it may have been executed will appear in the following pages.

Three classes of changes have been made: (1) Those which were clearly indicated in the author's notes already mentioned. These I have made without hesitation, as being certainly what he himself would have done. (2) Some changes not particularly noted by him, but concerning which I have distinct recollections of conversation, or concerning which on other accounts I feel reasonably sure that he would have made the alterations adopted. (3) There are also some changes wherein I have had to rely upon my own judgment, believing that they would be for the better. It is right for me to say that these are comparatively few, and, further, that I have made no changes without consultation with members of the author's family, from whom valuable help and suggestions have been received.

As most of the alterations are the author's, I beg to say distinctly that whatever improvements may be noticed in the book should be ascribed to him, and the editor will cheerfully take the responsibility of any changes which may not meet the approval of the reader.

It is my earnest prayer and hope that this book, which has been so useful for twenty-seven years, shall go forth in its new form on a mission of continued and larger usefulness to those whose blessed work it is to preach the unsearchable riches of Christ.

E. C. DARGAN

Louisville, Ky., December, 1897.

ACKNOWLEDGMENTS

Special acknowledgment is due the following publishers and authors for the use made of quotations from their copyrighted books:

Charles Scribner's Sons.
A. E. Garvie, *The Christian Preacher.*
H. H. Farmer, *The Servant of the Word.*
M. P. Noyes, *Preaching the Word of God.*

The Oxford Press.
Samuel McComb, *Preaching in Theory and Practice.*

Henry Holt and Company.
R. S. Woodworth, *Psychology.*

Abingdon-Cokesbury Press.
D. C. Bryan, *The Art of Illustrating Sermons.*

University of Chicago Press.
Ozora S. Davis, *The Principles of Preaching.*

Willett-Clark and Company.
C. S. Patton, *Preparation and Delivery of Sermons.*

Macmillan and Company.
S. Parkes Cadman, *Imagination and Religion.*

AUTHOR'S PREFACE
to the First Edition

◇◇

THIS work is designed, on the one hand to be a text-book for classes, and on the other to be read by such ministers, younger or older, as may wish to study the subject discussed.

As a teacher of Homiletics for ten years, the author had felt the need of a more complete text-book, since a course made up from parts of several different works would still omit certain important subjects, and furnish but a meagre treatment of others, leaving the class to a great extent dependent entirely upon the lectures. The desire thus arose to prepare, whenever possible, a work which should be full in its range of topics, and should also attempt to combine the thorough discussion of principles with an abundance of practical rules and suggestions. When the labor involved in teaching this and at the same time another branch of Theology became excessive, and it was necessary to relinquish Homiletics—though always a favorite branch—the author determined, before the subject should fade from his mind, to undertake the work he had contemplated.[1]

The treatise is therefore a result of practical instruction, but it is not simply a printed course of lectures. The materials existing in the form of brief notes have been everywhere rewrought, the literature of the subject carefully re-examined, and the place which had been occupied by text-books filled by an independent discussion.

Those who may think of employing the work as a text-book are requested to note, that it is divided into independent Parts, which, while arranged in the order indicated by the nature of the subject, may be taken up in any other order required by the exigencies of instruction. Some would prefer to begin with Arrangement, in order that students may at once have the benefit of this in preparing sermons or sketches. Others might begin with Style, in order to general exercises in composition; and possibly others with Delivery. The

[1] [This relinquishment was only temporary, being required by the author's state of health, though he at the time supposed it would be permanent. After one year he resumed Homiletics, and taught it with enthusiasm and success to the end of his life.—D.]

author would himself prefer if using the book, to take, after the Introduction, the first three chapters of Part I., and then Part II., and perhaps other portions before completing Part I. The cross references from one part to another will be found somewhat numerous. In the plan of the work, a few instances occur of departure from a strict technical distribution of the topics, for the sake of practical convenience. Thus the matters embraced under Illustration, Expository Preaching, or Imagination, would strictly belong to several different parts of the work, but it is practically better to discuss all at the same time. So with Occasional Sermons.

It may be necessary to explain the introduction of copious chapters on the Interpretation of a Text, and on Argument. The former subject is discussed in treatises on Hermeneutics. But besides the fact that not a few of those who use this book will not have previously studied Hermeneutics, those who have done so may be interested and profited by a discussion bearing more directly on the work of preaching; and such students will be able to read the chapter rapidly. Much improvement has been made during the past century in respect to pulpit interpretation, but it is a point as to which our young ministers still need to be very carefully guarded. The subject of Argument is thought by some to be out of place in a treatise on Homiletics or on Rhetoric in general. But preaching and all public speaking ought to be largely composed of argument, for even the most ignorant people constantly practise it themselves, and always feel its force when properly presented; and yet in many pulpits the place of argument is mainly filled by mere assertion and exhortation, and the arguments employed are often carelessly stated, or even gravely erroneous. Treatises on Logic teach the critical inspection, rather than the construction of argument, and so the latter must be discussed in works on Rhetoric, if anywhere. The well-known chapters of Whately have been here freely employed, but with very large additions, and with the attempt to correct some important errors. The examples of argument given are nearly all drawn from religious truth. With these explanations it is left to instructors to use or omit these portions of the work at their pleasure.

But the great mass of young ministers, particularly in some denominations, never study Homiletics under a teacher, whether they have or have not enjoyed a Collegiate education. The attempt has been everywhere made to adapt the present work to the wants of these students, as well as to the purposes of a text-book. They will choose for themselves what portions to take up first, but such as have had no College education may be urged not to abandon the book without reading the discussion of Arrangement and Style, as well as of Interpretation, Subjects of Preaching, and Argument.

Those who have had much experience in preaching often find it interesting and useful to examine a treatise on the preparation and delivery of sermons. New topics and new methods may be suggested, things forgotten or hitherto neglected are recalled, ideas gradually formed in the course of experience are made clearer and more definite, and where the views advanced are not deemed just, renewed reflection on some questions need not be unprofitable. Moreover, the desire for high excellence in preaching may receive a fresh stimulus. Such readers will remember that many practical matters which to them have now become obvious and commonplace, are precisely the points upon which a beginner most needs counsel. And while there are in the present treatise numerous divisions and subdivisions, so marked as to meet the wants of students, the attempt has been made to preserve the style from becoming broken and unreadable.

The author's chief indebtedness for help has been to Aristotle, Cicero, and Quintilian, and to Whately and Vinet. The two last (together with Ripley) had been his text-books,—and copious extracts are made from them on certain subjects. A good deal has been derived from Alexander, Shedd, Day, and Hoppin, from Coquerel and Palmer, and a great variety of other writers. Besides quotations, there are numerous references to works in which may be found some impressive statement of similar opinions, or further considerations bearing on the subject in hand. Only such references have been given as it was thought really worth while for the student to consult. At the close of the Introduction,[2] there is a list of the principal works forming the Literature of Homiletics, with brief notices of their character and value. It is believed that to give in a treatise some account of previous works on the subject, as judged from the author's point of view, is a thing appropriate and calculated to be useful. Such notices, in the case of contemporary writers, ought not to be reckoned discourteous if they frankly express disapprobation in some respects as well as praise in others. Were they somewhat more extended, these critical appreciations would be more useful. Besides this general account of the literature, essays and treatises upon particular branches

[2] [It was thus in the earlier editions; but in this, the Bibliography will be found at the end of the book.—D.]

of Rhetoric or Homiletics are briefly characterized in foot-notes, upon the introduction of the respective topics. Two important and valuable works, McIlvaine on Elocution (New York, 1870), and Dabney's Sacred Rhetoric (Richmond, 1870), were received after the Introduction was stereotyped, but are noticed in Part IV., chapter ii., and were made useful in that and the following chapters. Two articles published by the author in the Baptist Quarterly for January, 1869, and January, 1870, have been incorporated into the work, with the necessary rewriting; and some articles forming other portions of it have appeared in the Religious Herald, and the Central Baptist. The author is grateful to his colleagues and his pastor,[3] for sympathy in his undertaking and for valuable suggestions. The Index has been prepared by the Rev. John C. Long, of Virginia.[4]

Special pains have been taken, at the proper points of the treatise, to give practical suggestions for extemporaneous speaking. Most works confine their instruction as regards the preparation of sermons to the case of writing out in full; and many treat of delivery, as if it were in all cases to be reading or recitation. The effort has here been to keep the different methods in view, and to mention, in connection with matters applicable to all alike, such as apply to one or another method in particular.

As to many of the practical questions connected with the preparation and delivery of sermons, there is much difference of opinion; and an experienced preacher in reading any treatise on the subject, must find points here and there which he would prefer to see treated otherwise. He would decide whether, notwithstanding, the work is likely to be useful. In the present case, criticism, whether favorable or adverse, would be welcomed. Where the author is in error, he would greatly prefer to know it. Where the views presented are just, they may become more useful through discussion.

No one could prepare a work on this subject without feeling, and sometimes deeply feeling, the responsibility he incurred. It is a solemn thing to preach the gospel, and therefore a very solemn thing to attempt instruction or even suggestion as to the means of preaching well.

July, 1870.

[3] [The Rev. Dr. Wm. D. Thomas, then the beloved pastor of the Greenville, S. C., Baptist Church, now Professor of Philosophy in Richmond College, Richmond, Va.—D.]

[4] [Afterwards Professor of Church History in Crozer Theological Seminary, Upland, Pennsylvania, and since deceased.—D.]

CONTENTS

◇◇◇

II. ARGUMENT

III. ILLUSTRATION

IV. APPLICATION

Part IV. THE STYLE OF THE SERMON

I. GENERAL OBSERVATIONS ON STYLE

V. IMAGINATION IN PREACHING

Part V. METHODS OF PREPARATION AND DELIVERY OF SERMONS

I. PREPARATION OF SERMONS

*On the Preparation
and Delivery of Sermons*

❖

INTRODUCTION

PREACHING is characteristic of Christianity. No other religion has ever made the regular and frequent assembling of the masses of men, to hear religious instruction and exhortation, an integral part of divine worship. Judaism had something like it in the prophets, and afterwards in the readers and speakers of the synagogue; but preaching had no essential part in the worship of the temple.

In the Graeco-Roman world of the first century A.D. the preaching philosopher, employing the finely polished instrument of Greek rhetoric, was not an unfamiliar figure.[1] But neither Jewish religion nor Greek philosophy gave to preaching the significance it has in Christianity where it is a primary function of the church. Following the successes of Christian preaching, and especially in modern times, other religions and sects have adopted preaching in a limited way, but it remains true that as a basic service of the church in its history and significance preaching is a peculiarly Christian institution.[2]

I. THE PLACE AND POWER OF PREACHING

In the ministry of Jesus preaching occupied a central place. Although greatly tempted to give primacy to other methods of approach to the world, he "came preaching." In the synagogue at Nazareth he described himself as having been divinely ordained "to preach good tidings to the poor . . . to proclaim release to the captives . . . to proclaim the acceptable year of the Lord" (Luke 4:16-21). And all the gospels give unforgettable pictures of the itinerant Preacher, in the synagogues, on the mountains, by the seaside, going from village to village, drawing after him almost unbelievably large crowds, and amazing the people by his words of grace and the authority of his teaching. John, writing many years afterwards, remembered vividly his Lord's preaching in the temple during one of the great feasts. Of one day he reported that "Jesus cried in the temple, teaching

[1] Angus, *The Early Environment of Christianity*, pp. 74 ff.
[2] See H. H. Farmer, *The Servant of the Word*, Chap. 1.

and saying . . ."; and of another, the last day of the feast, that he "stood, and cried, saying, "If any man thirst let him come unto me and drink" (John 7:28, 37). His preaching was a cry, urgent in its compassion and masterful in its urgency.

The fact, so often referred to by modern educators, that the oral ministry of Jesus is more often called teaching than preaching is easily misunderstood and made the basis of erroneous distinctions. The general term for preaching in the New Testament is κηρύσσειν, to proclaim or herald. Another word εὐαγγελίζεσθαι emphasizes the nature of the proclaimed message as good news. A third word διδάσκειν is used to indicate the purpose of imparting to men divine truth and instructing them in righteousness. This last word is applied to other methods of instruction, but is freely used also of preaching to crowds. For example, Jesus taught (ἐδίδασκε) the Sermon on the Mount. In proclaiming the good news of the Kingdom of God, he went on to show its relation to Scripture and history, to moral purpose and social conduct, and to the destiny of man. In one discourse he proclaimed, evangelized and taught. The proper distinction is not between preaching and teaching, but between the evangelic and didactic emphasis or element of preaching; and even this distinction is not absolute. Preaching in the meaning and purpose of Jesus included all elements calculated to stir the mind in all its functions and lead men to see, to feel, to evaluate, and to make moral decisions.

Thus our Lord preached. And for their mission after him he bequeathed to his apostles the same strategy.[3] Preaching was in his announced purpose for them when he chose them. And at the end of his ministry he gave the Great Commission which, according to Mark, was a simple command to go everywhere preaching the gospel, and according to Matthew the purpose was to be threefold: to make disciples, to lead to confession in baptism, and to instruct in Christian living according to his commands. In the book of the Acts and in the Epistles of the New Testament, as well as in the strength of the church at the end of the apostolic period, the record and power of their preaching are to be found.

In the power of the same Spirit they and those who came after them faced the pagan world with the message of salvation (κήρυγμα) and a theology and ethic (διδάχη) that in three centuries made Christianity the foremost religion in the Roman Empire. And in the centuries since those early triumphs of the gospel the quality of preach-

---

⁴ Mark 3:14 ff., 16:15; Matt. 28:18-20.

ing and the spirit and life of the church have advanced or declined together. If preaching, never wholly free from the pressure of world movements, has often faltered in periods of spiritual crisis, it has always led in the periods of revival. Of every age it is true that there has been no great religious movement, no restoration of Scripture truth and reanimation of genuine piety without new power in preaching.

2. PREACHING AND ITS COMPETITORS

The great appointed means of spreading the good tidings of salvation through Christ is preaching—words spoken to the individual or to the assembly. And this, nothing can supersede, although methods of communicating truth have been greatly multiplied and refined. The vast output and availability of books, magazines, and newspapers, the reach of the radio, the appeal of the motion picture, have seemed to many to make preaching of less importance. They are, indeed, a challenge to intelligence, freshness, relevance, and reality in preaching; they must be utilized for the ends of preaching, but they cannot be substituted for it. When a man who is apt in teaching, whose soul is on fire with the truth which he trusts has saved him and hopes will save others, speaks to his fellow-men, face to face, eye to eye, and electric sympathies flash to and fro between him and his hearers, till they lift each other up, higher and higher, into the intensest thought, and the most impassioned emotion—higher and yet higher, till they are borne as on chariots of fire above the world,—there is a power to move men, to influence character, life, destiny, such as no printed page, radio cabinet, or silver screen can ever possess. Radio centers have their auditoriums, and crowds go to see the performers; the personal appearance of the movie actor draws a larger attendance than the picture alone; the broadcasting of operas has not closed the Metropolitan Opera House but rather advertised it. The abundance of speech and literature does not call for a moratorium on preaching but for fresh passion, improved skill, and spiritual power.

Inside the church preaching faces in our day a new insistence upon the importance of work and worship. Ecclesiastical history has tended to follow a cyclical pattern: Church expansion through strong preaching, organization and stabilization, crystallization of forms of worship and service, decline of preaching and loss of spiritual objectives, revival, and then new expansion through strong preaching, and so on.

Social determinists would say that such cycles are inevitable; but intelligence and spiritual passion, conscious of super-social resources of power, need not surrender to the dogmas of naturalism, or to the downgrade pressures of a particular period. That the church and preaching have so yielded in the past does not constitute a necessity but a forewarning and forearming. With the emphasis today upon the institutional program of the church, pastoral visitation, counseling and administration, the proper use of ceremonial and ritual in worship, these tend to become competitors of preaching and to disparage the hearing of the Word which is the secret of power in all. The passion for preaching, on the other hand, easily discounts the value of the other functions of the church. All these activities—preaching, worship, service—are proper functions and should be co-ordinated. In competition they work against spiritual power and permanent effectiveness. In balance and unity they make for spiritual and institutional progress.

Pastoral work, for example, is of immense importance, and all preachers should be diligent in performing it. But it cannot take the place of preaching or fully compensate for lack of power in the pulpit. The two help each other, and neither of them is able, unless supported by the other, to achieve the largest and most blessed results. When he who preaches is the sympathizing pastor, the trusted counselor, the kindly and honored friend of young and old, of rich and poor, then "truths divine come mended from his lips," and the door to men's hearts, by the magical power of sympathy, will fly open at his word. But, on the other hand, when he who visits is the preacher, whose thorough knowledge of Scripture and elevated views of life, whose able and impassioned discourses have carried conviction and commanded admiration and melted into one the hearts of the multitude, who is accustomed to stand before them as the ambassador of God and is associated in their minds with the authority and the sacredness of God's Word,—when *he* comes to speak with the suffering, the sorrowing, the tempted, his visit has a meaning and a power of which otherwise it must be destitute.

Ceremonies of worship, also, are instructive and impressive and should be clothed in such beauty and dignity and meaning as to lead the worshiper into the presence of God with reverence and a pure heart. But let it be remembered that true preaching is as essential and necessary even as ritual and song and, properly done, is itself an act of worship. Let Dr. A. E. Garvie[4] express the thought:

[4] *The Christian Preacher*, see p. 4.

It is at least as important that we should know God's will as that we should make our wishes known to God. God is worshiped in the humble and obedient acceptance of His preached Word as in the offering of prayer and praise. . . . Where devotion is divorced from truth, it is to be observed that the external aids—'the dim religious light' of the pictured window, the symbolism of the sculptured stone or the carved wood, the suggestion of human costume, picture, and gesture, the stimulus of music and song —become and must become more prominent. Can it be doubted that the appeal to the conscience, reason, and affections through the declaration of the truth and grace of God will be more effectual in inspiring true devotion than the excitement of devout feelings through fair sights and sweet sounds? . . . The writer feels justified in vindicating the claim of preaching to the foremost place in the Christian Church, in insisting that worship cannot supplant preaching, which is, rightly understood, itself worship, without danger and loss to Christian life.

It follows that preaching must always be a necessity, and good preaching a mighty power throughout the world. The dilettante men of letters who every now and then fill the periodicals with sneers at preaching no doubt judge most unkindly and unjustly, for they purposely compare ordinary examples of preaching with the finest specimens of literature, and they forget their own utter lack, in the one case, of that sympathetic appreciation without which all literary and artistic judgment is necessarily at fault; but we who love preaching and who try to preach are better aware than they of the deficiencies which mar our efforts and the difficulties which attend our work. We know that preaching deserves the highest excellence since it is the chosen instrument of the Savior of the world, who himself came preaching. And the admonition of the apostle to the younger preacher remains an unceasing challenge: "Give diligence to show thyself approved unto God, a workman that needeth not to be ashamed, rightly dividing the word of truth."

3. REQUISITES TO EFFECTIVE PREACHING

What, then, are the requisites of effective preaching? Phillips Brooks said that preaching is

the communication of truth by man to man. It has in it two essential elements, truth and personality. . . . It must have both elements. It is in the different proportions in which the two are mingled that the difference between two great classes of sermons and preaching lies. It is in the defect of the one or the other element that every sermon and preacher falls short of the perfect standard. It is in the absence of one or the other element that a discourse ceases to be a sermon, and a man ceases to be a preacher altogether.[5]

To this Dr. A. E. Garvie adds what was no doubt in the mind of Brooks:

> Preaching is not merely a communication of knowledge. As it exercises the whole personality of the preacher, so it is addressed to the whole personality of the hearer as a moral and religious subject. As the truth with which it deals concerns God, freedom, and immortality, so its end is to evoke faith, stimulate to duty, and sustain hope.[6]

The subject of preaching is divine truth, centrally the gospel as revealed and offered in Jesus Christ. Its object is eternal life,—in the words of Jesus, "that they may have life and may have it abundantly." Surely the preacher, the agent of this high function, must not consent to the omission of any discipline of heart and mind and conduct required for preaching effectively. Among the requisites piety must be placed first, then natural gifts, knowledge, and skill.

(1) *Piety.* Piety is a quality of soul. It is moral earnestness rooted in a continuing experience of fellowship with God. It is reverent devotion to the will of God. It is not a pose that is struck. It is not austere but moves with the glow and warmth of the Christian graces. It is not otherworldly in any sense of proud withdrawal from human interests but mingles with life in the strength of Christian virtues. It is not weak but heroic and is the inspiration of that heroism which is the "brilliant triumph of the soul over the flesh." It is spiritual reality that entertains no simulation, and spiritual realism that recognizes and challenges the moral and spiritual enemies of life. It is not too much to say that this quality of spirit is the prime requisite to effectiveness in preaching. It inspires the preacher himself with ardent zeal, and keeps the flame alive amid all the icy indifference by which he will so often be encompassed. It gains for him the good will and sympathy of his hearers, the most ungodly of whom will feel that devout earnestness on his part is becoming and entitles him to respect. And to this is promised the blessing of God upon the labors which it prompts. Much false theory and bad practice in preaching is con-

[5] *Lectures on Preaching*, p. 5 f.
[6] *The Christian Preacher*, p. 12 f.

nected with a failure to apprehend the fundamental importance of piety in the preacher. Just rhetorical principles, as well as other and far higher considerations, imperatively require that a preacher of the gospel shall cultivate personal piety. It is *bad rhetoric* to neglect it.

(2) *Natural gifts*. The preacher needs the capacity for clear thinking, with strong feelings, and a vigorous imagination; also capacity for expression, and the power of forcible utterance. Many other gifts help his usefulness; these are well-nigh indispensable to any high degree of efficiency. Each of these can be improved almost indefinitely, some of them developed in one who had not been conscious of possessing them; but all must exist as natural gifts.

(3) *Knowledge*. There must be knowledge of religious truth and of such things as throw light upon it, knowledge of human nature in its relations to religious truth and of human life in its actual conditions around us. It was a favorite idea of Cicero that the orator ought to know everything. There is, of course, no knowledge which a preacher might not make useful. We may thankfully recognize the fact that some men do good who have very slender attainments and yet may insist that it should be the preacher's lowest standard to surpass, in respect of knowledge, the great majority of those who hear him, and it should be his sacred ambition to know all that he can learn by lifelong and prayerful endeavor.

Piety furnishes motive power; natural gifts, cultivated as far as possible, supply means; knowledge gives material; and there remains—

(4) *Skill*. This does not refer merely to style and delivery but also to the collection, choice, and arrangement of materials. All who preach eminently well—and the same thing is true of secular speakers—will be found, with scarcely an exception, to have labored much to acquire skill. Henry Clay became an accomplished orator by diligent cultivation of his natural gifts. In an address to some law students at Albany towards the close of his life he mentioned that during his early life in Kentucky, he

commenced, and continued for years, the practice of daily reading and speaking upon the contents of some historical or scientific book. These offhand efforts were made sometimes in a cornfield, at others in the forest, and not unfrequently in some distant barn, with the horse and the ox for my auditors.

We are told that the Indian orators of the Six Nations were known to practise their speeches beside a clear pool as a mirror.

Patrick Henry, the most illustrious example of natural oratory, so far as there is any such, went through a course of training in his daily studies of human nature as drawn out by himself in his little shop, his every-day trials on his lingering customers of the power of words, his deep and enthusiastic investigations into history, and particularly his patient and continued study of the harangues of Livy and the elaborate translations he made of them, which, to say the least, is very uncommon.[7]

Henry Ward Beecher, the premier orator of the American pulpit, serves as an outstanding example of the value of studying the principles of rhetoric and oratory. He mastered the classic textbooks of rhetoric, took special training in speech, studied the sermons of great preachers. "He was always alert to discover what other masters of pulpit discourse could teach him about the fine points of his profession."[8] Anyone whose good fortune it has been to be intimate with some of those noble American preachers who, beginning with hardly any education, have worked their way up to the highest excellence in their calling will have seen ample proofs, particularly in their unrestrained private conversation, that their power of clear and precise expression and of forcible and attractive delivery is the result of sharp, critical attention, of earnest and long-continued labor. The difference between skill and the lack of it in speaking is almost as great as in handling tools, those, for example, of the carpenter or the blacksmith. And while no real skill can be acquired without practice—according to the true saying, "The only way to learn to preach is to preach,"— yet mere practice will never bring the highest skill; it must be heedful, thoughtful practice, with close observation of others and sharp watching of ourselves, and controlled by good sense and good taste.

Now in respect of skill, preaching is an *art*; and while art cannot create the requisite powers of mind or body or supply their place if really absent, it can develop and improve them and aid in using them to the best advantage. To gain skill, then, is the object of rhetorical studies, skill in the construction and in the delivery of discourse.

4. RELATION OF HOMILETICS TO RHETORIC

Like the Greek language, Greek rhetoric was a ready instrument for the proclamation of the gospel to the gentile world. By the latter part of the fourth century B.C. it had reached its highest development

---

[7] Day's *Art of Discourse*, p. 18.
[8] Crocker, *Henry Ward Beecher's Preaching Art*, p. 53.

among the Greeks in the oratory of Demosthenes and in Aristotle's famous treatise on rhetoric. Later contributions were made by Roman orators, particularly Cicero and Quintilian. In the Graeco-Roman world into which Christianity came, rhetoric was the crown of a liberal education.

Grammatic (the study of literature) imbued the student with the wisdom of the past and developed his literary aptitudes; *Dialectic* trained his reasoning powers; and *Rhetoric* taught him to turn his equipment to account, especially in the law-court and the Senate, by instructing him in the art of ready utterance, appropriate expression, and moving appeal.[9]

But the adaptation of rhetoric to the ends of Christian preaching was a gradual process, waiting upon conditions and needs. Christian preaching began in Palestine. Its first preachers and audiences, its background and spiritual affinities, were Jewish. It was natural, therefore, and necessary that the manner of preaching should follow the pattern of the Old Testament prophet and the teaching rabbi. Moreover, in the hands of unscrupulous lawyers and false teachers rhetoric had fallen into disrepute, being associated with sham and sophistry and regarded as a subtle instrument for making the worse appear the better reason. It was true, also, that among many Jews anything Hellenic was regarded as a threat to the very substance of Jewish life. Accordingly, early preaching was after the manner of Jewish rather than gentile culture. The sermon was called, as indeed it was, a "homily," a familiar discourse, or talk.

There were two influences, however, that gradually drew Christian preaching toward rhetorical forms. One was the extension of the gospel to gentile populations among whom Jewish traditions and forms were not well known. Recall the criticism of Paul by some of the people at Corinth, and their delight in Apollos, which, David Smith says, was "the first intimation to the ambassadors of Christ that, if they would win the world, they must address to it a congenial appeal.[10] The second influence was the conversion of men who were already trained in rhetoric. An increasing number of such men became preachers, and naturally they used their rhetorical gifts in the proclamation of the gospel. Add to these influences the fact of decline in Jewish Christians and Jewish preachers, and one can see how the "homily" (although the term was commonly used until the third century) gave way to the more elaborate sermon.

[9] David Smith, *The Art of Preaching*, p. 45.
[10] *The Art of Preaching*, p. 58.

And the change must be viewed as an advance. It gained a wider and more favorable hearing for the gospel. The principles of discourse were the tested ways of convincing and persuading men and in the hands of devout men like Basil, Gregory, Chrysostom, Ambrose, and Augustine became, to a degree not reached by the older Greeks, an instrument of spiritual power among cultured and uncultured people alike. These men ennobled the art by filling it with the distinctive reality of Christian faith and the Christian message and devoting it to Christian ends. Thus arose the science of "homiletics," which is simply the adaptation of rhetoric to the particular ends and demands of Christian preaching.[11]

5. DANGERS OF RHETORICAL STUDIES

Attention must be called to the fact that in the adoption of rhetorical methods all was not gain. Paul's early fears, that with "persuasive words" would also come insincerity and pride of sower, were not empty. The tendency of the new preaching was to set the preacher at a distance from his hearers, making him an orator and master of assemblies instead of a witness and fellow-worshiper. The sermon tended to become an oration to be applauded rather than a message to be believed and acted upon. And history records the tragic story of ambitious and praise-loving men in the pulpit, who became mere public entertainers, converting the sacred service into a trivial and sensational show. This, of course, is no condemnation of rhetoric itself. Like any other art it takes its character from the artist. But the tendencies have proved themselves so persistent, and the preacher's temptations are so recurrent, that it is quite worth-while for the student to be reminded of the dangers that will stalk his preaching ministry.

(1) *Overemphasis on rules and forms.* There are two things to be said about homiletical rules. First, they are the result of experience. They are sometimes spoken of as if they had been drawn up by would-be wise men who undertook to tell, on general principles, how one ought to speak. But they simply result from much thoughtful observation of the way in which men do speak when they speak

[11] For a history of the development of homiletics see Dargan's *The Art of Preaching in the Light of Its History*. Note also Hoppin's definition (*Homiletics*, p. 9): "Homiletics is the science that teaches the fundamental principles of public discourse as applied to the proclamation and teaching of divine truth in regular assemblies gathered for the purpose of Christian worship."

really well. They are tested methods. In the second place, it must be said that, however judiciously they may be framed, rules are not superior to principles; they are never as flexible or as universal. It is necessary, therefore, for the fullest freedom and effect, that the preacher should put more emphasis on principles than rules. The preacher's aim is to convince the judgment, kindle the imagination, move the feelings, and give a powerful impulse to the will in the direction of truth's requirement. There are certain facts about the functions and processes of the human mind that give rise to principles of approach. It is much more important that the preacher should master those principles than that he should memorize and slavishly follow rules. There will be occasions, and as regards some rules, many occasions, in which one may violate the rule and yet be really conforming to the principle. Differences of circumstance, the individuality of the preacher, the occasion, the character of the audience, make it necessary that rules be kept in the position of servants, not masters, and that forms be always flexible and variable. To follow rules slavishly is the mark of superficiality. The highest compliment of a sermon is not that it is "homiletical" but that it moves souls toward the Kingdom of God and his righteousness. It is lamentable to see how often the remarks upon preaching made by preachers themselves, in conversation and in newspaper critiques, are confined to a discussion of the performance and the performer. Unsympathizing listeners or readers have, in such cases, too much ground for concluding that preachers are anxious only to display skill and gain oratorical reputation. Oratory is not primarily technique, but, in the words of H. W. Beecher, "truth bearing upon conduct and character, set home by the living force of the full man."

(2) *Imitation.* All are aware that there is both a conscious and an unconscious imitation. That which is unconscious is of course not so blameworthy, but it cannot fail to be injurious, and it is a subtle evil which should be guarded against with the sharpest self-inspection. Everyone observes, too, that imitators are especially apt to imitate a man's faults. The reason is easily seen. The excellencies of a good speaker are apt to be symmetrical, while his faults are salient, prominent. The latter, therefore, will most readily attract unconscious imitation. As to the conscious imitator, he is sure to be a superficial observer who will think that what he notices most in some admired speaker is the secret of his power and will go to imitating that, when, as a matter of fact, no one characteristic is the secret of a great man's

power. The secret is an original combination of traits and hidden experiences, which no imitation can accomplish. There is no standardized pattern of excellence, and no mere copyist ever created a masterpiece, though every color and feature was borrowed from a master. The preacher must have his own voice and tone and must follow his own emotions and sense of emphasis; his sermons must follow the path cut by his own thinking. Dr. Jowett used to imagine, in his study, how this or that great preacher would approach a subject, but not in order to imitate them. He wrote:

> While I am advising you to consult other minds, I must further advise you not to be overwhelmed by them. Reverently respect your own individuality. I do not advise you to be aggressively singular, for then you may stand revealed as a crank and your influence will be gone. But, without being angular, believe in your own angle, and work upon the assumption that it is through your own unrepeated personality that God purposes that your light should break upon the world. Reverently believe in your own uniqueness, and consecrate it in the power of the Holy Spirit. Be yourself and slavishly imitate nobody.[12]

(3) *Artificiality*. There is much artificiality which ought not to be called by the odious name of affectation. The speaker's motives are good; he merely errs in judgment and taste and in the pulpit becomes another man. But a great error it is. In all speaking, especially in preaching, naturalness, genuineness, even though awkward, is really more effective for all the highest ends than the most elegant artificiality. "But it is the highest art to conceal art." Nay, no art can conceal art. We may not perceive it, but we dimly, instinctively feel that there is something the matter, and perhaps wonder what it is; somehow, the preacher's well-meant efforts are failing to reach their aim. The danger of artificiality in speaking is very great. When one begins, he is apt to feel awkward in the new and strange situation. As one unaccustomed to riding on horseback must learn to sit naturally and feel at ease in the saddle, so very many speakers, perhaps all, have to learn to be natural. They must not only reject all intentional artificiality but must carefully guard against that which is undesigned and unconscious. To forget self, because of living desire to do men good, is the great means of being natural. It follows that a preacher ought never to preach merely for practice; this will inevitably tend to encourage artificiality. The first few efforts of a young man—which will

---

[12] *The Preacher: His Life and Work*, pp. 127 f.

often go much farther than he is at the time aware to form his habits for life—ought to be genuine, *bona fide* preaching. If he preaches in the presence of none but his fellow-students and instructors, it ought to be only upon a subject thoroughly suited to their religious wants, and with a most earnest and prayerful effort to do them good.

As regards all that pertains to preaching, and especially delivery, our efforts at rhetorical improvement must be mainly negative. We endeavor to gain correct general principles and some idea of the errors and faults to which speakers are generally liable. We then speak, aiming to be guided by these principles and to correct our faults as they may arise. It is unwise to set up at the outset some standard of excellence and aim to conform to that. If one should take a fancy that cedar trees are more beautiful than oaks and attempt to trim his oaks into the shape, and color them into the hue, of cedars, the result could only be ridiculous. Let the young cedar grow as a cedar and the young oak as an oak, but straighten, prune, improve each of them into the best possible tree of its kind. And so, as to speaking, be always yourself, your actual, natural self, but yourself developed, corrected, improved into the very best you are by nature capable of becoming.

6. THE STUDY OF HOMILETICS

It is evident that both to the student for the ministry and to the active pastor attention to this subject is of utmost importance. It is proposed to offer here some suggestions toward a profitable pursuit of the study.

The literature of homiletics is ample and worthy. There are multitudes of able and good books of all ages and languages, books which bear more or less directly upon the subject. General treatises on rhetoric, elocution, and kindred topics abound, and many of these are well worthy of the preacher's careful reading. In recent times, with the revived interest in the study of English in our colleges and universities, there has been put forth a large number of rhetorical treatises. From these back to the still useful works of the ancient masters there is a long line of excellent discussions of the fundamental and permanent principles of rhetorical science.

Then there is a very complete, and for the most part valuable, literature of homiletics proper. These treatises discuss preaching from almost every conceivable point of view. Many noble and useful works have been produced in our own country, and they are noted for prac‑ tical value and thoroughness of treatment. There are also a few works, but not so many nor so good as could be wished, on the history of oratory and of preaching, that are helpful in the study of homiletics. For a brief critical survey of the best known and most useful works in this department the student is referred to the bibliography at the end of this volume.

Besides treatises on preaching, the chief sources of instruction in homiletics are as follows: (1) The preaching that we hear, when heard with fraternal sympathy and prayerful desire for spiritual benefit, and yet with critical attention. (2) Published sermons, the value of which is readily acknowledged. (3) Biographies of preachers, which, to one having a general knowledge of homiletics, are often surpassingly instructive. (4) The criticism of instructors or judicious hearers upon our own preaching. (5) Careful observation of our faults, as developed in actual practice, with resolute and patient effort to correct them.

Part I

FOUNDATIONS OF THE SERMON

❖◇◇◇◇◇◇◇◇◇◇◇◇◇◇◇◇◇◇◇◇◇◇◇◇◇◇◇◇◇◇◇◇◇◇◇◇◇❖

CHAPTER I

THE TEXT

I. MEANING OF THE TERM

THE word "text" is derived from the Latin *texere*, to weave, which figuratively came to signify to put together, to construct, and hence to compose, to express thought in continuous speech or writing. The noun *textus* thus denotes the product of weaving, the web, the fabric, and so in literary usage the fabric of one's thinking, continuous composition. The practice arose of reading the continuous narrative or discussion of some author and adding comments, chiefly explanatory, or of taking the author's own writing and making notes at the sides or bottom of the page. Thus the author's own work came to be called the "text," as distinguished from the fragmentary notes and comments of the editor or speaker. This use of the word still survives, as when we speak of the "text" of ancient authors or others, meaning their own original composition; and "text-criticism" is the science of determining what was their exact language. Now, early preaching was of the nature of familiar running commentary on the connected train of thought, or text, of Scripture, which was so named to distinguish it from the preacher's comment or exposition. As the practice grew of lengthening the comments into an orderly discourse and of shortening the passage of Scripture expounded, the word "text" has come to mean the portion of Scripture chosen as the suggestion or foundation for a sermon.

The history of the word, like that of "homiletics," points back to the fact, which is also well known otherwise, that preaching was originally expository. The early Christian preachers commonly spoke upon passages of considerable length and occupied themselves largely with exposition. Frequently, however, as was natural, they would find a brief passage so fruitful as to confine themselves to it. Usage tended more and more toward the preference of short texts. In England in the seventeenth century it was not uncommon to make many sermons on some brief passage. Thus John Howe has fourteen sermons on a part of Rom. 8:24, "We are saved by hope"; seventeen on I John 4:20; and eighteen on John 3:6. The object was to make a complete discussion of some great topic and to bind all the discourses into a whole by connecting all with the same text. But this practice conflicted with the natural love of variety. It is usually much better to make a series appear such by the manifest relation of the subjects and to choose for each discourse a separate text, which presents the particular subject or view there discussed. This is at present the common practice, it being a somewhat rare thing now to preach more than one sermon on the same brief text. There is also a tendency at present to return to the more frequent use of long texts.

2. ADVANTAGES OF HAVING A TEXT

Taking a text is an old and well established custom from which there seems to be no good reason for departing. Moreover, the custom is founded in excellent reason and has marked advantages.

It is manifest that to take a text gives a tone of sacredness to the discourse. But more than this is true. The primary idea is that the discourse is a development of the text, an explanation, illustration, application of its teachings. Our business is to teach God's Word. And although we may often discuss subjects and aspects of subjects which are not presented in precisely that form by any passage of Scripture, yet the fundamental conception should be habitually retained, that we are about to set forth what the text contains. When circumstances determine the subject to be treated and we have to look for a text, one can almost always be found which will have some real, though it be a general, relation to the subject. If there be rare cases in which it is otherwise, it will then be better to have no text than one with which the subject has only a fanciful or forced connection.

There are several advantages in regularly taking a text. (1) It constantly recalls the fact just mentioned, that our undertaking is not to guide the people by our own wisdom, but to impart to them the teachings of God in his Word. This fact enables us to speak with confidence and leads the people to recognize the authority of what we say. (2) If the text is well chosen, it awakens interest at the outset. (3) It often aids the hearer in remembering the train of thought, having this effect wherever the sermon is really evolved from the text. (4) It affords opportunity of explaining and impressing some passage of Scripture. (5) It tends to prevent our wandering utterly away from scriptural topics and views. (6) Greater variety will be gained than if the mind were left altogether to the suggestion of circumstances, for then it will often fall back into its old ruts; and this variety is attained just in proportion as one restricts himself to the specific thought of each particular text.[1]

Objections to the use of texts have commonly arisen from one of two or three causes. (1) The grievous laxity in the interpretation of texts which has so widely prevailed, leads some men to regard the employment of them as wrong or useless. This is the old story— the abuse of a thing causing men to question the propriety of its use. (2) Again, persons who have little or no true reverence for Scripture, or appreciation of its riches, speak of the text as a restriction upon freedom of thought and flow of eloquence. (3) As a third ground of objection to texts, some able and devout preachers, disliking expository and even textual preaching, and wishing that every sermon should be a philosophical discussion or an elaborate discourse upon a definite topic, incline to regard the custom of always taking a text as an inconvenient restriction.

It is sometimes not unsuitable to have two texts, or even more. Thus with Heb. 9:22, "And without shedding of blood is no remission," there might be united I John 1:7, "The blood of Jesus Christ His Son cleanseth us from all sin." Or with Isa. 6:3, "The whole earth is full of his glory," may be taken Ps. 72:19, "And let the whole earth be filled with his glory"; to angelic eyes it is so—the human mind can only pray that it may be so. (Compare Hab. 2:14) Spurgeon has a sermon on the words, "I have sinned," as occurring seven times in the

---

[1] Dr. Henry Sloane Coffin (*What to Preach*, pp. 21 f.) suggests three values in having a text: (1) "It keeps a preacher in line with the historical spiritual past which he is seeking to continue." (2) "It sums up in striking and memorable form the main point of his message." (3) "It almost invariably enriches the sermon from the wealthy life with God in the Bible with suggestions which were not in the preacher's mind before." See also Garvie, *The Christian Preacher*, p. 282, and David Smith, *The Art of Preaching*, p. 147.

Bible, and gives interesting views of the different circumstances and states of mind in which they were uttered.[2]

In this whole matter of taking texts the law is value, not custom. Let the preacher decide. The important thing is that the sermon shall be Christian in content and spirit and purpose. One may take a text and still preach a sermon that misses the mark of being Christian; on the other hand, a sermon without a text and without formal Scripture reference may be thoroughly Christian. And merely to follow a cult of novelty or to copy some admired rebel against convention is quite as bad as following tradition. Let the preacher have a reason for what he does. Sometimes he may omit a text because no suitable text can be found for what he wants to say. But this should rarely occur, for, as Dr. Coffin suggests,

if within the ample range of the biblical literature a preacher cannot find a text for what he wishes to say, the chances are that he is deviating from the historic faith of which he is a teacher.[3]

Occasionally he may see value in preaching without a text for the sake of variety. Or again he may deal with a number of passages, no one of which is suitable for a central text. But as a general rule the objectives of the sermon are better served with a well-chosen text.

3. RULES FOR THE SELECTION OF A TEXT

The proper selection of a text is a matter of great importance. A felicitous choice will animate the preacher throughout the preparation and the delivery of his sermon and will help him to gain at once the attention of his hearers. There are few points as to which preachers differ more widely in talent and skill than the selection of texts, and few in which diligent and systematic effort will be more richly rewarded. The minister, or student for the ministry, should keep a note-book for lists of texts. In reading the Scriptures and books of theology, in reading collections of sermons, biographies, and newspaper notices, in casual reflection, and in the preparation of other sermons passages will be constantly occurring upon which it strikes one that he could make a sermon. Let these be at once written down in the list. Let the preacher constrain himself to do so until it becomes a habit. And he

---

[2] Amer. ed. of Spurgeon's *Sermons, Third Series*, p. 241. See also David Smith, *The Art of Preaching*, pp. 147-150, for other suggestions concerning the use of multiple texts.

[3] *What to preach*, p. 21. See also pp. 23 f.

should by all means put down at the same time, however briefly, the
proposed outline of the discourse, or any specially valuable view or
illustration of it that may occur to him. Otherwise, he will afterward
find many passages in the list that it will seem strange he should ever
have noted, because the association will have been broken, the point
of view will have disappeared. At some times the mind is in a highly
creative mood, and plans of sermons or suggestive texts or topics will
rapidly succeed one another as the preacher reads, reflects, or visits
from house to house. These fruitful germs should be carefully hus-
banded, and the lines of development indicated. And often when one
is cold and lifeless and could at the moment produce nothing, some
good thought which was struck out in a happier mood will fall into
his mind like a spark and presently set it all on fire. Many an admirable
text and many a golden thought, given to men in their better
moments, are lost forever, when a brief record, or even some little
effort to associate them in mind with other things might have made
them a permanent possession.

To aid in the selection of texts, there are offered the following rules.

(1) *The text should not be obscure.* It ought, as a rule, to exhibit its
meaning readily. Otherwise, the people either will be repelled by what
they see no sense in, or will be apt to feel a merely idle curiosity to
know what in the world the preacher will make of that. Still, there
are important exceptions here. If the preacher is satisfied that he can
explain an obscure passage and can show that it teaches valuable truth,
he may take it. If the passage is one about which many are known to
feel interested, and he is really able to make its meaning clear and
bring out useful lessons, it may be very wise to employ it. But observe
the stress that is laid on the practicability of making the passage instructive and useful. To explain merely for the sake of explaining, is
a task for which the preacher scarcely has time.[4]

(2) *One must be careful as to employing texts "marked by grandeur
of expression. They seem to promise a great effort."*[5] And if great
expectations are excited at the outset, it is of course very difficult to
meet them. Yet no one would say as a rule that such texts must be
avoided. Many of the noblest and most impressive passages of Scripture rise into a natural grandeur of expression, and there would be
serious loss in habitually avoiding these. Sometimes we may find a

---

[4] Compare Phelps, *Theory of Preaching*, pp. 84-91, for a very sensible and more
extended treatment of the comparative advantages of perspicuous and obscure texts.

[5] Ripley, *Sacred Rhetoric.*

simpler text that presents the same subject, and the grander passage can be introduced somewhere in the course of the sermon. But when such a passage is made the text, we may prevent any undesirable effect by announcing it with unaffected modesty, and by the general tone of the introduction. We must carefully avoid whatever course would savor of display but must not fastidiously shrink from treating any passage which we may hope to make useful.

(3) *Caution should be exercised in choosing texts that will seem odd.* The quest of the unusual may sacrifice a higher value for a small gain in initial interest. The text should indicate not only a central concern of the message but something of its tone also. It should embody or suggest qualities of thought and emotion that may with profit be sustained and advanced as the message unfolds. This does not mean that one should be content with the much used or standard texts, but only that in the pursuit of novelty the significance and high purpose of the text should not be violated. The elements of surprise and shock, of humor and oddity have their values in preaching, but they have much less value in the text than in the midst of the sermon.[6] Dr. Austin Phelps commends the choice of novel texts as preferable to hackneyed or standard texts because they excite interest, freshen up old truth, promote variety, impress truth more deeply, and stimulate the preacher in the composition of his sermon.[7] But novelty is not necessarily oddity, and Dr. Phelps warns against the trivial and anything that would violate the dignity of the text by suggesting low or ludicrous associations, or that would shock the sensibilities of the audience.

(4) *Do not avoid a text because it is familiar.* What has made some texts familiar to all, but the fact that they are so manifestly good texts? It is a very mistaken desire for novelty which leads a man to shrink from such rich and fruitful passages as "God so loved the world," etc.; "This is a faithful saying," etc., which Luther used to call "little Bibles," as if including in their narrow compass the whole Bible. He who will turn away from the tradition of the pulpit as to the meaning and application of such passages and make personal and earnest study of them will often find much that is new to him and his hearers, as the skilful gold-hunter in California will sometimes follow in the very track of many searchers and gain there his richest harvest. Be-

---

[6] For a good discussion of the value and use of humor in preaching, see Dr. C. R. Brown's *The Art of Preaching*, pp. 135-142.

[7] *Theory of Preaching*, pp. 95-102.

sides, what we need is not absolute novelty but simply freshness. If we can manage, by prayerful reflection, to obtain such views and provide such illustrations of a familiar text as will give it a fresh interest to ourselves and the hearers, then all the riches of the passage are made available for good. Alexander[8] calls attention to the fact that of the great sculptors and painters many took the same themes; and so with the Greek tragedians. He remarks: "Some, anxious to avoid hackneyed topics, omit the greatest, just as if we should describe Switzerland and omit the Alps." In point of fact, the great preachers, all the best preachers, do preach much upon the great texts and the great subjects. How is a feebler man ever to develop his own strength unless he grapples with great themes? One may show skill and add somewhat to the harvest by cultivating out-of-the-way corners and unpromising ledges of rock; but the bulk of the crop by which the family are fed must come from the broad, open field.

(5) *Do not habitually neglect any portion of Scripture.* Some neglect the Old Testament thus losing all its rich unfolding of God's character and the methods of his Providence, all its unnumbered illustrations of human life and duty, and its many types and predictions of the coming Saviour. Others preach on the Old Testament almost exclusively. These are either men who take no delight in the "doctrines of grace," in the spirituality of the gospel, or men devoted to fanciful allegorizing, who do not enjoy the straightforward teaching of Christ and his apostles so much as their own wild "spiritualizing" of everything in the Old Testament history, prophecies, and proverbs.

Let us not neglect either of these great divisions of God's own Word. And so as to particular books. In the course of a good many years a preacher ought to have taken some texts from every portion of Scripture, though he will of course choose most frequently from those books to which attention is directed by his peculiar mental constitution and tastes or by their comparative richness in evangelical and practical matter.

(6) *Do not take spurious passages.* Those which are certainly spurious may be avoided by the use of the American Standard Version of the Bible. The revisers were very conservative as to the text, and any passage omitted in that version may be safely assumed to be spurious. In regard to doubtful passages further help may be had from West-cott and Hort's Greek Testament and from the revision published by the American Baptist Publication Society. Following are some

8 *Thoughts on Preaching,* pp. 10-12.

examples of texts to be avoided. A favorite text with many is Acts 9:6, "Lord, what wilt thou have me to do?" This is unquestionably spurious, and these words should never be quoted as Scripture; yet essentially the same thought is expressed in Acts 22:10, "What shall I do, Lord?" as uttered on the occasion of Paul's conversion. The famous passage in I John 5:7, "There are three that bear record in heaven, the Father, the Word, and the Holy Ghost: and these three are one," is also spurious beyond question. The passage in Acts 8:37, "And Philip said: If thou believest with all thy heart, thou mayest. And he answered and said, I believe that Jesus Christ is the Son of God," has the evidence so overwhelmingly against its genuineness that it ought not to be used as a text. Very doubtful are the passages, John 7:53—8:11, concerning the woman taken in adultery, and Mark 16:9-20.[9]

(7) *The sayings of uninspired men, recorded in Scripture, ought not to be used as texts,* unless we know from other teachings of Scripture that they are true, or unless we propose to find instruction in the fact that those men made the statements given, or that the statements are untrue. Many such sayings found in the Bible are in themselves utterly untrue, inspiration being responsible only for the fact that they were actually spoken. No one, for example, would think of treating as true the vaunting speech of Rabshakeh (II Kings 18). However, the question of the scribes (Mark 2:7), "Who can forgive sins but God only?" we know to be a just question, and as such we might make it a text. In John 7:46, "Never man spake like this man," we likewise recognize a truth, and at the same time find significance in the fact that the officers sent to apprehend Jesus were thus impressed. The well-known words of Gamaliel (Acts 5:38, 39) are very instructive as his saying under the circumstances, but the principle laid down is not true without qualification. That there is much need for such alert discrimination is quite evident when we consider books like Job and Ecclesiastes, which portray in drama and sermon intellectual and moral problems in the process of solution. In the Book of Job many of the things said by the three friends are quite erroneous, and a few of Job's own utterances are tinged with error, as is shown

---

[9] There is no more occasion for uneasiness at the fact that errors are found in the common text of Scripture, than in the current translations. Men who are well aware of the latter fact and not disturbed by it are sometimes shocked at the former, because it is new to them. But neither in text nor in translation do our common Bibles present any such errors or uncertainties as would alter or modify any doctrine of Scripture. Still, that we ought not to employ as Scripture what is known to be spurious is a proposition which would seem to need no proof.

in the latter part of the book. These ought not to be treated as un-qualified truth, while as a part of the discussion they are highly interesting and instructive. So with some particular sayings in Eccle-siastes, which are not the present, affirmations of the inspired writer, but only a record of things which he had said in some former wrong mood, and which the argument of the whole book serves to correct. Yet texts from both these books are sometimes preached upon, which, regarded in themselves, present erroneous and morbid views of life. Let all sayings which, though a part of the inspired record, are yet only the utterances of uninspired men, be scrutinized in the light of their connection and of Scripture in general before they are used as texts.[10]

(8) *In the course of pastoral labor, several considerations should be borne in mind when selecting texts.* One is the present condition of the congregation. Mr. Beecher[11] insisted very strongly, and none too strongly, on the importance of this, and said:

You will very soon come, in your parish life, to the habit of thinking more about your people, and what you shall do for them than about your sermons and what you shall talk about. That is a good sign.

A second consideration is the character of the texts recently discussed. We have to guard against monotony in the subjects chosen, as well as in the mode of treating them, and to seek after such a relation between the successive sermons as will cause them to help each other's effect. It is sometimes well to look forward and mark out a series of sermons in advance; but it is always well to glance backward, at each new step, and keep in suitable relation to what has preceded. For this purpose, as well as on other accounts, a preacher should from the outset keep a list of sermons preached, including date, place, and text. A third and very important consideration is to select that in which we can at the time take interest, as otherwise we shall not deeply interest others. These three considerations will sometimes more or less con-flict; we must endeavor to maintain the balance among them as judiciously as possible.[12]

[10] See some examples in Vinet, *Hom.*, p. 109, and a very sensible discussion of the whole matter in Fisk's *Manual of Preaching*, pp. 68-70. Professor Fisk mentions several ways in which texts of this kind may be used: (1) As illustrations of God's character; (2) of his works; (3) of the imperfections of good men; (4) of the character of bad men; and (5) of the power of conscience in bad men.

[11] *Yale Lectures, First Series*, pp. 40 ff.

[12] It is interesting to note that Phillips Brooks (*Yale Lectures*, pp. 153 ff.) discusses, more at length and with excellent judgment, these same three points.

CHAPTER II

INTERPRETATION OF TEXTS

I. OBLIGATION TO INTERPRET CAREFULLY AND STRICTLY

TO interpret and apply his text in accordance with its real meaning is one of the preacher's most sacred duties. He stands before the people for the very purpose of teaching and exhorting them out of the Word of God. He announces a particular passage of God's Word as his text with the distinctly implied understanding that from this his sermon will be drawn, if not always its various thoughts, yet certainly its general subject. If he is not willing to be bound by this understanding, he ought to reject the practice which commits him to it and preach without any text. But using a text and undertaking to develop and apply its teachings, he is solemnly bound to represent the text as meaning precisely what it does mean. The remark may be here added that, where a text in its connection admits of more than one meaning, we shall do well either to avoid it as too ambiguous for our purpose or to indicate that we take the more probable sense and confine attention to its lessons as thus understood. The plan of taking up in succession several different senses and making a practical application of each cannot be approved. We must bring to bear upon men's minds as a part of God's Word only what the text really means as best we can ascertain it.

This would seem to be a truism. But it is often and grievously violated. Not only is there much contented ignorance as to interpretation and much careless neglect on the part of persons well able to interpret correctly and much wild spiritualizing of plain words, but by a violent method of "accommodation," Scripture sentences or phrases are employed as signifying what it is well known, and perhaps even declared at the time, that the sacred writer did not mean to say and has not at all said. "The original meaning of these words, as used by the inspired writer, is—so and so; but I propose on the present occasion to employ them in the following sense." That is to say— honored brother, see what you are doing—you stand up to teach men from a passage of God's blessed Word and coolly declare that you propose to make the passage mean what it does not mean. "But the words might have that sense." They might, but as a part of the Bible, as a text of Scripture, they do not. If we take the passage in a sense entirely foreign to what the sacred writer designed, as indicated by his connection, then, as we use it, the phrase is no longer a passage of Scripture at all. It is merely words of Scripture, used without authority to convey a different meaning, just as truly as if we had picked out words from a concordance and framed them into a sentence. "But the language of Scripture is so rich, its pregnant sayings often mean so much, that I think perhaps this expression may convey, among other things, the sense which I propose." If it really does, there is no objection whatever to using it so. But a mere vague "perhaps" is a slender and tottering excuse for a preacher, who is looked up to by the people as authority in this matter, who is supposed to have studied his text and to know its meaning, and whose statements will, for that reason, be accepted by many without question. Such a man is verily guilty before God if he does not honestly strive to understand that which he interprets and give forth its real meaning and no other.

Phelps[1] has a good discussion of accommodation. He distinguishes three kinds: (1) that based on mere resemblance of sound, as where a man preached on the duties of judges from the words, "Judge not, that ye be not judged." This he justly condemns as puerile and characterizes as "play upon a jewsharp." (2) that founded on metaphorical resemblance. This he also wisely rejects. It is merely spiritualizing, which will be considered further on. (3) that which "rests on the ground of resemblance in principle between the text and the theme." This he considers to be, with cautious use, admissible.[2]

Phillips Brooks[3] has an admirable passage on this subject, the closing sentences of which are as follows:

Never draw out of a text a meaning which you know is not there. If your text has not your truth in it, find some other text which has. If you can find no text for it in the Bible, then preach on something else.

And to the same purport Phelps[4] says:

That is a distorted ministry which deals in any large proportion with subjects which are not logically presented in the Scriptures. It is not a biblical ministry.

[1] Theory of Preaching, pp. 114 ff.
[2] Compare also Hoppin, *Hom.*, pp. 314-318; and Fisk, *Manual of Preaching*, pp. 74 ff.
[3] *Yale Lectures*, pp. 162, 163.
[4] Theory of Preaching, p. 124.

In one direction, however, the idea of strict interpretation may be carried too far. It is certainly best, as a general rule, to confine the sermon to the precise subject and aspect of a subject which the text in its connection sets forth. But we are not necessarily restricted to this. Some principle may be presented by the text in one application, and we may with perfect propriety make other applications of it. If this is all that is meant by accommodation, it is not a perversion of the Scripture, for the text really teaches the principle, and the new applications are avowedly made by ourselves, guided by the general teachings of Scripture. The apostle Paul often states a broad principle as bearing on some particular question of truth or duty. For example, Gal. vi. 7, "Whatsoever a man soweth, that shall he also reap," is said with special reference to the duty of contributing to the support of religious teachers, but it is given as a general truth and admits of many applications which it is lawful for us to make. Again, sometimes a very general admonition may properly be applied by the preacher to some particular case, provided he is sure it really covers the case. For example, it is perfectly legitimate to apply to a large variety of special cases the noble counsel of Paul in I Thess. 5:21, 22, "Prove all things; hold fast that which is good; abstain from every form of evil." Such texts as these are a great comfort to the conscientious preacher who is really anxious to use the Word of God accurately and sincerely. With this text a man can preach against any form of evil, provided he can prove that it is in truth an evil. Of course, if there is some text which specifically condemns the evil it is better to take that, but sometimes it may not be easy to find just the text that suits. In other cases we may start from the precise point given by the text and advance to related truths. We thus extend the application of the text, but in a direction not foreign but akin to the sacred writer's specific design. In Amos 4:12, "Prepare to meet thy God," the prophet gives warning of impending temporal judgments upon the nation and calls upon Israel to prepare to meet God in these. Yet, it is lawful for us, after pointing out this, to show that if we continue in sin we must all meet God, not only in temporal judgments but in the vengeance of the great day, and so we may call on our hearers to prepare for eternity. It thus appears that one may preach from a text on any matter which it presents to the mind, whether directly or indirectly, by statement, presupposition, or inference, provided that in some way it really does mean what is claimed; and where this meaning is only indirectly presented it will be better, in some simple way, to point out the fact, so as not to encourage in the people loose notions of interpretation. Very different from this was the course of a preacher who once gave a missionary sermon from the words of the young ruler, "What lack I yet?" inquiring what we lack for greater success in the missionary enterprise. This is an extreme case; but thousands of sermons are preached in which the real meaning of the text is just as completely, though not often so manifestly, violated.

Is it ever allowable to use a text simply as a motto? This is questionable. Hoppin[5] squarely opposes the practice. Phelps[6] discusses the matter very wisely and thinks that with some distinctions and cautions motto-texts may sometimes be used. But what is meant by a motto-text? It is like the quotations on the title-page or at the chapter headings of books; the words only remotely suggest the treatment. As Hoppin says, in this way the "text" often becomes only a "pretext." But still an occasional use of a text in this way is conceivably proper. Let us put the case thus: Occasion arises for the discussion of some particular subject for which the preacher can find no exactly suitable text. He must not pervert Scripture to make it suit his theme. Then he must either make an address without taking a text or use the text as a motto for his discourse. Which should he do? Sometimes one and sometimes the other. In the first case he should explain that he prefers to make an address rather than to preach from a text. In the other case he ought to interpret his text carefully, giving its real meaning and application. He should then show how the text, as properly interpreted and applied, comes to suggest at least the subject or to have a fitting connection with it. Thus in preaching a historical sermon before the Southern Baptist Convention on one occasion, the preacher chose as his text the promise to Naphtali in Deut. xxxiii. 23, "O Naphtali, satisfied with favor, and full with the blessing of the Lord; possess thou the west and the south." As a motto the beautiful appropriateness of this is apparent; but the preacher did not pretend that the tribe of Naphtali was in any sense a "type" of Southern Baptist or that Moses might have had these in his prophetic view when he pronounced this blessing.

Now supposing in the preacher an earnest desire to interpret his text correctly, he will not always find it an easy task. Apart from the loose notions, bad examples, and previous wrong practice, which often becloud the mind with reference to interpretation, it has some

---

[5] *Hom.*, p. 318.
[6] *Theory of Preaching*, pp. 126 ff.

intrinsic and serious difficulties which can be overcome only by thoughtful effort. While, therefore, the whole great subject of biblical interpretation does not belong to a treatise on homiletics, it seems proper and necessary to give some account of the errors to be avoided by a preacher in interpreting his text.

2. CHIEF SOURCES OF ERROR IN THE INTERPRETATION OF A TEXT

(1) Erroneous interpretations often arise from *misunderstanding the phraseology of the text itself*. Language even when chosen for precision of expression, can scarcely avoid the possibility of being misunderstood; and an easy, colloquial style is especially apt to involve a number of ellipses, broken constructions, words of various and not well-defined meaning, and other causes of ambiguity. If, then, a revelation is to be given in the language, idioms, and thought forms of those who are first to receive it, and to be expressed for the most part in that familiar style which will make it "come home to men's business and bosoms," it must be an inevitable condition of such a revelation that questions may often arise as to the exact meaning of its details. The general drift of a narrative, argument, or exhortation may be obvious enough, and its practical impression upon a docile and susceptible mind may be very distinct, and yet those who come to criticize the details, especially if they come with prepossessions and prejudices, may find numerous expressions capable of being variously interpreted, and perhaps some whose exact sense is really doubtful. Far better this, it is evident, than the idea of a revelation presented in a uniformly didactic and rigorously scientific style, which must at last fail of absolute precision, while it would be thoroughly devoid of interest for the ordinary human mind. Let us, therefore, cheerfully accept the necessity of exercising great care when we interpret the language of Scripture, as we are compelled to do with all other language.

Moreover, there are in our task some peculiar conditions. Many of us have to interpret a translation. Now the best translations are necessarily imperfect. It is rarely, if ever, the case that two words in different languages will contain precisely the same bulk of meaning in the same form and carry with them the same atmosphere of association and suggestion. Idiomatic differences of construction, too, will sometimes introduce ambiguity in a translation where the original was precise, or make too definite what in the original was only general. Especially frequent are the cases in which our language fails to indicate the emphasis, which in the Hebrew or the Greek may be distinctly marked. Yet with all this, there is nothing to discourage or to excuse the preacher from earnest efforts to ascertain the true meaning of his text. By working himself, through extensive, constant, and devout reading of the Bible, into thorough sympathy with its characteristic modes of thought and forms of expression, by throwing himself upon the current of the general connection of his text, so as to be borne over any particular difficulties, by comparing it with various other passages in which the same or a kindred subject is treated, and by consulting the works of learned and really judicious expositors, the intelligent preacher who uses only translations will have great success in the interpretation of Scripture. Witness the sermons and the writings of hosts of ministers who have become trustworthy expositors. Witness Andrew Fuller, who had practically no knowledge of the original languages, and yet his interpretations of Scripture are clear and safe in a degree very rarely surpassed.[7]

If, on the other hand, one uses the original languages in his interpretation, there is the danger of being misled by superficial knowledge or hasty examination. To ascertain the exact meaning of words and phrases in those languages, a thorough acquaintance with them is obviously necessary. An acquaintance with the original language will enable us to judge, with greater confidence and correctness, among the various interpretations of difficult passages, though it be not likely that we shall strike out anything new without a profounder knowledge than is often attained. Such an acquaintance will also sometimes save us from the disheartening notion that scholarship would make it all plain in cases which have at last to be decided by reference to the connection and the general teachings of Scripture. But as to the great bulk of Scripture, even the slightest knowledge of the originals is of service in helping us to enter into intellectual sympathy with the sacred writers and to catch the vividness and flavor so often lost in translation.

Moreover, interpreters must take account of various significant characteristics of the language of the Bible. In the first place, it is

---

[7] Dr. Chalmers, in urging his favorite counsel that students and ministers who know the original ought also to make regular and extended study of the English version, somewhere refers to Andrew Fuller as a striking example of the extent to which a man may carry his knowledge of Scripture by the use of the English version alone. Some brief and good suggestions on exposition are given by Fuller, *Works* (ed. Am. Bapt. Pub. Soc.), Vol. I., p. 712.

pervaded by a Hebraistic spirit, marked by Oriental modes of conception, which are in many respects quite different from those of our own people. Again, there is a certain number of important words, key words, in the Bible that have a well-defined and constant meaning which one must learn from the Bible itself.

If we confine ourselves purely and simply to the usual signification of the terms which the translator uses in rendering such words into our language, we are in great danger of committing serious errors. Thus, as to the words *flesh, soul, heart, fear, faith, understanding, foolish, light, darkness, just, righteousness, salvation, grace, good man, wicked.* The translator has translated for you the words; you must translate the ideas for yourselves.[8]

The technical sense in Scripture of such leading terms we partly learn from general observation in reading but may more precisely ascertain through a comparison, by help of the concordance, of many passages in which they are employed.

Further, it is to be observed that the language of Scripture is, as a general thing, not philosophical but popular, not scientific but poetic, not so much an analytical language, fond of sharp discriminations and exact statements, as a synthetical language, abounding in concrete terms, the representatives not of abstractions but of facts of actual existence and experience, which in their meaning gradually shade into each other without any definite line of distinction. This character leads to some peculiar forms of expression, which abound in the Bible, and are important for the interpretation of many texts.

For example, the language of the Bible delights in alternately diminishing and augmenting expression, in stating as absolute that which is relative and relative that which is absolute, in synonyms and parallelisms, in classifying persons and qualities without scientific purpose, and in symbols and metaphors.[9]

The interpreter of Scripture must remember that he is interpreting a literature whose style reflects the modes of thought of each of the epochs represented in it and of each of the authors who contributed to it. He must remember that the instruments of divine inspiration were living minds, Hebrew and Greek minds, and that the language of inspiration possessed the qualities and forms peculiar to those

---

[8] Vinet, *Hom.,* p. 111.
[9] Vinet, *Hom.,* pp. 113, 114. See for examples: Luke 14:26; I Cor. 13:2; Gen. 44:8; Jer. 7:22, 23; Exod. 20:16; Pss. 51:12; 119:105.

minds. It follows that the preacher must acquaint himself, if not with the original languages, at least with sound principles of interpretation that have emerged from an understanding of Hebrew and Greek modes of thought and expression.

(2) Erroneous interpretations arise from *disregarding the connection of the text.* In some cases, a sentence taken apart from its connection would give a positively wrong sense. For example, "Nevertheless, being crafty, I caught you with guile" (II Cor. 12:16). In others, it would be hopelessly ambiguous or utterly vague. In nearly all cases, a thorough understanding will require that we examine the connection. Even in those portions of Proverbs, where the several sentences appear wholly disconnected, one may sometimes derive help from observing what seems to be the general class of topics which the writer or collector has here in mind. In the Psalms, even Psalm cxix., there is always a general drift by which we may be guided. In the narratives, poetical treatises, discourses, epistolary arguments, etc., which make up almost the entire Bible, the connection is obviously important. It might in fact seem needless to insist on this. No man of sense, in dealing with any other book, would think of interpreting a single sentence here or there, in entire disregard of its connection.

Why, then, do men of sense so often neglect, or even knowingly violate, the connection of a Scripture text? Partly from the long-continued and widespread practice of allegorizing—to be discussed below—which is often most easily managed by cutting loose from the context, and which has encouraged men to think that the language of Scripture is so very different from all other language as to be independent of the principles which ordinarily govern interpretation. A second cause is the exclusive use of short texts. Men of ordinary powers cannot always find short passages which, interpreted in the light of the connection, will furnish them material enough for a sermon; and they are tempted to make some additional application of the words which the connection does not admit, or even to break a sentence away from its connection and give it an entirely new application which would make it a striking text. Under such pressure, and encouraged by the example of good and honored brethren, they interpret as suits them; and the habit thus formed is perhaps confirmed by indolence, seeing that it is often troublesome to study the context.

And there is yet another cause. Some six centuries ago there began

the present division of the Bible into chapters, and some three centuries ago the subdivision into verses. Both were made for convenience
in reference, just as somewhat similar divisions and subdivisions
have from time to time been made in the text of many Greek
and Latin authors. The divisions were very carelessly made and often
sadly disregard the connection and obscure the sense. And even if the
verses were better divided, the separate printing of brief sentences and
parts of sentences must of necessity make it more difficult to keep up
the general connection, particularly as we are accustomed, in all other
books, to a division into paragraphs, which mark the connection
clearly. The result has been to lead both preachers and hearers to think
of every chapter and every verse as a sort of separate whole. It is
curious to observe how rarely we hear read in public the latter part of
one chapter and the earlier part of the next, though the slightest care
for the real connection of narrative or argument would often require
this; and how awkward it would seem to take the last words of one
verse and the first words of another as a text. To dispel this illusion,
which makes every verse a paragraph and every chapter almost a
distinct book, is a matter of serious importance for all persons, ministers or others, who wish really to understand the Bible. Much advantage may be derived from habitually reading a paragraph Bible. The
American Standard Version and other modern translations, particularly of the New Testament, have in this respect an advantage
over the King James Version.

It would seem plain from what has been said, that the preacher
who wishes to deal fairly with his own mind and with God's Word
must determine that he will never interpret a text without careful
regard to its connection.[10] The considerations presented may explain
how it is that many devout and sometimes able brethren have been
led to do otherwise, and censure of their course is not proposed; but
when a man's attention has been distinctly called to the matter, he is
solemnly bound to give heed to it in practice. How shall one reconcile
it with the responsibility of his position, to stand before men in God's
name and say that a passage of the blessed Bible means anything else
than what he is satisfied, from the phraseology and the connection, it
really does mean?

(3) A third source of error in the interpretation of texts is *improper
spiritualizing*.

We have no other means of representing spiritual things than by

---

[10] See below, § 4, Rule (2).

metaphors derived from things temporal; and our very conceptions of the unseen world depend upon images furnished by the world in which we now live. The Scriptures appear to teach that there really is much of intimate connection and much of close correspondence between these two great spheres of existence. And the allegorical, in the broad sense of that term, is very widely and variously employed in the Scriptures of truth. The prophets frequently employed objects or events near at hand to picture realities belonging to the messianic age. Zion, the capital city and representative of Israel, furnished a favorite prophetic image in depicting the future of the spiritual Israel. In the New Testament numerous sacrifices and purifications, the priesthood, certain individual personages, as Melchizedek, Moses, and David, and the history of Israel as a whole are represented as having an analogical and sometimes a designedly typical relation to Christ and his church. The relation between husband and wife afforded an oft-recurring image of the relation between God and the chosen nation, between Christ and his Church. Even the enmity of Sarah and Hagar pictured the opposition between bondage under the law and liberty in the gospel.

With such a foundation in the nature of things, and with so much support in the actual usage of the Bible, it is not strange that there has always been on the part of some men a tendency to spiritualize, widely and wildly, the language of Scripture. It is common to speak of Origen (third century) as the father of Christian allegorizing; but it abounds already in some writers of the second century, and Origen learned much of it, as regards the Old Testament, from Philo the Jew, a contemporary of our Lord; the Alexandrian Jews having long been engaged in this sort of speculation. Origen's transcendent ability, learning, and power of creative imagination contributed much to make fanciful allegorizing popular among Christians. Most of the great Fathers, who have ever since their own times exerted so powerful an influence on Christian thought and practice, are grievously infected with this evil. After them many of the greatest preachers followed the method freely without any consciousness of violating the meaning of the text. Augustine, for example, is said to have represented the drunken Noah as a symbol of the shame of the manhood of Christ on the Cross.[11] With the rise of the historical method of interpretation in modern times allegorizing has fallen into disrepute; and today it is thoroughly discredited in theological edu-

[11] A. E. Garvie, *A Guide to Preachers*, p. 13.

cation. Nevertheless, there is still much ignorance to overcome, and too many able and honored ministers continue sometimes to sanction by their potent example the old-fashioned spiritualizing. It is so easy and pleasant for men of fertile fancy to break away from laborious study of phraseology and connection, to cease plodding along the rough and homely paths of earth, and sport, free and rejoicing, in the open heaven; the people are so charmed by ingenious novelties, so carried away with imaginative flights, so delighted to find everywhere types of Christ and likenesses to the spiritual life; it is so common to think that whatever kindles the imagination and touches the heart must be good preaching, and so easy to insist that the doctrines of the sermon are in themselves true and scriptural, though they be not actually taught in the text,—that preachers often lose sight of their fundamental and inexcusable error, of saying that a passage of God's Word means what it does not mean. So independent, too, one may feel; so original he may think himself. Commentaries, he can sneer at them all; other preachers, he has little need of comparing views with them. No need of anything but the resources of his own imagination, for such preaching is too often only building castles in the air.

The tendency to error in this direction is also increased by the fact that it is impossible, in respect to spiritualizing, to draw a line of unquestionable distinction between what is and what is not allowable. A good and safe rule to follow is that, while probable allegorical or spiritual meanings may be adduced as probable, no allegorical meaning shall be made the basis of a sermon without clear warrant in Scripture usage. But, practically, as to texts, we can never feel safe in going beyond this rule; anything not thus used in the New Testament can only be spoken of as possibly, or, at most, as probably, having an allegorical meaning; and while possible or probable interpretations, when distinctly stated to be such, may be properly used as yielding part of the argument or illustration of a sermon, the text, which is the foundation or source of the whole sermon, ought in the preacher's judgment really to have, beyond peradventure, the meaning assigned to it. Let us add that portions of Scripture which cannot be interpreted as having a spiritual meaning may yet be employed in various ways for teaching spiritual truth. They may embody principles, capable of an application to spiritual things, though such an application must be made by the preacher on his own responsibility and received by the people on their own judgment, not as a part of the teachings of Scripture. Or they may furnish illustrations of spiritual truth, just as we may derive illustration from everything in nature, history, and common life.[12]

And observe: In the case of *figurative passages* which really have a spiritual meaning, there is danger of pressing the figure too far, of fancying a spiritual sense in aspects or details of the figure which are not really within the scope of the inspired writer. When our Lord says, "Take my yoke upon you," we have no right to hunt up all manner of details as to yokes and oxen and run a fanciful parallel as to each particular; the general meaning is plain enough, and that is all. When he says, "Be ye wise as serpents," or "I will make you fishers of men," and in thousands of Scripture passages, the same principle holds. We must inquire what the sacred speaker or writer designed by the figure; so much it means, but beyond that, as a part of Scripture, it means nothing. Especially common are errors of this kind in the interpretation of our Lord's parables. The stories which were told by the Great Teacher are illustrations of unrivaled beauty and impressiveness, but still they are illustrations. Like the illustrative comparisons and incidents which we employ, some of them are founded upon a closer, and others upon a more remote, resemblance or analogy; some run parallel for a long distance to the subject compared with them; others barely touch it at a single point. When Christ's coming is said to be like that of a thief in the night, the resemblance extends only to unexpectedness; as to the character and objects of those who come, and almost everything else that is involved, the illustration and the thing illustrated are utterly unlike. And when it is said, "The kingdom of heaven is like leaven, which a woman took, and hid in three measures of meal, till the whole was leavened" (Matt. 13:33), what sense is there in looking for some spiritual truth illustrated by the number "three," or in saying that the woman represents the church, when as a matter of course a woman and not a man would be introduced in a story as making up bread? In undertaking to interpret a parable, we must learn from the connection what subject our Lord used it to illustrate—must then notice what light the parable as a whole throws on that subject, what aspects of the subject it brings to our view—and finally inquire how far we may fairly regard the several details of the story as separately significant. In this last respect we must avoid extremes, exercise sound judgment, and constantly keep in mind that the parable

[12] Compare Vinet, p. 120.

is an illustration and founded on some resemblance or analogy which is at best only partial.

3. EXAMPLES OF TEXTS OFTEN MISAPPLIED

There has been during the present century considerable improvement in various quarters as regards strict interpretation in the pulpit. But to show how much laxity on the subject still prevails it is proposed to mention a few examples of passages which are often used by preachers as texts or in argument, and whose meaning is beyond question very different from that commonly attached to them. It is strange how powerful is the tradition of the pulpit; how often able and thoughtful men will go all their lives taking for granted that an important passage has that meaning which in youth they heard ascribed to it, when the slightest examination would show them that it is far otherwise. The examples here given are arranged in the order of the three sources of error as to interpretation which have been discussed in the foregoing section, though of course these will sometimes be combined in the same passage. Many of the texts to be noted have been corrected in the Revised Version, especially in the marginal renderings. The preacher should be very careful not to use any text without first consulting the Revised Version.

(1) *Misunderstanding the phraseology of the text itself.* Jer. 3:4, "My father, thou art the guide of my youth." This is very often used in preaching to the young and given as a motto on the title-page of books for the young, the idea being that young people should seek the guidance of our Heavenly Father. But this is to miss the Scripture use of the phrase, "guide of my youth," as well as to disregard the connection of the passage. In Prov. 2:17, it is plain that "guide of her youth" (more exactly, companion, associate of her youth, R. V., margin) denotes the husband. Here in Jeremiah it is the same Hebrew word. The whole connection of chapters 2 and 3 shows that God through the prophet is reproaching the nation as an adulterous spouse, who deserves to be utterly cast off; but still he invites her to return to him. "Wilt thou not from this time cry unto me, My father, thou art the guide of my youth?" Thou art my early husband, the companion of my youth (compare Jer. 2:2; Hos. 2:15), and I return unto thee. And the term "father" is just a respectful form of address used by the wife to her husband, as Naaman's servants called

him "my father" (II Kings 5:13). Thus the common application of the passage is utterly erroneous.

Eccles. 12:1, "Remember now thy Creator in the days of thy youth." Here the word "now" is often much insisted on. But the Hebrew is simply "and remember," R. V., "remember also," etc. King James' translators, not perceiving the propriety of the connection indicated by "and," and finding it entirely omitted by their favorite authorities, the Vulgate and Luther, used, as a sort of compromise, the particle of transition "now." The connection is really very fine. "Rejoice, O young man, in thy youth . . . and walk in the ways of thine heart . . . and know that for all these things God will bring thee into judgment. And remove sorrow from thy heart, and put away evil from thy flesh; for childhood and youth are a breath. And remember thy Creator in the days of thy youth," etc.

Prov. 8:17, "They that seek me early shall find me." This does not at all mean early in life, as it is so constantly taken. Our translators, following the Vulgate, understood the Hebrew to signify early in the morning, there being a cognate word which denotes morning; and the idea they intended to convey was similar to that of Jer. 7:13, "And I spake unto you, rising up early and speaking, but ye heard not." Their phrase thus gives substantially the same sense with the view of recent scholars, who suppose that there is no connection with the idea of morning, and explain the word as signifying to seek (so the Septuagint), or to seek zealously, earnestly (R. V., "diligently." Compare Prov. 1:28; Ps. 63:1; Hos. 5:15). Thus the passage has no specific, much less exclusive, reference to the young.

Ps. 23:4, "Yea, though I walk through the valley of the shadow of death, I will fear no evil." To many it would seem almost sacrilege to say that this passage has no direct reference to the time when one is drawing near to death. The shadow of death, the dark place where the dead are, is an image frequently employed in the Old Testament to denote the densest darkness. Thus in Amos 5:8, God is described as "He that maketh the seven stars and Orion, and turneth the shadow of death into the morning, and maketh the day dark with night." Here it means the darkness of night. In Ps. 107:10, "Such as sat in darkness and the shadow of death, bound in affliction and iron," the reference is to the darkness of a dungeon. In Jer. 2:7, "Where is the Lord that brought us up out of the land of Egypt, that led us through the wilderness . . . through a land of drought, and of the shadow of death, through a land that no man passed through," the darkness of a gloomy desert is meant. In Isa. 9:2, "The people that walked in darkness have seen a great light, they that dwell in the land of the shadow of death, upon them hath the light shined," it is the darkness of destitution, ignorance, and affliction. (Compare Matt. 4:16.) The phrase is used in various other passages, but always meaning dense darkness, literal or figurative, and nowhere having any reference to dying. Now in Ps. 23:4, the image is that of a flock led through a deep, narrow, very dark valley, such as abound in Judea, with wild beasts lurking in the thickets on either hand, where the timid sheep would fear hurt unless protected by the shepherd; the Psalmist says that though walking in the darkest valley (R. V. margin, deep darkness), dark as the grave he will fear no evil, etc. And the image will naturally suggest any season or experience of life in which the believer would naturally feel alarm and distress but may be safe in his Shepherd's presence and protection. Such are temptation, sickness, bereavement, and death too, not because the word "death" is employed but because the image of passing through a valley dark as the grave naturally applies to death, and not as the single application, but as one of many. Thus a correct understanding of the passage does not destroy but widens its significance.[13]

Rom. 12:1, "Present your bodies a living sacrifice." Here many will begin to speak of making sacrifices, in our derivative sense of that term. But the thought of the text is that, as men presented at the altar the bodies of beasts as sacrifices, so we must consecrate ourselves unto God; and this is a "reasonable service," a worship of the rational or spiritual nature, and not a mere bodily worship, made up of outward acts and offerings.

I Tim. 2:8, "I will that men pray everywhere," etc. The Greek gives "the men" (as R. V.) and has the peculiar word which signifies man as opposed to woman. The apostle is giving directions for the conduct of public worship and says that the men must pray in every place, lifting up holy hands, without wrath and disputing. These phrases embody the special dangers with reference to men when engaging in public worship; and in the next verse he says that women, for their part, must not dress too fine, but be adorned with good works.

II. Tim. 2:15, "Study to show thyself approved unto God," etc. This

---

[13] Bunyan in the *Pilgrim's Progress* uses the image correctly, making his pilgrim pass through the valley of the shadow of death some time before he reaches the river.

is often quoted and sometimes made a text, as teaching that a minister must study, namely, study books, especially the Bible—study nature, human nature, etc. The real meaning of our version, as of the original, is endeavor; studiously endeavor to present thyself approved unto God. The Revised Version has "give diligence."

Heb. 7:25, "Wherefore he is able to save them to the uttermost that come to God by him," is a favorite text as showing that Christ is able to save the worst sinners. The real meaning of the phrase— as the connection also might show—is to save to the utmost, to the full extent of saving. As our High Priest does not transmit his office to successors and leave to others the work he has begun, but ever lives to intercede for those who come to God through him, he is able to save them completely—not merely to begin their salvation but to carry it forward in life and death till in eternity it is complete.

(2) *Disregarding the connection.* Col. 2:21, "Touch not, taste not, handle not." These words have been a thousand times blazoned on banners and quoted by impassioned orators, as a precept of Holy Writ against the use of intoxicating drinks. The slightest attention to the connection would show in the first place, that they are not spoken with any reference to that subject, and in the second place, that they are given by the apostle as an example of ascetic precepts to which we ought not to conform. "If ye died with Christ from the rudiments of the world, why, as though living in the world, do ye subject yourselves to ordinances, Handle not, nor taste, nor touch, . . . after the commandments and teachings of men?" (R. V.) There are many passages of Scripture which enjoin temperance, but this is certainly not one of them.

Heb. 6:1, "Let us go on unto perfection," is a favorite text with some of those who maintain the possibility of sinless perfection in this life. But the sacred writer is speaking of knowledge, and urges prog- ress toward maturity of knowledge. The word in the preceding verse (v. 14) rendered "of full age" is literally "perfect"; so that the two verses have a close verbal connection besides the general connec- tion in sense.

I Cor. 2:9, "Eye hath not seen, nor ear heard, neither have entered into the heart of man, the things which God hath prepared for them that love him," is constantly quoted as referring to the glory and blessedness of heaven; but the connection leaves no doubt that the apostle refers to the profound wisdom of the plan of salvation, which no human mind could have perceived or imagined, but which "God has revealed unto us by his Spirit."

Mark 9:8, "Jesus only." To make these words a text and discourse upon Jesus only as Prophet, Jesus only as Priest, Jesus only as King, etc., is an extreme instance of disregarding the context. At the close of the transfiguration, "suddenly, when they had looked round about, they saw no man any more, save Jesus only with themselves." Now it is very true that we must have Jesus only as Prophet, Priest, and King, but who will say that this passage teaches that or even fairly suggests it? And the mere words, taken entirely apart from what the sacred writer meant by them, are no more a saying of Scripture than if "Jesus" had been taken from Mark, and "only" from Romans and the two combined as a text.

Isa. 1:5, 6, "The whole head is sick, and the whole heart faint. From the sole of the foot even unto the head there is no soundness in it; but wounds, and bruises, and putrefying sores," etc. This is sometimes used as a text and perpetually cited as a proof-text to show the total depravity of man. But look at the connection. The nation of Israel had been stricken with the divine judgments till it was like a man beaten with the terrible Oriental scourging, from head to foot, and with wounds and stripes unhealed; the country was desolate, the cities burned, and Jerusalem stood alone in a wilderness. And the prophet asks, Why should ye be stricken any more? If it is done, you will revolt still more. Already you are beaten from head to foot, but punishment makes you no better; it even seems to make you worse. Now this would be an excellent text for showing how often nations, communities, individuals, refuse to be subdued by afflictions and go on in their wickedness; and there is in this respect a proof here of the depravity of man. But the image, the whole head is sick, etc., is clearly not at all designed to set forth depravity, but severe chastisement.

Isa. 63:1-3, "Who is this that cometh from Edom, with bright-red garments from Bozrah? . . . I that speak in righteousness, mighty to save. Wherefore art thou red in thine apparel? . . . I have trodden the wine-press alone." How often this is held to denote our Saviour as shedding his blood and suffering alone for our salvation. And yet what can be plainer than that this is a conqueror, stained with his enemies' blood and fighting alone? In the same sentence he says, "For I will tread them in mine anger and trample them in my fury; and their blood shall be sprinkled upon my garments."

(Compare also verses 4-6.) Here the speaker is the conqueror of Edom and deliverer of Israel. If understood as applying to Messiah, it must be to him as conquering his people's enemies, and mighty to save in this sense. In Rev. 19:11-16, the same imagery is employed in describing the Word of God; yet there too it is not a sufferer but a conqueror.

I Kings 18:21, "How long halt ye between two opinions?" The favorite use of this text is to reproach men with indecision and hesitation as to becoming Christians. But the Israelites were not undeceived as to whether they would serve Jehovah or Baal; they were trying to serve both, to conform to the fashionable court-religion and yet retain the religion of their fathers. Elijah reproaches them with this effort to do both. Serve Jehovah, or else Baal, not first one and then the other. (Compare "Ye cannot serve God and Mammon.")

(3) *Improper spiritualizing, etc.* Amos 6:1, "Woe to them that are at ease in Zion." Here Zion is the church, those at ease in Zion are the slothful, worthless members of the church, and away we go. But the prophet adds, "and trust in the mountain of Samaria"; what is the "spiritual sense" of that? The chiefs of Judah trusted in the strong fortifications of Jerusalem and those of the northern kingdom in Samaria, and so they were not alarmed by the prophetic warnings that enemies would come and destroy those capitals, as other great cities had been destroyed. Woe to them, if quietly confiding in Jerusalem and Samaria, they did not repent of their wickedness and trust in God. The application of this in time of war is manifest and important. The principle might also be applied to any reliance upon human instrumentalities or outward agencies instead of relying on God. The do-nothing members of a church deserve severe scourging, but this text does not touch them.

Exod. 2:9, "Take this child away, and nurse it for me, and I will give thee thy wages." And some able men actually make this a text in preaching to parents, or to Sunday-school teachers. "God says to you, Take this child," etc. But he says no such thing. He simply tells us that the daughter of Pharaoh said this to the mother of Moses. God does not address these words to anybody. To find here a spiritual meaning is so wholly unwarranted, so utterly arbitrary, as to be beyond the reach of argument. If the preacher says that he takes the words in the sense proposed, then they are not Scripture at all,— not God's saying, but his saying,—and ought not to be called a text, for that means Scripture. It would be just as appropriate to take

Prov. 23:30, "Tarry long at the wine," as a divine precept, or Ps. 14:1, "There is no God," as a declaration of Scripture. Whether as allegorizing or as "accommodation" such an application of the text is indefensible, and when once a man's attention has been called to the matter, it would be inexcusable.

Jonah 1:6, "What meanest thou, O sleeper?" How *can* a preacher tell us that these words refer to sinners as spiritually asleep? Jonah, worn out with his hasty and anxious journey to Joppa, and now safe aboard, was soundly sleeping; and the ship-captain alarmed and impatient, shouts at him, "What are you about, fast asleep? Arise, call upon thy God, as all the rest are doing." A minister can utter these words to sleeping sinners, but he may not say that God addresses this question to them or to anyone. God's Word simply narrates the fact that the ship-captain thus spoke; he does not himself speak the words at all. As merely the minister's words, they would not be a part of Scripture. As to any properly allegorical meaning hidden in the words, it is a sheer figment and must be proven, not recklessly assumed.

Prov. 18:24, "There is a friend that sticketh closer than a brother." It is commonly held that in the eighth chapter of Proverbs there is some allusion to Christ,—which is not at all certain,—and hence any passage in Proverbs at will is taken as referring to Christ. But at chapter x there begins a manifestly distinct collection, containing a number of detached proverbs, exceedingly instructive and useful for our practical guidance in life, but having not the slightest appearance of a mystical character. The proverbs which here immediately precede and follow and the other half of this proverb are about common matters. Verse 21, power of the tongue; verse 22, blessing of finding a wife; verse 23, the poor entreats, the rich answers roughly; and as to the succeeding proverbs, verse 1 (next chapter), the poor who walks in his integrity, and the perverse fool, etc., etc. Verse 24 is rendered, "A man that hath friends must show himself friendly; and there is a friend that sticketh closer than a brother." The first half is in the Hebrew obscure, but most probably means "a man of [many] associates will ruin himself," by misplaced confidence, or "will prove bad," cannot be faithful to them all. However that may be, the general subject is plainly the common friendships of life; and there is no hint of allusion to Christ. And then it is added that there are some close and permanent friendships, there is a friend (literally, "lover") that sticketh closer than a brother not referring to any particular individual, but meaning that such a thing does exist. We need not condemn the poet's use of this expression,

> One there is above all others
> Well deserves the name of friend:
> His is love beyond a brother's, etc.;

but the license of poetical adaptation is a very different thing from interpretation. One might take this proverb as a text, and speak of the friendships that are close and faithful and then pass by analogy, on his own responsibility, to speak of Christ as a friend; but that is not saying that this passage refers to Christ.

It has seemed necessary to discuss the above passages with some care, because the inexperienced reader might naturally be slow to believe that so many favorite texts have been utterly misunderstood by himself and by many preachers around him. No infallibility is claimed for the particular interpretations here given. The thing urged is to form the habit of carefully studying every text, even the most familiar and apparently obvious, to see if it really does mean what the preacher has hitherto supposed. This practice will rob him of many texts but will enrich him with many others. Most of those above considered, when the common application has been set aside, are found to have a sense that may be made interesting and useful. And by careful examination many another passage will develop unsuspected riches. If strict interpretation of texts brought unmitigated loss of material, we ought still to practice it, for the sake of dealing honestly with our own minds, and with God's Word; but the habit of strict interpretation will give far more than it takes away. If one knows the Hebrew or the Greek, let him never preach upon a text without carefully studying it and its context in the original. Otherwise, let him search the best translations and good explanatory notes, determined that he will never say a passage of God's holy and precious Word means so and so, without personal, honest, patient effort to ascertain the fact.

4. SUGGESTIONS FOR THE STUDY OF TEXTS

Though we have discussed at length the chief sources of error in the interpretation of texts and illustrated them by many examples, it seems best to give, positively, some account of the principles upon which one must proceed if he would interpret correctly. Good treatises on interpretation are accessible,[14] and it is sufficient here to give a few brief suggestions. In regard to interpretation, we must distinguish the preliminary study of a text with a view to preaching upon it from that general study of the Bible which should be a part of every preacher's regular work, and also from the popular explanation of the text which forms part of the sermon. This will be treated later.[15] The suggestions here offered are intended to aid the preacher in getting from himself the exact meaning of the passage of Scripture which he proposes to use as the text for his sermon. And this is surely what every preacher should feel in conscience bound to do. Whatever helps he may use, in the way of commentaries, lexicons, grammars, books of illustration and the like, he should see to it that the interpretation which he adopts is his own. That is, the meaning of the text which he proposes to unfold and enforce in his sermon should be in all cases his own carefully formed view of the passage, —the fruit of earnest reflection and study. Hints that may prove of service in making such a study will now be given in the form of rules.

(1) *Study the text minutely.* Notice carefully both the grammar and the rhetoric of the text. (*a*) Endeavor to ascertain the precise meaning of the words and phrases used in the text. Inquire whether any of them have a peculiar sense in Scripture, and whether such peculiar sense holds in this passage. If there are key-words in the text, or words of special importance, examine, by the help of a concordance, other passages in which such word is employed. This is best done in the original, because our version will often have the same word where the Hebrew or Greek is different, and the same Greek or Hebrew word will be used in important passages where our version renders differently. But for those who are limited to the English language there are available excellent concordances, translations, and commentaries that will be found most helpful.

Grammatical study of the text can scarcely be made too minute or protracted. Whately used to say, "Before writing your sermon, look at your text with a microscope,"[16] and Shedd justly remarks:

Every particle of care in first obtaining an excellent text and then getting at, and getting out, its real meaning and scope, goes to render the actual

---

[14] Such as Fairbairn's *Hermeneutical Manual* (for the New Testament), Davidson's *Biblical Hermeneutics* (particularly full on the History of Interpretation), Angus' *Bible Hand-Book*, Barrow's *Companion to the Bible* (new, cheap, and on this subject very good) Horne's Introduction.

[15] See Chapter VI § 2.

[16] *Life and Remains of Whately*, p. 402.

construction and composition of the sermon more easy and successful. Labor at this point saves labor at all after points.[17]

(b) Pay special attention to any figures of speech that may occur in the text or its connection. Wherever it is clear, from the nature of the case, from the connection, or from precisely similar expressions in other passages, that the literal sense is not designed, then we must understand figuratively. In the language of Scripture, as in all other language, the presumption is in favor of the literal sense. To explain away as figurative whatever seems to conflict with doctrinal prejudices, or with fanciful notions and morbid feelings as to ethics or æsthetics, or with hasty inferences from imperfectly established scientific facts is to trifle with that which we acknowledge as an authoritative revelation. Still, there is very much in Scripture that is clearly figurative and very much more which might so readily be thus understood, in the light of other Scripture usage, that we ought to be careful about building important theories upon its literal sense. This is especially true as regards prophecies of things yet to come, in which it is of necessity quite difficult to distinguish beforehand between literal and figurative, though the fulfillment will some day make it plain. And remember that language may be highly figurative without being fictitious. Only ascertain what the figures of Scripture were designed to mean, and that meaning is as certainly true as if stated in plain words. Thus the "fire that cannot be quenched" may be called a figure if you choose; yet it assuredly means that in hell there will be something as bad as fire, something as torturing as fire is to the earthly body—nay, the reality of hell, as well as of heaven, does no doubt greatly transcend the most impressive imagery that earthly things can afford.

(2) *Study the text in its immediate connection.* The connection of thought in which a text stands will of course throw light upon its meaning and is usually indispensable to understanding it. The immediate connection or context will usually embrace from a few verses to a few chapters before and after the text; and of this context the preacher should not only have a general knowledge but should make special examination when examining his text; and we must resist the common tendency to imagine that this context begins or ends with the chapter in which the text stands. The extent to which such study of the connection should be carried will of course be very

[17] Shedd, *Hom.*, p. 176.

different in different cases; but there are scarcely any texts with reference to which it can with propriety be entirely neglected. It should be remarked that besides the importance of studying the logical connection in order to obtain a thorough understanding of the text, an exposition of the context often forms a good, and sometimes a necessary, introduction to the sermon.

(3) *Study the text in its larger connections.* These remoter relations of the text are also very important to its correct interpretation. They commonly embrace the three following particulars. (*a*) Sometimes the logical connection will really be the entire idea to which the text belongs. There are few sentences in Hebrews or in the first eleven chapters of Romans which can be fully understood without having in mind the entire argument of the Epistle. Of course this is not so strikingly true in most of the books, but each of them has its own distinctive contents, connection, and character. Few things are to be so earnestly urged upon the student of Scripture as that he shall habitually study its books with reference to their whole connection. Then he can minutely examine any particular text with a correct knowledge of its general position and surroundings.

(*b*) Apart from the logical connection of discourse in which a text is found, there is often important aid to be derived from general historical knowledge. In the narratives which make up the larger part of Scripture we have constant need of observing facts of geography which would throw light on the text. So as to the manners and customs of the Jews, and other nations who appear in the sacred story. Thus much is obvious, though these helps for understanding texts are seldom used as diligently as they should be. But there is also much to be learned by taking account of the opinions and state of mind of the persons addressed in a text. We need to remember the relations between the speaker or writer and those whom he has specially in view. In order to do this, we must not merely know the previous relations of the parties, as in the case of Paul's Epistles, but must endeavor to ascertain what errors or evils existed among them which the inspired teacher is here aiming to correct. This can often be gathered from the book itself. No trouble need ever have been felt as to the supposed contradiction between Paul and James with regard to justification, if attention had been paid to the theoretical and practical errors at which they are respectively aiming. In the case of our Lord's teachings, much may be learned from the Gospels and also from the Jewish writings and the modern works founded on them, concerning the wrong notions and evil practices existing among the Jews and to which his sayings have often a very direct and specific reference. With respect, for example, to divorce, to oaths, to the Sabbath, or to the duty of paying tribute, his teachings will be imperfectly apprehended unless we understand the practical abuses and vehement controversies which existed among his hearers as to those subjects. On such points the best commentaries give some information. Or, to take a different kind of example, the words "No man can come to me, except the Father which hath sent me draw him" (John vi. 44), were not spoken as a mere general, didactic utterance; much less were they addressed to humble and anxious inquirers but were aimed at an utterly unspiritual rabble, who were following him not from any elevated motives but from mere fanatical excitement, and in the hope of continuing to be fed without working for it—who called themselves his disciples and talked about forcing him to set up an earthly kingdom. The recollection of all this does not weaken the force of what he said, but it helps us to appreciate his specific aim at the moment and gives us an important example as to the adaptation of doctrine. The more one attends to the subject the more he is likely to become convinced that almost everything in the New Testament, as well as much in the Old, is really controversial or apologetic in its specific design, and that we must constantly inquire what errors or evil practices are aimed at in order to appreciate the precise bearing given, in any text, to the principles it may contain and the modifications of statement which may be necessary in turning these principles towards new applications.

(c) We must interpret in accordance with, and not contrary to, the general teachings of Scripture. These teachings are harmonious and can be combined into a symmetrical whole. If a passage may have two senses, owing to the ambiguity of some word or construction, to the doubt whether some expression is figurative, etc., then we must choose one which accords with what the Bible in general plainly teaches rather than one which would make the Bible contradict itself. It is a gross abuse of this principle—though one often practiced —to force upon a passage some meaning which its words and constructions do not grammatically admit of, in order that it may give the sense required by our system. But between possible grammatical meanings we are compelled to choose upon some principle, and certainly one important principle to be considered is that the teachings of Scripture must be consistent. Where the grammatical probabilities are pretty evenly balanced, a comparatively slight preference in the respect mentioned must turn the scale; and even a much less probable sense—provided it be grammatically possible, and sustained by some corresponding usage of language—may be preferred to a more probable and common sense, if the former would perfectly accord and the latter would grossly conflict with the acknowledged general teachings of Scripture. In order to apply this principle with propriety and safety, it is manifestly necessary that we should bring to bear no narrow and hasty views of Scripture teaching but the results of a wide, thoughtful, and devout study of biblical theology.

It is necessary also that we should keep in mind the fact that revelation was progressive. Light grew from less to more. There is a marked advance of knowledge as we move more from Abraham to Moses and the prophets and from the prophets to Christ. This holds true in matters of theology and also of ethics. This fact means two things for the interpreter: first, that the teachings of the Old Testament must be interpreted in the light of the New; and, secondly, that the use of proof-texts must be made with great care. The finality of any text or portion of Scripture must be judged by the total revelation. Scriptural authority has been claimed for many erroneous ideas by failure at this point. The law of Moses, for example, recognized polygamy and made provision for divorce, which Jesus declared to be unideal and contrary to the high purpose of God. The imprecatory prayers of certain psalms cannot be properly evaluated apart from the injunction of Jesus, "Love your enemies." Many of the ideas of Ecclesiastes and Job are but the transient groping of men struggling toward the light.

The careful examination of Scripture "references" in studying a text is also a matter of great importance. These will often help in the grammatical part of interpretation by showing how the same words and phrases are elsewhere employed; and in the historical, by showing how the same subject was presented under different circumstances, or what was the peculiar state of things in which the text was uttered. They may also assist us by presenting parallel or analogous Scripture usage, in determining whether expressions of the text ought to be taken as figurative or as allegorical; and there are cases in which even a few other passages will so far set forth the general teachings of Scripture on the subject involved in the text as to be of service in choosing among the possible meanings of its language. They will also help the preacher to form his own opinion as to the meaning of his text, without depending too much on commentaries and other helps. Moreover, the "reference" passages will very often furnish useful material for the body of the sermon, suggesting to us new aspects, proofs, illustrations, or applications of the subject treated. The young preacher should make it a fixed rule to consult the references to his text; and many men and women have become "mighty in the Scriptures" by the diligent use of references in their daily reading.

CHAPTER III

THE SUBJECT

THE sermon may or may not have a text. It must have a subject. Definitely it must be about something, some significant truth bearing upon religious life—a doctrine or ethical principle, some moral problem, personal or social, some human need such as the need to be saved, encouraged, or guided in religious living. Whether the subject or the text is first chosen will of course depend upon circumstances and the preacher's turn of mind. In considering the condition of the congregation or looking back over the sermons recently preached, one will be more likely to decide upon a subject, for which he must then find a text. In reading the Bible or running over his growing list of texts, he will be more apt to light upon some text which interests him, and from which he will proceed to evolve a subject. It has been thought best to discuss the text first, because the primary conception of preaching is to bring forth the teachings of some passage of Scripture. The approach does not greatly matter. The points to be insisted on are these: When the subject is first selected, then carefully look for a text which will fairly, and if possible exactly, present that subject. If the text comes first, then seek to work out from it some definite subject.

I. RELATION OF SUBJECT AND TEXT

The relation between the subject and the text should be clear and unquestioned. The final reason for the choice of a text, granted that it fulfills such requirements as those discussed in Chapter I, is that it expresses or suggests ideas that yield a worthy subject or support in a legitimate way a subject already chosen. Dr. A. E. Garvie's discussion of the connection between the two is worthy of study.[1] Text and subject may stand in the relation of principle and application, or general and particular truths. For example, one desires to speak on some social practice of doubtful moral character

[1] A. E. Garvie, *The Christian Preacher*, pp. 385-389.

50

or consequences; if he is familiar enough with his Bible he will recall Paul's words, "Whatsoever is not of faith is sin" (Rom. 14:23). Or beginning with a text such as "Whatsoever a man soweth that shall he also reap" (Gal. 6:7), one may preach on some particular moral débâcle or triumph, either personal or social. In such instances the subject is a deduction from the text. On the other hand, the subject may be a particular fact or judgment or experience, and the subject a generalization upon it or induction. For example, Luke 12:19-20 may be the text for a sermon on the futility of covetousness; so also the experience of Simon of Cyrene is a legitimate basis for the subject, Burdens That Are Blessings. Numberless texts are particular instances of divine power, providence, love, mercy, wrath, and redemption, as many others express great principles that speak to numberless subjects pertinent to life.

Garvie points out further that subject and text may have an analogical relation, suggesting, for example, that a sermon on the perils to Christian ideals incident to war may have for its basis Ps. 137, and that Matt. 18:15-17 may quite legitimately be used to discuss ways of preventing war, the method of resolving personal differences having a bearing upon the problem of group differences. Or again the text may be related to the subject through suggestion. Horace Bushnell read the sentence, "Then went in that other disciple also" (John 20:8) saw one man influencing another unconsciously, and wrote his great sermon on Unconscious Influence. The connection of text and subject is real, though indirect. To Bushnell also the text, "I have girded thee [surnamed thee, A.R.V.] though thou hast not known me" (Isa. 45:5), was a sufficient basis for the subject, Every Man's Life a Plan of God.

If a man has a fanciful wayward mind, if he is imperfectly instructed in the Holy Scriptures and Christian truth, it will be at his peril that he will follow the suggestions of his text, for as a rule they will be will-o'-the-wisps leading him into a mental bog. But if a man has adequate knowledge and disciplined judgment, suggestion, even when it cannot be reduced to strict logical form, may be a helpful guide.[2]

This is especially true of the details of the parables of Jesus, which are full of suggestions but must be used with great care and restraint, else that which began as a suggestion may become a "hidden meaning."

[2] *Ibid.*, p. 387.

It is legitimate also to use as a text for a sermon on some character or chapter of history a passage that reveals a central point of interest or that would serve as a starting point. The text, "And the Lord turned, and looked upon Peter" (Luke 22:61), for example, is an excellent taking-off point for a sermon on Peter's fall and recovery. In this whole matter the preacher needs a good imagination, good judgment, a high regard for his own integrity, and above all a purpose of dealing honestly with the Scriptures and with his audience.

2. STATEMENT OF THE SUBJECT

Later we shall study various sermon forms. Let it be said now that whatever the form, it is important for the sermon to have unity of subject.

A preacher may take a text, and say a great deal about the words, phrases, and clauses of the text, without fixing his own mind or the minds of his hearers on any one subject. There are sermons which are like a rudderless ship on a wide sea, driven hither and thither, and making for no haven.[3]

To state one central idea as the heart of the sermon is not always easy, especially in textual and expository preaching. But the achievement is worth the effort. Even when a text presents several ideas, all of which should be incorporated in the sermon, it is desirable to find for them some bond of unity, some primary idea that will serve as focus or axis or orbit. One may fix attention on one of the ideas as subject and consider the others in relation to it. The text in Heb. 2:3 suggests three subjects: the Great Salvation, the Evil of Neglecting the Gospel, and the Problem of Escape, any one of which might well be chosen, depending upon purpose and circumstance. The other two will mightily enforce its consideration. Or it is possible to state a general idea that will include all the main points of the text, as, for instance, in dealing with such texts as I Pet. 1:8-9. There are four verbs—love, believe, rejoice, receive. What is the text about, four things or one thing in four aspects? Let one preacher answer:

What he (the apostle) is trying to do here is something rather daring: it is nothing less than to define *the central Christian experience* in a single sentence; and you will observe that he has packed it all into four words,

[3] *Ibid.*, p. 42.

four short, decisive verbs. "Ye love—ye believe—ye rejoice—ye receive." That, he declares, is *what it means to be a Christian*. That, throughout the ages, has been *the high road of salvation*.[4]

The italicized words show the possibilities in expressing a unifying idea. Dr. W. L. Watkinson preached a sermon on I Cor. 15:32-34, his subject being The Personal Equation in Christian Belief. Let him tell how he arrived at it:

Our text seems to be an interruption to the great argument (concerning resurrection), and at the first glance it appears somewhat irrelevant and misplaced. Yet a little reflection shows that it is a parenthesis quite in place, and one of weightiest signification. The apostle reminds his readers that faith in the great future is not simply a question of logic, but also a question of the state of mind we bring to the consideration of the subject. He emphatically declares that it is possible for men so to live that their vision may be blurred, their sensibilities dulled, and they themselves become incapable of great ideals and hopes.[5]

Hence his subject. Another might have stated the same idea as Moral Barriers to Great Faith. The whole point is that the preacher can and ought to preach on one subject, clearly apprehended by himself and so presented to his audience.

Great care should be taken in the statement of the subject. Being the focal idea of the sermon it calls for the simplest rhetorical statement, for example, Salvation by Grace, The Wages of Sin, the Assurance of Hope, Christ—the Unfailing Light, The Goodness and Severity of God, Abounding Grace, The Expulsive Power of a New Affection, The Royalty of Service, The Sense of What Is Vital, The Son in the Home. Notice that there are two or more terms in each of these subjects: Salvation and Grace, Assurance and Hope, etc. They are all general terms, but by the use of prepositions, adjectives, conjunctions, or participial forms they are all brought together in some definitive relation, so that we have not broad generalities but particular ideas.

3. TITLE AND PROPOSITION

Besides the simple rhetorical expression of the central idea or the relation of ideas to be discussed in the sermon, two other ways of

[4] James S. Stewart, *The Gates of New Life*, p. 125.
[5] W. L. Watkinson, *The Shepherd of the Sea*, pp. 53 f.

stating the subject must be considered,—as title and as proposition. The principal function of the title is to attract and interest the public. In a day of church calendars, bulletin boards, and newspaper advertising this is of great importance. Dr. Ozora Davis makes the observation that as the success or failure of a book is often determined by its title, "so the attractiveness of a sermon is conditioned largely by the choice of the title."[6] Often the well-phrased subject will serve, but more often, perhaps, the preacher will desire in his public announcement another form. So most modern books of sermons would indicate. A review of a few of these volumes will serve to point out at once the value of the title and some of the principles that ought to be observed in its formulation. One finds all sorts of titles— titles that promise more than the sermons give, titles trivially stated, dull titles, sensational titles that smack of super-salesmanship, magnetic, majestic, poetic titles, titles that are simple, positive and unadorned. All depends on the imagination, taste, and high purpose of the preacher, and in these things preachers are not all equal. Some titles are in technical theological terms, others in untechnical words ranging from good vernacular to slang. They are in the form of questions, exclamations, prepositional phrases, contingent clauses, single words, short dogmatic statements, as well as in conventional subject form. A few writers have the ability to frame a title that gives an adequate sense of the subject in phraseology that strikes the moods, the perplexities, the tendencies, and the manner of speech of the modern man. They know contemporary life, vocabulary, and psychology.

It is a rare gift that enables a preacher to select such titles as will be vital, interesting, timely, and also conform to the laws of good taste and dignity. With careful thought and continued practice a preacher ought to become resourceful and accurate in the phrasing of sermon titles; certainly this involves one's best possible thought and practice.[7]

The Proposition deserves more attention than is given by many preachers. It is a statement of the subject as the preacher proposes to develop it. It is subject (idea) and predicate. The subject answers the question, What is the sermon about? The proposition answers the question, What is the sermon? Phelps likens the proposition to the trunk from which the body of the sermon expands, the root

[6] *Principles of Preaching*, p. 199.
[7] *Ibid.*, p. 200.

being the idea in the text.[8] "The discourse is the proposition un-
folded, and the proposition is the discourse condensed" (Fénelon).
Its form should be one complete declarative sentence, simple, clear,
and cogent. It should contain no unnecessary or ambiguous words.
"It should contain all that is essential to the sermon, no less and no
more, and no other than the truth of the subject, stated in cumulative
order."[9] It is important to distinguish between the proposition and
the objective. The latter has to do with the desired ends of the sermon
in the character and conduct of the hearers; the former, with the
form and substance of the message.

A few examples will serve to make the meaning clear. In the
sermon already referred to, Every Man's Life a Plan of God, Horace
Bushnell announced the following proposition:

The truth I propose then for your consideration is this: That God has a
definite life-plan for every human person, girding him, visibly or in-
visibly, for some exact thing which it will be the true significance and
glory of his life to have accomplished.[10]

Bushnell's sermon on Unconscious Influence has for its proposition,

Thus it is that men are ever touching unconsciously the springs of
motion in each other, (so that) one man without thought or intention or
even a consciousness of the fact is ever leading some other after him.[11]

Phillips Brooks' sermon on the Light of the World contains two
statements of the proposition, the one brief, the other more explicit:

[1] That the soul of man carries the highest possibilities within itself,
and that what Christ does for it is to kindle and call forth these possibilities to actual existence.
[2] Christ when he comes finds the soul or the world really existent,
really having within itself its holiest capabilities, really moving, though
dimly and darkly, in spite of its hindrances, in its true directions; and what
he does for it is to quicken it through and through, to sound the bugle of
its true life in its ears, to make it feel the nobleness of movements which
have seemed to it ignoble, the hopefulness of impulses which have seemed
hopeless, to bid it be itself.[12]

The student will readily see that the briefer is the better statement.

---

[8] *Theory of Preaching*, p. 308.
[9] Davis, *Principles of Preaching*, p. 206.
[10] *Sermons for the New Life*, p. 10.
[11] Davis, *Principles of Preaching*, p. 21.
[12] As reprinted in Davis, *Principles of Preaching*, pp. 43 ff.

Turning to sermons of our own day, notice first a sermon by Dr. G. G. Atkins. The text is Ps. 119:109; the title, Craftsmen of the Soul; the proposition, "In a true sense we hold our souls in our hands as an artificer the materials upon which he works, and the creative shaping of them to high uses and enduring ends is our master task"[13] (Parts of two sentences). From Dr. H. E. Fosdick we have the following: text, Philem. 4:22; title, Christians in Spite of Everything; proposition, "Christianity essentially means a spiritual victory in the face of hostile circumstance." In a recently published volume by A. A. Cowan a sermon on the institution of the Lord's Supper has for its texts Exod. 12:26 and Matt. 17:5; for its title, The Banquet of Liberty; and for the proposition, "What Jesus and his disciples celebrated in the Upper Room was a new future prepared by divine love for believing hearts and assuring them that they would be freed from all enslavements."[14] In a sermon on the Escape from Frustration, James Reid, using Luke 5:4, 5, 10 as his text, states his proposition as follows: "The way out of life's frustrations is found, not by resenting our limitations, but by accepting the place of frustration as the sphere of God's purpose.[15]

The proposition is the gist of the sermon. A reading of the best sermons reveals that often the preacher repeats more than once the comprehensive sentence, and every paragraph serves in some way to enforce or prove or explain or illuminate it in its deep significance. It is observed also that the proposition varies in its character; sometimes it is a thesis calling for logical argument in proof of it; sometimes it is a truth to be explained, or appraised and applied. Often it is not formally stated with any such introductory words as "I propose to show," but is incidental; and sometimes it does not appear at all in the sermon. But usually the reader, or hearer, is more interested if in the introduction or early in the sermon there is a revealing statement of the heart of the message. It may be well to conceal the steps to be taken and to employ the element of surprise, but it should be in the process of unfolding and in the application of truth rather than in hiding the truth that burns in the preacher's heart. So the proposition is of value in the delivery of the sermon, adding greatly to its effectiveness. It is of greater value in the prepara-

---

[13] *Craftsmen of the Soul*, Chap. I.
[14] *Crisis on the Frontier*, Chap. 6.
[15] *Facing Life with Christ*, Chap. 8.

tion. To write out a proposition as one begins to compose the sermon, even though it may have to be revised more than once as one proceeds, is to give point and direction to the writing. It will serve as a sort of magnet to keep one on the main track. And not the least service is to deliver the preacher from monotony and staleness, for few men will consent to platitudes and repetitious sermons if they stare at him week after week from the written sentence. The preacher is not wasting time when he searches for a vital statement of his theme. He can get along much better with it than without it.

Though it be but a fragment in form, it is an index to the whole style of thinking which underlies the form. Without it, the most valuable style of thinking is impracticable in the pulpit; and with it, all styles may be at command.[16]

4. CHOICE OF SUBJECTS

Year in and year out the minister of a congregation is faced with the task of choosing sermon subjects. What kinds of subjects are legitimate? What limitations should be recognized? What principles of selection should guide? We suggest two broad principles, so broad as hardly to be called limiting, yet definite enough often to invoke restraint.

(1) The first is in terms of the object or purpose of preaching, which is *life*. Preaching is unto life—life in the meaning of Jesus: spiritual, eternal, abundant, dynamic. "Nothing is a sermon which is out of the range of the religious necessities of the people."[17] The preacher is limited by the high conception, not only in his choice of a subject, but in all that he says about it. But it is a broad boundary. All that serves to introduce men into the fellowship of God, all that opens up to them the plenteous pastures and eternal springs, all that helps them to lay hold of the resources of faith and to possess the sinews and energies adequate to combat the evil and serve the good,— all, in short, that promotes life in the spirit of God is the field of the preacher's appropriate concern. He may preach about anything, if he knows what he is about and forgets not that he is a messenger of God calling men to life in him. He may preach about the bread that perishes, or possessions that deceive, or the temporal and transient, but only to lead on to life that is more than food, to treasure in

---

[16] Phelps, *Theory of Preaching*, p. 294. For an elaborated discussion of the proposition see Chaps. 20-26 of this great treatise.

[17] *Ibid.*, p. 9.

heaven, and things unseen and eternal. Adherence to this high objective is the only justification for preaching at all. And by this rule every subject must pass the criterion of relevance to the religious needs of the spirit of man.

In the analysis of those needs the preacher will come unfailingly upon a wide range of particular objectives that will clamor for his attention. Basic among them may be mentioned the need to be brought into fellowship with God, to grow in the knowledge of God and in devotion to the Kingdom of God, to be instructed in righteousness in the midst of complex moral situations, and to be guided in the appropriate expression of Christian faith and life. When these and other such needs are contemplated in the light of varying individual experience and different community situations, it begins to appear that it is abundance and not scarcity that makes the choice of subjects difficult.

(2) The second principle is in terms of the subject or contents of preaching, which is *truth*. Recall Phillips Brooks' characterization of preaching as the communication of truth through personality. He used the most general terms, but, as his own comment shows, he meant Christian preaching, Christian personality, and Christian truth. "Here [in the fact that the preacher should regard himself as a messenger] is the primary necessity that the Christian preacher should be a Christian first, that he should be deeply cognizant of God's authority, and of the absoluteness of Christ's truth."[18] Perhaps the best-known definition of a sermon is that of Dr. Austin Phelps: "An oral address to the popular mind, on religious truth contained in the Scriptures, and elaborately treated with a view to persuasion." Here the general subject of preaching is limited to biblical truth, i.e., truth which has biblical sanction, either by express statement or by implication, as Phelps explains. The Bible is the touchstone of all true preaching, and every subject worthy of a Christian pulpit will establish a highway between its teachings and the needs of life. From the earliest centuries this has been the high conscience of men in whose hearts dwells the spirit of the Word Incarnate. The modern preacher has no warrant for departing from it. Let him select for his sermons only subjects that lend themselves to the proclamation of divine truth. The surrender of the vanity of originality and the smartness of modernity for timeless truth will be rewarded by a new breadth and depth of knowledge, and by richness and effective power in his ministry.

[18] *Lectures on Preaching.* p. 16.

CHAPTER IV

CLASSIFICATION OF SUBJECTS

THERE is no single principle for classifying sermons that is wholly satisfactory. Phelps mentions seven principles of classification and then proceeds to show the inadequacy of six of them and to make a considerable defense of the seventh, which is based on the method of treating a subject with no reference to the nature of the subject, form, or vital objective of the sermon.[1] Any sermon, if well conceived, may be variously classified with equal justification. For example, a sermon on the Love of God might be at once doctrinal, textual, persuasive, and evangelistic; or, again, ethical, topical, illustrative, and devotional. Perhaps the nearest approach to simplicity would be to think in terms of primary and secondary classifications, the former on the basis of the subjects and the objectives of the sermon, the latter on the basis of the form and the method of treatment.

Attention is now directed to the classification of subjects. And the first thing to be said is that any classification is necessarily imperfect, as the classes will in certain cases overlap, and the number of classes will vary with men's gift of generalizing. One preacher will classify his subjects under a few general headings; another will require more. But the habit of referring every subject to a class will be found useful, contributing to unity and consistency of treatment, and to variety of topics. There is general agreement upon a minimum of four classes—doctrinal, moral, historical, and experimental;[2] and the discussion of these classes furnishes occasion for practical suggestions upon matters of no little importance.

I. DOCTRINAL SUBJECTS

The phrase "doctrinal sermon" is constantly used by some to denote sermons on points of denominational peculiarity or controversy. Such a limitation, implying that these are the only doctrines, or that we cannot discuss doctrine otherwise than polemically, is a really grave error, and should be carefully avoided and corrected.

[1] *Theory of Preaching*, Lecture III.
[2] Vinet (*Hom.*, p. 75) classifies subjects as doctrinal, moral, historical, as drawn from the contemplation and study of nature, and as psychological.

Doctrine, i.e., teaching, is the preacher's chief business.[3] Truth is the life-blood of piety, without which we cannot maintain its vitality or support its activity. And to teach men truth, or to quicken what they already know into freshness and power, is the preacher's great means of doing good. The facts and truths which belong to the Scripture account of sin, Providence, and redemption, form the staple of all scriptural preaching. But these truths ought not simply to have place after a desultory and miscellaneous fashion in our preaching. The entire body of Scripture teaching upon any particular subject, when collected and systematically arranged, has come to be called the "doctrine" of Scripture on that subject, as the doctrine of sin, of atonement, of regeneration, etc.; and in this sense we ought to preach much on the doctrines of the Bible. We all regard it as important that the preacher should himself have sound views of doctrine; is it not also important that he should lead his congregation to have just views? In our restless nation and agitated times, in these days of somewhat bustling religious activity, there has come to be too little of real doctrinal preaching. To a certain extent it is proper that we should conform to the tastes of the age, for they frequently indicate its real wants, and always affect its reception of truth; but when those tastes are manifestly faulty, we should earnestly endeavor to correct them. The preacher who can make doctrinal truth interesting as well as intelligible to his congregation and gradually bring them to a good acquaintance with the doctrines of the Bible is rendering them an inestimable service. Doctrinal preaching is not necessarily dry. In fact, properly presented doctrine, didactic instruction, may be the most interesting kind of preaching. Men wish to know, delight in knowing. All depends on the way in which it is done. The dry preacher will make all subjects dry; dull anecdotes and tame exhortations have sometimes been heard of.

And let us preach especially on the great doctrines.[4] True, they are familiar, but sermons upon them need not be commonplace. The sunlight is as fresh every morning as when it shone upon our first parents in their paradise; young love is still as sweet and

---

[3] There are good discussions of this subject in Dabney's *Sacred Rhetoric*, pp. 50 ff; and in Phillips Brooks' *Yale Lectures*, pp. 128, 129. Dabney says, "It was a golden maxim of the Protestant fathers, that 'doctrines must be preached practically, and duties doctrinally.'" Brooks says, "Preach doctrine—preach all the doctrine that you know, and learn forever more and more; but preach it always, not that men may believe it, but that men may be saved by believing it."

[4] See Jowett, *The Preacher: His Life and Work*, Lecture III; also Coffin, *What to Preach*, Lecture II.

parental grief as heart-rending as was theirs. And so the great doctrines of the gospel, to him who has eyes to see and a heart to feel them, are forever new. Our task is, loving these truths ourselves, to make others love them. Many a preacher could tell how in the early months or years of his untutored ministry he was sometimes driven from sheer lack of a novel topic to fall back upon repentance, regeneration, or the like and make what he felt to be a poor sermon; and how, long afterwards, he heard of fruit from those sermons rather than from others which he at the time considered much more striking and impressive. Of course one should not make a hobby of a particular doctrine, as some men do with the doctrine of election or of baptism and some others with perfection, the witness of the Spirit, the second coming of our Lord, and the like. In regard to preaching unpopular doctrines, such as election before some audiences, future punishment, depravity, and even missions, before others, one comprehensive rule may be given: Be faithful and fearless, but skillful and affectionate.

While, however, we ought to preach much upon the great doctrines, it is not often advisable, especially for a settled pastor, to embrace the whole of such a doctrine in a single sermon. This would contain the mere generalities of the subject and be very difficult to the hearer, or, more frequently, quite commonplace. It is a common delusion of inexperienced speakers or writers, to think that they had best take a very broad subject so as to be sure of finding enough to say. But to choose some one aspect of a great subject is usually far better, as there is thus much better opportunity for the speaker to work out something fresh and much better prospect of making the hearers take a lively interest in the subject as a whole. Alexander, writing to a son at college, says:

The more *special* the subject, the more you will find to say on it. Boys think just the reverse. They write of virtue, honor, liberty, etc.; it would be easier to write on the pleasures of virtue, the honor of knighthood, or the difference between true and false liberty—which are more special. Take it as a general rule, the more you narrow the subject, the more thoughts you will have. And for this there is a philosophical reason, which I wish you to observe. In acquiring knowledge, the mind proceeds *from particulars to generals*. Thus Newton proceeded from the falling of an apple to the general principle of gravity. A great many particular observations were to be made on animals, before a naturalist could lay down the general law, that all creatures with cleft hoofs and horns are graminivorous. . . . This process is called generalization. It is one of the last to be developed. Hence it requires vast knowledge and a mature mind to treat a general subject, such as virtue, or honor, and it is much better to begin with particular instances.[5]

And this applies not merely to the preacher's power of treatment but to the hearer's power of comprehension. When he becomes fully able to discuss large subjects in a single discourse, the great mass of his hearers will still be unable to follow him, unless the discourse be so long as to include copious details. And besides all this, the settled pastor cannot often afford to consume so much material in a single sermon. The exceptional cases, as a series of sermons on several great doctrines, the existence of special interest in some one doctrine, etc., will of course be treated as exceptions.

The specific aspects of a great doctrine may sometimes be chosen according to the natural divisions of the subject itself. For example, repentance: its nature, necessity, season, evidences, relation to faith; or regeneration: its nature, necessity, author, relation to baptism, faith, and the like. In this matter, and in all that pertains to preaching upon doctrinal subjects, we must carefully bear in mind the distinction between a theological treatise or lecture, and a popular sermon. The scientific analysis and elaborate logic of the one is seldom appropriate to the other. The parts of a subject which require most attention and excite most interest on the part of a systematic student may be least suitable to preaching, and vice versa. The knowledge presupposed by the theological teacher cannot usually be taken for granted as existing in a congregation. Young ministers often help to make doctrinal subjects unpopular by the fact that their sermons too closely resemble the treatises they have been studying or the lectures they have heard. We must assume a different point of view, must consider which aspects of a doctrine will awaken interest in the popular mind, and at the same time help to give just views of the whole. Besides the important differences between the merely didactic and the oratorical mode of treatment, there is here a previous difference as to the choice of subjects and parts of subjects to be treated.

Or, instead of selecting according to the logical divisions of the doctrine, we may take the aspect of it presented by some one text. Thus on repentance one might preach upon its nature, its results, the obligations to it, etc., hunting up a text for each; or he might begin

[5] *Thoughts on Preaching*, p. 522.

by selecting among the texts which treat of repentance. For example, Mark 6:12, "And they went out and preached that men should repent," would suggest a general view of repentance, or an inquiry into its obligation; Acts 5:31, "Him hath God exalted a Prince and a Saviour, to give repentance to Israel, and forgiveness of sins," presents repentance as a gift of Christ; Acts 20:21, "Testifying . . . repentance toward God, and faith toward our Lord Jesus Christ," brings up the relation between repentance and faith; and Matt. 3:11, "I indeed baptize you with water unto repentance," that between repentance and baptism. Various distinct and impressive motives to repentance are exhibited by Rom. 2:4, "The goodness of God leadeth thee to repentance"; Acts 3:16, "Repent . . . that your sins may be blotted out"; Luke 13:3, "Except ye repent, ye shall all likewise perish"; Acts 17:30, 31, "God . . . now commandeth all men everywhere to repent, because he hath appointed a day in which he will judge the world in righteousness"; Luke 15:10, "There is joy in the presence of the angels of God over one sinner that repenteth." And Matt. 3:8, "Bring forth therefore fruits meet for repentance," would lead one to speak of the appropriate effects of repentance.[6] A person well acquainted with the whole doctrine of repentance could treat the view presented by any one of these texts as a part of the whole, so as gradually to give a complete knowledge of the entire subject, while each sermon would have the freshness and force belonging to a specific topic.

Besides the properly doctrinal, i.e., didactic, there are apologetical and polemical subjects.

Apologetics, that is, the evidences of Christianity and its defense against assailants, is a class of subjects not often requiring, in our ordinary preaching, to be formally treated. Robert Hall[7] in a striking passage justly criticises the too great readiness of some preachers to discuss this class of subjects. Such preachers often do harm by suggesting difficulties which their arguments do not remove. He also calls attention to the fact that the argument for Christianity is a cumulative one and cannot be properly presented in so brief a discussion as a sermon.

But informally, incidentally, we may all make very frequent and profitable use of Christian evidences. Without at all treating the question of the truth of Christianity as an open one, and without

---

[6] Compare Ripley, *Sacred Rhetoric*, p. 32.
[7] *Works*, Vol. II, p. 299.

undertaking any full and regular discussion of its claims or refutation of objections to it, we may introduce into ordinary sermons
some subordinate division or passing remark that will vividly exhibit
one of the evidences or strikingly refute some particular objection.
This course meets any rising doubts in one mind or another and
precisely suits the mental wants and habits of most men and is thus
the fairest way of bringing the subject before them. Even if one
sees cause for an expressly apologetical sermon or series of sermons,
he had better select some part of the great subject and barely allude
to, or rapidly touch, the others. Whatever matters are distinctly
brought forward ought to be thoroughly discussed. Let us beware
how we merely mention some striking form of error or plausible
objection to truth without meeting it very squarely, if not at all
points. Everyone has observed what Mr. Hall intimates, that the
error often remains in the mind, while the imperfect refutation is
forgotten; and the reason for this is not far to seek. Errors often find
their chief power in the fact that they consist of truth torn away from
its connection and held up in an excessive prominence, or without
the limitation and modification which would be given by its related
truths. A fragment of truth thus held up may make its delusive
impression in a single moment. The apologist must carefully replace
the truth and bring the hearers to look closely at all the surrounding
truths and consider their relation to that which has been dislocated.
But this is often a work of time, requiring wider knowledge than
the audience possess or he can readily impart, and more reflection
than the heedless many are willing to bestow. It is unfair to the
truth if we neglect this fact and expect a brief statement of some
novel and seductive error to be sufficiently met by an equally brief
reply.

The internal and experimental evidences may be very readily
preached upon with advantage. The beautiful harmony of the sacred
books, with all their rich diversity, the effects of Christianity
upon civilization, the adaptation of the gospel to the wants of an
awakened conscience, the believer's testimony on the ground of
experience, the blessed results of piety, and the powerful example of
the truly pious are topics which may be widely and freely used.

Polemics, or controversy with other professed Christians, presents
subjects which demand faithful and careful handling. The spurious
charity, now so much talked of, which requires that we shall not
assail error in our fellow-Christians, the indifference to truth so

widely prevailing, which prates of the "good in everything" and urges that a man's belief is of little importance if he is intellectual, or amiable, or moral and devout,—these make some men unwilling to preach upon polemical topics, especially to discuss the errors of other evangelical denominations. The natural love of conflict, which even in preachers is sometimes so strong, the lively interest which the ungodly will take in a fight among Christians, the hearty support and laudation which a man's own party will give him, often precisely in proportion as he flatters their self-conceit and unfairly assails their opponents,—such causes as these contribute to make another class of men excessively fond of controversy. And then the two classes really stimulate and encourage each other. The former, being greatly disgusted at what they reckon bad taste and a wrong spirit, are thus all the more disposed to shrink from such topics; and the latter, being fired by what appears to them cowardice or worldly policy, are all the more bitter against the common foe and inclined to assail their friends besides. In this way two tendencies often arise in a denomination, each toward a very hurtful extreme. Is there not a golden mean? It would seem to be a just principle that a preacher should never go out of his way to find controversial matter or go out of his way to avoid it. He who continually shrinks from conflict should stir himself up to faithfulness; he who is by nature belligerent should cultivate forbearance and courtesy. When the text or topic naturally leads us to remark upon some matter of controversy, we should not, save in exceptional cases, avoid it because esteemed Christians are present who differ with us on that point. We should of course be mainly occupied with the advocacy of positive truth; but the idea that a man can always "talk about what he himself believes, and let other people's opinions alone" is impracticable, even if it were not improper. In many cases we cannot clearly define truth save by contrasting it with error. And since errors held and taught by good men are only the more likely to be hurtful to others, we are surely not less bound to refute them in such cases than when advocated by bad men. Paul employs terms of terrible severity, as his Master had done, in speaking of some who taught utterly ruinous error and from bad motives.[8] Paul also withstood to the face, before all the brethren, his beloved but not erring fellow-apostle,

[8] Philem. 3:2; Gal. 6:12; I Tim. 4:1, 2; II Tim. 4:14; Compare Matt. 23:33; III John, 10.

using against him hard arguments but soft words.[9] Afterwards, in speaking of the matter, he charges Peter with dissimulation, a charge justifiable because he knew with certainty that it was true. We, who are so liable to err in judging, ought to be very slow to impugn the motives of those whom we believe to be lovers of Jesus. No doubt Satan rejoices, as we know that wicked men do, to see Christians adding abuse to argument. While faithfully and earnestly opposing error, even as held by Christian brethren, let us avoid needlessly wounding the cause of our common Christianity.

It is not unfrequently the wisest policy, as regards certain forms of error, to leave them unnoticed. In the excitement about Romanism, which its boldness and boasting have awakened in our country, there is reason to fear that many will fall to preaching against the Romanists where they are little known and thus only help to bring them into notice. While well assured that their grievous errors can be refuted, we ought to remember that those errors are subtle and to some minds seductive, and that here, just as in the case of infidel theories and objections, slight and hasty refutation is often worse than none. So, too, there are some minor religious denominations whose vital breath is controversy and who will most surely die when they are most severely let alone.

2. SUBJECTS OF MORALITY

We sometimes hear pious men speak with severe reprobation of "moral sermons." It has often been the case that morality would be preached with little or no reference to the atonement and the work of the Spirit, a mere morality taking the place of the real gospel. This has established an association in many minds between moral discourses and opposition to the doctrines of grace. But our Lord's personal teachings consist mainly of morality; and Paul and Peter, while unfolding and dwelling on the salvation which is by grace through faith, have not merely urged in general a holy life but have given many precepts with reference to particular and sometimes minor duties. No one among us will question that we ought constantly to exhort believers to show their faith by their works and to be holy in all their deportment, seeing that theirs is a holy God. But there is in many quarters a reluctance, for the reason just mentioned, to preach much upon particular questions of moral duty. A preacher of the gospel certainly ought not to preach morality apart

[9] Gal. 2:11-21.

from the gospel.[10] He may present other than strictly evangelical motives, but these must be manifestly subordinate to the great motive of grateful love to Christ and consecration to his service. We should exhort men to keep the law of God, for thus they may be brought to Christ; but to incite unregenerate people to a so-called "moral life" on the ground merely of interest, of regard for the well-being of society, and even of love for their children, etc. is for the preacher unsuitable save in very peculiar cases. He must first, as an ambassador for Christ, call men to be reconciled to God, must insist upon the indispensable need of regeneration through the Holy Spirit. Then, speaking to those who are looked upon as regenerate, he must, with all his might, urge them to true and high morality, not only on all other grounds, but as a solemn duty to God their Saviour. For Christianity has a distinctive ethics as well as a theology, and the preacher cannot escape the twofold responsibility of making clear the moral principles that are basic in Christian living and of guiding his people in the application of those principles to personal and social problems.[11] The only question is, how far he ought to go into details. As above intimated, our Lord and his apostles did go into details very freely. And our preaching often suffers from the fact that, while inculcating Christian morality in general, we do not bring the matter home to the hearts and daily lives of our brethren, do not so delineate their practical experiences, and indicate their duty in practical questions, as to make them feel stimulated and encouraged in the actual pursuit of holiness. At the same time, these questions are innumerable and often complicated and difficult, and we are compelled to select.

Now certain limitations, as to the preaching of particular morality, appear to be important. (1) We must not make formal discussion of very minute topics.

Represent to yourself, for example, sermons on neatness, on politeness, etc. Some topics of this sort, doubtless, may be approached, but it must be done incidentally; they should never furnish the subject of a sermon. Particular morality is not to be excluded, but such details of it may have their place in more general matters, or in historical subjects.[12]

[10] Compare Phillips Brooks, *Yale Lectures*, pp. 136-140; and Dabney's *Sacred Rhetoric*, pp. 243 ff., where the relation of the imagination to moral suasion is well brought out.

[11] For valuable discussions of this task see Buttrick, *Jesus Came Preaching*, Chap. IV; also C. R. Brown, *The Social Message of the Modern Pulpit*, and H. S. Coffin, *What to Preach*, Lecture III.

[12] Vinet, *Hom.*, p. 83.

It is one of the advantages of expository preaching, whether doctrinal or historical, that it gives occasion for many useful incidental remarks upon minor morals, for which we might never find a place in formal subject-sermons. (2) A second limitation is, that the inculcation of morality must not consume a disproportionate part of our time, for there are other needs of men that must not be neglected, e.g., to be converted, to be instructed in doctrine, to be inspirited, etc. Be it also remembered that the doctrines of grace are the great means of making believers "careful to maintain good works."[13] (3) And it is a third limitation that we must not so enter into particular questions of morality as to make the preaching of the gospel merely tributary to secular interests and apparently to sink the preacher in the partisan.

Political preaching has long been a subject of vehement discussion in America and presents questions of great importance. In Europe the almost universal connection of church and state has embarrassed the subject with complications from which we are comparatively free. Government here does not interfere with religion, to support some or to persecute others; and we have in this respect no occasion to discuss governmental affairs. Still, political measures often involve, and are sometimes almost identical with, great questions of right and wrong.[14] The notion that political decisions are to be regularly made on grounds of mere expediency is dishonoring to the religion which many of us profess, and would ultimately ruin any nation. That truly pious men shall carry their religion into politics, shall keep religious principle uppermost in all political questions which have a moral character, is an unquestionable and solemn duty. Of course, it is right that the preacher should urge them to do so, and should urge it with special earnestness in times of great political excitement, when good men are often carried away. Now we have observed above that in other matters it is well not merely to insist upon morality in general but to go somewhat into details, thus illustrating general truth and offering hints for practical guidance. Why, then, it may be asked, shall we not do likewise in reference to political matters, where it is often as difficult as it is important for a good man to decide upon his duty? Why shall not the preacher go somewhat into details here? The great difficulty is that it is almost impossible for a preacher to do this without becoming partisan in

[13] See Titus, iii 3-8, an important passage on this subject.
[14] Compare Phillips Brooks, *Yale Lectures*, p. 141.

spirit. In a country where party feeling runs so high as in ours, to take sides at all in public discourse will cause the preacher to be at once swept away by the rushing tide. He ceases to sustain an impartial relation to all the people over whom he is shepherd, and becomes, in a matter which with many is more important than religion, the friend of some, the foe of others. The irreligious, and many of the brethren, forget all about the religious aims of his preaching in the one absorbing inquiry how much he will help or harm their party. Thus has many a good man, who was honestly striving to bring politics under the control of religious principle, been brought, before he knew it, into the position of a recognized political partisan. Upon perceiving such a result, some preachers at once draw back, wiser from their experience; but others, proud of consistency, resolved to conquer opposition, or unable to see just what their mistake is and how to correct it, persevere with deplorable results. The association which once connected them in the popular mind with unworldly feelings and eternal interests is broken. Their power of turning men's eyes away from the things which are seen to the things which are not seen is seriously diminished. They become comparatively unable to accomplish the great object which a good man in the ministry must cherish, the object of saving souls. Besides, the temporal benefits of Christianity are greatest just in proportion as there is most of true spirituality. Preachers do men most good as to this world in proportion as they bring them to care most for the "things that are above." In losing this higher power, then, one has likewise actually lost the most effectual means of advancing those lower ends at which he was aiming. While striving to bring some of the motive power of his engine to bear upon one subordinate work, he has left the boiler to burst and now can do neither the greater nor the less.[15]

Many persons insist that the minister must have nothing to do with politics, not even to the extent of voting, or of the formation and private expression of political opinions. Some take this ground from false notions of the "clergyman's" position; but a Christian minister is no more a priest than a Christian layman, and nothing is intrinsically wrong to the one which is not to the other. A well-informed man in this country cannot avoid the formation of opinions upon politics; and in voluntary ignorance of current affairs more is

[15] Compare Vinet, *Hom.*, pp. 71-74, and 86, 87; and Shedd, *Hom.*, pp. 248-249, for similar views.

lost by the working pastor than gained. The minister ought to have his opinions and ought to vote; and he may state his views in private conversation with more or less reserve according to circumstances. He should in the pulpit urge and conjure his Christian hearers to be controlled in their political action by Christian principle. To go into details and suggest how they ought to vote in a particular issue is lawful but in general highly inexpedient; the little good done will almost certainly be overbalanced by the harm that in various ways must result. If a preacher ever takes such a course at all, it should be in very peculiar and extraordinary cases, and even then his discussion should be brief, well considered, and temperate, and gladly abandoned for other themes.

There are other very important and difficult topics of particular morality, such as temperance and the question of amusements; but a few remarks upon these must suffice. The preacher should by all means *avoid ultraism*. Some things not sinful in themselves, it is yet best to abstain from because they so readily and widely lead to sin. But here there is at once seen to be room for difference of opinion. Not everything should be avoided which is often grossly abused; and however clear it may seem to us that some particular thing should be avoided, another man may perhaps judge otherwise. Even though vehement in condemnation, we must not be indiscriminate. And if in the natural desire to take strong ground we represent the use of intoxicating beverages, dancing, and games of amusement as in themselves sinful and under all circumstances wrong, we assume an extreme and false position which must eventually weaken our cause. If discriminating and considerate views, leading to a regard for their example and influence and a recognition of possible danger to themselves and their families, will not restrain men in these respects, then extravagance and violence, even if controlling a few, will in general but repel and provoke, stimulating the wrong practices in question and driving many away from the gospel. The world is full of great and dreadful evils, which may well excite both grief and indignation and which call loudly for correction; but one evil is not to be cured by another. Again, we must not merely condemn the wrong but exhort to the right. Preaching on these subjects too often consists merely in vehement assaults. Much more may be accomplished if we also encourage the right-minded to a proper course and affectionately point out to them the beginnings of evil against which they must guard. The latter course may not afford so much occasion for impassioned and boisterous "eloquence," but it will hardly be on that account the less useful. Severe censure is sometimes necessary, but encouragement to do right is always in place and often more potent. "Reprove, rebuke, exhort, with all long-suffering and teaching."[16] And finally, it is usually better to treat these subjects in the course of our ordinary preaching than to make set sermons upon them. These may draw a crowd, if that is all, but the formal discussion invites criticism and awakens opposition, and, even if really convincing, finds the persons most concerned particularly hard to convince. Arguments and appeals from time to time, as suggested by the subject or the occasion, will make no unfavorable impression, and steady perseverance will gradually call back and win over all whom it is possible to influence. Only, let not the preacher make any particular vicious practice or social usage his hobby; for then folks will but smile at all he can say.

3. HISTORICAL SUBJECTS

It would be necessary to urge that history is attractive for all who read and full of varied instruction for all who read thoughtfully. And the most instructive history is that of the Bible. A leading writer[17] on the philosophy of history has declared that no such philosophy can be constructed save by the recognition of a providential purpose which pervades all events and links them into unity. In the Bible the designs of Providence are not left to be judged of by our sagacity but are often clearly revealed, so as to show us the meaning of things obscure and the real co-working of things apparently antagonistic. Thus the Bible histories act like the problems worked out in a treatise of algebra, teaching us how to approach the other problems presented by the general history of the world. The oft-quoted saying of an ancient writer that "history is philosophy teaching by example" applies nowhere so truly as to the inspired records, which are God himself teaching by example.

Moreover, nothing so interests us all as a person. No inanimate object or general proposition will make much impression upon mankind at large unless it is personified or impersonated or invested with some personal interest. The poet, delighting in nature, instinctively feels as if communing with a person. Even so abstract a thing as a

[16] II Tim. 4:2.
[17] Schlegel.

system of philosophy is usually remembered in connection with a personal teacher. A benevolent enterprise seldom takes much hold on the popular mind unless it is associated with some honored man, its embodiment and representative. A celebrated lecturer[18] on history once stated in conversation that he found it difficult to interest a popular audience, if he presented merely historical events, periods, or lessons; these must be associated with some person. Now the Bible not only consists very largely of history, but the greater part of its history is really biography, the story of individual lives, exhibiting the most various and instructive examples of character, both good and bad, of both sexes, and of every condition in life. And this great historical picture groups all its figures around one Person, to whom some look forward with longing and others look back with love and whose very enemies unwillingly stand connected with him.

All this being true, it would seem that historical subjects of preaching ought to be much more frequently employed than is actually the case. Several reasons for the comparative neglect of them may be suggested. The greater part of devout ministers unwisely overlook the human elements in Scripture history. If not carried away by the passion for finding "types of Christ" so as to care little for the persons and events that cannot possibly be thus regarded, they still fail to study these histories as history. They do not trace the progress of events in the history of Israel as in that of any other nation, allowing for the occasional miraculous interferences and searching amid the mingled web of Israel's affairs for the golden thread of providential purpose. They do not analyze the character and motives of inspired men as "men of like passions" with ourselves, men who struggled, as we have to do, with their own infirmities and the thronging temptations of life. They shrink from contemplating the genuine but sinless humanity of the glorious central Person, which makes him so real and so unspeakably valuable an example for us, at the same time that he is our divine Redeemer. Another reason is, few ministers gain that minute and familiar acquaintance with Scripture geography, with the manners and customs of the Jews and related nations, and with the secular history connected with biblical events which would enable them to realize the scenes and reproduce them with vivid coloring so as to kindle the imagination of their hearers; nor do they cultivate, as all preachers should, the power of description. On the other hand, some make historical sub-

[18] John Lord.

jects simply the occasion for displaying their descriptive powers or exhibiting their archæological learning, without teaching any useful lessons, and thus establish an association in the minds of many hearers between historical sermons and mere "word-painting." And further, preachers who know or suppose themselves to have little talent for description are apt to forget that one of the chief benefits of historical preaching is derived from the analysis of character and motive. We all find it so hard to understand our fellow-men or ourselves that it is a great blessing to have in some Scripture examples the veil taken off and the real motives and true character of men laid bare to our inspection, and, in many other cases, to have suggestive and reliable indications to provoke and encourage inquiry. Living instances could be mentioned of very able men who had rarely attempted historical subjects, because they are conscious of possessing little talent for description. But when the simple suggestion was made that they could bring to bear their analytical powers upon the character of some Scripture personage or the motives of the actors in some Scripture scene, they soon found themselves much interested in historical discourses and found, too, that they could throw in excellent touches of description by the way.

The history of Christianity outside of the Bible, from the earliest times to our own, furnishes much instructive and interesting material for preaching; but to draw the subject of a sermon from this source would be unwise. A sermon upon the life and character of Augustine, Calvin, Wesley, Fuller, Hall, or Judson might be really useful, but the tendency would be towards one of the abuses of Romanism: substituting panegyrics of the saints for biblical preaching. Yet sometimes week-night lectures might be devoted to the delineation of great and instructive Christian characters, particularly notable missionaries.

4. EXPERIMENTAL SUBJECTS

Historical subjects manifestly include doctrinal and moral elements; and yet those subjects have really a distinct character. In like manner experimental subjects partake of the doctrinal, the moral, and the historical, but are so distinct, and of such importance, as to deserve separate classification and notice. The actual experiences of men in receiving the gospel and living according to it ought to be delineated; always under the guidance of Scripture doctrine, precept.

and examples, but still delineated as we find them to be. Such matters will enter largely into the substance of many discourses whose *subject* is doctrinal, moral, or historical; but the chief phases of religious experience deserve to be somewhat frequently made the subject of special and careful discussion. Material for this purpose is to be drawn from the Bible, from treatises bearing on the subject, and biographies, from the preacher's own experience, and with particular advantage from frequent conversation with richly experienced Christians, making allowance for their peculiarities of temperament and theological opinion, and for their degrees of culture. The preacher, like the physician, ought in addition to what is learned from books, to "study cases," as they arise in his practical labors. Few things are more interesting and helpful than studies of actual life situations. They rarely fail to supply freshness and to give to preaching a connection with life that more easily carries the truth home.

It would surely be very useful sometimes to depict the life of an irreligious man, as it is now going forward on week-days and Sundays, in business and in society and at home; to do this without exaggerating in order to make a striking picture, without ignoring the man's better impulses, good intentions, kindly affections, etc.,— to make him out, so far as possible, just what he is. After pondering the matter and asking a good many thoughtful questions of some intelligent brethren as to their personal recollections, a preacher might be able, modestly and with good success, to treat such a subject. It is not uncommon to describe conviction of sin, the various methods in which it is wrought, and the causes by which it is often weakened and brought to nothing. So with conversion. Accounts of conversion in persons differing in temperament, religious education, etc., carefully analyzed so as to distinguish the general from the peculiar, are always interesting and may be made exceedingly profitable. The early Baptist preachers who traveled from New England to Georgia, preaching depravity, atonement, and regeneration to an ignorant and gainsaying people, often made a great impression and gave most important instruction by telling their own experience. And then the varieties of experience in the Christian life—what subjects they afford for preaching! The Christian's Conflicts, Backsliding and Progress, Despondency and Assurance, Sickness and Bereavement,—these are often discussed in every evangelical pulpit.

To speak at all of our own experience is a task to be performed with special prayer for humility and delicacy, lest we injure our own character and repel hearers of fastidious tastes. Many shrink too readily from this duty; but not a few go to the other extreme and speak too much and not wisely of their own experiences, and this is the worse evil of the two. Let us in this matter, as in so many others where discretion and good taste are involved, earnestly strive to find the proper middle course. The apostle Paul has spoken frequently, and sometimes at great length, of his conversion, the trials, conflicts, and consolations of his subsequent life, and of his present purposes and hopes; and the Psalms consist almost entirely of recorded experiences. In speaking of our own experiences, we ought to be careful not to tell the same thing over too often, nor indeed should we speak too often of ourselves at all. We should never do so out of mere egotism, but with careful selection of such things as will be really appropriate to the subject and helpful to the hearers. One thing, however, is to be specially guarded against in all attempts at depicting religious experience and especially in allusions to our own: we are very apt to imagine, or at least to speak as if we imagined, that all experiences will be like ours. Thus Chrysostom, always moral and inclined to be devout from a boy, taught that we get all the grace that we are willing to receive; while Augustine, very wicked and powerfully converted, preached sovereign and irresistible grace. A preacher or other Christian whose conversion was consciously sudden will almost always speak of conversion as sudden; one in whom the work was gradual and slow will give a corresponding description. So with the hopeful and the desponding, the fully assured and the often doubting, and the like. We are prone to forget that Christian experience, like the human countenance, will in no two persons be precisely alike, and often presents many and striking differences, though the great characteristic features are always the same.

CHAPTER V

GENERAL MATERIALS OF THE SERMON

OF BASIC importance in preaching is the ability to lay hold of appropriate materials by use of which the subject may be amplified into a full sermon,—the power to discern new relations of ideas and to join them together in effective discourse. In rhetoric this selection and arrangement of materials is called "invention." Aristotle and Quintilian gave considerable space in their famous works to this part of the subject, and Cicero devoted to it a special treatise. In some modern rhetorical books the subject receives scant attention, more consideration being given to style. But latterly our rhetoricians are coming again to bestow more care upon the matter of invention. And this is well, for it is evidently a matter of the utmost importance. If important to every speaker, it is supremely important to the preacher to have something to say. Vapid nothings, no matter how well said, should have no place in a sermon.

I. INVENTIVE PRODUCTION

Much in regard to invention will be said incidentally as we proceed with the discussion of materials and particularly in the chapter on Imagination. But a few words as to the inventive power itself and the best means of cultivating it may be appropriate here.

Rhetorically, invention is the selection of materials out of a fund of knowledge and experience and their arrangement for purposes of discourse; logically, it is a line of reasoning concerning identities as between a subject and predicate by means of middle terms; psychologically, it is response to stimuli that originate in past and present experience. That is to say, there are two steps in the inventive process, one having to do with knowledge, experience, stimuli; the other with selection, relation, response.

Typically, the preliminary stage consists in recall; and association by similarly, bringing together materials from different past experiences, is very important as a preliminary to invention. Facts recalled from different contexts are thus brought together, and invention consists in a response

76

to such novel combinations of facts. The two steps in invention are, first, getting a combination of stimuli, and second, responding to the combination.[1]

It is evident, to start with, that some minds are more creative than others, and the same mind varies in this matter according to the stage of its culture and even according to its moods. If a man has no power of invention, he has mistaken his business when he proposes to be a preacher. But if he has some natural ability in this direction it is capable of indefinite cultivation. Clearly it is every preacher's imperative duty to train this faculty to do its best. Next to character and piety it is the most important element of his outfit.

In the development of the power of inventive thought three processes are absolutely necessary: acquistion, reflection, exercise. The homely illustration of a mill may help us to see this more clearly. For the production of meal there must be the grain, the motive power, and the actual movement of exerting the one upon the other by means of the machinery. So in developing the inventive powers of the mind there must be knowledge, thought, and constant use. These are the essentials in the production of sermons.

The chief materials of a sermon are in the great mass of cases not really invented at the time of preparation; they are the results of previous acquistion and reflection. This is true even of much that seems to the preacher himself to have then for the first time a place in his mind; it is in fact the revival of something forgotten or the development of something already known. In this respect inexperienced and comparatively uncultivated young preachers are often greatly deceived. Their early sermons are made with ease. Ardent, zealous, excited, they find that thought springs spontaneous in the mind and feeling flows like a torrent. They imagine that it will always be easy to find something to say which will interest themselves and their hearers. But they are like men who have inherited a fortune in cash and who spend their principal as if it were but income. Rejoicing in his facility of speech, the young preacher is not aware that he is drawing upon all that he has thought, felt, and seen, all that he has read and heard, since his childhood. And not a few go on for some months or years, consuming all their store, and evoking all that their minds are so constituted as readily to produce, and presently begin to wonder and lament that they find it so much harder than formerly to make a

[1] Woodworth, *Psychology*, p. 519.

sermon. In like manner, preachers who are growing old sometimes complain that people will not listen to them as in other days, when the difficulty is that they have ceased to maintain activity of mind and good store of fresh thought; and unable to interest themselves, they of course cannot interest others. These somewhat frequent and very painful experiences only illustrate the proposition—we draw our sermons mainly from what we have wrought out or learned beforehand. And when the preacher speaks from great fullness of thought, then what he says borrows power from what is in reserve, as the head of water gives force to that which strikes upon the wheel. It follows that, next to the cultivation of personal piety, there is nothing for which the preacher should so earnestly labor from his first call to the close of his life as the acquistion of abundant general materials for preaching and constant practice in composition.[2]

2. SOURCES OF MATERIAL

These materials will of course be drawn from every source. No kind of knowledge can be utterly useless to a preacher, and reflection, upon whatever subjects, will always leave him something which may hereafter be turned to account. But it may be well to remark upon the principal sources from which materials for preaching are derived.

(1) The Scriptures themselves should at every period of his life be a preacher's chief study. When we meet a young brother who has just become convinced that it is his duty to preach and who is inquiring about preparation for the work, our first word ought to be, the Bible,—not so much, at the outset, the profound study of doctrinal epistles or prophetical books, as the familiar and accurate knowledge of historical facts, the analysis of biblical characters, the memorizing of devotional passages and of precepts, the acquisition of a general familiarity with the contents of particular books and of the entire sacred collection. Young ministers, even graduates of colleges, are often found sadly deficient as to this general knowledge of the Bible; while the best Sunday schools, as well as the most admirable family instruction, have usually but laid the foundation for such knowledge as the preacher should make haste to gain.

---

[2] See Shedd (*Hom.*, p. 108), who says that a preacher should "acquire and cultivate a homiletical habitude." Everything he comes in contact with should turn to sermon Compare also Brooks' *Yale Lectures*, p. 157.

And every stage of culture and experience as life goes on presents fresh occasion and new facilities for studying the Bible—in the originals if possible, in the English version at any rate. By the rapid reading of large portions, by the thorough study of a given book, by the minute examination of particular passages, and sometimes even by looking at sentences here and there as we turn over the leaves, by reading in company with others for discussion or for sympathy, by reading when alone with our beating hearts and our God, by adopting new methods for variety, and by steadily maintaining old methods till they become habitual; by reading when we enjoy it as a pleasure, and, when at the beginning we do not enjoy it, as a duty,—in every way and continually let us keep up, freshen, extend our acquaintance with the precious Word of God. Every kind of knowledge we gain should lead to further examination of that which is for us the center of all knowledge, and the various experiences of life should be constantly bringing us back to find new meaning, strength, and consolation in God's Word. And we must constantly beware lest we fall into the habit of reading the Bible only as a perfunctory matter, a professional duty. In the spirit of personal devoutness, with a desire for personal benefit, and with the constant prayer that God would bless us in learning and in teaching, let us study the Bible that we may "both save ourselves, and them that hear us."

(2) Systematic theology is of unspeakable importance to the preacher, indispensable if he would be in the best sense instructive and exert an abiding influence over his hearers. This enables him to speak with the boldness of assured conviction, giving him a confidence in the great system of inspired truth which no minute criticism can shake.[3] This prepares him to urge one doctrine or to unfold and apply one text without the fear of offending against another,—a fault into which many ministers are grieved to remember how often their early sermons fell. This renders it practicable to discuss particular aspects of a doctrine in different sermons in such a way as by degrees to impart a good knowledge of the doctrine as a whole. And the manifest possession of a systematic acquaintance with revealed truth gives him authority with the people. They readily listen to one who has definite, positive, and well-considered opinions; and no uninspired man, even of the highest genius, has a right to be so

---

[3] R. W. Dale, *Yale Lectures*, pp. 7 ff., has some excellent remarks on the advantages of studying theology.

authoritative in his utterances upon moral and spiritual truth, as a preacher of humble powers, who speaks from a thorough and systematic study of God's Word.[4] Exegesis and systematic theology properly go hand in hand. Neither is complete, neither is really safe, without the other. And while a man will be apt to feel himself specially attracted towards one of them, according to his mental constitution and training and will naturally work extensively at that one, he ought also diligently, regularly, and through life to pursue the other. A preacher ought always to have on hand some able treatise of theology, which he is regularly studying, or some particular topic of divinity, which he makes the subject of much reading and reflection.

(3) The closely related field of philosophy and ethics will give to theological and ethical beliefs a necessary comprehensive setting. The preacher comes to men with a Christian proposal for faith and thought and conduct. Should he not know what other proposals are being made? Will it not make his own convictions stronger and his own statement of truth clearer and more convincing if he has faced and answered for himself, through the good offices of great Christian thinkers, the claims of humanism and naturalism? Many men, unfamiliar with the language of philosophy, follow a humanism that has no place for God and a naturalism that eliminates both God and a distinctive humanity. They are indeed "of this earth, earthy," and have beneath their feet only "the firm foundations of unyielding despair." If the preacher has not only a cry of alarm but also an understanding of the riddle men are trying to solve and of the road between their wilderness and the temple of God, his ministry will be broadened and deepened among the learned and the unlearned alike. The world needs that kind of preacher, one who knows the geography of man's wilderness and understands why the philosophies and programs of atheism and animalism are no abiding habitats of the soul, and who believes with all his soul that the God and Father of Jesus Christ is the One Eternal "out of whom and through whom and unto whom are all things."

(4) Nor can the preacher forget that science has unearthed a wealth of fact which he may ignore only unto poverty. He may, and sometimes must, reject theories, but he must welcome facts. Facts will always serve him; and the better they are related and organized, the better they will serve. Read the sermons of a man like W. L. Watkinson to see how the facts of natural science enrich preaching

[4] Compare Shedd, *Hom.*, pp. 26 ff.

by manifold illustration of moral and religious truth. "The works of God throw light upon the Word of God; or rather, all the great discoveries of man in art, science, and morality are so many words of God to him."[5] "The heavens declare the glory of God" and "the whole earth is full of his glory." The new sciences of psychology and sociology are of special value. Psychology is a study of man in his mental life; sociology is a study of man in his social relations. The one is a study of personality; the other, a study of community. And each is discovering more and more its need of the other. The preacher needs both, for the gospel is for the whole man; it has two commandments, speaking to man as an individual standing before God, and as a co-individual indissolubly related to his fellow-men. The gospel of the eternal and abundant life must find its way into the souls of men as they are constituted. And it is of inestimable value to the preacher to know the normal mental and social processes, to have an intelligent approach to the ills and problems that disturb men's mental life, to be acquainted with the problems of social relations, both pathological and normal. Both the search for souls and the cure of souls are set forward by intelligence.

(5) History and biography constitute another continent of material of great variety and vital worth. Church history does not usually receive from working ministers the attention it deserves. Especially does the history of doctrines assist one in understanding the truth and in comprehending those objections and erroneous tendencies which under different forms reproduce themselves in every age. Every religious denomination has certain characteristic or favorite doctrines which its standard works bring out with clearness and prominence. Thus, apart from the necessary provision for polemical preaching and from the common stock of Christian theology, there is much to be learned by studying the peculiar opinions of different denominations. Such a study will save the preacher from false representations which are at once unjust to others and destructive of his own influence as a man and his power to convince others of the truth of his own beliefs. As for biography, what can yield greater insight into human nature and more telling illustrations? What is more inspiring to the preacher's own heart and imagination?

A genuine biography enables us to see into the motives on which man has built his life, the ideas with which he started, the enemies with whom

[5] McComb, *Preaching in Theory and Practice*, p. 33.

he had to contend, the faith and the aspiration which gave him the victory.[6]

Thus we may make companions and counselors of the nobility of the ages.

(6) The study of sermons is not only very useful with reference to the art of sermonizing but also affords much valuable material, provided it be not borrowed directly but assimilated by reflection and made part of one's own thinking. The careful analysis and thorough and repeated examination of a few rich and impressive sermons is much better, in every respect, than the cursory reading of many.

(7) It can only be mentioned that many have found in imaginative literature rich tributaries to their preaching. The poetry of the Bible cannot be surpassed in its devotional power. The great poets of the centuries have caught the timeless treasures of human life and thought, and clothed them in language that stirs men's hearts. Fiction also, tested and carefully chosen fiction, gives insight into typical human experience, together with the circumstances in which it was born, and its fruits, good or evil.

The novel like the drama holds up the mirror to nature and life, and the more the preacher knows of the soul as reverent students of the soul have revealed it, the better will he be able to minister the truths of religion, the forgiving and regenerating grace of God in Christ Jesus.[7]

(8) But there are other sources of materials for preaching besides books. Personal experience, for its importance, might have been mentioned second and repeated after each succeeding paragraph. A preacher's firsthand knowledge of human nature and of the world, his experience of life, and especially of the religious life, his conversation with those around him upon religious and upon general themes, his perpetual reflection upon everything felt, observed, or heard,—these afford a large part of his most valuable materials. And all his previous preaching, if rightly managed, has but enriched the mind to meet further demands. If one merely scrapes together thoughts around a subject so as to make a sermon, then every sermon consumes part of his material and leaves him poorer. But if he habitually penetrates into a subject and masters it, every sermon leaves him richer; not that he can shortly preach again upon the same topic or text, but that he is better prepared for treating others

[6] *Ibid.*, p. 25.
[7] *Ibid.*, pp. 29 f.

akin to it. There is a fertilizing production. In this sense, too, "there is that scattereth, and yet increaseth."

3. THE QUESTION OF ORIGINALITY

In its absolute sense originality means bringing into existence thoughts which the world never knew before, which had never arisen in any human mind. Of course, this must be very rare. "The ancients have stolen all our best ideas" is one of the sayings of the great Edinburgh Reviewer which cannot soon be forgotten. And Goethe said: "Very little of me would be left, if I could but say what I owe to my predecessors and my contemporaries." But not in modern times alone has this been felt. Hear Chaucer:

> For out of the old fieldes, as men saithe,
> Cometh al this new corne fro yere to yere,
> And out of olde bookes, in good faithe,
> Cometh al this new science that men lere.

And Confucius, five centuries before our era, proclaimed himself only a student of antiquity. Yet, even in this absolute sense, originality is possible, and we should not despair. Progress in some directions the world's thought does slowly make. Among all the uncounted millions of men, patient thinkers are far from numerous; and he who will patiently think, why may he not light upon some thought unknown to those who have gone before him?

(1) *In its relative meaning any man may be "original," and to some extent every man is so.* For no two men are likely to have identically the same idea. It will have in each mind a differential quality. As we contemplate our world, we produce thoughts which were not by us derived from any other mind.

The same phases of nature and experiences of life awaken in us much the same reflections they have awakened in many others; and seed-thoughts attain in us much the same developments. Here there is everything to encourage. Much of the mental quickening, the conscious vigor, and buoyant self-reliance, which result from absolute originality, may also be wrought in us by thoughts relatively original although the mental elation may not be so great.

Moreover, it is not within the purpose of preaching to be absolutely original, since it must come from Scripture. But the preacher may be original in several ways. He may have original views of the meaning of Scripture. It is entirely possible that any one of us should attain more just conceptions of the meaning of some passage or certain aspects of a doctrine than have ever before been gained. And to interpret and ponder for ourselves, in the sense of relative originality, is the privilege and the duty of all. We have no right to take for granted that commentators and theologians are correct in their opinions; and in fact theological discords and conflicts, with all their evils, have this advantage, that they compel the most trusting and the most slothful of us somewhat to feel the necessity of thinking for ourselves. What freshness, what power there is, in truths which the preacher has himself wrought out from Scripture, drawing with his own bucket, as Lord Bacon says, "immediately where it springeth." The student of physical science must observe nature for himself; and so in theology we must open our own eyes to behold and contemplate the teachings of God's Word. There is no limit to the relative originality which may in this respect be achieved. Again, the combination of Scripture teachings with the facts and truths which we derive from nature, Providence, human nature, life, affords large room for originality. Here in every direction the mind may expatiate, bringing all things into relation to the Word of God. And then in the choice of topics, the construction of discourse, the illustration and application of truth, a preacher may perpetually devise what shall be in some respects fresh and, relatively to him, original. And, in fact, a man has his own way of presenting any subject whatever, which derives power from association with his personality; and other things being equal, this is for him the best way. "Put honor upon your individuality."

Originality is sometimes aimed at in unworthy ways or made matter of affectation. Men of a certain character will take up with some heresy, merely to display independence, to show that they, forsooth, are not tied down to the old opinions just as some men will stick to an old opinion just to display orthodoxy. Paradox may be properly employed, as it is by some able teachers and preachers, as it was by our Lord himself, to awaken attention to truth; but there are those who deal in the paradoxical as showing originality. Oddity and sensationalism in ideas, expressions, or manner, are mere caricatures of originality in order to obtain a spurious freshness. To say that such and such a preacher is "an original" is to use the term in a very degraded sense. Young men, and even older ones, sometimes pretend not to read lest it should impair their originality.

We have seen the works of a painter, who would see no Raffaelles or Van Dycks, lest he should spoil his native manner. He has certainly succeeded in avoiding all that one beholds in these great masters.[8]

(2) *Why is originality so desirable?* We may answer, first, that independent thinking more than anything else will develop, discipline, and strengthen the mind. In the matter of mental improvement, it must never be forgotten, the hardest way is the easiest way, the slow way the swiftest.

Again, remember that originality renders discourse greatly more attractive and impressive. On the one hand, an original thought interests the speaker more. It is his offspring; it awakens in him a parental affection and perhaps a thrill of paternal pride. It is his possession; he is no dispenser now of other men's bounty but gives of his own; and in knowledge, as elsewhere, "to give is happier than to receive." But no analogies will do justice to the feeling—the pleasure, the confidence, the hopefulness and earnestness—with which a man utters what is even relatively original. On the other hand, it interests the audience more. As simply new, it gratifies their natural love of novelty. If they consider the thought original with the speaker, there arises a heightened admiration of him and a higher regard for all that he says. And then they sympathize with the speaker's own feeling. Whatever makes his mind glow will warm theirs. In general, no man can interest others save by that which exceedingly interests himself. Thus the two causes combine. And no doubt there are other causes. Analysis cannot fully reach the secret of that delight with which we regard what comes as a new creation, a fresh existence. But even a little reflection should make us feel more deeply the importance of original thinking.

It is an obvious inference that we ought to think out for ourselves the most familiar topics and exhibit them in our own manner. In discoursing upon matters so commonplace as the pleasures of piety or the danger of delay, one should strive by long and earnest reflection to gain views of the subject or a method of presenting it which will be his own. Happy the preacher who can thus give to momentous but too familiar themes some heightened interest, some new impressiveness. Yet the warning must here be repeated: mere oddity is a very different thing from originality, and it is better to be commonplace but in earnest than to be manifestly straining after novelty.

[8] Alexander, *Thoughts on Preaching*, p. 362.

Another inference is that even ideas which have been borrowed ought to be so thoroughly thought over as to become a part of our own thinking. Otherwise they will commonly fail to take a firm hold of ourselves or of the hearers. As a government often takes foreign coins and passes them through its own mint, so the thoughts derived from others should receive the stamp of our own minds, which will give them newness of aspect, full value, and ready acceptance.

(3) *Obstacles to originality.* These are numerous and powerful, as might be taken for granted when we remember how desirable it is to be original, and yet how rarely it is found in any high degree.

Erroneous views of the nature of originality prevent many persons from attaining it. Some imagine that there can be nothing worth the name, unless it be absolutely original, new to the human race; and as this can, of course, be very seldom achieved, they despair and content themselves too commonly with taking ideas at second hand. Others wrongly think that wide reading interferes with originality, and, confining themselves within the narrow limits of their little minds, thus condemn themselves to great mental barrenness. It would be as wise to avoid conversation. Who does not know the quickening, fructifying power of talk with an intelligent friend upon a subject which we have been studying? Though nothing be directly borrowed, yet new thoughts are often suggested, and we are led to see more clearly what we had but dimly perceived. The same effect may be produced by reading. In general, we ought vigorously and patiently to think upon the subject before either reading or conversing upon it; otherwise, the mind is in danger of merely following the track which others have marked out, instead of approaching the subject in its own manner. But after such personal reflection, then reading and conversation may be found highly stimulating and suggestive, leading to much that is really our own, but which without this contact with other minds would not have occurred to us. A third class, by mistaking oddity or eccentricity for originality, misdirect and pervert their aspirations and powers, and so fail to accomplish what they might have done. Still others, especially aspiring young minds setting out in pursuit of originality, are sometimes led to seek it in affectations of style, rather than in genuine, clear thinking. Well says Phillips Brooks:

Be yourself by all means, but let that good result come not by cultivating merely superficial peculiarities and oddities. Let it be by winning a true self full of your own faith and your own love. The deep originality is noble, but the surface originality is miserable. It is so easy to be a John the Baptist, as far as the desert and camel's hair and locusts and wild honey go. But the devoted heart to speak from, and the fiery words to speak, are other things.[9]

A second hindrance is found in native indolence. Original thinking is difficult, laborious, and usually slow, the hardest work that men ever attempt. Who can wonder that easy borrowing, or even shameless stealing, is so often substituted?

A third obstacle, especially at the present day, is the vast extension of literature and the attractive forms which new books and periodicals assume, seducing us by their charm or imposing on us unreal claims to our acquaintance. Reading accompanied by honest thinking is promotive of originality; but we are tempted to waste ourselves upon a species of reading which does not demand reflection or leave time for it. One who is inclined to free indulgence in light literature must curb himself with a very steady hand, or he will never achieve much as a thinker, nor be in any respect worth much to the world. Even of books upon religious subjects, very many of the most attractive that appear are by no means so stimulating, so provocative of good thinking, as the older books from which they were mainly drawn.

And the pressures of the age upon the preacher are in many respects unfavorable to profound thought. The demand is for quick processes and so-called "practical" results. His administrative functions in church and community multiply. The inevitable temptation is to substitute readiness, variety, boundless surface knowledge, with brilliancy, and point and paradox for deep thinking and thorough acquaintance with a few subjects. We must constantly remind ourselves that real knowledge has three dimensions, length, breadth, and depth. Our acquisitions in that noble domain should not be confined to the surface of things, but should correspond to the old law as to the tenure of land, by which possession extends up to the sky and down to the center of the earth. Such knowledge is the handmaid, nay, the sister of original thought.

Two remarks may be made here in conclusion. One is, that the preacher should not desire to originate any part of the fundamental material of his preaching. He should not only submit but rejoice to take this from the Word of God. Too many preachers are in

[9] *Lectures on Preaching*, p. 24.

these days seeking after originality and other novelty by forsaking the Scriptures. The other remark is that we must not aspire after originality in the spirit of pride or selfish ambition but as a means of doing more to benefit men and to glorify the Redeemer.

4. PLAGIARISM AND BORROWING

A plagiary among the Romans was a kidnaper, one who stole free men and made slaves of them, also one who stole or enticed away another man's slave to use or sell as his own, and this secondary sense appears to be that which gave rise to the literary usage. A late Roman writer, by a natural analogy, applies the odious name to one guilty of literary theft, stealing and using another man's ideas; and the languages derived from Latin retain the word in this sense. Plagiarism has from the earliest times been censured and satirized, and no man defends it any more than other stealing would be defended.[10] But then what is plagiarism, and what is lawful borrowing? Some practice the former who design only the latter, and some, through morbid dread of that which is disgraceful, shrink from what is innocent and helpful. There are two questions to be considered, the proper use of other men's thoughts, and the proper acknowledgment of such use.

(1) What use is it proper to make, in preparing a sermon, of ideas derived from others? The question is in principle the same, as regards what we have read, and what we have heard; though many persons who are much more strict as to the fruits of reading use with great freedom what they have heard, in the pulpit, the lecture room, or in conversation.

(a) Never appropriate an entire discourse, whether with or without acknowledgment. It might be lawful, under peculiar circumstances, to read to an audience some choice sermon, avowedly as reading; as an occasional exercise, by a good reader, and with a congregation who fancy it this might do good. But to preach, as preaching, a

---

[10] Chrysostom, in his beautiful treatise on the Priesthood (§ 451), makes a slightly humorous complaint as to the charges of plagiarism against preachers, sometimes even for repeating what was their own. And Augustine does defend the practice in a strange fashion (De Doct. Christ., Lib. IV., xxix., n. 62), saying that one must not be accused of theft or plagiarism for preaching alienos sermones if he lives according to the teachings they contain, for thereby it becomes his own; "for the word of God is not alien to a man who obeys it." Strange what quibbling sophistry great minds sometimes permit themselves to use!

discourse which we acknowledge to have been borrowed from others is so incongruous and unpleasing a thing as to be very rarely done. The real practice, with some preachers, is still worse. They shrink from acknowledging what they do but still allow themselves to do it. It is wonderful how those who boast of being gentlemen can practice an appropriation which is condemned by the guilty pains they take to hide it. And such a usage on the part of men who profess to be Christians could never have arisen save in connection with radically wrong ideas as to the very nature of preaching.

(b) Never appropriate without acknowledgment the complete outline of a discourse.[11] Many persons in our country appear to think this perfectly lawful. Ludicrous stories are often told of sermons pursuing the same train of thought with one shortly before preached at the same place; and sometimes the real author incurs the blame. But one rebukes himself for being amused at such stories, for they have a grave side which is humiliating. Does the evil of stealing depend on whether one is caught at it, as the Spartans taught their boys? Shall a Christian minister, in the very performance of his solemn duties, deliberately do what he would be ashamed to confess? Let anyone try the experiment, if he likes, of acknowledging that the plan of his sermon is derived from so and so and see to what an extent, save in very peculiar cases, it will diminish the interest. The people do not merely come to hear a discourse,—they come to hear a living man, communicating to them his earnest thought and feeling; and if the principal ideas of the sermon are from another preacher, they regard themselves as only hearing an absent or dead man. If, then, it would be bad policy to proclaim the borrowing, how can it be honesty to conceal it? The power of custom, including the known practice of some good men, the seductions of sloth, and the overwork to which ministers are often subjected have wrought in many minds a confusion of ideas on this subject which can alone account for the frequent cases of unacknowledged appropriation.

The books of "Sketches and Skeletons," which are so often published and so widely bought, are, unless honestly and wisely used, an unmitigated evil and a disgrace to the ministry of the gospel. And it is a fair question whether such books can be honestly and wisely used. For they are likely to prove a snare even to those who

[11] Dean Howson says: "If the plan is your own, the sermon is your own in a truer sense, and you are likely to preach it with more heart than if you were to take the framework from someone else and then fill in the empty spaces."

wish to be honest and are sure to be a temptation to all who use them to depend too much on the suggestions of others rather than on their own thinking. If it be said that they may be profitably studied as specimens of sermonizing, there is the obvious answer, that it would be much more profitable to analyze for ourselves the full sermons of really great men. There is no excuse for such books, and no minister should suffer one of them to remain in his library. But they are deplorably common.

(c) But may we borrow? Certainly, we may and sometimes ought to borrow. There are two extremes. On the one hand, a mistaken desire for originality and independence causes some able men to abstain from reading anything on the text or subject. Such a man deceives himself, for many of the thoughts which his own mind now furnishes were originally derived from reading or hearing. True, these are more likely to have been digested and assimilated than what is read just at the time of preparation. But this difference does not necessarily hold, for many thoughts are long retained by the memory in a perfectly crude state, and what results from reading at the time should not be used until after thoroughly working it over in our own mind. And besides this self-deception, he deprives himself of what would often prove valuable help in contemplating the subject on every side and presenting it in the most effective manner. The other extreme is that of reading instead of thinking, just cramming the mind with a medley of other men's thoughts, and constructing a discourse out of these.[12] Such a method of preparation, though often adopted, is exceedingly objectionable. But can we avoid the latter extreme only by rushing to the former?

There is surely a middle course. We may both think and read. On most texts and subjects think long and laboriously before reading at all (except it be the commentaries as to the meaning of the text). Put down in writing some statement of your principal thoughts and make out the plan of the discourse. Afterwards, read whatever bears upon the subject as far as you have time or see occasion, and in reading think for yourself still, not only weighing carefully what the author says but following out any trains of thought which he may suggest to your own mind. On some subjects concerning which we lack information it may be well to read widely before constructing

[12] Pascal has somewhere a fine sarcasm to the effect that when a preacher of this sort says "we," he means himself and the man from whom he has stolen.

the plan of the sermon. But one will not often determine to preach upon a subject until he has gained some general knowledge of it. And now if we have found an idea, or remember one formerly met with, which can be easily wrought into our plan of discourse and which would make the sermon more instructive, interesting, or impressive, why, let us use it,—of course, with proper acknowledgment. The question is, which will be better, on the one hand for your general improvement as a preacher and on the other for the effectiveness of the present sermon, that you should use this idea or should omit it.

Everything thus borrowed must have been fully comprehended and made a part of our own thinking, and must take its place naturally as a part of the discourse. A discourse is a structure, and extraneous matters which do not fit into it and subserve its objects will, however admirable in themselves, be offensive and hurtful, as would be such additions to a dwelling house or a steam engine.

(2) In what cases, and in what ways, shall one make acknowledgment of having borrowed?

When the remark is obvious or belongs to the common stock of religious ideas so that it might have occurred to ourselves, although it happens to have been drawn from another, then it is often unnecessary to make any acknowledgment. When the idea is at all striking, so that hearers would give any special credit for it as a good thing, then we must not take a credit which is undeserved but must in some way indicate that the thought was derived from another.

In what cases shall we mention the precise source? When the author's name would give greater weight to the idea or in some way attach interest to it: for example, Bacon or Bunyan, Whitefield or Spurgeon. Again, when we may hope thereby to lead some hearer to read the book mentioned. Or generally, when to name the source would do any good. It is well to be sure that one can pronounce the author's name correctly or else to omit it. Many French and German names occur in our religious literature, and many hearers know enough of those languages to make the effect quite bad if the preacher ludicrously mispronounces them.

Otherwise, it is enough merely to indicate that the thought was derived from some source. Avoid a parade of honesty about acknowledging. Avoid, too, an ostentatious display of wide reading. Let the acknowledgment interrupt as little as possible the flow of thought, —detract as little as possible from the interest which the idea is likely to awaken. If it would decidedly interrupt or detract, then omit the acknowledgment and the thing borrowed. In general, the method of acknowledging calls for the exercise of judgment and good taste. Without formality or set phrases and with graceful simplicity, state, indicate, or even merely intimate that the idea was derived from some other person.

It is certainly important that on the whole subject of borrowing, one should have just principles, and that he should early in life establish such principles, and form correct habits from the beginning. Otherwise, there either will be a wrong practice continued through life, with very injurious results to a man's character and influence, or, when he comes to see more clearly, there will be much to regret in his past course. It is a good rule never to make use of another's contribution in a way that would be embarrassing to confess in public or that would be embarrassing if the author were present. Professor Phelps truly says:

A young man has gained one of the prime elements of scholarship when he has learned of the worth of artlessness in his literary dealings with himself. Play no tricks upon yourself. Do not be hoodwinked into an imitation of the tricks of authors. Be honest in your secret literary habits. Keep yourself always on the safe side of plagiarism in your sermons. Be assured that you will plagiarize unconsciously quite as much as is consistent with the rights of authorship. As a specimen of the care which should be practised in this respect, if you quote in your sermon, see to it that you put the signs of quotation into your delivery as well as into your manuscript. . . . There is such a thing as intellectual integrity. The price of it is above rubies.[13]

[13] *Men and Books*, p. 199.

Part II

FORMAL ELEMENTS OF THE SERMON

◇◇◇

CHAPTER I

IMPORTANCE OF ARRANGEMENT

THE effective arrangement of the materials in a discourse is scarcely less important than their intrinsic interest and force. This is a distinct part of the speaker's work and should be contemplated and handled as something apart from invention on the one hand and from style on the other, albeit closely connected with both. In fact, the task calls for a specific talent. Some men exhibit from the very outset a power of constructing discourses which is quite out of proportion to their general abilities; and other men find nothing so difficult to acquire or exercise as skill in arrangement. And here, as in everything else that demands specific talent, there is need of special training and practice.[1]

In this respect the speaker is an architect. Out of gathered materials he is to build a structure and a structure suited to its specific design. The same or nearly the same materials may be made into a dwelling, a jail, a factory, a church. But how different the plan of the building according to its design, and how important that it be built with special reference to the design. In like manner, substantially the same materials may be wrought into a story, a dialogue, an essay, or a speech; and several speeches on the same subject, embodying much the same thoughts, may make a very different impression according to the plan of each.

Or the speaker's task may be compared to the organization of an army and then the concentration of its several divisions upon one objective point.

---

[1] See a sensible discussion of Arrangement in Genung's *Practical Rhetoric*, pp. 260 ff.

I. VALUES OF A PLAN

(1) Arrangement is of great importance to the speaker himself. It reacts upon invention. One has not really studied a subject when he has simply thought it over in a desultory fashion, however long-continued and vigorous the thinking may have been. The attempt to arrange his thoughts upon it suggests other thoughts and can alone give him just views of the subject as a whole. Good arrangement assists in working out the details, whether this be done mentally or in writing. Each particular thought when looked at in its proper place develops according to the situation, grows to its surroundings. If one speaks without manuscript, an orderly arrangement of the discourse greatly helps him in remembering it. One reason why some preachers find extemporaneous speaking so difficult is that they do not arrange their sermons well. And not only to invention and memory but to emotion also is arrangement important. Whether in preparation or in delivery of sermons, a man's feelings will flow naturally and freely only when he has the stimulus, support, and satisfaction which come from conscious order.

The speaker who neglects arrangement will rapidly lose, instead of improving, his power of constructing, organizing, a discourse; and he will have to rely for the effect of his sermons entirely on the impression made by striking particular thoughts or on the possibility that high emotional excitement may produce something of order. For passion does sometimes strike out an order of its own.

I know that nothing is as logical, after its own manner, as passion, and that we may depend upon it for the direction of a discourse of which it is the principal inspiration. The beginning we may be sure will be good, and the beginning will produce all the rest. It will be repetitious, it will retrace its steps, it will digress, but it will do everything with the grace and felicity which always accompany it; and it would be less true and consequently less eloquent if it were more logical in the ordinary sense of the word. It naturally finds the order which suits it, and it finds this precisely because it does not seek after it. The rapid propagation of ideas, their concatenation by means of thoroughly vital transitions, which themselves constitute the movement of the discourse, suffice for the eloquence of passion.[2]

This sort of thing is not infrequently observed in the best efforts

[2] Vinet, *Hom.*, p. 271.

of some uncultivated but gifted men; and many a pastor has had occasional experience of it when forced to preach with inadequate preparation, and unusually helped by passionate emotion. It is very proper that a preacher should sometimes give himself up, for a small portion of a discourse, to the suggestions of deep feeling, should throw himself upon the current of emotion; and in social meetings he may sometimes speak without any immediate preparation and yet, if he becomes deeply stirred and gains the sympathies of his audience, may speak with spontaneous order and with powerful effect. But to rely on this habitually is surpassingly unwise.

(2) Still more important is good arrangement as regards the effect upon the audience. It is necessary, first, in order to make the discourse intelligible.

Hearers generally, when the preacher has a poor plan, feel the difficulty, though they may not be able to trace it to its real source; and one of the reasons why a man of truly philosophical mind is able "to make things plain" even to illiterate hearers is that he presents clear thoughts in a proper order.[3]

Many persons appear to think that intelligibility is altogether an affair of style, when in fact it depends quite as much on clear thinking and on good arrangement as on perspicuous expression. It is melancholy to think how large a portion of the people, even in favored communities, really do not understand most of the preaching they hear. Not a few would say, like Tennyson's "Northern Farmer," if they spoke with equal frankness, that they had often heard "parson a bummin' awaäy,"

An' I niver knaw'd whot a meän'd, but I thowt a 'ad summut to saäy,
An' I thowt a said whot a owt to 'a said, an' I comed awaäy.

And not merely is this true of the comparatively ignorant and stolidly inattentive, but many sermons are not understood by the better class of hearers.

The audience keep nothing of the discourse; they carry away, in retiring, an indistinct mass of remarks, of assertions, of appeals, which nothing co-ordinates in their memory, and the impressions received are summed up in the saddest criticism that can be made by a devout person who came to hear with attention: I do not know exactly what the preacher preached about.[4]

[3] Ripley, *Sacred Rhetoric*, p. 185.
[4] Coquerel, *Observ. sur la Préd.*, p. 160.

Besides, something worse may happen than that the discourse should not be understood; it may be misunderstood, utterly, and with deplorable results. We must strive to render it not merely possible that the people should understand us but impossible that they should misunderstand.

Again, it greatly contributes to make the discourse pleasing. "Order is heaven's first law." Even those phenomena in nature which seem most irregular and those scenes which appear to be marked by the wildest variety are pervaded by a subtle order, without which they would not please. Chaos might be terrible but could never be beautiful. And discourses which are pleasing but appear to have no plan will be found really to possess an order of their own, however unobtrusive or peculiar. An ill-arranged sermon may, of course, contain particular passages that are pleasing, but even these would appear to still greater advantage as parts of an orderly whole, and the general effect of that whole must be incomparably better. Let it be added that a well-arranged discourse will much more surely keep the attention of the audience. And this not merely because it is more intelligible and more pleasing but also because, being conformed to the natural laws of human thinking, it will more readily carry the hearer's thoughts along with it.

Further, good arrangement makes a discourse more persuasive. Both in presenting motives and in appealing to feeling, order is of great importance. He who wishes to break a hard rock with his sledge does not hammer here and there over the surface but multiplies his blows upon a certain point or along a certain line. They who lift up huge buildings apply their motive power systematically, at carefully chosen points. So when motives are brought to bear upon the will. And the hearer's feelings will be much more powerfully and permanently excited when appeals are made in some natural order.

We may, by a word or an isolated act, give a movement to the soul, inclining it immediately to a certain object, to perform an act of will; but this movement is only a shock. By the same means we may repeat, multiply these shocks. . . . Eloquence consists in maintaining movement by the development of a thought or proof, in perpetuating it, according to the expression of Cicero, "What is eloquence but a continuous movement of the soul?"[5]

And finally, it causes the discourse to be more easily remembered.

[5] Vinet, *op. cit.*, p. 289.

Hearers are edified, other things being equal, just as the sermon sticks. No food feeds the flock as that which is distinctly remembered, which the mind can carry away from the sanctuary for the heart to feed on afterwards. This sometimes makes the difference, and all the difference, between failure and success in a pastorate.[6]

2. QUALITIES OF GOOD ARRANGEMENT

The importance of arrangement may be further seen by observing what are the principal qualities of good arrangement. They appear to be unity, order, and proportion.[7]

(1) *Unity*. It might seem quite unnecessary to urge the importance of unity in a discourse, but it is very often neglected in practice, particularly in text-sermons and expository sermons, which are frequently made up of two or three little sermons in succession. Whether the unity be that of a doctrinal proposition, of an historical person, or of a practical design, in some way there must be unity.

A work of art may express a variety of ideas, but it cannot remain a work of art unless this variety is held together by the unity of a single idea. The sermon, too, may and should present a variety of thoughts; yet it dare not be a barrage of heterogeneous and arbitrarily assembled elements but must form an organic unity.[8]

(2) *Order*. All that is said might be upon the same subject, while the several thoughts by no means follow one another according to their natural relations, or according to the design of the discourse.

We know not how to name a composition without order. It is disposition, it is order which constitutes discourse. The difference between a common orator and an eloquent man is often nothing but a difference in respect to disposition. Disposition may be eloquent in itself, and on close examination we shall often see that invention taken by itself, and viewed as far as it can be apart from disposition, is a comparatively feeble intellectual force. "Good thoughts," says Pascal, "are abundant." The art of organizing them is not so common. . . . I will not go so far as to say that a discourse without order can produce no effect, for I cannot say that an

[6] Johnson, *The Ideal Ministry*, p. 342.

[7] Genung (*Practical Rhetoric*, p. 263) gives as the requisites of composition, distinction, sequence, and climax; Reu (*Homiletics*, pp. 390-394), unity completeness, order, and simplicity; Davis (*Principles of Preaching*, pp. 224 f.), mentions as the outstanding qualities of eight selected sermons of great preachers, progress, moving toward climax, and proportion of parts.

[8] Reu, *Homiletics*, p. 390.

undisciplined force is an absolute nullity. We have known discourses very defective in this respect to produce very great effects. But we may affirm in general that, other things being equal, the power of discourse is proportional to the order which reigns in it, and that a discourse without order (order, be it remembered, is of more than one kind) is comparatively feeble. A discourse has all the power of which it is susceptible, only when the parts proceeding from the same design are intimately united, exactly adjusted, when they mutually aid and sustain one another like the stones of an arch. . . . This is so true, so felt, that complete disorder is almost impossible, even to the most negligent mind. In proportion to the importance of the object we wish to attain, or the difficulty of attaining it, is our sense of the necessity of order.[9]

Good order requires first of all that the various ideas comprising the unit of consideration be carefully distinguished from one another; secondly, that they follow one another in true sequence, so making for continuity; and, thirdly, that the order of thought shall move toward a climax.

The climactic arrangement is especially in place when the appeal is to the will, so that each successive point will bear with stronger and ever stronger impact upon the will until the last crowns the whole. . . . This should be borne in mind especially by beginners, who commonly bring up their heaviest troops first, only to be left later in the lurch; unless they husband their resources they will give out before reaching the conclusion, and their powers will be spent when they should be at their height.[10]

What Horace said, speaking of poetry, is also true of the sermon: that the power and the beauty of order consist in saying just now what just now ought to be said, and postponing for the present all the rest.

(3) *Proportion*. This involves two things. The several parts of the discourse, whether they are distinctly indicated or not, must be so treated as to make up a symmetrical whole. Not that they are to be all discussed at the same length, but at a length proportioned to their relations to each other and to the entire discourse. And besides this proportion of natural symmetry, there is that of specific design. One may treat substantially the same topic in essentially the same manner and yet greatly vary the length of particular parts and the stress laid upon them, according to the object then and there had in view; just as two animals are often found constructed according to the

---

[9] Vinet, *op. cit.*, pp. 264, 265.
[10] Reu, *op. cit.*, p. 393.

same plan and with equal symmetry, while yet certain bones are of exceedingly different size, being adapted to special functions.

Disregard for proportion is one of the faults apparent in the sermons of younger ministers, especially those who do not write their sermons. In the ardor of the discussion they give so much time to the less important points that they do not have the necessary time for those of greater weight. Writing the sermon and constant care in the delivery, if the style is extempore, are the most useful ways by which to avoid the danger.[11]

Coquerel says that the lack of method is the most common fault of preaching, and the most inexcusable because it is usually the result of insufficient labor.

A man cannot give himself all the qualities of the orator; but by taking the necessary pains he can connect his ideas, and proceed with order in the composition of a discourse.[12]

Without specific talent for building discourse, one will not find it an easy task, and may never become able to strike out plans that will be remarkably felicitous; but a fair degree of success in arrangement is certainly within the reach of all, provided they are willing to work.

3. STUDY OF ARRANGEMENT

The importance of studying arrangement is accentuated by the fact that for greatest effectiveness every preacher must be the author of his own forms. The patterns, the blueprints found in textbooks are not final. They were arrived at through the experience of many orators and long study of the best ways to bring truth home to the hearts of men; and they are subject always to further experience and fuller knowledge. No one form is adequate in all circumstances. And no set of forms can anticipate changing mental habits and satisfactions. Forms, therefore, are but suggestive helps and should be regarded as flexible. They will naturally be influenced by the individual preacher's manner of thinking, the peculiar requirements of an audience, and the various purposes of particular sermons. In the forms as well as in the materials of preaching there is room for originality and freedom. Rules are instruments, not masters. The essential qualities of discourse—unity, order, proportion—are the

---

[11] Davis, *Principles of Preaching*, p. 225.
[12] Coquerel, *Observations on Preaching*, p. 163.

limiting factors; the form is their servant, as they in turn are the servants of the moral and spiritual ends of preaching.

For the preacher, however, to possess the freedom, such as that of an artist, to create forms that satisfy his own sense of proper expression, he must accept the disciplines of an art student. He must be familiar with the formal elements essential to every sermon and become a master of the principles of construction that are illustrated in typical forms. Thus to know the causal why of historic forms will not only give the preacher an appreciation of their worth but will give him authority to venture in expressing a new, effective how. But to venture without knowledge, merely in rebellion against old forms, whether we call it vanity or anarchy, is a perilous assertion of freedom. Hence the next four chapters will be devoted to a study of the formal elements—introduction, discussion, and conclusion—and of certain typical sermon forms.

CHAPTER II

THE INTRODUCTION

IT CAN scarcely be necessary to argue at length to the effect that
sermons ought generally to have an introduction. Men have a
natural aversion to abruptness and delight in a somewhat gradual
approach. A building is rarely pleasing in appearance without a porch
or some sort of inviting entrance. An elaborate piece of music will
always have a prelude of at least a few introductory notes. And so
any composition or address which has no introduction is apt to seem
incomplete. But there is more than an aesthetic reason for an introduction. A book needs a preface to introduce to the reader the subject,
the author's reason for writing, his point of view, the approach,
plan, etc. So the subject of a sermon usually needs to be introduced
as a significant idea into the conscious mind of the hearers. Dr. Oman
observes that

even if your subject need no introduction, your audience does. If for
nothing else, they need a little time to settle down. But also they start
the better for being first drawn both to you and your subject, and they
will travel more hopefully if they can survey the scene for a little before
taking the road.[1]

Moreover, the preacher himself needs, for the sake of self-possession, certitude, and deliberate movement, to walk or step into his
message rather than to plunge headlong into it.

I. OBJECTS OF THE INTRODUCTION

The introduction has two chief objects: to interest our hearers
in the subject, and to prepare them for understanding it.

(1) As to the former, a preacher may usually, it is true, count on
a certain willingness to hear. Not many come who are hostile to the
truth, but very many, alas! who are sadly careless about it. And a
much more lively attention may be secured by an interesting introduction.

[1] *Concerning the Ministry*, p. 155.

We all know how much depends in the ordinary affairs of life upon first impressions. The success of his sermon often depends upon the first impressions which a preacher makes upon his hearers in his exordium. If these impressions be favorable, his audience will listen to the remaining part of his discourse with pleasure and attention and, consequently, with profit.[2]

Our aim should be to excite not merely an intellectual interest but, so far as possible at the outset, a spiritual and practical interest—to bring our hearers into sympathy with our own feeling and attune their minds into harmony with the subject we design to present. One may sometimes expressly request attention, as did Moses (Deut. iv. 1), Isaiah (xxviii. 14), Stephen (Acts vii. 2), and our Lord (Matt. xv. 10); but such a request, if often repeated, would lose its force, and it is usually best to aim at saying something which will at once interest the hearer's mind. "What is the best way," asked a young preacher of an older one, "to get the attention of the congregation?" "Give 'em something to attend to," was the gruff reply.

(2) The other object, to prepare the audience for understanding the subject, is obviously very important and to some extent can often be effected. But our efforts in this respect must be carefully guarded against the danger of anticipating something which properly belongs to the body of the discourse. What such preparation involves will be suggested later in the consideration of sources of introduction.

The German preachers very often give an introduction before announcing the text. This fashion appears to have originated in the fact that most of them are required to take their text from the *"pericope,"* or lesson appointed for the day, so that it may be assumed as to some extent known already before it is announced. Frequently the same fashion is observed in the American pulpit, sometimes, one is inclined to think, as a timid compromise with some moderns who eschew texts altogether. The habitual practice of thus beginning with an introduction is apt to make it too general, or pointless, or far-fetched; but some introductions of this sort are exceedingly felicitous, and the practice is well worthy of occasional adoption.

There are cases in which it is best to dispense with introduction and plunge at once into the discussion; for example, when the sermon must needs be long, or when nothing has been struck out that would make a really good introduction. In familiar addresses, as at prayer meetings, Sunday-school meetings, and the like, this course is quite

[2] Potter, *Sacred Eloquence*, p. 97.

often preferable. In all preaching let there be a good introduction or none at all. "Well begun is half done." And ill begun is apt to be wholly ruined.

2. SOURCES OF INTRODUCTION

The sources from which the preacher may draw introductions are extremely numerous and various. There may, however, be some advantage in classifying them as follows:

(1) *The text.* Wherever the meaning of the text requires explanation, this explanation may of course form the introduction. So, too, when an explanation of the context would throw light on the meaning of the text. These seem to be very natural sources; and Robert Hall, with his severe taste, commonly began with some explanation of the text or the context, preferring this to more ambitious introductions. And if not for explanation proper, there may be occasion for illustration of the text by means of historical and geographical knowledge such as will make its meaning, though not more clear, yet more vivid and interesting. In other cases, some account of the writer of the text or of the condition of any particular persons whom he addressed (as in the case of Paul) may serve to interest hearers in the text or to prepare them for understanding it.

(2) *The subject to be discussed,* if obvious from the mere statement of the text, or if announced at the outset, may then furnish an introduction in various ways. We may remark on its relation to some other subject, e.g., "to the genus, of which the subject is a species," or to some opposed or similar subject, or one related to it as cause, or consequence, or case in point. Where the sermon is designed to be explanatory or practical, an introduction on the relevance of the subject to some present need or problem will often be appropriate; where the sermon is to establish the truth of a proposition or to exhibit its importance, the introduction will frequently explain the nature of the subject involved. The preacher

may state the intellectual advantages to be derived from discussing such a theme. The subject may be the doctrine of moral evil or that of divine sovereignty. It may be stated at the beginning that these are the greatest problems of the human mind meeting the philosopher as well as the theologian, that they have called forth the strength of the best intellects of the race, that no problems are more difficult and therefore none more deserving of the attention of thinking minds. He may state the connections of the subject with other more practical spiritual truths. He may remove the prejudice that the doctrine has no immediate practical bearing or utility, even as depravity, for instance, or the doctrine of sin lies in one sense at the base of the whole Christian system, of the atonement, regeneration, holiness, and the Christian life. He may make some *historical allusion* naturally connected with the theme, which always forms an attractive introduction.[3]

And so in many other ways.

(3) *The occasion.* If the sermon has reference to some particular season of the year or is preached at some special religious meeting, in connection with the administration of an ordinance, or the like, we may begin by remarking upon the occasion. So with allusions to the character of the times in which we live or to recent events or existing circumstances, as showing why the particular text or subject has been chosen, or as tending to awaken a livelier interest in it.[4] Or we may speak of doubts known to exist as to the question involved, or hostility to the truth in this respect, or of some common mistake, or some prevailing or growing error, or evil practice, with reference to this subject. In other cases allusion is made to the religious condition of the church or congregation or cheering news from some other church or part of the country. Sometimes one may refer to a subject or subjects heretofore discussed, as furnishing occasion for presenting today the present subject; and the hymn which has just been sung or a passage of Scripture (not containing the text) which has been read will occasionally afford an interesting introduction. In rare cases the preacher may begin by speaking of himself, whether it be of his feelings as a preacher, of his interest as a pastor, of some particular epoch in his connection with this church, or of something belonging to his personal experience as a Christian.[5] Only, let the preacher beware of apologies. These often create the suspicion of insincerity where it is undeserved because they are sometimes in fact sincere and because the preacher who feels at the outset oppressed by ill health or unfavorable circumstances may, quite unexpectedly to himself, rise to the subject and succeed remarkably well. Let a preacher never say he feels unusually embarrassed on the present occasion, as we hear it so often. Apologies are like public rebukes for disorder in the congregation in that one will very seldom regret

---

[3] Hoppin, pp. 342, 343.

[4] For example, Wesley's sermon on the Great Assize.

[5] To this class belongs an exceedingly felicitous introduction of Spurgeon's, First Series, Sermon I.

having omitted them, however strongly inclined at the moment to speak. When there is any real occasion, whether in beginning or ending the sermon, for what might be called apology, let it never proceed or seem to proceed from anxiety as to the preacher's reputation; let it be brief, quiet, and, as it were, incidental.

The question will often require to be decided whether any of these remarks upon the occasion shall be made in the introduction or in the conclusion. We must consider whether a particular remark of this kind is better suited to awaken interest in the discussion, or to deepen the impression made by the application. Affecting personal illusions, in which the preacher might be interrupted by his emotions, are in general better reserved to the conclusion.

(4) There is an immense variety of other sources, which do not admit of classification and can only be set down as miscellaneous. The preacher's inventive genius should be freely and widely exercised, in seeking for every particular sermon the most thoroughly appropriate introduction.

3. QUALITIES OF A GOOD INTRODUCTION

(1) The introduction must present some thought closely related to the theme of discourse, so as to lead to the theme with naturalness, and ease, and yet a thought quite distinct from the discussion. Inexperienced preachers very frequently err by anticipating in the introduction something which belongs to the body of the discourse; and the danger of doing this should receive their special attention.

The design of the introduction is altogether preparatory. The preacher will often find himself tempted, especially in introductions drawn from the text or context, to remark in passing upon interesting matters which are somehow suggested but are foreign to his purpose on that occasion. This temptation should be resisted, except in very peculiar cases. You have determined to carry the audience along a certain line of thought, hoping to arrive at a definite and important conclusion. Do not first wander about and stray awhile into other paths, but lead on towards the route selected and enter it.

(2) The introduction should generally consist of a single thought; we do not want a porch to a porch. But there are many exceptions to this rule, and it is frequently appropriate to present some introductory thought and afterwards give an exposition, which in such cases

becomes a part of the body of the discourse or else constitutes a sort of halt, while we clear the way for the discussion.

(3) It is desirable to avoid the practice of beginning with some very broad and commonplace generality, as with reference to human nature or life, to the universe or the Divine Being. Of course, there is sometimes real occasion for this, but many preachers practice it as an habitual method, and it is apt to sound like an opening promise of dullness, a platitude to start on.

(4) On the other hand, the introduction must not seem to promise too much in its thoughts, style, or delivery. Let it be such as to excite interest and awaken expectation, provided the expectation can be fairly met by the body of the discourse. It should not be highly argumentative or highly impassioned. As to the latter, it must be remembered that even if the preacher is greatly excited at the outset, the audience usually are not, and he had better restrain himself so as not to get beyond the range of their sympathies. When Cicero broke out with his opening words against Catiline, the Senate was already much excited; and so with Massillon at the funeral of Louis the Great.[6] Such exceptional cases must be decided as they arise.

It is the privilege of talent and the fruit of study and experience, to know when to venture and when to abstain. It cannot be allowed to teaching, strictly so called, to set aside talent or anticipate the dictates of experience.[7]

Moreover, while earnestly seeking to make the introduction interesting and engaging, we must shun the sensational and the pretentious. Whatever savors of display is exceedingly objectionable in a preacher, and particularly at the outset. And he should begin not merely with personal modesty but also with official modesty, reserving for some later period of the sermon anything which it may be proper to state with the authority belonging to his office.

(5) A good introduction would, in general, be exclusively adapted to the particular discourse. In some cases, a certain general thought might with equal propriety introduce several different subjects. Thus some account of Paul might form the introduction to sermons on various passages of his writings; yet the account must in almost every case be at least slightly varied if it is to be exactly adapted to the design. So with the description of a Scripture locality; and so,

---

[6] "My brethren, God only is great" were his first words.
[7] Vinet, op. cit., p. 105.

to some extent, with introductions personal to the speaker. Lawyers make many speeches on very similar subjects or occasions; and this fact partly explains Cicero's statement that he kept some introductions on hand for any speech they might suit—as was also done by Demosthenes.[8] We should beware of set phrases and stereotyped forms of introduction; the people very soon begin to recognize them, and the effect is then anything else than to awaken interest and excite curiosity. Nowhere is it more important to have the stimulus and charm of variety, and this is best attained by habitually seeking to give the introduction a specific and exact adaptation.

(6) The introduction must not be long. An eminent preacher, much inclined to this fault, was one day accosted by a plain old man as follows: "Well, you kept us so long in the porch this morning that we hardly got into the house at all." And it was said of John Howe by some one: "Dear good man, he is so long in laying the cloth that I lose my appetite, and begin to think there will be no dinner after all." Of course the introduction may sometimes be much longer than would be generally proper; and the attempt of some writers to tell how many sentences it should contain is exceedingly unwise. But "where one sermon is faulty from being too abruptly introduced, one hundred are faulty from a long and tiresome preface."[9]

(7) The introduction, though simple and inelaborate, should be carefully prepared. Quintilian remarks that a faulty proem may look like a scarred face; and that he will certainly be thought a very bad helmsman who lets the ship strike in going out of the harbor.[10] The extemporaneous speaker should know exactly what he is to say in the introduction. But it is very doubtful whether he ought, as is frequently recommended and practiced, to have the introduction written, when the remainder of the discourse is unwritten. It is too apt to seem formal, and the transition to the unwritten to be abrupt and precipitous, something like stepping from a wharf into deep water, as compared with quietly wading out from the shore. However, it is good advice that at least two sentences should always be written: the first sentence, that the preacher may be sure of his beginning; and the last, that he may be sure of his ending. It will sometimes happen that at an early stage of the preparation, an introduction will occur to the mind; more commonly, it has to be struck out or selected

[8] Compare Vinet, *Hom.*, p. 301.
[9] Shedd, p. 182.
[10] Quintilian, IV. 1. 61.

after the principal materials have been gathered. That is, its materials may be the last to be gathered. But as to the composition of the sermon in detail (whether it be written or unwritten composition), the introduction should be composed before the body of the discourse. This is the natural order, and the finished introduction will assist the preacher in composing the remainder, somewhat as it will help the hearers. An introduction to a discourse is quite different from a preface to a book.

The discussion of this subject may close with a useful remark from Vinet:

Among experienced preachers we find few examples of exordiums alto-gether defective; we find few good ones among preachers at their begin-ning. We hence naturally infer, that there is in this part of the discourse something of special delicacy, but nothing which demands peculiar facul-ties.[11]

[11] *Op. cit.,* p. 297.

CHAPTER III

THE DISCUSSION

THE discussion, or body of the discourse, must be constructed on some plan, or it is not a discourse at all. Though there be no divisions and no formal arrangement of any kind, yet the thoughts must follow each other according to the natural laws of thought. Men who rely on their powers of absolute extemporizing or who imagine themselves to possess a quasi-inspiration usually stagger and stray in every direction, following no definite line and accomplishing very little, save where, as we have seen, passion comes in and strikes out an order of its own.

The plan of a discourse in the broadest sense includes the introduction and the conclusion, but as these are here considered separately, we may for convenience speak of the plan as belonging rather to the discussion, or body of discourse, with its divisions and subdivisions.

It is not well to call the body of the discourse the "proof" as a general name, though some able writers have done so. The treatment frequently consists of proof in whole or in part, but frequently also of explanation or the impressive exhibition of a theme without any process of proof. In hortatory sermons there is a series of motives, but to bring these to bear on the will is a very different thing from proving, though often confounded with it. After excluding the introduction and conclusion, the remainder is called by various names, as the "division," the "development," the "argument," the "treatment"; but the "discussion" seems to be, upon the whole, the best term. But our present concern with this is to consider the fact that it must have a plan.

I. THE PLAN

Sometimes a plan will occur to us with the subject or on very little reflection. In other cases we only get a variety of separate thoughts. It is well then to jot them down as they occur, to make the thoughts objective so that we may draw off and look at them, and sooner or later a plan of treatment will present itself. This effort to make out an arrangement will often suggest to us new thoughts which otherwise we should never have gained.

One ought to seek not merely for some plan but for the best.

There are plans, energetic and rich, which, applying the lever as deeply as possible, raise the entire mass of the subject; there are others which escape the deepest divisions of the matter and which raise, so to speak, only one layer of the subject. Here it is, especially here, in the conception of plans, that we distinguish those orators who are capable of the good from those who are capable of the better—of that better, to say the truth, which is the decisive evidence of talent or of labor. . . . Every one should strive, as far as possible, for this better, and not be content with the first plan which may present itself to his thought, unless, after having fathomed it, he finds it sufficient for his purpose, suited to exhaust his subject, to draw forth its power—unless, in a word, he can see nothing beyond it.[1]

The plan ought to be simple, not only free from obscurity but free from all straining after effect, and yet ought, so far as possible, to be fresh and striking. So many sermons follow the beaten track, in which we can soon foresee all that is coming, as to make it a weary task even for devout hearers to listen attentively. One feels inclined to utter a plaintive cry, "Worthy brother, excellent brother, if you could only manage to drive us sometimes over a different road, even if much less smooth, even if you do not know it very well—I am so tired of this!" And it is only a plan which strikes that has any chance of being remembered. Still, we must carefully avoid mere sensational, odd, or "smart" plans. A sermon might excite much interest and be remembered long by reason of such qualities, without doing half as much real good as another that was heard quietly and soon forgotten but made, so far as it went, a salutary impression. We must also avoid great formality of plan.

Robert Hall,[2] in a striking passage, criticizes very justly the stiff and minute method of analysis and statement prevalent in his day. Many of the older English and American preachers doubtless erred in this direction. There has been much improvement during the present century, but many preachers are still stiff, uniform, and monotonous in their plans.

In making the plan, a well-formed proposition is an almost indispensable aid. Although it does not mark out the pathways and

---

[1] Vinet, *op. cit.*, pp. 276, 277.

[2] Sermon on the Discouragements and Supports of a Christian Minister, *Works,* Vol. I. p. 140.

intersections of thought, it does fix the boundaries, thus promoting unity and proportion. Often, also, it will be directly suggestive of the order of presentation itself. It would be well at this point in our study to review the discussions of the proposition and the qualities of good arrangement.[3]

2. THE QUESTION OF DIVISIONS

It is a question of much practical importance whether the plan of a discourse ought to include divisions. The Greek and Roman orators, greatly concerned to make the speech a finished work of art and often anxious to hide the labor bestowed upon the preparation, seldom made clearly marked divisions. Yet, in all cases they followed a definite plan and advanced in an orderly manner. In much the same manner the Christian Fathers preached. But the great Schoolmen of the Middle Ages, applying the most minute logical analysis to all subjects of philosophy and religion, established a fashion which was soon followed in preaching also. The young preachers, being trained by the books they read and by the oral teaching at the universities to nothing else than this minute analytical discussion, made the mistake, so often made still, of carrying lecture-room methods into the pulpit. Analysis became the rage. Scarcely anything was thought of but clear division and logical concatenation, and to this was to a great extent sacrificed all oratorical movement and artistic harmony. Too much of the preaching of all the modern centuries has been marred by this fault. Analytical exposition of topics and elaborate argumentation have been the great concern to the comparative neglect of simplicity and naturalness, of animated movement and practical power. Preachers, especially the educated, have too often regarded instruction and con- viction as the aim of their labors, when they are but means of leading men to the corresponding feeling, determination, and action. And the custom being thus established, it has been followed, simply because it was the custom, by many practical and deeply earnest preachers who limited and overcame the evils of the method as best they could.

Two centuries ago, when the excessive multiplication of formal divisions and equally formal subdivisions was almost universal in France as well as in England, Fénelon inveighed vehemently against the whole fashion, urging a return to the methods of the ancient

[3] See pp. 54-56 and 97-99.

orators,[4] and on this question almost all subsequent writers have taken sides. Yet, a certain formality of division and of general order has continued to be common in France and Germany, and for the most part in England and America. Dr. Arnold of Rugby set the example and urged it upon others of avoiding divisions and making the sermon a very informal address, and since his time many preachers in the Church of England have followed that course. But it is worthy of special notice that the two ablest and most generally admired preachers the Church of England has recently produced, Robertson and Liddon, both regularly make divisions and commonly indicate them in passing, while the former frequently states his divisions beforehand and also marks numerous subdivisions. Dr. John Watson, better known as Ian Maclaren, says:

> Three detached sermonettes do not make one sermon; but, on the other hand, a handful of observations tied together by a text are not an organic whole. It all depends on whether the heads advance, ascend, cumulate, or are independent, disconnected, parallel.[5]

Concerning the tendency of his time in America Phillips Brooks makes the following observation and judgment:

> One prevalent impression about sermons, which prevails now in reaction from an old and disagreeable method, is, I think, mistaken. In the desire to make a sermon seem free and spontaneous there is a prevalent dislike to giving it its necessary formal structure and organism. The statement of the subject, the division into heads, the recapitulation at the end,— all the scaffolding and anatomy of a sermon is out of favor, and there are many very good jests about it. I can say that I have come to fear it less and less. The escape from it must not be negative but positive. The true way to get rid of the boniness of your sermon is not by leaving out the skeleton but by clothing it with flesh. True liberty in writing comes by law, and the more thoroughly the outlines of your work are laid out, the more freely your sermon will flow, like an unwasted stream between its well-built banks.

From these principles and facts, what are we to conclude?

(1) While not necessary, distinctly marked divisions will usually be of service, not only in making the train of thought plain to the hearers but also in serving to the preacher himself, both as compelling to logical correctness and completeness of preparation and as helping him to remember in extemporaneous delivery. In every par-

---

[4] Fénelon, *Dialogues on Eloq.*, Dial. II.
[5] Cure of Souls (*Yale Lectures* for 1896), pp. 41 f.

ticular sermon or class of sermons, we must decide the case upon its own merits; but it will commonly be best to make divisions.[6] Whether they shall be slightly or broadly marked and how carefully the entrance upon a new division should be indicated must also be decided according to the merits of the case. Where the subject specially requires explanation and argument, it will commonly be advantageous to have clearly stated divisions and frequently sub-divisions also; but these must not be so multiplied or so stated as to prevent the discourse from standing out as a living whole, or to interrupt its progressive movement towards the practical end in view.

(2) As to the number of divisions, we must consult simplicity and, at the same time, vividness and variety. It is of course more simple to have but few, and in many cases two divisions will be most natural and pleasing. But as a uniform method, the twofold arrangement scarcely presents the requisite variety. It is also highly desirable that the divisions, as stated, should be interesting, having the vividness which belongs to concrete or specific thoughts, and this can often be attained only by having several divisions, since the reduction to a smaller number would render them abstract or general.

Take the topic, *In what consists the glory of gospel preaching?* In that it (1) is appointed by the Son of God; (2) makes known the will of God; (3) promises the grace of God; (4) is performed in the strength of God; (5) is attended by the blessing of God; and (6) leads souls to the presence of God. The division might be simplified: (1) in its establishment; (2) in its subject; (3) in its operation and effects. But the former is to be preferred because more striking.[7]

Yet, when the heads become as many as five or six, they must follow each other in a very natural order, or the average hearer will not easily retain them in mind. Accordingly, judicious and skillful preachers seldom have more than four heads of discourse.

We are thus prepared to understand why it is that sermons oftener have three divisions than any other number. This is a fact long observed and made the subject of small wit—"three heads, like a sermon." No doubt many preachers have tried to make out three divisions, even where nothing called for it, simply from habit or

---

[6] Oman (*Concerning the Ministry*, p. 151) suggests these benefits of divisions: "They help the preacher to clarify and develop his thought, to proceed easily from one part to another, and to secure a right proportion of the whole; and they give the hearer resting places and points of outlook by the way, and help to recall what he hears."

[7] Otto, *Prak. Theol.* s. 355.

from blindly following a custom. But the custom itself must have had some natural origin. Now a principal reason for it is seen from the considerations stated above; three divisions will give a goodly variety without distracting attention or burdening the memory. And in many directions we meet with similar or analogous facts. Thus one of the commonest schemes of discourse will naturally be, What? Why? What then? i.e., explain, prove, apply. A syllogism, when fully stated, furnishes three propositions. There cannot be a climax without at least three steps. Three gives the idea of completeness,—beginning, middle, end. When men start in a race, the signal is always "One, two, three," neither more nor less. The Scriptures often use a threefold repetition as the most emphatic and impressive: Holy, holy, holy; Ask, seek, knock; etc.[8] Often logical and rhetorical reasons combine to fix three as the number. Thus, The resurrection of the body is (1) possible, (2) probable, (3) certain. To carry religion into daily life is (1) possible, (2) desirable, (3) obligatory. Piety is for every young man (1) a thing to be respected, (2) a thing to be desired, (3) a thing to be sought. These considerations go to show that it is not accidental and not strange that elaborate discourses so often have three divisions. The fact that this is the commonest number may incline us to avoid it unless required by the natural arrangement of the subject; but when it is so required, as must very frequently be the case, let us employ it without hesitation. In general, then, one should make the most natural division, considering the subject and the practical design of the discourse.

3. CHARACTER OF THE DIVISIONS

The character of the divisions must be determined by their relation to the subject proposed and to each other. (1) As to the former, it is obvious that no one division should be coextensive with the subject; and yet inexperienced sermonizers sometimes unconsciously have it so. More important is the inquiry whether the divisions should exhaust the subject. This depends upon what we mean by the subject. The general subject treated will very seldom be exhaustively divided in a sermon; but the view of it proposed in the discourse ought to be exhausted by the divisions. That is to say, they ought to exhaust the proposition or, we might say, the subject proposed. Yet, even

---

[8] Phelps thinks that the threefold division was due (as in part no doubt it was) to a desire on the part of medieval preachers to honor the Trinity.

in this narrower sense the oratorical division and subdivision of a subject will not commonly exhaust it as a logical analysis would do. The latter must rigorously set forth "all and singular" the contents of the proposition. The former requires that its divisions shall with a certain general completeness cover the whole ground of the proposition, so as to make the discourse a structure, but does not always demand scientific accuracy in that respect; and, as to subdivisions, it is very easy to extend analysis beyond what conduces to practical effect in speaking. The complete logical analysis of a subject, dividing and subdividing, will sometimes be useful as a part of the preparation for preaching on it; but the oratorical division is distinct from this and often very different, especially as to subdivisions.[9]

(2) As regards the relation of the divisions to each other, they must be distinct and symmetrical. It is not uncommon for unpracticed speakers to have one division that really includes another,[10] and very common to see one that includes some part of what also comes under another. We are sometimes greatly tempted in treating one branch of a subject to go on with some closely related matter which yet properly belongs to another branch. The incongruity is not always obvious and requires attention. Sometimes, in fact, it is difficult to decide where such or such an idea more properly belongs; but it must be confined to one head or fairly divided between the two, so that, in whatever way, the heads shall be kept distinct. Furthermore, ideas are frequently set forth as distinct divisions which are not sufficiently distinct to be divided at all; and ideas which are distinct will be so stated as to glide into each other, without any clear line of demarcation.

Words the most different do not always convey essentially different ideas, as in this division: "It is characteristic of Christian faith, that it excites, guides, supports." To prove successively that a thing is contrary to good sense and contrary to our own interests is to condemn ourselves to be in presence of nothing after finishing the first part.[11]

Besides being distinct, the divisions should be symmetrical. It is little to say that they must not be incongruous, though preachers of

[9] The author once received, as a homiletical exercise, the sketch of a sermon containing four divisions, but with subdivisions and divisions of these again and again, till the whole numbered more than a hundred and twenty. The analysis was almost faultless, but it would have made an intolerable sermon.

[10] Thus Cicero (De Inventione, I. 23) points out how improper it would be to undertake to show that from the opposite party's cupidity and audacity and avarice, many ills had befallen the state, because avarice is really one kind of cupidity.

[11] Vinet, op. cit., p. 282.

some ability do at times throw together matters which have as little congruity as the human head, a horse's neck, a body composed of parts brought from all directions and covered with many kinds of feathers, and the whole ending in a fish's tail—according to the well-known warning of Horace.[12] But the important precept is that the divisions must all sustain the same kind of relation to the subject proposed. Nothing is more common among the faults of inexperienced preachers than to see three divisions, one of which is not co-ordinate with the other two but only with some other proposition of which those two are really subdivisions; some of the divisions are branches of the tree, and others are but branches of branches. This fault should be carefully guarded against. In some respects, the idea of symmetry is often pushed too far. Of course the subdivisions of any one division should all sustain to it the same relation. But pains are often taken to give each division the same number of subdivisions in order to make the plan symmetrical. Even when this is natural, it is very apt to appear artificial, particularly if the number of divisions and sub-divisions be considerable; and when it is really artificial, the effect is not good. Pascal compares such matters inserted merely for the sake of symmetry to false windows in a building, a poor attempt to hide internal lack of symmetry, offending as soon as we know what they are. Another mistaken notion of symmetry requires that each division and sometimes even each subdivision should be discussed at about the same length. When natural, this is pleasing. But it will not often be natural. A mere external symmetry is far less important than proportion to the internal relation of the topics and to the specific design of the discourse.

4. PROBLEMS OF ORDER AND MANAGEMENT

(1) The order of the divisions will be controlled not merely by logical but also by practical considerations. Even where instruction and conviction are especially aimed at, there is always in preaching a practical effect proposed, and usually instruction and conviction are quite subordinate to the object of impressing the feelings and determining the will. As to instruction, it is obviously proper that those divisions should precede, which will help to understand the succeeding ones; and it is commonly convenient that negative considerations should precede the positive. So far as conviction is concerned, a

[12] *Ars Poetica*, 1.

sermon should arrange arguments according to the general principles which regulate the order of arguments, and which apply here not less than in the essay or treatise. And in respect to practical effect, we must endeavor clearly to discern the particular end proposed and then must consider what selection and arrangement of points will be most likely, by kindling the imagination and warming the passions, to induce the hearers to resolve and to act as the truth requires. For this purpose the abstract must precede the concrete, the general precede the specific or particular, and commonly instruction and conviction must precede appeal. The appeal, however, may either come in mass after the whole body of instruction and argument, or it may immediately follow each leading thought as presented. This last course, to apply as we go, has sometimes considerable advantages. The successive waves of emotion may thus rise higher and higher to the end. And besides, while thought produces emotion, it is also true that emotion reacts upon and quickens thought, so that the impressive application of one division may secure for the next a closer attention. Yet, the interest must steadily grow as we advance, or the effect will be bad; and where we cannot feel sure that it will thus grow, point by point, then application had better be postponed till towards the close.

The preacher who repeats a sermon ought to consider whether he cannot advantageously rearrange it or, at any rate, improve the plan.

(2) The statement of the divisions and subdivisions, like that of the proposition, ought to be exact, concise, and, as far as possible, suggestive and attractive. Without straining after effect, one may often state a division in terms so brief and striking that the hearer's attention will be at once awakened. It is well that the several divisions should be stated in similar forms of expression where this can be done without artificiality. Such similarity of statement brings out the symmetry of the divisions, rendering them clearer and also more pleasing. Alliteration is often quite felicitous in making the divisions memorable. But one must always guard against artificiality and inaccuracy.

It is dangerous, and p is a specially dangerous letter, though q runs it hard. The result is apt to be what an address which had two heads with p's and two with q's was called, "a very peculiar speech." But while it is a fond thing to search for alliteration, there is no reason for rejecting it if it arrive for a better reason than ingenuity.[13]

[13] Oman, *Concerning the Ministry*, p. 152.

(3) Shall the divisions be announced beforehand? This was once almost universal, and is still the regular practice of many preachers. At one time in some parts of Germany, the plan of the sermon was printed and either published in the newspaper of the previous week or handed in slips to the congregation as they entered the church.[14] To make a minute announcement of divisions and subdivisions and repeatedly recall them in passing is very appropriate when lecturing to a class on some difficult subject, where the object is not persuasion but only instruction and conviction. But in preaching, rightly regarded, these are commonly subordinate to persuasion. Now three cases may be noted, in which it is desirable to announce the divisions at the outset. First, when the train of thought is difficult, and the announcement may aid in following it. Sometimes this would but increase the difficulty, the hearer finding it easier to comprehend each division by itself as it is presented. But, in other cases, the divisions when placed side by side will throw light on each other. Secondly, when it is particularly desirable that not merely the practical impression should be permanent but that the successive steps in the exposition or argument should be remembered. Thirdly, when we judge that the announcement would awaken interest and attention rather than abate them; and here every case must be decided upon its own merits.[15] Unless one of these three conditions exist, no previous announcements should be made. It must be remembered that there are many different methods of announcing, beginning with the formal statement of numbered divisions (and sometimes of subdivisions also), and extending through numerous gradations to the perfectly informal and perhaps very slight mention of the divisions as the points it is proposed to consider. Between these limits there may be devised a great variety of methods by the exercise of power of invention and of judgment and good taste. Shedd thinks[16] that, as a general thing, recapitulation is better than preannouncement, as being more intelligible, more impressive, and more easily remembered. In many cases, this is true. In many others, the preannouncement is best. Sometimes, it is even well to employ both. To announce at the outset the subdivisions, also, would be scarcely ever desirable, and that only in very peculiar cases where the train of thought was in itself very important.

[14] Hagenbach, *Hom.*, ser. 122.
[15] Compare Phelps, pp. 411-414, and Brooks, p. 177.
[16] *Hom.*, p. 195.

5. TRANSITIONS

The transitions from one part of a discourse to the next are most felicitous when least noticeable. The ideal of excellence would be that the parts should fit perfectly together, "like well-cut stones, needing no cement," to use Cicero's image, or that each should grow out of the preceding by a process of natural development. This ideal can seldom be realized; but in all cases transition will be easy in proportion as the subject proposed has been thoroughly studied and the thoughts to be presented have been well arranged. No good transition can be made between topics that have not a real and natural relation, such as to make it appropriate that they should stand in immediate succession. When, therefore, we find the transition difficult, it is well to inquire whether the arrangement is not defective. Often, indeed, the difficulty arises from the fact that we are attempting to work in some idea or passage which has no natural place in the train of thought. Buffon has remarked, "Those who fear to lose isolated thoughts and who write detached passages at different times never combine them without forced transitions."[17] And the difficulty is even greater with scraps gathered from reading. These should be introduced only when they can be thoroughly incorporated into the discourse. Otherwise, no matter how sensible, striking, or pleasing, it would be better to omit them; if really so good, they will soon find their place somewhere else. A discourse is not a mere conglomeration or accretion of foreign matters. From whatever source its materials may have been derived, they must be made to unite and grow together. Like sap in the plant or blood in the body, the vital current of thought must flow through the whole discourse, giving it animation, flexibility, strength.

Still, it will frequently happen that the practical design of a sermon or the exigencies of preparation will require us to bring together thoughts between which there is not a perfect fit or a spontaneous vital connection. It may then be necessary to interpose some third idea, related to both and forming an easy transition.[18] Such an idea must not have any separate prominence or, in fact, attract to itself any attention from the persons addressed, though a critical observer would perceive that it is appropriate and properly introduced. In most cases

[17] Quoted by Vinet.
[18] Compare Vinet, *op. cit.*, p. 317.

the transition can be effected by a single brief sentence. To manage this with simplicity, grace, and variety is a task of some delicacy, but due attention and practice will enable anyone to perform it with tolerable success. One of the most distinguished preachers of America[19] is known to have remarked that the transitions, the articulations, of a discourse give the highest proof of oratorical skill. If under articulation we comprise the adjustment of successive thoughts to each other, this would naturally include arrangement, and, taken with this breadth of meaning, the remark is unquestionably correct.

But whether the transition be in itself mediate or immediate, it is often desirable to employ some form of expression which, in conjunction with the natural change of tone and manner, shall cause the hearer to observe that we are here passing to another thought. This is sometimes done by numbering the divisions and subdivisions and then introducing each by a mention of the number, which, besides the formal statement, can be made in a variety of informal ways. And without numbering or without stating the numbers, we may use any of those numerous expressions which indicate progress from point to point. Among the most common are: again, in addition, besides, furthermore, still further, moreover, another point, in the next place, and not only this but, on the other hand, once more, finally, etc. But let not the inexperienced preacher imagine that there are any set phrases which propriety requires him to adopt. Let him notice what relation exists between the foregoing and following thoughts and indicate the transition by any appropriate and simple expression, without hunting after novelty, and without neglecting variety.

If the sermon is unusually long, the transition to one of its later divisions may in some simple and quiet way acknowledge the fact, perhaps slightly apologize for it; if any particular portion, from its difficulty or its importance, requires special attention, this also may be indicated in the transition; and in rare cases a word may be thrown in to arouse flagging attention. The propriety of all such passing remarks, humorous and otherwise, and the method of making them must be determined by good sense and good taste. If not well managed, they are much worse than nothing.

As to this whole matter of the plan of discourse, we may rejoice that in the present age, and especially in our country, there is no established and dominant custom but a good degree of freedom. The

---

[19] The late Richard Fuller.

preacher, particularly in his youth, had better not make haste to conclude that he is superior to general experience but should study and practice different methods, following mainly those which he finds best suited to his powers but frequently exercising himself in others; thus he will let no one method become a necessity to him, but will broaden and vary his cultivation and adapt himself to differences of taste among his hearers. On the other hand, he need not be always following the fashions of his time but, taking due account of the nature and design of pulpit discourse, should give free scope to his individuality and sometimes strike out methods of his own, observing how they affect him and his hearers. He should be neither solicitous to appear independent and original nor afraid to try experiments, under the control of good taste and devout feeling.

CHAPTER IV

THE CONCLUSION

PREACHERS seldom neglect to prepare some introduction to a sermon but very often neglect the conclusion; and yet the latter is even more important than the former. John Bright, who was one of the foremost political orators of the present age, stated that however little preparation he may have made for the rest of a speech, he always carefully prepared the conclusion. Lord Brougham said that the conclusion to his celebrated speech before the House of Lords in defense of Queen Caroline was composed twenty times over, at least. The peroration of Burke's first speech at the trial of Warren Hastings was worked over sixteen times.[1] The great orators of Greece and Rome paid much attention to their perorations, seeming to feel that this was the final struggle which must decide the conflict and gathering up all their powers for one supreme effort. But how often we find it otherwise, especially on the part of preachers who extemporize. The beginning and earlier progress of the sermon show good preparation and do well. But towards the close the preacher no longer knows the way; here he wanders with a bewildered look, there he struggles and flounders. Another, feeling excited at the close, launches into general exhortation and, proceeding till body and mind are exhausted, ends with what is scattering, feeble, flat. The conclusion ought to have moved like a river, growing in volume and power, but, instead of that, the discourse loses itself in some great marsh or ends like the emptying of a pitcher with a few poor drops and dregs.

I. THE BASIC RULE: CAREFUL PREPARATION

A group of travelers in China went one day in rickshaws to see a famous pagoda that was located several miles from the railway station. Unused to being hauled about by men instead of motors, they watched the coolies, as they traveled along, with an uncertain feeling that soon crystallized into pity. For with the miles the pace lagged and shoulders drooped. Finally, returning, they came again in

[1] See Macaulay's Essay on Warren Hastings.

sight of the railway station. Suddenly, to the surprise of every rider the coolies straightened their shoulders, lifted their heads and trotted briskly to the journey's end. Why? Because they wanted, by ending well, to get a friendly tip and more business. To end well was their best strategy. Many preachers are careless about the way they end their sermons because they don't have a coolie's understanding of the importance of ending well. Rhetorically, psychologically, and spiritually the conclusion is, next to the introduction, the most vital part of the sermon.[2] It is not an addition to the sermon but an organic part of it, necessary to its completeness of form and effect. It gathers up the various ideas and impressions of the message for one final impact upon the minds and hearts of the hearers. "The conclusion gives the supreme opportunity to the orator. The rhetorical conclusion makes possible the oratorical drive."[3] In most cases it is the place of the sermon's climax—or anticlimax.

Let us lay down the rule, then, that the conclusion, or at least some conclusion, should be carefully prepared. We shall often find occasion to modify it in delivery, according to the state of feeling which has then been reached by ourselves and the hearers. But one can usually determine, when preparing, precisely the thoughts with which the sermon ought to conclude, though he may leave the mode of stating them to be controlled by the feelings of the moment. He ought in every case to have ready, and well prepared, something that will make an appropriate and effective conclusion. Where the subject will naturally lead to passionate exhortation, we can almost always foresee a certain range within which such exhortation must be restricted, if it is to be kept in relation to the subject, and can commonly fix some point beyond, towards which this emotional expatiation shall tend, and where we may close with some comprehensive statement or final appeal. The difficulty encountered as to the conclusion is only a higher degree of that which everywhere presents itself in the best forms of speaking and which we must learn to overcome; namely, how shall we combine the most thorough possible preparation with the largest liberty in delivery?

As to the time of preparation, the general character of the conclusion ought to be determined before the detailed composition (whether written or unwritten) of the discourse is begun. Then the development of the details may be suitably limited and directed by

[2] Blackwood, *The Fine Art of Preaching*, p. 125.
[3] Ozora Davis, *Principles of Preaching*, p. 217.

the use which it is proposed to make of the whole in concluding. If the other materials have been provided and arranged and no conclusion has yet suggested itself—a thing which will not often happen— we may look again over the train of thought drawn out, asking ourselves distinctly the question what will be the most suitable conclusion to all this. Or perhaps a renewed examination of the text or of its connection or of parallel passages will furnish something suitable. The problem is not to find some conclusion, but that one which will be most appropriate and effective. It is plain that the conclusion cannot be composed in detail till we reach it in composing the discourse. In fact, some better conclusion than was originally contemplated may have presented itself in the course of composition, which it is proper to substitute. And the same thing may happen in the course of delivery. The great requisite is that the body of the discourse and the conclusion shall each be adapted to the other; and this may be accomplished by fixing the general contents and design of the conclusion when laying out the plan of the discourse, and then allowing the style and tone of the conclusion to be modified, or its very character changed, in any way that may have been suggested in the progress of composition or of delivery. This relation of the conclusion to the whole sermon is well expressed by Dr. Oman.

As the introduction should be like the porch, first in execution and last in conception, the conclusion should be like the spire, last in execution but first in conception. As you have to prepare for the spire by laying foundation strong enough to bear it, and erect thereon pillars, buttressed by the whole building, able to support it, so every word you say should not only be leading up to the conclusion, but have throughout power to sustain it. Though preaching is more than mere pleading, there is a sense in which, like a barrister addressing a jury, you should be out, from the beginning to end, for a verdict. And the conclusion should only be, like his most impressive, most telling appeal, to clench all that has been already said.

2. GUIDING PRINCIPLES

In reference to the sermon, the purpose of the conclusion is to bring the discussion to a fitting end. Like love among the virtues, it is to complete and fasten all together. In reference to the hearers, its function is to relate the truth helpfully and abidingly to life as they face it. In reference to the preacher, the conclusion is a taking leave, in which he commits vital and eternal issues to the decision of those who have heard him through. It is his "finally," throwing the responsibility of action squarely upon them. And he can be at peace only as he has said his best word. Consulting the requirements of these three points of reference we arrive at the following principles:

(1) The conclusion should be a natural and appropriate termination of the discussion. It should seem to the congregation to be the inevitable thing to be said, a logical end of all the arguments, a worthy proposal in the light of all the facts. The most effective conclusion rests wholly upon the cumulative force of the discussion without the introduction of new or extraneous material. Any deviation from this rule is apt to divert the audience at the moment when concentration is desired, and so to lose the full impact of the line of thought pursued in the discussion. The true connectives between discussion and conclusion bear the meaning of such words as "therefore," "so," "consequently," "surely then,"—words that may not be spoken but are nevertheless felt by those who hear.

(2) The conclusion should be unmistakably personal in its aim. Preaching is personal encounter. It is through man to men. Sometimes in the midst of the sermon the preacher, becoming conscious of his oratory, gets "off the beam" and soars around impersonally to the delight of himself and his audience, making little progress toward his destination. But, whatever he may do elsewhere, in the conclusion the preacher must be very conscious of his hearers and must speak very directly to them. He is a messenger and advocate of God, beseeching, exhorting, persuading, counseling, guiding, challenging. His conscious aim is not oratorical but personal and spiritual. "I remind you," "I beseech you," "I plead with you," "I challenge you" are the words of his heart. The second personal pronoun will be in his mind and often upon his lips. Dr. Herbert H. Farmer[4] in his discussion of the sermon as personal encounter says:

If there is no point where you can say 'you,' then it is strongly suspected that your discourse is not a sermon but an essay or a lecture. It is at the points of focus, where you seek to draw your message together and drive it home in challenge or appeal or succor, that the pronoun 'you' is indispensable.

(3) The conclusion should be alive and energetic. "It is not enough just to stop, . . . words of wisdom are to be as nails fastened in a sure place and your last word should be the right word to fasten

4 *The Servant of the Word*, p. 64.

them."[5] Weakness in manner, thought, or words draws the nails instead of driving them deeper. Deep passion, thoughts that burn, strong words are the instruments required, whether the conclusion be a direct drive on the will[6] or an appeal to the heart. Crooning at the last is altogether out of place. Strength, of course, does not mean bombast or uncontrolled emotion but life and energy, by which deep passion may express itself in throbbing compassion as well as in compelling challenge, and thoughts may burn with tenderness as well as fury, and words may have the power of gravitation as well as the shock of an earthquake. It is a fault of some energetic speakers that they exhaust themselves before they reach the conclusion and come up panting and hoarse and with no banner but a moist handkerchief. Some end weakly through lack of forethought or lack of courage; and still others, because in the sermon they have laid no strong foundations. If the preacher has any regard for the vital effect of his sermon he ought to conclude strongly. No better examples of what this means can be found than in the conclusion of Joshua's address to his people (Josh. 24:14-16) and the closing paragraph of the Sermon on the Mount (Matt. 7:24-26).

(4) The conclusion should be definite and clear in thought and expression. Precision is a proper standard for the preacher at every point in the sermon. It cannot be abandoned in the conclusion. If there is any place for clear statement and definite counsel along carefully chosen lines, it is there. It is easy for the extemporaneous preacher who does not write his sermons, after he has fixed upon his main ideas or divisions, to leave the conclusion to the inspiration of the moment. That bespeaks indefiniteness concerning the objective of his message and is an unnecessary hazard. Without accurate cutting beforehand (i.e., precision) the conclusion may become a confusion of generalities. Unexpected circumstances may blunt for the moment the keen edge of thought and make one's vocabulary a printer's pie. In the emotion of the moment words that wound may appear where words of healing ought to be, and soft words where there ought to be manly challenge. If one has self-mastery and keen sensitivity, and can think accurately on his feet, and has a large and intelligible vocabulary at tongue's end, one has less to fear. But no preacher should gamble with "the moment." To go into the pulpit knowing precisely to what ends he seeks to guide his people and having con-

---

[5] Oman, *Concerning the Ministry*, p. 158
[6] See Davis, *op. cit.*, p. 219.

ceived those ends in terms that they will understand gives to the preacher, all the way through, an invigorating confidence and liberty. It is there, not in haphazard, that one finds unction.

3. METHODS OF CONCLUSION

One element in the conclusion of a sermon will often be recapitulation. If the discourse has consisted chiefly of careful explanation or argument, and if it is important that its several divisions should be remembered, and doubtful whether they will be, then the divisions and occasionally even certain subdivisions may be distinctly restated. But this must be so managed, to use a phrase of Cicero, "that the recollection may be revived, not the speech repeated." Labored recapitulation is as unnecessary as it is tedious. Though perhaps anxious at the moment to enlarge anew upon some favorite point, we must confine recapitulation to its proper office. In most sermons, however, we do not care to reproduce the several thoughts and fix them separately in the hearer's mind, but rather to gather them all together and concentrate their force upon one final effort of conviction or persuasion. In such cases it is not well to make any formal recapitulation, but in a freer way to recall the train of thought or the principal points of it, sometimes using very different forms of statement. This appears to be what Vinet would call *résumé*, as distinct from recapitulation.[7] For properly oratorical purposes, it is commonly much to be preferred. The recapitulation or the *résumé*, especially the latter, may sometimes form the entire conclusion; but in most cases it only draws the whole message together in one focal point of light whose glow and heat will support the preacher's final word. It is often better, particularly where the discourse includes many points, to give some recapitulation before reaching the conclusion, usually when passing to the last division.

The conclusion will, for the most part, consist of application, i.e., pointing out the bearing of the truth preached on the lives of the hearers in some particular manner or at some particular point. Application usually includes also practical counsel in reference to some opportunity, duty, or challenge that emerges from the truth of the sermon.

It is often made elsewhere than in the conclusion, sometimes, indeed, forming a large portion of the sermon, enlarged at some point

[7] Vinet, *Hom.*, p. 323.

or distributed throughout. Yet, it is evident that the application concentrates itself, so to speak, in the conclusion. This concluding application requires, even more than the other parts of the discourse, that the preacher should have strong faith, warm religious experience, intense earnestness.

Often the claim of the sermon will be articulated in a direct appeal. Prophetic and apostolic preaching abounded in it. And it is no good sign that many preachers have lost the shameless urgency of importuning men on behalf of God. Appeal is necessary, particularly in evangelical preaching. In many American churches the appeal is made in the form of an invitation to men to confess Christ publicly or to repent of unfaithfulness and pledge themselves to faithful living. Too often this method, one fears, becomes a custom without a sense of timeliness and without any inspiring emotion.

It is quite wrong to suppose, as some preachers appear to do, that every sermon must end with a very pathetic or overwhelming appeal. It is not infrequently best to end quietly, yet still so as to impress. And whatever the subject might require, let a man not speak in an emotional manner unless he really feels it. An effort to work oneself up into feeling because it is desirable at this point will usually fail; and if it succeeds as to the preacher himself, it will be apt to make anything else than a good impression on the hearers. If an impassioned conclusion was prepared and the speaker now finds that his own feelings and those of the audience have slowly subsided till there is no good prospect of exciting them, let him omit the prepared conclusion or modify its tone so as to attempt nothing but what can be achieved. Few things are so painful or so injurious as the reaction produced by passionate words which are not felt by the hearers or even by the speaker. "Do not preach the corpse of an appeal."[8] And let it never be forgotten that we must not aim to excite emotion merely for its own sake, as if that were the end in view, but to make it a means of determining the will and stimulating to corresponding action. Even love to God will not subsist as a mere feeling.

Again the conclusion may center in pastoral exhortation, encouragement, or warning. A concluding exhortation ought, as a rule, to be specific, keeping itself in relation to the subject which has been treated. There is great danger that a fluent and fervid speaker will wander into mere general appeals, equally appropriate to almost any other subject or occasion. This may be sometimes allowable, but a more specific exhortation would almost always be more effective. When the sermon has been one of solemn warning, it is sometimes well in concluding to speak words of comfort and encouragement in view of the divine promises; or when the discourse has dealt mostly with earnest invitation, it might be best for the conclusion to speak frankly of the difficulties of discipleship to Christ, so as to discourage a hasty profession. The preacher must judge in every case, whether this combination will deepen the general impression, or whether the two will neutralize each other in the hearer's mind, and leave him unaffected by either. It may be added that warnings, and all that is alarming in gospel truth, should be uttered not as if we delighted in denunciation, but with especial tenderness, showing that we speak in the faithfulness of love.

The final words of the conclusion may sometimes consist of a comprehensive and impressive restatement of the subject which has been discussed.

It is very effective when, in our final appeal, we can strongly and vividly reproduce the leading idea of the whole discourse. It has a very great effect upon our hearers, after so many solid proofs and so many skillful strokes of oratory have been devoted to it, to see the great leading truth, the parent idea, appear once more at this crowning moment in all the force of its beautiful simplicity, in all the strength of its unity.[9]

Or the text itself may be the last words. When the discourse has been developed out of the text and has exhibited all its wealth of meaning, then the emphatic repetition of the text in closing will impressively sum up all that has been said. Or we may end with another passage of Scripture, or with part of a hymn, or a poem.[10] There seems to be an increasing tendency in America to close sermons either with a story or a poem. Neither should become a habit. And the requirements for their effective use are great. One must have good taste for choosing, skill in the telling, and a pure heart to keep his motive high and centering outside his own vanity. Story or poem ought to hit squarely the thought that should be uppermost, without the necessity of a build-up. And it ought to be brief and clear. Again, to close with an invocation of the divine blessing is sometimes natural and impressive but should never become a regular form. Very often,

[9] Potter, p. 228.
[10] Ozora Davis suggests that a poem should not be used more frequently than once in six or seven times (*Principles of Preaching*, p. 220).

however, the general contents or design of the conclusion will require that we close with some particular thought. The last sentence,
of whatever it may consist, ought to be appropriate and impressive,
but its style ought not to be elaborate and ambitious. In most cases it
ought to be the preacher's own. It is a very solemn moment. Do not
be thinking of your reputation but of your responsibility and of your
hearers' salvation.

4. RELEVANT QUESTIONS

Attention must be given briefly to three questions: (1) How long
should the conclusion be? (2) Should it be announced? (3) And
should it always register a positive note? The length of the conclusion,
like that of the introduction, is dependent on circumstances, and no
rule can be laid down.

(1) Because of the limited time allotted to the sermon in the modern service of worship, the tendency is toward brevity in conclusion,
so much so that one recent writer[11] issues a warning. He says:

> Most conclusions are too brief. To impress people properly with any
> idea, it is not enough to state it clearly or beautifully; one must repeat it
> often enough and long enough to let it sink into their minds. Twenty-nine
> minutes of sermon and one minute of conclusion is not a good proportion
> —not if it has been a real sermon from which a real conclusion can be
> drawn.

But there is great danger of making it too long, especially in
hortatory appeals and in sermons which have not been thoroughly
prepared. The feeling of the speaker inclines him to continue, but
the feelings of the hearers cannot be long kept up to a high point.
If the sermon has been long, the conclusion should certainly be brief,
save in very peculiar cases. Sometimes the close of the last division
really brings the whole train of thought to an end and gives it a
practical turn; any extended conclusion is then unnecessary and commonly undesirable. Sometimes an abrupt conclusion is very effective,
when well managed, with good taste and unaffected solemnity. Sometimes the preacher will be overcome by emotion, and then tearful
silence will be more powerful than speech.

Excessive length is a common fault of the conclusion of extemporaneous
preachers and writers; in fact, of all who do not govern themselves both

[11] C. S. Patton, *Preparation and Delivery of Sermons*, p. 54.

in the preparation and delivery of sermons by well-defined plans. New thoughts occur to them, and they are hitched on to what has gone before. What is worse, sometimes the preacher becomes conscious that he has failed to accomplish the object of his discourse, or to awaken the degree of interest he ought to have excited, and he struggles on in the vain endeavor to compensate the fault, until at last he is forced to terminate further from his object than when his conclusion began.[12]

(2) It is generally better to use some other connective than "Now, in conclusion" to mark the transition from the discussion. Phillips Brooks began the conclusion of a sermon by saying, "Thus, then, I have passed through the ground which I proposed. See where our thoughts have led us." Other examples are: "We are not proposing, then, this Christmas Sunday morning, an easy thing—to let him in, to make room for him—but we are proposing a glorious thing";[13] "But what of this sense of guilt, this inward sense of shame that comes down on the soul like a great shadow? Can that ever be lifted? Ought we to want to have it lifted?";[14] "Now, all this gives me what I am always so glad to find, a new fresh way of conceiving our function as believers in our own particular age."[15] The stereotyped "In conclusion" is often spoken for no reason at all, which is an excellent reason for not saying it. Any announcement of a conclusion inevitably calls attention to time and to the stage of the sermon at which the preacher has arrived. Whether anything is gained by that the preacher must judge. As with illustrations, it is usually best to proceed with the conclusion without calling attention to the fact. Pause and vocal inflexion, a single transitional word or sentence will be enough. Certainly the conclusion ought not to be announced if, already, the last point of discussion has been announced with a "Finally." Most of all it is unwise to give indication that one is about to conclude and then start again or keep dragging on.

(3) In most instances the conclusion should be positive rather than negative. What Patton says is generally true:

Negative statements belong in the early part of the sermon. These may often be very important. We teach by contrast. It is frequently necessary to clear the ground before one can put up his own structure; but one

[12] Kidder, *Homiletics*, pp. 229, 230.
[13] H. E. Fosdick, *The Power to See It Through*, p. 247.
[14] James Reid, *Facing Life with Christ*, p. 57.
[15] John A. Hutton, *The Victory over Victory*, p. 121. In his conclusions Dr. Hutton often speaks in terms of what the truth of the sermon means to him.

should not still be clearing ground in his concluding sentences or bring in at that place things which he wants to warn his hearers away from.[16]

But there are times when one must leave off with a warning, to carry his people with him in a great condemnation of their own sin. Recall the conclusion of the Sermon on the Mount and Chalmers' sermon of Unconscious Influence whose final sentence is "I only warn you here of the guilt which our Lord Jesus Christ will impute to them that hinder his gospel." In every such case, however, the preacher must make sure his love and solicitude are not concealed.

[16] *Preparation and Delivery of Sermons,* p. 64.

CHAPTER V

CLASSIFICATION OF SERMON FORMS

CLASSIFICATION of sermon subjects as doctrinal, moral, historical and experimental has already been considered. Another basis of classification has regard to form or, as it is commonly called, "homiletical structure." On this principle sermons may be designated as subject-sermons, text-sermons, and expository sermons. Phelps adds also inferential sermons. These are the standard artistic patterns, and like all such they are flexible in the hands of masters. Examination of the sermons of great preachers is almost always disappointing to the student seeking perfect examples of any one of them. They are always secondary to purpose and utility. They are tools, and in the shaping of tools and the techniques for handling tools experimentation and invention are desirable. But these require intelligence and faithfulness to underlying principles. The streamline automobile preserves the essential elements of an oxcart. The student of preaching must not despise but rather master the sermon patterns, following them closely in the days of his apprenticeship. Accordingly, this final chapter in connection with the formal elements of the sermon is a presentation of the peculiarities of the several patterns with practical suggestions as to their management.

The distinction between subject-sermons and text-sermons has to do simply with the plan of the discourse, especially with the source of its divisions. It is only in this respect that they constitute different species, and yet the difference is one of considerable practical importance. The phrases in question—for which some substitute topical and textual sermons, or topical and textual division of sermons—have not been generally employed with great precision or uniformity. A very obvious application of them, and one which can be consistently carried through, would be as follows: Subject-sermons are those in which the divisions are derived from the subject, independently of the text, while in text-sermons the divisions are taken from the text. In the latter case as well as in the former, there may be a definite subject, distinctly and even formally stated; but this subject is not divided according to its own nature, but only such divisions are made as are presented by the text. Sometimes the two plans may coincide. Beginning with a subject, one may find so appropriate a text that the logical divisions of the subject will all be contained in the text; or, beginning with a text, he may state its subject in so felicitous a form of proposition that the several divisions presented in the text will also constitute a complete logical division of the proposition. But they will not often thus coincide, and the fact that they sometimes do will not make them less distinct in principle.

I. SUBJECT-SERMONS

In subject-sermons, then, we have to do with a subject. If it is drawn from a text, then the text, having furnished the thought, has no further part as a formative force in the plan of treatment pursued in the sermon, but the subject is divided and treated according to its own nature, just as it would be if not derived from a text.

This form of treatment has important advantages. It better insures unity, which is indispensable to the best effects of discourse. It trains the preacher's mind to logical analysis, and few kinds of power are so valuable to him. It is more convincing and pleasing to a certain order of minds in the audience, especially among cultivated people, such a treatment having a more logical character and also a more manifest completeness. Besides, there will often be practical occasion for thus thoroughly discussing a subject. The needs of the congregation will make the preacher wish to present a full view of some doctrine or some topic of general or particular morality, and not merely the special aspects of it which one text or another may exhibit. The Scriptures do not present truth in a succession of logical propositions, any more than the objects of nature are found grouped according to scientific classification. This suits the design of the Bible as a book to be read and also leads to a rich variety in textual preaching. But it is frequently instructive and satisfactory to discuss some collective subject.

It is usually better that the subject should be not general but specific. This, as was seen in the discussion of doctrinal subjects, not only promotes variety in successive sermons but really makes each subject more fruitful. And if in addition to being a theme specific in its logical character, it be the specific theme of the text from which it is drawn, this removes, in part, one of the objections to subject-sermons, namely, that in them the text does not perform so important a part as it ought to in preaching. Too often the text is only a starting point, with which the sermon afterwards maintains not only no formal but no vital connection. Sometimes, indeed, it is made simply a motto, a practice of extremely doubtful propriety. Of course, a text which presents a specific aspect of some subject may be lawfully used as suggesting the general subject, or we may draw from a comprehensive text its general subject and then avowedly confine ourselves to one department of it. But, as a rule, it is greatly better that the subject should be precisely that which the text most naturally presents and which most thoroughly exhausts its meaning. A good example of such specific subjects is found in Robert Hall's three sermons: Reasons for a Judgment to Come, Character of the Judgment to Come, Remembrance in Youth of Judgment to Come.[1] And a text is in each case taken which is supposed to present the specific topic. The first is Acts 24:25, "As Paul reasoned of righteousness, temperance, and judgment to come," though this is probably an unwarranted interpretation, as the word properly signifies "discoursed"; the second is Heb. 6:2, "Eternal judgment"; and the third, Eccles. 11:9, "Rejoice, O young man, in thy youth . . . but know thou that for all these things God will bring thee into judgment." Mr. Hall's biographer states that he was fond of thus confining himself to one aspect of a subject. In like manner, South has a number of distinct sermons on Deliverance from Temptation.

The subject will be divided according to its own nature and to our practical design in treating it. This design will usually lead us either to explanation (whether by analysis or by comparison), to proof, or to application of the subject and in many cases will require some combination of these. The practically different methods of dividing are extremely numerous and various, and here the analytical and imaginative powers of the preacher may be freely exercised.

Although the philosopher's categories of thought are too formal to be followed strictly in preaching, one who is familiar with them will find them helpful. In fact, as Garvie points out,[2] we are constantly using them, though unconsciously. For instance, when we discuss a subject under its various aspects, we are using the category of substance and attribute, as also when we discuss the essential and accidental or nonessential qualities of, say, conversion or some other Christian experience. Again, we proceed in terms of genus and

---

[1] *Works*, Vol. IV. p. 304.
[2] *The Christian Preacher*, p. 433.

species when we show how parent virtues like love and justice express themselves in such other virtues as kindness and veracity. What the preacher needs is to know various ways of approaching and treating subjects, what questions may be asked in order to get at their reality, character, values, relations, meanings, uses, etc., whether he consults the categories or learns, as he finally must, by the empirical route of his own practice and careful study of the sermons of others. Some men's preaching becomes stale and monotonous because they ask one question and travel one road. It may be the question of truth and the road of argument, or the question of understanding and the road of explanation, or the question of utility and the road of application. There are many roads and many questions. Dr. Garvie is helpful here:

An abstract idea may be illustrated by concrete instances, scriptural, historical, biographical, literary. A personality may be sketched as regards heredity, environment, development, capacity, character, career, reputation. An event may be examined as regards time, place, antecedents, consequents, human conduct, or divine Providence. A nation's history falls into periods separated by crises. The moral quality of an action may be judged as regards motive, method, manner, intention, result; its religious significance may be determined in its conditions and issues as regards the relation of God and man. A vice, virtue, or grace may be analyzed psychologically as regards thought, feeling, will. A statement may be broken up into its parts; e.g., Evil company doth corrupt good manners (I Cor. 15:33). (1) What is evil company? (2) Wherein do good manners consist? (3) How does the first corrupt the second? The enquiry might be extended thus. (4) Why does it corrupt? The expansiveness and pervasiveness of personal influence would be the answer. (5) How is this corruption to be prevented? A subject can be dealt with in its various relations, as love in relation to God, self, neighbor. The various reasons for a thesis may be stated in order, as for the statement that Christ is divine: (1) his sinlessness and perfect moral character, (2) his unique and absolute consciousness of divine sonship, (3) the constancy and efficacy of his mediatorial function.[3]

Subject preaching is the orator's method par excellence. It lends itself to finished discourse. But it has its dangers. The preacher easily becomes interested in finding subjects that are interesting and readily yield a good oration rather than such as have a sure Christian and scriptural basis or such as come close home to the needs of his people. He is tempted to think more of his ideas and his sermons than of "rightly dividing the word of truth" and leading men into the

[3] *Ibid.*

Kingdom of God. He is in danger also of preaching in too narrow a field of truth and human need, since of necessity he will be drawn to those subjects that interest him personally or with which he is already familiar. Unless, therefore, he is constantly widening his horizon by diligent study, he will soon exhaust his resources. Accordingly, at the very beginning, the student should be warned against too exclusive use of this type of sermon.

2. TEXT-SERMONS

These ought to be governed by the same general principles as subject-sermons. They must always have a plan, and commonly divisions; and the principles laid down as to divisions in the foregoing chapter apply, in general, to text-sermons as well as others. Text-sermons include two distinct varieties, those which present a single subject and those which discuss several subjects.

(1) A single subject is drawn from the text and stated, whether formally or informally, and then is discussed under such divisions as the text furnishes. We have seen that this may sometimes coincide with a complete logical division of the subject itself, but in those rare cases it would still be called a text-sermon, if the divisions were actually derived from a contemplation of the text. In general, such plans are quite different from those which a logical analysis of the subject would suggest. Text-sermons of this sort are by some writers confounded with subject-sermons, because in both cases there is a definite subject. Others call them "textual-topical."

The divisions thus drawn from the text, while not commonly forming a complete analysis of the subject in itself considered, must yet be so related to the subject and to each other that they together form a structure, a symmetrical whole. Otherwise, the discourse is felt to be incomplete and fragmentary.

A well-constructed text-sermon of this kind has most of the advantages possessed by subject-sermons and the great additional advantage that it is much more intimately in contact with the text, drawing from it not only the subject treated but all the leading thoughts of the treatment. This method, accordingly, is very largely adopted. It gives ample opportunity for variety, freshness, originality.

A tact is needed in the preacher to discover the hidden skeleton. This tact will be acquired gradually and surely, by everyone who carefully cultivates himself in all homiletic respects. Like all nice discernment, it comes imperceptibly in the course of training and discipline, and therefore no single and particular rule for its acquisition can be laid down. It must be acquired, however, or the fundamental talent for textual sermonizing will be wanting. Moreover, this tact should be judicious. It is possible to find more meaning in a text than it really contains. . . . This talent for detecting the significance of Scripture must be confined to the gist of it—to the evident and complete substance of it.[4]

The German preachers, who have to preach many times in successive years upon the same passage, often show great ingenuity in striking out new plans for the same text,—plans which shall make a complete section of the whole passage but in a new direction.

Take, for example, the history of Peter's denial. I can set out either from the fact of the denial itself, considering it as to its causes, its consequences, etc.; or from the danger into which one gets who warms himself with the world; or from the thought that in this world everything helps when a disciple is to be brought to fall; or from the repentance of Peter, which presupposes as well love as weakness of love; or I can set forth the power of the love of Jesus in his look at Peter, (a) how it humbles him, better than law and penalty could do, (b) how it makes a new man of him. In all five sermons the whole of the text would have place, but every time in a different light.[5]

One of our Lord's miracles of healing may be considered either from the point of view of the divine grace glorifying itself in this history, in which case Christ's mode of action is made to illustrate that of God (for example, he delays, indeed, with his help, but at last he does help); or the history may be chiefly considered from the ethical standpoint, and then Christ is the example according to which we are to act in similar cases; or, finally, we consider the conduct of the persons themselves on whom the healing is performed, who are set before us as an example of faith (for example, the centurion of Capernaum).[6]

Among English preachers, Melvill is famous for the ingenuity with which he develops a rich meaning from passages which to most persons would suggest nothing.

Here, as in the case of subject-sermons, we hear sometimes merely a series of observations or remarks upon the subject, which could

---

[4] Shedd, p. 152.
[5] Palmer, *Hom.*, s. 378.
[6] Hagenbach, p. 120. Compare the plans of Krummacher, in his "David," and the sermons on the Temptation of Christ by Krummacher and by Monod, in Fish's *Select Discourses from the French and German.*

hardly be called divisions of it. The following example is from Bed-dome: Acts 9:4, "Saul, Saul, why persecutest thou me?" (1) It is the general character of unconverted men to be of a persecuting spirit. (2) Christ has his eye upon persecutors. (3) The injury done to Christ's people, Christ considers as done to himself. (4) The calls of Christ are particular.[7] The fourth might be omitted. Such remarks suggested by the text would seem a more satisfactory treatment than topical remarks, but one should not very often allow himself to construct sermons in so loose a fashion.

The preacher must exercise his judgment with reference to every particular discourse, as to whether it is better to make a textual division of the subject or to treat the subject independently, according to its own nature.[8]

(2) In other text-sermons, there is not one definite and comprehensive subject, but several topics presented by the text are successively treated. These, though they do not admit of being combined into one, ought to have such a mutual relation as to give the discourse unity. The same sentence of Scripture might suggest several entirely distinct topics, and a sermon upon these would be really several sermons in succession. A discourse that has not unity both offends taste and lacks power—in fact, is not a discourse at all. The unity, however, may be that of subject or of person or of place, provided in the latter cases there be also some internal connection so that all may blend in the general effect of the discourse. Thus topics apparently so diverse as suicide, ingratitude, avarice, and remorse might all be treated in a sermon upon Judas, because they not only pertain to the one person but were in his case intimately connected, as will be apparent from stating them in a different order, avarice, ingratitude, remorse, suicide. After pointing out that in him they were thus connected, one might even treat of them in some other order if oratorically more convenient, and the topics, though separate, would at least seem tied together into a kind of unity. Such an example shows that it is allowable to go quite far in this direction; but, as a rule, we ought to have as close an internal relation among the topics of the discourse as possible. It is the great fault of this variety of text-sermons that they are apt to be desultory and rambling, to resemble the scattering fire

[7] Quoted by Shedd, p. 150.
[8] Some preachers, for example, South, are very fond of sermons which draw some divisions directly from the text, but others from the nature of the subject. This might seem an incongruous mixture, but is often well managed and effective.

of irregular soldiers rather than the systematic and concentrated dis-
charge of a disciplined body. We avoid this fault by refusing to include
in the sermon any topic suggested by the text which will not take its
place in a connected series, though the topic in itself might be interesting and instructive.

In both these varieties, especially in the second, the divisions may
sometimes be stated in the very words of the text. Thus the young
convert is commended to God (Jude 24), (1) that is able to keep
you from falling, (2) and to present you, (a) faultless, (b) before
the presence of his glory, (c) with exceeding joy. In Gal. 5:6, what
it is that in Christ Jesus avails is (1) neither circumcision nor uncir-
cumcision, (2) but (a) faith, (b) which worketh, (c) by love. The
order of the clauses may be varied if deemed oratorically more suitable. Luke 23:43, (1) Thou shalt be in Paradise. (2) Thou shalt be
with me in Paradise. (3) Today thou shalt be with me in Paradise.
When one thus takes up the successive words or clauses of a text and
"enlarges" upon them, the process closely resembles musical variations
upon a familiar tune, possessing similar advantages and being liable
to the same faults. It is often so managed as to be wearisome, what
Schleirmacher called "spelling" the text; sometimes it is offensive, as
when a passage is so dissected as to destroy the very life of it. But
when the text is happily chosen and the treatment, while natural, is
fresh, instructive, and animated, with a manifest connection in the
topics and a sustained oratorical progress to the end, such a sermon
may be highly effective. The people love to have their minds kept
in close contact with the text if it is done in an interesting and
impressive way. Let it be said, however, that, although texts, like the
examples above, may furnish in their very words the ideas of an
outline, in the composition and delivery of the sermon the ideas
should be expanded in the preacher's own words into an intelligible
and impressive statement at every point.

Or the divisions may be stated in different terms, though following
the order of the text; or both in different terms and in a different
order if this would give a more oratorical arrangement. The statement must commonly be thus varied, in text-sermons upon a single
definite subject; and much will depend upon the skill with which
the divisions are drawn from the text and enunciated. Ezek. 11:19, 20,
"And I will give them one heart," etc. Genuine religion, developed
in four particulars: (1) its author, (2) the disposition it produces,

(3) the obedience it demands, (4) the blessedness it insures.[9] Ps. 73:24,26, God is the pious man's all in all, (1) his guide through life, (2) his support in death, (3) his portion forever. Sometimes very little departure from the words of the text is necessary. Rom. 5:1, 2, the believer's happy state: (1) he may have peace with God, (2) he may stand (i.e., stand fast) in the grace of God, (3) he may exult in hope of the glory of God.

It often happens that the thoughts of a text can be very thoroughly and neatly drawn out by a series of questions, the answers to these forming the divisions of the sermon. Examples of this are familiar.

In treating the details of a text-sermon, it is not necessary to confine ourselves strictly to views presented by the text. Any one of the topics may be developed and applied according to its own nature or according to the specific design of the sermon. Yet, it is always pleasing, when effected without artificiality, to see all the lines of development kept within the limits of the text.

3. EXPOSITORY SERMONS

The name of this species of sermons is derived from a peculiarity in their materials, namely, the fact that they are mainly occupied with exposition. But their homiletical peculiarities belong to the matter of construction, to that oratorical arrangement and adaptation which should distinguish an expository sermon from a commentary or an exegetical essay. The present, therefore, seems to be the appropriate place for discussing this important variety of sermons.

Almost every preacher one meets, if asked whether he often makes expository discourses, will answer, "No, I have long believed there ought to be more preaching of that kind; but the attempts I formerly made in that direction were quite unsuccessful, and it seems I have no talent for it." But comparatively few have ever fairly tried to develop such a talent. Men labor for years to acquire the power of producing a good topical sermon. All the rhetorical training and all their practice are directed to that end. Then they try the experiment of expository preaching, which requires a different kind of practice and perhaps even a different method of studying the Scriptures, and wonder that their first attempts prove a comparative failure. This is as unreasonable as the course of those who, after training themselves

---

[9] Jay, quoted by Kidder, p. 206. Jay is particularly fond of this species of sermons and often felicitous in his plans.

to read sermons, make a timid and ill-prepared effort to preach without writing and infer from the almost inevitable failure that they have
no talent for extemporizing.

(1) It is not thought necessary to discuss at any length the advantages and disadvantages of expository preaching. The former are to
some extent obvious and generally recognized, and they have been
admirably presented by Alexander, in his *Thoughts on Preaching*.[10]
As stated by him, they are as follows: (*a*) This method better corresponds with the very idea and design of preaching. (*b*) It is the primitive and ancient method. (*c*) It insures a better knowledge of the
Scriptures on the part of preacher and hearers, and of the Scriptures
in their connection. (*d*) It causes sermons to contain more of pure
Scripture truths and scriptural modes of viewing things. (*e*) It gives
occasion for remarking on many passages of the Bible which otherwise might never enter into one's sermons, and for giving important
practical hints and admonitions which might seem to some hearers
offensively personal if introduced into a topical discussion, but which
are here naturally suggested by the passage in hand. (*f*) And it greatly
diminishes the temptation to misinterpret texts by excessive allegorizing, by "accommodation," etc.; for men are often driven into such
misinterpretation by the difficulty of finding for every sermon a short
passage which will legitimately afford the requisite amount of
material.[11]

(2) It might be more desirable to discuss the objections to this
method,[12] for these often appear more serious than they really are.
There is, in many quarters, a popular prejudice against expository
preaching, arising from the fact that it is so often badly managed and
from the notion that it is a labor-saving contrivance. On rainy Sundays or on week-nights the preacher who has no sermon prepared or
wishes to save his elaborate preparation for a more auspicious occasion
will frequently undertake to "read a passage of Scripture, and make a
few remarks"; he feels that this enterprise is attended by no risk,
because, as some quaint old preacher expressed it, if he is "persecuted
in one verse, he can flee to another." Hence the people rather naturally
conclude that whenever one takes a long text, it is an expedient to
dispense with labor. Besides this prejudice against the method, which

---

[10] Pp. 272-313.
[11] W. M. Taylor, *Ministry of the Word*, pp. 161-175; Hoyt, *The Preacher,* Chap. 14;
Coffin, *What to Preach*, Lecture I; Brown, *The Art of Preaching*, Chap. 2.
[12] H. E. Fosdick, article in *Harper's Magazine*, July 1928, pp. 133ff.

a judicious and laborious preacher can soon overcome, it has inherent disadvantages. Our people, it is to be regretted, seldom follow that excellent Scottish fashion of keeping a Bible in hand during the sermon; and so they find it hard to remember the general drift and connection of the long text, as they are accustomed to do with a short one. This difficulty one must bear in mind, seeking to overcome it as far as possible. Some persons, too, in our extremely restless age, object to continuous exposition on the ground that it lacks variety; they grow tired of hearing the preacher, Sunday after Sunday, announce the same book and perhaps the same chapter. Others really care so little about the Bible that they take no interest in explanations of it; they wish the preacher to make his text merely a point of departure and to give them "something fresh." Others object that the expository sermon cannot present those connected arguments in which the human mind so greatly delights; but it may trace and unfold the argument of an inspired writer, which ought to be more interesting than one constructed by the preacher himself. If it be still further objected that a discourse which is mainly or largely occupied with explanation of the text can leave but little room for application, we may answer that the impressiveness of an application depends very largely upon the interest which the hearers have been previously brought to feel in the subject applied, and that a brief and even unexpected application or appeal is often more impressive than one which gives notice, and throws men on the defensive.

Shedd takes the ground[13] that

there is somewhat less call for expository preaching than there was before the establishment of Sabbath schools and Bible classes. . . . It is the duty of the preacher, occasionally, to lay out his best strength in the production of an elaborate expository sermon, which shall not only do the ordinary work of a sermon, which shall not only instruct, awaken, and move, but which shall also serve as a sort of guide and model for the teacher of the Sabbath school and the Bible class.

But it is worthy of inquiry whether the Sunday-school teaching does not actually prepare people to receive expository preaching with higher appreciation and profit. The great difficulty in the way of making it effective is not knowledge of Scripture but ignorance of it. One sometimes fancies he could point out, after preaching to a congregation of strangers, those who are engaged in the regular study of the Bible, from the greater interest with which they listened

13 *Hom.*, p. 157.

to any explanations of Scripture that may have occurred in the sermon. Robert Hall found his regular Sunday morning expository sermon very acceptable at Cambridge; but at Leicester he lamented to a friend that the congregation, being generally less intelligent, could not be brought to like this method, and he was annoyed at having to change his habit and hunt up two separate texts for every Sunday.

(3) But the thing here specially proposed is to offer practical suggestions as to the proper management of expository preaching. It is in several respects a peculiar variety of discourse, requiring peculiar treatment; and yet the treatises of homiletics, while never failing to urge that this method has great advantages, seldom furnish the student with any directions for his guidance in attempting it. The hints which follow are derived from some experience and observation, from conversation with other ministers, and from the study of the best specimens within reach.

An expository discourse may be defined as one which is occupied mainly, or at any rate very largely, with the exposition of Scripture. It by no means excludes argument and exhortation as to the doctrines or lessons which this exposition develops. It may be devoted to a long passage, or to a very short one, even a part of a sentence. It may be one of a series, or may stand by itself. We at once perceive that there is no broad line of division between expository preaching and the common methods, but that one may pass by almost insensible gradations from textual to expository sermons.[14] We see, too, that men often preach expository sermons which they would not call by that name. Moreover, it is common to apply the term only to discourses upon the doctrinal, preceptive, and devotional portions of the Bible, and not to those which treat of the narrative portions. Now the methods of exposition appropriate to Scripture history are of course quite different from those applied to the other portions. But whenever the discourse is not merely a discussion of certain thoughts suggested by a Scripture story or scene, but in the first place, spends much time in bringing out clearly and vividly the scene or story itself, that is really historical exposition. And this is surely a highly important class of expository discourses. A very large portion of the Bible consists of narrative, and in this, as in other respects, the Bible is adapted to its purpose; for narrative possesses an unfailing interest, for old and young, cultivated and ignorant, converted and unconverted. But ser-

---

[14] Nearly all that has been said above, § 2, upon text-sermons, applies directly to expository preaching. See also §§ 1, 2, as to the plan of discourse.

mons on historical passages are very apt to err, in one of two directions. In the one case the preacher makes haste to deduce from the
narrative before him a subject or certain doctrines or lessons and
proceeds to discuss these precisely as if he had drawn them from some
verse in Romans or the Psalms; thus sinking the narrative, with all
its charm, completely out of sight. In the other case, he indulges in a
vast amount of the often ridiculous thing called "word-painting,"
overlaying the simple and beautiful Scripture story with his elaborate
descriptions and showing no desire or having no time to give us any
glimpse of the lessons which the narrative teaches. There is certainly
a middle course. Without consuming our time in exhibiting over-
wrought pictures of his own, the preacher may seek to throw light
on the Bible picture, so as to make us see it plainly and vividly, and
may either indicate the lessons as he advances from point to point
or group them in the latter part of his discourse. What we insist on is
that there ought to be such a method of preaching upon the narrative
portions of Scripture as should be distinctively appropriate to narrative, while yet it is preaching.

What, now, is the prime requisite to the effectiveness of an expository sermon? Our answer must be unity.[15] Unity in a discourse is
necessary to instruction, to conviction, and to persuasion. Without it,
the taste of enlightened hearers cannot be satisfied, and even the
uncultivated, though they may not know why, will be far less deeply
impressed. But unity in an expository discourse is by many preachers
never aimed at. They conceive of it as a mere series of disjointed
remarks upon the successive verses. It was to this kind of "homilies"
that Schleiermacher referred when he said that they are composed
of little sermons of the common form tacked together.[16] But it is
not at all necessary that an expository sermon should exhibit this fault.

The difficulty as to unity, presented by this kind of discourse, never
amounts to impossibility. We do not, at random, cut from the general
text of the sacred book the particular text of a homily. The selection is
not arbitrary. The limit of the text is predetermined by reference to unity,
which, therefore, we shall be at no loss to discover in it.[17]

In making a single, detached expository discourse, one can easily
see to it that the passage selected shall have unity. In continuous

[15] On the importance of unity, compare Phelps, *Theory of Preaching*, pp. 178, 179;
and Dabney, p. 109.
[16] Palmer, *Hom.*, s. 380.
[17] Vinet, p. 148; compare Shedd, p. 153.

exposition of the same book, it may sometimes be necessary to take a passage in which this is not the case; but even then, we may gather from it such thoughts as can be framed into one plan and pass over the remainder or notice them very briefly. Let there be unity at whatever cost. And not only this but structure. Thanks to the influence of the Schoolmen, the modern mind greatly delights in analysis and in the regular construction of the materials which analysis has furnished and hence the great preference of many for topical discourses. The homilies left us by the Fathers are frequently quite deficient in respect of orderly structure and sometimes even destitute of unity. And some persons appear to imagine that we can have no "homilies" except upon the model of the Fathers, and with a total disregard of modern taste and modes of thought. But a discourse upon an extended passage of Scripture, well chosen and well handled, may have a definite topic and a distinct and orderly plan and yet not fail to be an expository discourse, dealing largely in explanation of the text. Let us carefully observe, then, that an expository sermon may have, and must have, both unity and an orderly structure; for the frequent practical neglect of these requisites is one principal cause of those failures to which allusion was made at the outset.

When an inexperienced preacher begins to think of attempting expository preaching, his mind is very apt to turn at once toward the idea of continuous exposition. He must get up a series.[18] But why should not the preacher first discipline himself in this kind of preaching and accustom his congregation to it by the exposition every now and then, of detached passages? It will be time enough for a series when he has gained a little more practice, yea, and has made repeated and very mature study of the book to be treated. And let it be urged that first attempts shall not be made upon a Psalm, as is very generally the case; for with occasional exceptions the Psalms are comparatively lacking in manifest unity and in distinct connection and regular progress, so that it requires practice to handle them successfully. It will also sometimes be well to take an extended passage and merely make a text-sermon on a long text, gathering several thoughts from it and using them as in the ordinary text-sermon upon a short text. Or a brief text may be announced and the sermon be occupied with a discussion of the entire paragraph in which it stands. This, indeed,

---

[18] The author has recollections, more vivid than pleasing, of a first attempt, which consisted in a series upon Colossians and which was declared by a preacher's best adviser to have been on the whole a decided failure.

is often done by men who have no thought that they are preaching expository sermons. By such means the people cease to imagine that expository preaching is entirely different from other methods and become accustomed and attached to all alike. Then, whenever a series is attempted, there will be little feeling of strangeness about it and much less difficulty in sustaining the interest.

We turn now to the case of continuous exposition. Here, as has been intimated, the first thing to be done is to make a careful study beforehand of the entire book or other portion of Scripture to which the series is to be devoted. To view every book as a whole, to grasp its entire contents, and then trace in detail the progress of its narrative or argument is a method of Scripture study far too little practiced. It is one of the benefits of expository preaching that it compels the preacher to study in this way. We may say, in general, that no man will succeed in expository preaching unless he delights in exegetical study of the Bible, unless he loves to search out the exact meaning of its sentences, phrases, words. In order to do this, a knowledge of the original languages of Scripture is, of course, exceedingly desirable, but it is by no means indispensable. Andrew Fuller, who dealt largely and successfully in this method of preaching, had substantially no knowledge of Hebrew and Greek, and his writings were devoted not to commentary but to didactic and polemic theology. Yet, he loved to study the very words of Scripture. In all his works it is manifest that he did not content himself with gathering the general meaning of a passage but was exceedingly anxious to know its exact meaning. One of the most eloquent Baptist ministers of America, in the earlier part of this century, was never so happy, so charming, as in expository sermons.[19] He, too, was unacquainted with Greek and Hebrew and was not liberally supplied with commentaries; but he loved, above all things, to ponder and to talk about the meaning of God's Word. There appears to have been a change in this respect which is to be lamented. We have a great multiplication of commentaries, and an immense amount of more or less real study of the Scriptures in Sunday schools, we have many more ministers than formerly who know something of the original languages, but there is reason to fear that the close, thoughtful, lovingly patient study of the Bible is less common among the ministry now than it once was. As to conversa-

[19] [The author here alludes to his kinsman, the celebrated Andrew Broaddus, Sr., of Caroline County, Va., who, though a man of remarkable gifts and much sought after, preferred all his life a country pastorate.—D.]

tion about the meaning of this or that passage, such as once abounded when preachers were thrown together, it has gone out of fashion. A man who should raise such a question now among a group of ministers, sojourning together during the session of some association or convention, would be almost stared at. It will not do to say that we manage these questions better at home among our books. He who most zealously uses his books, at the same time thinking for himself as every man that is a man will do, finds the largest number of points arising upon which the books utterly disagree or are unsatisfactory and concerning which he would like to compare views with intelligent brethren. But not to dwell further upon this opinion, it is proper earnestly to insist that one great reason why many ministers find expository preaching difficult is that they have not been sufficiently accustomed to study the Bible. Our rapid general reading is very useful, our devotional reading of brief portions is indispensable to personal piety, but the downright study of Scripture is too often con-fined to the texts for next Sunday and their immediate context. The first thing to do, then, after determining to give a series of expository sermons upon a book or other portion of Scripture is to study it all over in advance, with some of the best explanatory commentaries, and with especial attention to the general contents and connection. To commit the book to memory would be no bad idea, but, at any rate, one should get the whole train of thought or series of facts, from beginning to end, firmly fixed in his mind.

Next, it would be well to mark out a scheme of sermons covering the whole ground. Previous experience in the exposition of detached passages will enable one to do this without any great difficulty, and, of course, there can be alterations if occasion for them should arise in the progress of the series. The great advantage of making out the scheme in advance is that we can thus distribute most judiciously the several topics of the book. In Romans, for example, various subjects are alluded to in the first three chapters, which are afterwards treated at some length. It would be awkward if one should go into any general discussion of these topics at the point of their first occurrence. They ought to be briefly considered there and reserved for more exten-sive remark where they are introduced again. It would very rarely be advisable, however, to promise at the outset a definite number of discourses. Indeed, it is not always best to announce a series at all. It may be added that one must beware of going too slowly. Let there be manifest progress, such as the restless spirit of our generation requires. But we may pause upon any specially interesting sentence or phrase, even to the extent, in some cases, of devoting a whole sermon to it. Thus there will be variety as well as progress; and hearers will be gratified to perceive that the preacher marks out passages not according to their mere external dimensions but according to the richness of their available contents.

But now the particular discourse is to be constructed. The passage before us has unity, and we note the heads which it presents, as we should do in a textual sermon. Thus we shall have a structure, a discourse, and not a scattering talk. But one of the principal difficulties in the entire task now presents itself, the proper handling of the details. If we simply take the topic and the heads which the passage affords and proceed to discuss them in our own way, that is not an expository sermon but a text-sermon. The exposition of some passages, particularly in the hands of some men, will constantly tend towards this form, and often with advantage. But what we are supposed to be aiming at is a strictly expository sermon, in which not only the leading ideas of the passage are brought out but its details are suitably explained and made to furnish the chief material of the discourse. In order to manage this, we need to study the details thoroughly, so as to master them, instead of being oppressed by them. We thus, too, enter more fully into the spirit of the passage, as the musician must who makes variations on a theme. Then we must select and group. Here the inexperienced preacher often errs. Having minutely studied the details of the passage and become interested in them, he desires to remark upon a greater number of points than the limits of his discourse will allow. Thus it becomes so crowded that the hearer follows with annoying difficulty, and none of the numerous points presented have time to impress themselves upon his mind. It is indispensable to select. Of course, one will aim to choose such details as especially require explanation and such as will at the same time yield important or interesting matter. Often points of no great intrinsic importance, slight traits in the narrative, or minor links in the argument will add greatly to the vivacity and vigor of the discourse. Everyone knows that in oratorical description we must seek the kind of excellence which is seen in certain descriptions by Demosthenes and Tacitus,—a few lines and touches, but those few eminently suggestive and stimulating to the imagination.[20] Is there not something similar in the oratorical exposition of an argument? Must we not labor,

[20] See Phelps on Picturesque Exposition, *Theory of Preaching*, pp. 165 f.

besides exhibiting the outlines, the prominent thoughts of our passage, to choose out those details which will cause the whole argument to stand forth in its completeness? Remember, we are not preparing a commentary, nor a dogmatic treatise but an expository sermon, and the whole treatment must be, in the good sense of that word, oratorical. In this respect, as in everything else pertaining to the art of discourse, practical effort, controlled by just principles, will not fail to bring skill.

A mistake sometimes made consists in the unduly multiplied and extended quotation of parallel passages. Thus the details of the text, too numerous themselves perhaps for oratorical purposes, are each surrounded by a mass of other passages, and the discourse is so loaded down as to be past endurance. It is a fault sometimes observed in other than expository sermons, though in these the temptation to it is particularly great. It is so easy for a preacher to persuade himself that he is putting honor upon Scripture by quoting thus largely, when sometimes he is only putting honor upon his own indolence. Of course, judicious quotation from other parts of Scripture is highly appropriate and often exceedingly valuable.

There is also danger of error as to the treatment of difficult passages occurring in the text. The preacher will, of course, study these with great care, for he cannot afford, as regards his personal habits, to slide over difficulties. But having thus become much interested in this difficult portion of his text, having become familiar with the different views which have been suggested and the arguments for one view and against another, he very naturally feels disposed to use the matter so laboriously wrought out, to discuss the question which appears so interesting. In this way many an expository sermon has been ruined. True, wherever the preacher is really able to clear up the difficulty and to do this by a comparatively brief and evidently satisfactory explanation, people will be glad to hear it. If he can show that the passage, as thus explained, presents some interesting and valuable truth, they will be delighted. If it is a passage which has been made prominent in religious controversies or has on any account attracted extraordinary attention, they might even like to hear something of the process by which this satisfactory explanation has been reached. But such cases are comparatively rare; and, in general, men grow weary of a long discussion of some *quaestio vexatissima* or *locus difficillimus*. If the preacher, by long study and a brief statement of the results, can throw any light on such a passage, very well; but the long study is his affair, not theirs. This is only one of many directions in which preachers are apt to err, in thinking the people will be interested by everything that interests them. And then, where the result of his researches is not satisfactory, where he does not feel that he can make the matter plain, let the preacher merely notice that there is a difficulty here and pass on to speak of truths which the passage certainly does teach, to handle what he is confident he understands.[21] It is a complaint often made against the commentaries that they say much about the easy places and little about the hard ones. Now where the book is designed not so much for explanation as for comment, in the strict sense of that term—and this is the case with most of the older works—it is obviously proper for the writer to spend his time in developing and applying the teachings of those passages which he understands. He has no right to develop and apply what he is not confident is the true meaning. Quite similar is the case of the expository preacher. To state at great length several different views as to the meaning of a passage, without being able to show cause why any one of them should be accepted or preferred, and then leave the matter in that unsatisfactory position is tiresome in a book and in a sermon intolerable.

In the progress of an expository discourse, it is often desirable to keep the connection of the whole text before the minds of the audience by somewhat frequently glancing back, as we proceed, upon the ground already traversed. Chrysostom sets us the example of managing this with skill. He also frequently throws in some lively question as to what comes next, calculated to arouse the hearers and make them notice it when stated. Our audiences, like his, do not commonly have the sacred text before them, and we must strive to supply the deficiency. By making the leading thoughts of the text quite distinct, by skillfully selecting and grouping the details, and by glancing backward and pointing forward as we proceed, this serious practical difficulty can be to a great extent overcome.

Much pains should be taken to point out and apply the lessons which the text may afford. The people need and desire to have these

---

[21] A celebrated Professor of Greek in one of our American Universities had a youthful assistant, who was one day unexpectedly called on to meet a class without having read over the lesson. When asked afterwards how he had got through, he said, "I just talked about what I understood and let alone what I didn't." "Pretty good plan," said the old gentleman; "I suspect you had better continue to do that as long as you live." [Well understood by intimates of the author to have been Dr. Gessner Harrison, of the University of Virginia, and himself.—D.]

distinctly stated, unless the application is exceedingly obvious. It will somewhat frequently be more convenient, particularly in historical exposition, to apply each division of the discourse as it is presented. But in many cases we can do as is common in other sermons—reserve the chief practical lessons for the conclusion. Of course, such lessons must, in general, be briefly indicated, as so much time is needed for exposition. But where there is a subject of special practical importance, it may be discussed and urged at length, even if some portions of the text have to be left unexplained. And if current events or the religious condition of the congregation should make it particularly desirable to discuss some practical topic which the text does not naturally suggest, it may be introduced in the way of remarks or of remote application of some general truth or duty. Here, again, Chrysostom presents us an example. Much as he delighted in explaining Scripture, he yet felt that, in preaching, the practical interest is paramount; and he not only points out many lessons by the way but is almost sure to find some practical subject for the conclusion, and this is not unfrequently treated at great length. Nor does he trouble himself much as to the association of ideas by which he shall reach any such important practical matter, but often uses a freedom which critics with strict notions of what we call "sermonizing" would be likely to condemn. In his sermon on the Transfiguration, for example, he wants to bear down on the moneylenders there at Antioch and reaches them as follows: The three disciples were happy in seeing Christ's glory on the mount—we may hope to behold him in a more splendid glory—but if we wish to do so we must take heed what manner of lives we are leading—we must not do this and that, must not oppress the poor—and so he comes to the matter of charging enormous interest, which is then discussed, for some time, with vehement denunciation and entreaty. By a still more roundabout process he passes from the feeding of the five thousand to an earnest attack upon the elaborately embroidered and curiously fashioned sandals which were then the rage. And he can frequently return to the same subject if it seems to require renewed censure or exhortation, managing to bring it in somehow. In one long series of discourses he rarely fails to inveigh against profanity; and his favorite topic of almsgiving may be expected to recur almost anywhere upon the slightest provocation. Now in all this his example is not faultless, certainly, but it is extremely instructive. We have seen that there is to be desired a much greater unity and much more of orderly structure and regular progress than is exhibited in Chrysostom's homilies. But the strictest notions in this direction must not prevent us from frequently and freely introducing matters of practical interest. In this way the people will be led to listen much more attentively to our explanations, being constantly on the lookout for some practical application to themselves; and they will also be constantly reminded of what men are so prone to forget, the intimate relation between Scripture truth and daily life. Pastors sometimes shrink from undertaking a series of expository discourses from the fear that they will not be able to adapt themselves to the precise condition and wants, week after week, of their people; but if the suggestions just made be acted upon, there will in this respect be no difficulty. Besides, where one preaches twice every Sunday, according to the common if not commendable fashion of the present day, he may of course have one sermon free for as much variety of specific adaptation as he pleases.

If the suggestions which have been offered are well founded, it will be obvious that expository preaching is a difficult task. It requires much close study of Scripture in general, and much special study of the particular passage to be treated. To make a discourse which shall be explanatory and yet truly oratorical, bearing a rich mass of details but not burdened with them, full of Scripture and abounding in practical applications, to bring even dull, uninformed, and unspiritual minds into interested and profitable contact with an extended portion of the Bible—of course this must be difficult. One cannot say, then, as is often said, try expository preaching first on week-nights till you and the people become accustomed to it. Nay, try it now and then for your principal sermon on Sunday without mentioning that you are about to do anything unusual, and lay out your best strength upon an earnest effort to make it at once instructive, interesting, and impressive. Then you and the people will gradually become accustomed to expository preaching as it should be. After repeating, more or less frequently, such occasional efforts, you will know how to prepare for an expository series. He who begins it as an easy thing will find expository preaching surpassingly difficult; but he who manfully takes hold of it as difficult will find it grows easier and more pleasant with every year of his experience. Not every man will find the expository method best suited to his mental endowments. But everyone ought to acquire the power of employing it with skill and success. Then, though it be better for this or that man to preach for the most part in other ways, he may continue to introduce expository sermons now and then and may also infuse a larger expository element into many of his textual and topical sermons. And it may be confidently asserted that many a one who now thinks this method of preaching unsuited to him needs nothing but diligent study and practice, upon some such principles as have been indicated, to make his expository sermons very profitable to his hearers and singularly delightful to himself.

Part III

FUNCTIONAL ELEMENTS
OF THE SERMON

◇◇◇

Chapter I

EXPLANATION

WHAT are the functions of preaching? The answer is to be found in the spiritual needs of mankind, which are many. Men need to be converted; they need to be instructed in the truth about God and man, about man's relation to God and to his fellowmen; they need to grow in character and spirit; they need to be enriched in their devotional life, sentiments, and ideals; they need to be inspirited and guided in Christian action, in home, church, and community life; they need to have the horizons of Christian interest and responsibility constantly lifted. It is among such needs as these that sermons must find point and purpose. The functions of preaching, therefore, may be classified as evangelistic, theological, ethical, devotional, inspiriting, and actional.

In order to fulfill any one or more of these functions a sermon must employ the instruments that are supplied jointly by psychology, logic, and rhetoric, which are explanation or exposition, argument, application, and, as largely auxiliary to the others, illustration.[1] These functional elements are not entirely distinct from one another; they often overlap. Thus certain processes which are always classed under explanation, as narrative and description, are often used at the same time, and even mainly for proof or persuasion. They are not, there-

[1] A full and in general valuable discussion of invention may be found in Day's *Art of Discourse*, pp. 42-207. He classifies materials according to the four objects of explanation, confirmation, excitation, and persuasion. His treatment of explanation is the most elaborate in existence (pp. 57-111), and although too formal in some respects, it will be found instructive and suggestive. See also Vinet, pp. 153-160.

fore, proper categories for the classification of sermons, although a sermon may be predominantly characterized by one or another. They are instrumental or functional elements to be used in the proportion that best suits the purpose of the particular sermon. For example, an evangelistic sermon will naturally appeal to emotion more extensively than a didactic sermon; a devotional sermon will be more explanatory and persuasive than argumentative; a theological sermon of the apologetic type will be largely argumentative, while the simple instructional type will be, in the main, explanatory; inspiriting sermons will be strengthened by illustrative examples. In order to be able, readily and properly, to adapt content to function the student should become thoroughly familiar with the elements discussed in this chapter and the three subsequent ones.

I. EXPLANATION IN GENERAL

There is in preaching very frequent need of explanation. Numerous passages of Scripture are not understood, or are even misunderstood, by our hearers; and many have become so accustomed to passing over these as to be no longer aware that they present any difficulty. Some of the most important doctrines of the Bible are in general very imperfectly understood; those who receive them need clearer views of what they profess to believe, and those who object to them are often in fact objecting to something very different from the real doctrine. The plan of salvation is seldom comprehended till one is really willing to conform to it, so that there is constantly arising new occasion for answering the great question, "What must I do to be saved?" And a thousand questions as to what is true and what is right in the practical conduct of life perplex devout minds and call for explanation. Preaching ought to be not merely convincing and persuasive, but eminently instructive. We often belabor men with arguments and appeals, when they are much more in need of practical and simple explanations as regards what to do and how to do it. And while some persons present may have repeatedly heard us explain certain important matters, we must not forget that there are others, children growing up, strangers moving in, converts entering the church, to whom such explanations will be new, and are in the highest degree necessary.

But just here the inexperienced minister may profit by several homely cautions. Do not attempt to explain what is not assuredly true. One sometimes finds great difficulty is working out an explanation of a supposed fact or principle because it is really not true. Do not undertake to explain what you do not understand. In preaching as well as elsewhere, this happens so often as to be ridiculous if it were not mournful. How can the housewife cook what has never been caught? How can the preacher explain what he does not understand? Never try to explain what cannot be explained. Some things taught in the Bible are in their essence incomprehensible; as, for example, the nature of the Trinity or the coexistence of absolute divine predestination with human freedom and accountability. In such a case it is very important to explain just what the Scriptures really do teach so as to remove misapprehensions; and it may sometimes be worth while to present any remote analogies in other spheres of existence so as perhaps to diminish the hearer's unwillingness to receive the doctrine; but attempts to explain the essential difficulty must necessarily fail, and the failure will react so as only to strengthen doubt and opposition. Do not waste time in explaining what does not need explanation.[2] A conspicuous instance is the nature of faith. Men frequently complain that they do not understand what it really is to believe, and preachers are constantly laboring to explain. But the complaint is in many cases a mere excuse for rejection or delay, and the real difficulty is in all cases a lack of disposition to believe. Elaborate explanations do not lessen this indisposition, do but strengthen the supposed excuse, and may even embarrass the anxious inquirer with the notion that there is something very mysterious about faith, when it is in fact so simple as not to admit of being explained. Our main duty is to tell the people what to believe and why they should believe it.

2. EXPLANATION OF TEXTS

To explain the Scriptures would seem to be among the primary functions of the preacher.[3] And there will often be occasion to explain not merely the text of the sermon but various other passages of Scripture which may be introduced into the discussion. The power of making such explanations attractive as well as clear will, of course, depend largely upon the preacher's turn of mind. But the most gifted in respect of this important task should seek constant

---

[2] Compare Vinet, *Hom.*, p. 166.
[3] Compare Exposition Sermons, Part II, Chap. V.

improvement, and they who have great difficulty must put forth diligent and hopeful efforts to overcome it. What nobler work is there than that of "opening" the Scriptures, as Paul did at Thessalonica? (Acts 17:3.)

(1) The exegesis of texts, as the process by which the preacher himself comes to understand them, has already received our attention.[4] Pulpit exegesis, or exposition, is in certain respects a different thing. We have here, save in exceptional cases, to present results and not processes. We must omit various matters which have perhaps greatly interested ourselves, because they would not interest the people or do not pertain to the object of the present discourse. Preachers sometimes allow themselves, in the introduction to the sermon or as a digression, to give long explanations of something in a passage or its connection, which has no bearing on their subject and thus impairs unity and distracts attention. There must, of course, be no parade of acquaintance with the original languages, and there should be no morbid fear of being charged with such parade. Commentaries may be mentioned if the people know something of them and would thereby be more readily satisfied, or if it is desirable to bring good popular authors to their notice. To repeat lists of strange and high-sounding names in favor of this or that interpretation is always useless and is in general a very pitiful display of cheap erudition, which with the help of certain books may all be gotten up at second hand in a few minutes. One may very easily indicate, without any array of authorities, that this is the view of the best writers, of some good commentators, etc. The great matter is to take the results of the most careful investigation in our power, select from them such points as are appropriate, and present these clearly, briefly, and in such a way as to be interesting. Sometimes the text or another passage introduced may be amply and admirably explained by a few words; but such words do not come of themselves; they result from close thinking and careful choice of expressions. Sometimes passages may be introduced in such a connection, as without a word of explanation to give them new meaning and preciousness. It is a fault in many able ministers that they comparatively neglect to bring in and explain the apposite sayings of Scripture which would both give and borrow light. And however congregations may shrink from elaborate exegesis or bungling and tedious attempts to explain, they will always

[4] Part I, Chap II.

welcome the felicitous introduction and quick, vivid elucidation of passages from God's Word.

(2) Narration has in preaching a peculiar character. Modern works on rhetoric treat of it almost exclusively as practiced in writing, historical, biographical, fictional, dramatic, and the like.[5] Ancient writers treat of oratorical narration and are therefore more valuable for our purpose,[6] though relating chiefly to the narrative in judicial oratory. The preacher, of course, narrates as a speaker and deals mainly with Scripture history. A speaker must always subordinate narration to the object of his discourse, the conviction or persuasion which he wishes to effect.[7] He must not elaborate or enlarge upon some narrative merely because it is in itself interesting, or follow the story step by step according to its own laws.

In demonstrative speeches the narration is not continuous, but given in scattered portions; for one must go over the actions out of which the speech arises; for a speech is a kind of compound, having one portion, indeed, independent of art, and another portion originating in art.

That is, the facts are independent of the speaker, but he breaks them up and presents them according to his object.

Owing to this, there are times when one ought not to narrate every fact successively, because this mode of exposition is difficult to remember. The one style of narration is too simple; the other has the grace of variety and is not so void of elegance. But what you have to do is to awaken the recollection of facts well known; on which account many subjects will stand in no need of narration—supposing, for instance, you would praise Achilles, because all are acquainted with his actions—but you must simply use the actions without narration. If, on the other hand, one wishes to praise Critias, it is necessary to narrate; for not many are acquainted with his exploits.[8]

And so when we preach with reference to the minor and less familiar personages of Scripture, it is proper enough to narrate all the facts concerning them. But when it is one of the great characters, we must choose between two courses. We may select the salient or characteristic points of his history and so narrate these as to exhibit the

---

[5] Thus, Day's *Art of Discourse*, and Bain's *Rhetoric*, and Genung's *Practical Elements of Rhetoric*.

[6] Particularly Arist. Rhet. III. 16, and Quintil. IV. 2, which will be found very suggestive.

[7] *Narratio est rei factæ . . . utilis ad persuadendum expositio.* Quintilian, IV. 2, 31.

[8] Arist. Rhet. III. 16, 1-3.

chief lessons of that history, introducing such details as are to the purpose and rigorously omitting all others. Thus the history of Joseph, of Job, of John the Baptist, may be conveniently treated. In such a case, every speaker will mention or enlarge upon different parts of the history, according to his particular object, as Stephen's speech, and that of Paul at Antioch in Pisidia sketch very differently the history of Israel, and as Paul in the two speeches which tell the story of his conversion expands in each of them certain matters which in the other are but slightly touched, adapting the narration to the character and wants of his audience.[9] But it is generally better to choose some one event of the man's history or some one trait of his character and narrate only what bears upon that. In preaching upon the meekness of Moses, there would be occasion to state briefly those circumstances of his training and career which were particularly unfavorable to the development of meekness and then to narrate, with vivid touches, the leading instances in which his meekness was exhibited, as well as those in which it temporarily failed; and the discourse would properly close with a somewhat extended application of the whole matter to ourselves. In this way the history of Moses would be much more impressively reproduced, than if one should attempt an outline of the whole.

Narration is often given in the introduction to the sermon. In so doing special pains should be taken not to have it too long, not to wander into parts of the story which have no bearing upon the design of the discourse, and not to pause, except in very rare cases for remarks upon outside topics which the narrative may suggest. Be sure, also, that the particulars of the narrative are at once interesting, plausible, and of evident value to the ends of the sermon. There is especial danger here of violating the laws of unity and proportion.[10]

Besides the instances in which some history in the Bible is our theme, there will be constant occasion to derive illustration from Scripture history and great demand for skill in the brief and interesting narration of events thus employed. Happy the preacher who can in this way keep ever fresh in the minds of his hearers those beautiful and sacred stories, which are not only sweet to the heart of childhood and full of instruction to youth but which, when rightly contemplated, assume new interest and meaning at every stage of life.

[9] Compare Acts 7 and 13.
[10] See Genung for a good discussion of the techniques of narration.

It is a rather common fault in the pulpit to narrate in a declamatory way. The preacher has become excited, and he states a plain fact or tells a simple story with such vehemence and boisterousness as to be extremely incongruous. Quintilian keenly satirizes those who think it beneath their dignity to set forth facts in everyday language, who do not seem to themselves eloquent unless they have thrown everything into agitation by boisterous vociferation, and, instead of simply narrating, imagine that they have here a field for showing off and "inflect the voice, set back the neck, and fling the arm against the side, and riot in every variety of ideas, words, and style."[11] Let us learn the lesson.

(3) Description is usually a necessary part of narration, separate scenes of the narrative being to some extent described. There is also frequent occasion to describe Scripture scenes apart from their connection in the narrative, as in the introduction to a sermon, in the employment of historical illustrations from Scripture, etc. And while we speak here of narration and description only as regards the events and scenes of the Bible history, it is obvious that the same skill may be applied to that great variety of illustrative matter from every other source, which must be vividly narrated or described in order to make any impression. A leading American preacher has said that "he who would hold the ear of the people must either tell stories or paint pictures."[12]

Power of description is of course partly a natural gift; but many intelligent men will marvel and lament that they cannot describe, when they have never fairly tried—never given themselves any general training in that respect, never really studied any one scene or object which they attempted to describe. Such men are aware that they cannot work out an argument without much previous thought but seem not aware that corresponding effort is necessary in order to achieve a good description.

He who would describe anything must have seen it, not necessarily with bodily vision but with the mind's eye. He must begin, then, with gaining correct information about the scene or object; and this information must extend, if possible, to details. As regards Scripture scenes, there is often need of a familiar acquaintance with biblical geography and with the manners and customs of the Jews. While

[11] Quintilian IV. 2, 37-39.
[12] H. W. Beecher. There is an interesting chapter on Word-painting in Potter's *Spoken Word*, p. 210 ff.

gathering such information and after doing so, he must fasten his mind upon the scene so that the imagination may realize it; he must look at it as he would at a landscape or a painting, first surveying the whole, then inspecting the most interesting details, and afterwards comprising all in a general view. This should be kept up, with the point of view varied and with repeated effort to imagine, till the whole scene stands out clear and vivid before the eye of the mind; only then is he prepared to describe it.

Remember now that a speaker is not to describe as the writer of a poem, a romance, or a book of travels might do but is to make the description brief and subordinate to the objects of his discourse; we may thus perceive in a general way how the description should be managed. The outlines of the picture should be rapidly drawn and may be rude, provided they are distinct. Then, certain prominent or characteristic points of the scene must be presented. And with some of these there should be given a few of the most suggestive details, which will arouse the hearer's imagination to fill up the picture. In this lies the great art of description, especially for speakers —to stimulate the hearer's imagination into seeing for himself. Sometimes there are a few details so characteristic that they need only the slightest indication of outline to make a picture, as in a caricature one or two peculiar features, somewhat exaggerated, and a few rude lines besides will be more amusing than a finished picture, because more suggestive. And even where no remarkably striking details present themselves, one may contrive slight touches here and there which will give life to the whole. If these are not afforded by our knowledge of the facts, they may be avowedly imagined, care being taken to have them suggest only what will harmonize with the facts. Thus in that remarkable homescene at Bethany, after describing Mary seated at Jesus' feet and hearing his word, one might imagine Martha as coming to the door of the room, her face heated with excitement and vexation, and, after vainly striving to catch Mary's eye and call her forth, at length stepping straight to the Master himself, with her complaining request; and this slight glance at her before she enters will help to realize the scene.

Avoid elaborate description. The preacher is expected always to cherish so practical a design, and feel such absorbing earnestness as not to have time for painting finished pictures. Hearers of good taste will always feel them to be out of place. As regards the temptation to give high-wrought descriptions to show one's talent in that respect, this must of course be resisted like all other temptations to display. But we cannot turn to the best account the historical portions of Scripture or use to advantage other narrative and pictorial illustration without cultivating our powers of narration and description; and he who will patiently strive, under the guidance of correct principles, first to see clearly and then to describe suggestively, may ere long surprise himself by the facility and pleasure with which he can bring out, in not many words, some story or scene from the Bible.

3. EXPLANATION OF SUBJECTS

Here again there will be included not merely the general subject of a discourse but any other ideas which enter into the discussion. Both the former and the latter must often require explanation. Many matters of truth and duty are obscure and, without help, practically unintelligible to the popular mind; many questions are sadly perplexing. To answer such inquiries, to clear up difficulties, and make as plain as possible the way of truth and the path of duty is, as well as the explanation of Scripture, an important part of the preacher's work.

(1) One means of explaining subjects is by definition.

Definition is defined by the etymology of the word. It marks the limits of an idea. To define definition positively, we say that it teaches of what elements an idea, as a whole, is composed. It consists in bringing together many general ideas, of which one is limited by the others. When the idea, so to speak, is fortified, entrenched, so that on all sides it repels ideas which would mix themselves with it, the object is defined. We must not confound definition and judgment. Definition does but verify identity; judgment expresses a relation. . . . Definition aims to make us know; judgment, to appreciate. Very often, however, definition appreciates, and involves judgment; and judgment is equivalent to a partial definition. We must not, however, confound with definition those judgments which give force to a characteristic of an object, and are only designed to excite toward it such or such a sentiment. Examples:
'Rivers are roads that move and carry us whither we would go.'
'Hypocrisy is a homage which vice pays to virtue.'
'Time is the treasure of the poor.'
'A tomb is a monument placed on the boundary between two worlds.'
'Love is the fulfilling of the law.'
When the notion of the attribute does not exhaust that of the subject, and one cannot be put indifferently for the other, we have not a definition, we

have a judgment. . . . A definition is indeed a judgment, but a judgment which contains or begets all the judgments which at any time may be pronounced upon an object. And reciprocally, by combining all the judgments which at any time may be pronounced on an object, we have a definition.[13]

Vinet proceeds to give examples of definition, including one which is very often called a definition but surely without propriety: "Faith is the substance of things hoped for, the evidence of things not seen." (Heb. 11:1.) Other judgments may be pronounced upon faith besides this. Faith is the substance of things hoped for, etc., just as love is the fulfilling of the law. It may be said that faith is the means of union with Christ; but that is not defining faith. In fact, as we have before observed, it scarcely needs definition, or admits of it.

In preaching we may sometimes most readily define an idea by connecting it with another idea, either in the way of distinction or of comparison.[14] And instead of or in addition to definition, it is often well to employ exemplification, for which see page 165.

Definition is not only a means of perspicuity, an element of instruction, the basis of argumentation; it is often the beginning of proof. Demonstration, at least, is firm and sure in proportion to the exactness and clearness of the definition.

Every one has observed how important it is in beginning a controversial discussion, public or private, that the question should be exactly defined; otherwise, confusion of ideas is inevitable. Now it is equally though not so obviously important in conducting a discussion alone that one should clearly define to himself the subject in hand. In fact, it is more important in this case, because controversy will sooner or later force the parties to perceive that they have not clearly understood the question or understood it in the same way, while the solitary thinker or the unanswered speaker may remain permanently involved in the confusion or error produced by his lack of well-defined conceptions at the outset. And the same thing applies to the definition of leading terms. But while we must always define to ourselves, it is not always necessary that we should define to the audience. The proposition of the subject, if felicitous, may often be sufficiently perspicuous and precise; or we may see that the discussion itself will most effectually give clear and definite views of the subject. In all definitions stated, we should eschew formality and "avoid

---

[13] Vinet, *Hom.*, pp. 161-163.
[14] See Vinet, p. 165.

too subtle distinctions and classifications, which assume a great habit
of abstraction and an exact knowledge of language on the part of the
hearer."[15]

(2) A second means of explaining ideas is by division. The methods
of dividing a subject and of stating divisions have already been discussed. See Part II, Chap. III.

(3) Exemplification is often necessary and almost always useful in
the work of explanation. The common mind does not readily apprehend general definitions, expressed in abstract terms; and even
to the most cultivated thinkers an idea will become more vivid and
interesting when there is added to a precise definition some apposite example. It would be difficult to present to a popular audience
a clear distinction between pride and vanity in the way of definition;
but by supposing certain circumstances and showing how the proud
man would act and how the vain man, in such a case, or by taking up
some particular action of a well-known character and inquiring
whether the motive here was pride or vanity, we may speedily make
the difference plain. So, instead of undertaking to explain faith, one
may describe a believer or, in addition to stating in general terms what
will make a Christian happy, may give an ideal portraiture of a
Christian who was happy. And still more useful are examples from
real life. Every preacher turns to account in this way his observation
of life, and some do so with very great effectiveness. But, besides
what we have personally observed, we have the wide fields of history
and especially of Scripture history from which to derive examples.
In selecting those to be used, the preacher must inquire not only what
is most apposite, but what will be most intelligible and interesting to
the particular audience and what he himself can most effectively
handle. Historical examples which would thrill one congregation
will make but little impression on another, not being familiar to them
or not linked to them by any ties of sympathy. In this, as in most
respects, examples from Bible history are the best. They are more
generally familiar than most others, and if any time be consumed
in bringing the example vividly before the hearers, it is time well
spent, because it promotes general acquaintance with the Scriptures.

(4) Among the commonest and most useful means of explanation
is comparison. With this may be classed contrast and also analogy,
which depends on a resemblance, not in objects themselves, but in
their respective relations to certain other objects. Analogy, however,

[15] Vinet, pp. 164, 165.

is more frequently employed for the purpose of proof and will be considered in the next chapter. Contrast needs no special remark.

The great mass of our Lord's parables are comparisons. "The kingdom of heaven is like," etc. "Unto what shall we liken this generation?" Some of them are thrown into the form of narrative; but others are mere statements of comparison, and he uses many striking comparisons which are never called parables. The comparison of his coming to that of a thief (Matt. 24:43, 44) is an instructive example of the fact that comparison is all the more striking where we have one point of resemblance between objects or events in other respects very different. Several of the parables are rather cases of exemplification than of comparison, as, for instance, the Rich Man preparing to take his ease, the Pharisee and the Publican, the Good Samaritan. Many of them are introduced for other purposes in addition to that of explanation. But they are chiefly comparisons and are mainly used to explain. They thus impressively exhibit to us the importance of explanation and the value of comparison as a means of effecting it. The same high example reminds us how desirable it is to derive our comparisons from matters familiar to our hearers.

CHAPTER II

ARGUMENT

EXPLANATION does not in itself meet the full requirement of preaching. Events must be related to present life situations and needs. Ideas made clear, if they are to have their full force, often must be established as true by relating them to other already accepted ideas in such a way as to win acceptance for them also. In thus relating ideas the preacher is expressing a judgment—that they are related, and in the manner set forth,—and, to quote Dr. Garvie,

it often happens that the connection between the two ideas in a judgment cannot be taken for granted, or be simply imposed by the preacher on his hearers. He must justify the connection; he must so present the connection as to win the assent of his hearers. He must, therefore, give reasons, or links of connection between the two ideas which are not obviously immediately related to one another.[1]

He must sometimes follow a line of reasoning, i.e., make an argument, to sustain his judgment and so establish the truth and justify the application he would make of it. Argument, therefore, in the logical and at the same time popular sense of the term, forms a very large and very important element in the materials of preaching. There are preachers, it is true, who seem to consider that they have no occasion for reasoning, that everything is to be accomplished by authoritative assertion and impassioned appeal. And this notion is not new; for we find Aristotle complaining that previous writers on rhetoric had concerned themselves only with the means of persuasion by appeals to feeling and prejudice. But preachers really have great use for argument, and there are many reasons why its importance in preaching should be duly considered.

I. IMPORTANCE OF ARGUMENT IN PREACHING

There are many gainsayers and doubters to be convinced, as regards both the truth of Christianity and the truth of what we represent to be its teachings. There are many who in both respects believe but

---

[1] *The Christian Preacher*, p. 398. For N. T. examples see Matt. 5:3-10; 13:52; Heb. 11:6; John 20:29.

whose religious affections and activity might be not a little quickened by convincing and impressive proofs that these things are so.

Even in the cases in which reasoning seems superfluous, it may be greatly useful, since its object is not so much to prove what is not yet believed as to fill the mind with the evidence, and, if we may so speak, to multiply the brightness of truth.[2]

And besides, there is in Christian countries a multitude of people who say they believe because they do not disbelieve or question, whose minds remain in a negative state towards the gospel, which is often the most fatal form of unbelief. Argument, as to the truth and value and claims of the gospel, as to the peril and guilt of their position, is often useful in arousing feelings of contrition and desire and is, therefore, one of the means by which we must strive to bring them, through the special blessing of the Spirit, into some real, some operative belief.

Some forms of error which exalt the intellectual at the expense of the spiritual gain much acceptance, particularly with a certain class of minds, by the argumentative garb in which they appear. The teachers of these errors come to men accustomed to a sleepy acquiescence in truths which they have never heard vigorously discussed, bring their powers of argument into agreeable exercise, and they are won. Even those who maintain sound doctrine sometimes support it by very unsound reasoning and thereby leave the way open for some shrewd opponent to overthrow their arguments, and thus appear to overthrow their doctrine.

Every preacher, then, ought to develop and discipline his powers in respect to argument. If averse to reasoning, he should constrain himself to practice it; if by nature strongly inclined that way, he must remember the serious danger of deceiving himself and others by false arguments. One who has not carefully studied some good treatise of logic should take the earliest opportunity to do so. It will render his mind sharper to detect fallacy, in others or in himself, and will help to establish him in the habit of reasoning soundly. The fact that, as so often sneeringly remarked, "preachers are never replied to" should make it a point of honor with preachers not to mislead their hearers by bad logic and should render them exceedingly solicitous to avoid those self-deceptions, which they have no keen opponent to reveal. One must constantly remind himself to argue for truth rather than

[2] Vinet. p. 176.

for victory and, as a rule, never to maintain a proposition which he does not really believe. The delicate perception of truth and the enthusiastic love for it will inevitably be impaired by a contrary course.

Yet in preaching we need not act as if everything had to be proved, and every proof to be a formal argument. Some things cannot be proved, some do not need to be, and others have been sufficiently proved before and should now be taken for granted. Elaborate argument which is not called for will only awaken doubt or lead to weariness and disgust. We may usually assume the truth of Scripture. And as to whatever the Scriptures plainly teach, while we must sometimes argue, it is often true, as Spurgeon has said, that the preacher should "dogmatize," being careful, of course, to remember that the dogmatic use of a passage as a "proof-text" must be approved in the light of the whole Scripture teaching.

The accent of true authority is welcome to almost every one. We are prepossessed in favor of men who, in this world of uncertainty and perplexity, express themselves on a grave subject with confidence and command. . . . The person of preachers is nothing, their message is the whole; and not for their person, but for their message, do they claim respect; but they would be as culpable not to demand this respect for the divine thought of which they are the depositaries, as they would be foolish and ridiculous to demand it for their own thoughts.[3]

But the right to speak with such authority will be acknowledged, among Protestants, only where the preacher shows himself able to prove whenever it is appropriate all that he maintains.

2. PRINCIPAL VARIETIES OF ARGUMENT

It is not proposed to give a formal analysis and classification of arguments but to explain the nature and use of the leading varieties. These are, in the order of their natural development and usage, testimony, induction, analogy, and deduction.

(1) *Argument from Testimony*. In establishing truth in the minds of one's hearers the most direct and simple way is to tell one's own experience of the truth and one's own observation of the truth. The preacher himself becomes a witness of what he himself has seen and heard and handled and tested out to a final faith. It has often been said that no one should go further. Preach only what you have experienced! Yet every preacher does go further, and must. He

---

[3] Vinet, pp. 228, 229.

expresses also his judgment. The man of experience inevitably becomes the man of opinion; having testified, "I was blind and now I see," and having given the details of the experience, he soon goes on to say, "He is a prophet." The testimony of fact is supplemented by the testimony of opinion or judgment.

The grain of truth in the old idea that we are to preach only what we have experienced is that we are not to preach anything that has not in some way become real to us. Guesses and hypotheses carry little weight. Speculations can never take the place of convictions. Yet, even speculation has a place in all human thought, religious or otherwise, and not all convictions are reached by experience.[4]

So in preaching we use the facts of our own experience and judgment and draw, also, upon the experience and judgment of others. This is the simplest proof, the beginning of argument. It is necessary in the use of testimony to distinguish clearly between fact and judgment or opinion. Common usage sometimes confounds these terms, even as men are very apt not to distinguish facts from their own judgments concerning them.[5] In the alleged "spiritual manifestations," of which so much has been said, there is unquestionable testimony that tables rise and move without the application of any apparent and adequate physical force, that certain peculiar rapping sounds are heard, and that other strange things occur. Now upon the testimony these matters of fact should be, without hesitation, admitted. But what causes these movements and sounds, whether some unknown physical force or some unknown spiritual agency, is purely matter of opinion. Those who have most frequently witnessed the phenomena are not thereby the best prepared to judge of their cause; while the supposed interpretation of the rapping noises and the correspondence of such interpretations with facts otherwise known are matters which open a wide door for all manner of self-delusions and impostures. We must accustom ourselves and educate the people to distinguish more carefully than is common between testimony as to matters of fact and mere judgments, opinions, and hypotheses as to their explanation.

It is not appropriate here to discuss the general subject of testimony as bearing upon the administration of justice. And, yet, a minister does well to consider carefully the rules of evidence in the courts of justice, endeavoring, in every case, to find the principle involved, that

[4] Patton, *Preparation and Delivery of Sermons*, p. 10.
[5] See Whately, pp. 79-83.

he may apply it with the necessary adaptations to the matters with which he is concerned. Those parts of the subject with which the preacher frequently has to deal will be briefly treated.

(*a*) In testimony as to matters of fact, the points to be considered are, on the one hand, the character and number of the witnesses and, on the other, the character of the things attested.

As to the character of the witnesses, we of course consider, mainly, their veracity, but also their intelligence, their opportunities of knowing the facts and their tendency to think in a certain way. A large number of witnesses will obviously make the evidence stronger, provided each speaks from his own knowledge and not from what others have told him. When there are several such independent witnesses, their testimony will differ as to some points of detail. Where the details are numerous, no man will be expected to remember and state them all; and each will select according to what he happened to observe, or what specially commended itself to his mind, or what he has had frequent occasion since to recall, or what falls in with the general design and drift of his statement or is suggested, point after point, by the natural association of ideas. If all were to agree in the details of an extended statement, we should feel sure that they had in some way learned from each other or had all drawn from a common source. These principles are familiar to the English and American mind. Had the Germans been accustomed to trial by jury (which they have had only since 1848) we should probably not have found so many able scholars among them denying the trustworthiness of the gospel narratives because of the "discrepancies" they present. These discrepancies, nowhere involving real contradiction, only show that the witnesses are independent and thus immensely strengthen their combined testimony to the substantial facts. The evidence is also strengthened by manifestly undesigned coincidences. A great number of such coincidences, clearly undesigned, between minor statements in the Epistles of Paul and in the Acts, have been exhibited by Paley, in his celebrated *Horæ Paulinæ* (Hours with Paul), a work which admirably fortifies the Christian evidences and presents the most useful lessons as to the value of testimony. And the less important in itself is the subject matter of such coincidences, the more certain will it be that they are undesigned. In such a case, the lightest matters are often the weightiest.

The unintentional testimony of adversaries is frequently of great value. Thus the opposers of Christianity in the early centuries, both heathen and Jewish, in endeavoring to account for the miracles of our Lord as wrought by magic, have shown that they felt it impossible to deny the reality of the occurrences.

On the other hand, there is to be considered the character of the things attested. Things in themselves improbable will, of course, require more testimony in order to gain our credence. Such is the case with miracles. Those who take the ground that miracles are impossible beg the question, and must be omniscient in order to make sure that their position is correct. But miracles are in themselves highly improbable.[6] That some spiritual force should so counteract the operation of great physical forces as for a time to prevent their otherwise uniform results is a thing which we are naturally slow to believe. This improbability, however, is greatly diminished where we see important occasion for such interference, as where miracles are wrought to authenticate a revelation. The Christian miracles have not only this but another advantage. The character and teachings of Christ are inseparably associated with miracles.[7] He who denies the miracles denies the supernatural origin of Christ's character and teachings and must then account for these as merely human and natural, which the ablest and most ingenious infidels, after a great variety of attempts, have utterly failed to do. So the question of antecedent probability is here reduced to this: Which is more improbable, that miracles should have been wrought, upon such occasion as the introduction of Christianity; or that the character and teachings of Christ should be merely human and of natural origin? Thus the general improbability of miracles is in this case much lessened by the adequate occasion for them and then is more than counterbalanced by a yet greater improbability if they be denied.

Moreover, the testimony of others to our Lord's miracles is not only strong and unquestionable in itself but has the unique and invincible reinforcement of our Lord's own testimony. Jesus professed to work miracles; he cannot by possibility have been deceived on the subject; and so either he did work miracles, or he was a bad man. Against his character all the objections to miracles must shatter, like surf against the rock. And this is not arguing in a circle—not

---

[6] The late Professor Huxley, in his controversy with Dr. Wace (1888), took the ground that the improbability of miracles was to great to be overcome by the evidence in their favor. But who is to judge as to the value of the evidence? It is not certain that a devotee of physical science will be a good judge of historical evidence.

[7] This argument is more fully presented in the author's *Jesus of Nazareth: Three Lectures.*

proving the miracles by Christ and Christ by the miracles. The concurrence of the two makes it easy to account for both; the denial of the miracles necessitates conclusions more improbable than the miraculous.

The testimony to our Lord's resurrection has been often and thoroughly discussed,[8] and shown to be irrefragable. It is especially strengthened by the great slowness of belief exhibited by the disciples; "They doubted, that we might not doubt."[9]

The evidence of Christian experience ought never to be overlooked. The believer finds a change wrought in him which testifies to the reality and power of Christianity, and he in turn bears witness to others that the change which they observe in him was wrought in connection with believing.

(*b*) Testimony as to matters of opinion, as distinguished from matters of fact, might be conveniently designated by the term "authority." But this term is sometimes applied to testimony as to matters of fact, especially where it is particularly strong and convincing testimony, and is also frequently used to denote some combination of testimony as to fact, and reliable judgment or opinion. But the basic distinction must not be overlooked. And it must be remembered that a reliable witness as to facts is not thereby necessarily reliable in judgment. The so-called "authority" of the Fathers must be differently regarded in different cases. As to the question, What books were of apostolic origin? they afford us testimony,—though in the case of all but the earliest Fathers it is not original but transmitted testimony,—and also the authority of their judgment as to the weight of the entire evidence known to them, only a part of which do they hand down to us. In respect to such questions they are known to have been very critical, and we may well attach great value both to their testimony and their authority. But concerning the interpretation of the sacred books, the question as to what Scripture teaches, we have only their authority, their judgment. Most of them were loose interpreters, and they were all greatly influenced by philosophical opinions, prejudices of various kinds, and especially, with rare exceptions, by an extreme fondness for allegory. Except, then, the cases in which familiarity with Greek, with ancient customs, and the like,

---

[8] Mention may be made of that piquant little work, Sherlock's *Trial of the Witnesses*, in which the evidence of the resurrection is examined according to the forms of law. See also Greenleaf and Milligan.

[9] Some of the views here presented as to testimony, and some others, will be found in Whately, pp. 78-104.

gives special weight to the opinions of a Father, their authority as to the meaning of Scripture is not great and, in fact, not justly equal to that of some later writers.

The Scriptures themselves are an authority, indeed. All that they testify to be fact is thereby fully proven, all that they teach as true and right is thereby established and made obligatory.

This is proof without arguing in the narrow sense. Somewhat similarly do all men prove by the direct appeal to consciousness. "You know that so and so is true" will in some cases settle the question. So, too, we frequently appeal to common sense, though it should be noticed that men often put forward as a judgment of common sense what is only some opinion of their own, some conclusion reached by a process of reasoning but by a process so obscure as to escape their consciousness and thus hide its fallacies from their view. But the Scriptures furnish a standard of final appeal having a far more frequent and extensive application. This does not at all enable us to dispense with argument. We have sometimes to prove that the Scriptures are such a standard; and to show what the various passages of Scripture teach on a subject often requires not merely exposition but argument. Many truths have to be established partly by argument on other grounds, reinforced and confirmed by indirect teachings of the Bible; and it is gratifying to believers, and demanded by unbelievers, that we should, wherever it is possible, exhibit the concurrence of reason and experience with the teachings of revelation. Thus we have constant need of argument. But in all our reasoning, care should be taken to treat the authority of Scripture as paramount and, wherever its utterances are distinct and unquestionable, as decisive. There are some subjects on which the Bible is our sole authority, such as the Trinity, justification by faith, the conditions of the future life, and the positive ordinances of Christianity, namely, baptism and the Lord's supper.[10] The Christian reasoner should seek fully to appreciate this unparalleled authority and should heedfully observe its proper relation to all other means of proof.[11]

The generally received opinions of mankind and the proverbs and maxims which express the collective judgment of many have a greater or less authority according to the nature of the case. Those, for example, which are readily attributable to human superstitions or selfishness or express only half-truths can claim but little weight.

[10] Compare Porter's *Hom.*, Lect. XI.
[11] Compare § 5, Order of Arguments.

(2) *Argument from Induction.* Induction has been variously defined. Thus Mills says: "Induction is that operation of the mind by which we infer that what we know to be true in a particular case or cases will be true in all cases which resemble the former in certain assignable respects." Professor N. K. Davis[12] defines: "Induction is an immediate synthetic inference generalizing from and beyond experience." Every term in this statement is important, and when they are well understood the definition will be found to be exact and complete.

Induction has also been very simply defined as "the process of drawing a general rule from a sufficient number of particular cases."[13] Finding something to be true of certain individual objects, we infer that the same thing is true of other objects or of the whole class to which those individuals belong. Induction is, in popular usage, the commonest form of argument. When carefully done it yields the surest knowledge and when carelessly done oftenest involves error. Men in general do not argue from general principles or previously established truths nearly so often as from examples. These examples they indolently observe, and without extensive comparison or careful scrutiny, they hastily infer that what a certain person did is right for them, that what is true of certain individuals, or of all they happen to have noticed, is true of all the class. When they are strongly impelled to wish it so, as by appetite, interest, or prejudice, and thus some powerful feeling combines with indolence, it is not wonderful, however deplorable, that a "hasty induction" is the result. In agriculture or in domestic medicine all manner of rules are upheld and followed among the masses of men on the ground of imperfect observation and hasty induction. In books of travel universal statements are constantly made as to the opinions, usages, and character of a people, which are founded on a very hasty induction, stimulated by prejudice, notable examples appearing in English books about America, in provincially minded authors when writing of sections of our country other than their own, also in reports of Foreign Missions made by some infidel or irreligious travelers. Certain choice specimens of what are called "uneducated" ministers surpass some very poor specimens of the "educated," and this is thought to prove that ministerial education is unnecessary; a half-educated young preacher

---

[12] *Elements of Inductive Logic,* pp. 6, 7, where a number of other definitions are given.

[13] Fleming, *Vocab. of Phil.,* p. 252.

makes a foolish display of something he learned at college or seminary, and this shows that education is injurious. But who could catalogue or even broadly classify the instances of hasty or otherwise unwarranted induction which make up so sadly large a portion of human reasoning? Let us earnestly strive, as a duty to our own minds and to our office as teachers of truth, to guard against this fruitful source of error.

The question of what is "a sufficient number of cases" to warrant our drawing a general rule depends upon the nature of the subject matter. In regard to physical facts a single example will sometimes suffice.

A chemist who had ascertained, in a single specimen of gold, its capability of combining with mercury would not think it necessary to try the experiment with several other specimens but would draw the conclusion concerning those metals universally and with practical certainty.[14]

But nothing like this applies to social facts or to moral and religious truth. In order for a safe induction, one must not merely aggregate a number of instances, he must analyze and compare them, so as to eliminate what is merely incidental, and ascertain the "material circumstances" in each case.[15] The more clearly we can discern a causal relation, accounting for the common element, the smaller the number of instances necessary to establish a rule. But the cause must be a real cause, not a mere hypothesis, not a matter having no real connection with the result in question, not an incidental circumstance. As an example of the last, it is frequently inferred that something found true in several cases of conversion will be true in all cases; but the question is whether this is something founded in the essential principles of human nature or merely the result of peculiar temperament, education, and other circumstances.

With due emphasis upon the dangers of faulty induction, it must be recognized with Garvie that rich values are to be found in this kind of reasoning.

There is a very wide scope for the preacher in taking the individual instances of morality enjoined in the prophets, the Gospels, and the Epistles so as to discover the general principles implied, and in then applying these principles to the instances of duty for his hearers.[16]

---

[14] Whately, p. 111.
[15] Compare Mill's *Logic*, Book V., Chap. v. § 4; and Hamilton's *Logic*, p. 453.
[16] *The Christian Preacher*, p. 407.

In his moral teaching our Lord laid down general moral principles which often were called forth by some concrete fact or experience, and also he gave particular teachings that fitted particular situations, leaving it to us to perceive and apply the embedded principle to other situations. For example, take his generalization about rich men following his experience with the rich young ruler. He laid down no abstract principle about private property, but all his remarks about wealth and greed and giving are particulars from which men may draw their conclusions. His generalization about paying taxes to Rome was based upon a fact of actual debtorship. The facts of human paternal love were his argument for faith in the beneficent love of the Heavenly Father. In the house of Simon the Pharisee his parable and subsequent remarks fairly crackled with facts from which that astonished man had to infer an embarrassing fact about himself. Christ's preaching was concrete, geared in closely with life situations; and its authority was strengthened by the fact that it claimed at every point the support of the facts of human experience. The preacher will do well to follow him in taking full cognizance of such facts. "Consider the lilies of the field," and "behold the birds of the heaven." And study induction—constructing strong bridges of facts that will bring men to some significant realization.

It is in the highest degree important that we should know how to correct those ten thousand erroneous inductions, whether in the arguments of other public speakers, in newspapers and conversation, or in their own thinking, by which the minds of our hearers are so apt to be misled. And it is highly important that we see and utilize the significance of assembled facts.

(3) *Argument from Analogy.*[17] Analogy is still too often confounded with resemblance, notwithstanding the earnest efforts of Whately and some other writers to confine the term to its original and proper sense. The primary meaning of the word is "proportion," and in this sense only is it employed in mathematics. It denotes not a resemblance between objects themselves, but a correspondence between their ratios or relations to other objects. The leg of a table does not much resemble the leg of an animal, but they are analogous, because the former sustains, in several respects, the same relation to a table

---

[17] Genung properly treats analogy as a form of induction, since it is inference from particular facts of relation. But its importance in preaching justifies separate treatment.

that the leg sustains to an animal. The foot of a mountain is analogous to that of a man, though scarcely at all similar.

An egg and a seed are not in themselves alike, but bear a like relation, to the parent bird and to her future nestling on the one hand, and to the old and young plant on the other.[18]

But analogous objects will frequently be similar, also, and this fact has helped to obscure to men's minds the distinction—that which is really due to the analogy being sometimes carelessly ascribed to the resemblance. Further, an analogy is often all the more striking from the fact that it exists between objects which in some other respects are utterly unlike. So it happens that failing to see clearly the difference between analogy and resemblance, and observing, besides, that the term analogy is often employed where there is in some respects a great dissimilarity, many persons have fallen into the habit of calling objects analogous which are similar in some respects, but have a recognized difference in others. Of course, an argument from a mere partial resemblance between objects can be worth but little. But very different may be the case where there is a resemblance (sometimes even an identity) in the relation which two objects bear to a third, or to two others, respectively. Understand analogy in this strict and proper sense, and the argument from analogy may have great force. It is exceedingly desirable that good usage should restrict the term to its proper meaning. The point to be guarded is, never to say there is an analogy between objects unless there is a correspondence (identity or similarity) in their relations to something else, however like or however unlike the objects themselves may be. Men are the slaves of words; and unless the thoughtful can discern, avoid, and correct such confusions in the popular use of important terms, reasoning to a popular audience will constantly become increasingly difficult.

It follows that we must carefully avoid the "error of concluding the things in question to be alike because they are analogous"; and that it is very unjust, when a man has argued from the analogy between two objects, to charge him with having represented them as similar. Moreover, the correspondence between the relations of objects which are seen to be analogous must not be presumed to extend to all their relations. Thus, because a just analogy has been discerned between the metropolis of a country and the heart of the animal body, the

[18] Whateley, p. 115.

inference has been sometimes made that its increased size is a disease, —that this may impede some of its most important functions or even be the cause of its dissolution.[19] The question is, In what respects are the relations between the objects similar?

A large proportion of the metaphors we employ rest not upon resemblance but upon analogy. For example, "He is the pillar of the State"; "Paris is the heart of France." All mental and spiritual states and operations are expressed by terms borrowed, by analogy, from the physical; all that we know of the future life, by terms derived from analogous objects or relations in this life. The sense of such metaphorical expressions has been in many cases fixed and defined by usage, so that, as commonly employed, they will not mislead; but whenever we begin to reason upon them, great care must be taken lest we extend the analogy to matters which it does not really embrace. So with the terms used to describe the attributes of God and his relations to his creatures. Thus we call God a Father, and in certain respects Christ reasons from earthly fathers to Him. Yet, if we infer from a father's forgiving his child upon repentance, without satisfaction, that our Heavenly Father will and must forgive us upon repentance, without need of an atonement, we extend the analogy more widely than is warranted. God is a Father, but is also a King, and His government is not a system of imperfect expedients but must consult the requirements of absolute justice.

Has the argument from analogy any positive force? It may certainly afford a probable proof of positive truth. When two objects are observed to be analogous in many important respects, it is assuredly more or less probable that they are also analogous in some other respect not observed. But it is very doubtful whether this can in any case be an absolute proof. Many results of induction, as we have seen above, are simply in a high degree probable; and they become certain only when, besides observing that the instances examined are all similar in a certain respect, we can also discern some cause of that similarity which will operate also in the instances not examined. Now the same thing must hold in the case of analogy. If two objects should correspond in all their relations to certain other objects so far as we can examine, and if we were able to discern some cause of the correspondence such as must produce a like correspondence in other relations not examined, then we might infer with certainty that in any of these other relations they do correspond. In many cases of induction, a

[19] Bishop Copleston, in Whately, p. 116, and pp. 492 ff.

cause or at least an explanation of the common element can be found. We leave it a question whether the same can ever be done in cases of analogy. Still, an argument from analogy will often add its force to that of other proofs and will make a result more or less probable, even where no other proof exists.

But chiefly for negative purposes, in the refutation of objections, is the argument from analogy of frequent and high utility, "like those weapons, which though they cannot kill the enemy, will ward his blows."[20] Butler, in his immortal work, has with great power refuted objections to natural religion by the analogy of nature and objections to revealed religion by the analogy of Providence. We must remember that Butler was arguing against the Deists, who admitted the existence of God as Creator and Moral Governor but brought objections against both natural and revealed religion. If men say it would be unjust in God to punish them for violating His law when they did not believe or did not certainly know that it was His law, we point them to the fact that this holds of physical laws,—that he who takes poison will be killed, even though he did not know or did not believe that it was poison. If they object that God could not with propriety make salvation dependent upon belief of the gospel, when there may be some doubt as to whether the gospel is true, we remind them that bodily life is often dependent upon sending for the physician, though there may be very great doubt as to whether he will understand and remedy the disease; we have to risk life upon a probability or take the consequences. If they object to the doctrine of original sin as incompatible with God's goodness, we point to inherited disease, inherited proclivities to vice, inherited dishonor. And so as to the doctrine of election. From the great inequalities which exist among men as to native physical powers, intellect, moral character, and the influences which have surrounded their childhood as well as their age, we could not with anything more than probability infer as a positive propostion that God would elect some men to be saved and omit others. As a positive argument it would be weakened by the fact that we cannot be certain of a universal analogy between God's operations in the sphere of creation and providence, and his operations in the sphere of grace,[21] and also by the fact that the widest inequalities of earthly life are

[20] Campbell, *Phil. of Rhet.*, p. 76.

[21] This is the fatal objection to much of the late Professor Drummond's argument in his famous book, *Natural Law in the Spiritual World*. He presses analogy to practical identity of law in the two spheres.

slight compared with the difference between salvation and damnation. But when to the doctrine of election as taught in Scripture men offer the objection that it is inconsistent with the divine justice to make such a distinction, we refute the objection by pointing to the immense distinctions which God certainly does make in this life.

When examples are invented to furnish argument (and not merely explanation, ornament, etc.), it must always be the argument from analogy. It is only necessary that the supposed case should be probable. Induction from unreal examples would, of course, be worthless; but merely probable cases may afford an analogy to the matter in hand which will be in a high degree convincing.[22]

The analogy of real and of invented examples is sometimes employed, not to prove but merely to explain or to render interesting.

(4) *Argument from Deduction.* The mental process called "deduction" is that by which we argue or infer from a more general truth. Its object, as involved in the etymology of the word, is to lead the mind down from some general truth to other truth, general or particular. It is obvious that much of all our reasoning is of this character. Syllogistic reasoning is deduction fully and formally expressed and by reason of its rigidity is not often effective in the pulpit; but often in deductive argument one or another of the steps is not fully stated but assumed, either as freely admitted, or so clear as not to need formal statement. Doctrinal preaching has been very largely of this sort, consisting chiefly in deductions or inferences from Scripture. Fully expressed, the preacher's syllogism would run somehow thus:

All Scripture is true and obligatory;
This particular doctrine is Scripture;
Therefore this doctrine is true and obligatory.

The major premise, All Scripture is true and obligatory, is usually and properly taken for granted and not expressed; the main contention in doctrinal preaching commonly is to establish the minor premise that the particular doctrine under consideration is scriptural, either by express statement or by legitimate inference.

Now such deductions must be made with great care. The reply often heard in conversational discussion, "Ah, but that is only an inference of yours," shows the common feeling as to the danger that our inferences will be far less certain than the truths from which we

[22] See Whately, pp. 129 ff.

infer. There is obviously need for great care that the deduction shall be strictly logical and, also, that what the preacher assumes to be a general truth shall be accepted by his hearers. If they are not with him in that, his argument is valueless. But another thing is important. In political economy, it is found that the results deduced by abstract reasoning from general principles must at every step be compared with facts, or they will at length be found to have gone astray from actual truth. And similarly in religious reasoning. We can very seldom take a general truth and make a series of deductions from it, as is done in geometry, and feel safe as to the results. We must constantly compare our conclusions with the facts of existence and with the teachings of Scripture. The love of purely abstract reasoning leads many minds astray as to religious truth. The idea of establishing some truth of religion by "a perfect demonstration" is commonly delusive. Human life is not really controlled by demonstrated truth, as to this world or the next. We must be content with those practical certainties which the conditions of existence allow us to attain; and while constantly drawing inferences, as it is right we should do, we must be content to compare them with fact and Scripture to make sure that they are correct.

Pure reasoning handles ideas and not facts. It is a sort of geometry of intellectual space. This geometry, however, is less certain than the other, the import of signs here being less invariable. Hence the necessity of not coursing entirely through the void, and of descending often to the earth, to set our feet on facts. Otherwise, we run the risk of proving too much, and losing, at length, the sense of reality. At the end of the most sound reasonings, when the reason of the hearer seems to be overcome, something more intimate than logic rises up within him, and protests against your conclusions.[23]

So precarious is the value of deductive reasoning in the pulpit, depending as it does on initial agreement, logical procedure, and the mental habit and mood of the hearer, that its use is becoming less general. Dr. Garvie says:

The deductive reasoning of the syllogism is out of place in the pulpit; and even argument from general principles is, as a rule, less effective than from concrete instances; for men want facts rather than ideas, observation rather than speculation.[24]

[23] Vinet, pp. 174, 175.
[24] *The Christian Preacher*, p. 402.

He adds, however, that there are general principles which are almost universally admitted, "from which the preacher may draw his inferences with the confidence that these will find general assent."

In respect to the whole matter of evidence and belief it is important to bear in mind the relation between belief and disbelief. As regards many truths of Christianity, he who disbelieves them is thereby compelled to believe something which shall take their place. He who staggers at the difficulties, real or alleged, which attach to the Christian evidences, must not forget the difficulties of infidelity. We must believe something, must believe something as to the problems of religion, and if we go away from Christ, "to whom shall we go?"

3. CERTAIN FORMS OF ARGUMENT

We have hitherto considered the principal varieties of argument as to their essential nature. But several of the forms which arguments, whatever be their material and character, often assume would seem to call for mention and explanation.

(1) An argument a priori is an argument from cause to effect, whether it be from a proper physical cause or from something in the general nature of things which necessitates a certain result or from something in the nature of a particular object or person which tends to produce a certain result. Thus deduction (argument from a general truth) is *a priori* when the general truth or major premise is necessitating or producing the conclusion; and induction (argument from particular facts) is a priori when the particulars are shown to account for a known cause, as when in a case of crime particular facts are adduced to establish some motive as a cause.[25]

With reference to the employment of arguments, whether a priori or not, bearing upon the relations of cause and effect, there are ambiguities in the familiar use of language which render necessary two distinctions. First, we must distinguish between logical and physical sequence. For example, "With many of them God was not well pleased; for they were overthrown in the wilderness." The fact that God was not well pleased with them is the logical consequence of their overthrow, being proved from it, but is, so to speak, the physical antecedent, being the cause of it. These two kinds of sequence are very often confounded, and very liable to be, from the fact that we use the same terms "for," "because," "therefore," "consequently,"

---

[25] See Genung, *Practical Rhetoric*, pp. 417 f.

etc., to denote both; yet they may coincide or be opposed to each other or may exist separately. Particularly frequent is the error of presenting that as the cause of something, which is only the proof of it.[26] Secondly, it is important to distinguish between cause and occasion. The inebriate says to the liquor-seller or to his boon companion, "You are the cause of my getting drunk," when these were but the occasion, and the cause was his appetite. To remove some of the occasions for any kind of vicious indulgence will be likely to lessen the evil, but we must not imagine that this is removing the cause.

(2) A posteriori designates an argument from effect to cause, i.e., an argument that "infers a yet unknown cause from observed facts recognized as effects." (See Luke 7:47 and I Cor. 10:5.)

(3) There is a form of argument known as a fortiori, i.e., from the proposition which has the stronger considerations against it to the proposition which has the weaker considerations against it. This shows that something is true in a less probable case, real or supposed, and then insists that much more certainly must it be true in a more probable case. This form of argument is a favorite one with orators and is very often found in the teachings of our Lord and the apostles, where the arguments are chiefly analogical or deductive in nature. "If ye then, being evil, know how to give good things to your children, how much more will your Heavenly Father," etc. "If God so clothe the grass of the field, which today is, and tomorrow is cast into the oven, shall he not much more clothe you, O ye of little faith?" "If they do these things in the green tree, what shall be done in the dry?" (Luke 23:31.) "He that spared not his own Son, but delivered him up for us all, how shall he not with him also freely give us all things?" (Rom. 8:32.) "For if the word spoken by angels was steadfast, and every transgression and disobedience received a just recompense of reward, how shall we escape, if we neglect so great salvation, which at the first began to be spoken by the Lord [i.e., the Lord Jesus], and was confirmed unto us," etc. (Heb. 2:2-4.) "For the time is come that judgment must begin at the house of God: and if it first begin at us, what shall the end be of them that obey not the gospel of God? And if the righteous scarcely be saved, where shall the ungodly and the sinner appear?" (1 Pet. 4:17, 18.)[27] These are but a few examples out of many. They should impress us with the suitableness of such arguments in addressing the popular mind.

[26] See more in Whately, pp. 75 ff.
[27] See Vinet, pp. 193-196.

(4) A form of argument from progressive approach has been pointed out and well illustrated by Whately. This is frequently a good form in which to put the argument from induction. In arguing the being of a God from the general consent of mankind, we observe that in proportion as men have become cultivated and civilized, their ideas of the unity and moral excellence of the Deity have risen higher; that there is a progressive tendency towards the most exalted monotheism, which is hence inferred to be true. Or as regards religious tolerance:

In every age and country, as a general rule, tolerant principles have (however imperfectly) gained ground wherever scriptural knowledge has gained ground. And a presumption is thus afforded that a still further advance of the one would lead to a corresponding advance in the other.[28]

(5) The dilemma presents two assumptions, of such a character that one or the other must be true, and yet whichever is considered true, there will follow, as a deduction, the result proposed. Such was Gamaliel's argument (Acts 5:38, 39.): "If this counsel or this work be of men, it will come to nought: but if it be of God, ye cannot overthrow it." It must be either from men or from God, and in either case the conclusion would be, "Refrain from these men, and let them alone."[29] The dilemma is most commonly but not exclusively employed for the purpose of refutation.

(6) In like manner, the *reductio ad absurdum* (reduction to the absurd) is most frequently but not always used for refutation, that is, in moral reasoning; Euclid uses it very frequently for indirect demonstration. When it is argued that we ought not to send the gospel to the heathen because if they reject it, their guilt and doom will be so much aggravated, we answer that upon that principle, the gospel ought not to be preached to the destitute at home or to anyone, and it is a pity there ever was a gospel. The principle which necessarily leads to such an absurdity must be, by analogy or deduction, in itself erroneous.

(7) The argument *ex concesso*, from something conceded by the opponent or known to be admitted by the persons addressed may be employed as a deductive argument not only for refutation, but also to establish positive truth, when we are satisfied that the thing admitted is really true.

(8) The argument *ad hominem* is legitimately employed only in refutation, and will be explained under that head.

[28] Whately, pp. 104-109.
[29] We are not here inquiring whether Gamaliel's assumptions are correct.

Arguments of different kinds, as to nature or form, will often be combined in one complex argument.

Different speakers will prefer one or another species of argument according to their mental constitution and other circumstances, and a man will be apt to manage best that which he prefers. But this preference should never become exclusive, or it will make the mind one-sided. Besides, it is necessary to consider what species of argument will best suit the mental constitution, intelligence, and tastes of the audience. We should therefore habitually seek to draw arguments from a variety of sources, and throw them into various forms.

4. REFUTATION

(1) It is frequently a sufficient refutation of error to prove the opposite truth; and this is then greatly to be preferred. The error, without mention, just falls away and is thought of no more. But such a course will not always suffice. The arguments of adversaries must often be met, and objections to the truth must still oftener be removed. In controversial sermons, though the preacher may have no actual antagonist, yet there are arguments well known to be used in favor of a different view, and which he must refute, "that he may be able with the sound teaching both to exhort and to refute the gainsayers. For there are many unruly vain talkers and deceivers . . . whose mouths must be stopped" (Titus 1:9-11). Right feelings towards those who are in error will render this necessary task a painful one. But naturally all men take pleasure in conflict.

We are more inclined to refute than to prove, to destroy than to build up. It is more easy, more flattering to self-love, more in accordance with our natural passions. Every one is eloquent in anger; love and peace seldom make men eloquent.[30]

The audience, too, are thus readily aroused. Everybody will run to see a fight. And he who assumes the character of a fearless defender of unpopular doctrines, a martyr-spirit, readily gains from the unthinking a species of sympathy and admiration. These things being so, we must carefully guard against the temptation to assail others where it is not really necessary. We must keep uppermost in our minds the desire to establish truth, and let refutation be strictly and manifestly subordinate.

[30] Vinet, p. 177.

But apart from controversy, and where we have no real antagonist, there will be, in preaching, very frequent occasion for refuting objections to the truth we advocate. It is better, whenever consistent with the known facts, to treat these as the objections not of a caviler but of an honest inquirer. Instead of assailing the supposed objector and attempting to conquer him, let us approach him kindly and seek to win him to the truth.

(2) In moral reasoning one cannot always, as in geometry, give a complete refutation of all objections. Sometimes they are too weak to be refuted. He who does not at once see their absurdity or nothingness can scarcely be made to see it at all. Or you perceive that the objection is really a pretence or a delusion on the part of men who are opposed to the truth on grounds they do not state—perhaps the last refuge of one determined not to yield.

Besides, there are objections to everything. Whately was fond of quoting a saying of Dr. Johnson, "There are objections to a plenum and objections to a vacuum; yet one or the other must be true." The reason for believing any proposition in moral truth consists of the arguments in favor of it, minus the objections, refuted as far as practicable.

It follows that we must not waste time in the refutation of trifling objections, or mention objections which would never trouble the minds of the hearers, and which furnish no sufficient ground for doubting the truth. Hervey well says: "Let obsolete errors alone, and reason against such only as are great, prevalent, and dangerous."[31] Nor should we attempt to refute objections unless we can do so satisfactorily. It is sometimes better to say, "Well, that is an objection to my propostion, I grant; but then the proposition must be true, as the arguments in favor of it show." If the objections or the arguments for a contradictory proposition are really convincing, it is the manifest duty of one who loves truth and would seem especially incumbent on a preacher to acknowledge himself convinced, and so far as this matter goes, to change his ground.

(3) When objections are discussed, they should be stated in full force. This is simply just, and is also obviously good policy.

Express it precisely as you believe it to be in the hearer's mind, so that, listening to your exposition of it, he may say to himself, 'That is exactly

31 *Christian Rhetoric*, p. 240.

my objection; that is precisely my difficulty, and I should wish very much to hear how the preacher will clear it up."[32]

(4) Refutation, whether of an erroneous proposition, or of an objection to the truth, will be accomplished by showing either that the terms are ambiguous, the premises false, the reasoning unsound, or the conclusion irrelevant. Sometimes that which is presented as an objection may be very true, but may not really conflict with the proposition under consideration.

We must know how to take the offensive, and, if possible, turn the objection into a proof. Prolonging the defensive enfeebles us; and to defend ourselves to advantage, we must make the attack. Great preachers have always observed this rule. In the error which we decompose or attack, we should find the very germs of truth.[33]

The Epistle to the Hebrews is an apposite Scripture example of thus turning objection into proof.

(5) Refutation of an error is sometimes strengthened by showing how the error may have originated. Thus an opposer of infant baptism, after disposing of such passages from the New Testament as may have been presented in proof of it, breaks the force of any argument derived from its present and long-continued existence, by pointing out how it may have arisen in the second or third century.

(6) It is often advantageous to have recourse to indirect refutation. The principal species of this, *reductio ad absurdum*, has been already discussed. The argument *ad hominem*, "to the man," can scarcely ever be properly employed to establish positive truth. An appeal to the hearer's peculiar opinions, position, or mode of reasoning, in order to make him believe something, is almost necessarily improper. But in refutation, in dealing with those unreasonable objectors "whose mouths must be stopped," it is perfectly appropriate and may be highly effective. Such is our Lord's argument in Matt. 12:27, "If I by Beelzebub cast out devils, by whom do your children cast them out?" He is not saying that the disciples of the Pharisees really do cast out demons, but simply shutting their mouths by an argument *ad hominem*. So likewise in I Cor. 15:29, "Else what shall they do which are baptized for the dead, if the dead rise not at all? Why are they then baptized for them?" the apostle silences certain objectors to

---

[32] Potter's *Sacred Eloquence*, p. 179. The sermons of the late Canon H. P. Liddon afford instructive illustration of this.
[33] Vinet, p. 179.

the resurrection of the dead by pointing to the superstitious practice encouraged by them, of baptizing living persons in behalf of those who had died unbaptized,—a practice which we know to have existed in the next century. He does not present this as an argument to prove the doctrine of the resurrection true, but simply as an *ad hominem* argument to stop the mouths of unreasonable opponents. And his own condemnation of the superstitious practice need not be stated, for at Corinth it would be well understood. This is one of the points to be guarded in using the form of argument in question; we must not seem to approve the position or practice to which we appeal. We must also take pains to use the argument fairly.

It is sometimes convenient to show that an opponent's premise is wrong, by showing that it "proves too much," i.e., "that it proves, besides the conclusion drawn, another which is manifestly inadmissible."[34]

Irony, as a means of making an opponent or an error ridiculous, is certainly allowable in serious discourse. Recall Elijah's address to the priests of Baal in I Kings 18:27. Though it be not true that "ridicule is the test of truth," it is certainly a very effective means of refuting pretentious falsehood. If a serious subject is involved, the persons refuted by means of irony will of course complain loudly that it is irreverent, and some good people may think likewise; but this only makes it proper to be careful that we do not say anything which really does make a serious subject ridiculous. It is obvious that an ironical passage in a sermon ought, save in very peculiar cases, to be quite brief.[35]

(7) Too elaborate and vehement refutation may sometimes defeat its own design, not only because it arouses deep-seated prejudices, but because, by overwhelming and utterly crushing an error, we may make persons unwilling to acknowledge that an opinion they have entertained is so preposterous, and therefore unwilling to admit that the refutation is just.[36] Thus in condemning the "accommodation" of texts, if one grows indignant and declares the practice to be inexpressibly foolish and wicked, some of those who have indulged in it are repelled and refuse to acknowledge that it is wrong at all.

(8) A successful refutation is apt to carry the sympathies of the hearers, as men usually sympathize with the victorious. And influenced

[34] Whately, p. 182.
[35] Compare Whately, pp. 183-187.
[36] *Ibid.* pp. 193-198.

by this feeling, they often overestimate the extent of the refutation. All the arguments advanced in favor of a proposition may have been refuted, and yet the proposition may be true, on grounds not mentioned. Now, since the preacher is not bent upon personal victory but truth, he should never sophistically manipulate arguments or claim to have fully established a truth or demolished an error when he knows that grave difficulties have been omitted. It is very easy to set up a straw man and proceed to knock him down. Too much preaching is of this debating and demagogic character. Let a man be honest in his choice of arguments, frank in his recognition of serious difficulties, and wise to arrange his reasoning so as to effect clear understanding and stable conviction, remembering always that his interest should be not triumph and praise but truth and life.

5. ORDER OF ARGUMENTS

The order of arguments is scarcely less important than their individual force. The superiority of an army to a mob is hardly greater than the advantage of a well-arranged discourse over a mere mass of scattered thoughts. The question what arrangement is to be preferred in any particular case, must depend upon a variety of circumstances. Here, as everywhere in rhetoric, we can only lay down rules as to what is generally best.

It is obvious that the several distinct arguments should be kept separate. But in the practice of inexperienced reasoners it is not uncommon to see portions of two different arguments combined, and two parts of the same argument separated by the interposition of other matter.

All arguments are used to prove one of three things: that something is true; that it is morally right or fit; that it is profitable or good. The appeal is to truth, duty, or interest.[37]

The consideration which must principally determine the order of arguments is their natural relation to each other.

Some proofs are explained by others, which must be previously exhibited in order to the full effect of the reasoning. Some proofs presuppose others. Some, once more, have great weight if preceded by certain others, and are of little moment unless preceded by them.[38]

Proofs which spring from the very nature of the proposition should

---

[37] Bull, *Preaching and Sermon Construction*, p. 185.
[38] Day, p. 153.

commonly come first, because the exhibition of these will involve a full explanation of the proposition, and "after such an explanation the relevance and force of every other proof will be more clearly seen."[39]

The order of arguments from inference (deduction, induction, analogy) should have regard, first, for their abstractness, the more abstract and general usually being introduced before those that are based on concrete and particular facts, thus moving from the purely intellectual toward an emotional and practical appeal. There are cases, however, as in sermons whose object is primarily intellectual, in which it is better to present first some more tangible and popular proof of a proposition, as from testimony or from example, and then show that this need not surprise us when we look at certain a priori considerations. Secondly, the order of inferences should have regard for the degree of probability which they establish. The more remote or weaker probability should precede the stronger.

The latter is in accordance with the general principle of climax. It is usually best, where nothing forbids, to begin with the weakest arguments used and end with the strongest, thus forming a climax, the power of which is well understood.

But we must sometimes depart from the order which would be fixed by the natural dependence of the arguments upon each other, because of the known disposition of the hearers. If they are unfriendly to our views, it is well to begin with one or more strong arguments, well suited to their minds, so as to command respect and secure attention. We may next, according to the precept of the ancient rhetoricians, throw in the less important matter and close with the strongest of all for the sake of the final impression; or, beginning with the strongest arguments, and adding less important but confirmatory considerations, we may at the close recapitulate in the reverse order and thus gain the effect of a climax.[40]

What position shall be occupied by arguments from Scripture, relatively to those drawn from reason and experience? When a thing has been proven by the Word of God, then for the preacher the question is settled; he cannot admit, he must not seem to admit, that there is any need of further argument. So far, then, it would appear that Scripture proofs should regularly follow others and so constitute the climax of proof. But there will be cases in which this is awkward;

[39] Day, p. 154.
[40] Compare Whately, p. 201.

and besides, to some of the hearers proofs from reason may be more convincing, or proofs from experience more impressive, than the plainest declarations of the Bible. To meet these conditions we may begin with the Scripture teachings and then observe that here, as in fact everywhere, reason and experience are in harmony with the Bible and so proceed to the arguments from those sources. In this way we conform to the hearer's mode of thinking and feeling and end with that which will make the strongest impression on him, without abandoning our own position as to the supremacy of Scripture,—a position which even infidels will feel that the preacher himself ought to maintain. To hold firmly our own ground and yet put ourselves as far as possible in sympathy with the persons we would win is a thing often demanded in preaching and is an achievement worthy of much thoughtful effort.

In what part of a discourse shall the refutation of objections be placed?

When an objection lies against the view advanced in a certain part of the sermon, it should obviously, for the efficiency of that part, be disposed of, though as briefly as possible, before passing to another point.[41]

If objections lie against the general sentiment of the sermon, and they can be refuted independently of the discussion, and briefly, it is advantageous to clear them out of the way before entering upon our line of argument. Where the refutation depends upon our argument or would occupy much time, it must be postponed to the close; and in that case, if some of the objections would be likely to occur at once to the hearer's mind, and interfere, as we proceed, with the effect of our arguments, it is well to intimate at the outset that we propose, before concluding, to notice some objections.

6. GENERAL SUGGESTIONS AS TO ARGUMENT

In concluding the subject of Arguments, it is proper to throw together a few practical hints, though some of them are indirectly involved in statements heretofore made.

(1) Let us note some suggestions as to cultivating the logical faculty of the mind. The importance of developing the reasoning powers is clearly enough involved in all the preceding discussions, yet some

---

[41] Ripley, *Sacred Rhetoric*, p. 81.

suggestions as to how it may be done will perhaps not be useless. Study books on Logic. Study other books logically. There are many books of distinctively argumentative character which it is incumbent on the preacher to read with care. He should make it his business to follow the arguments carefully, criticising, comparing, approving, or refuting, as the case may require. Besides this hard reading, even general literature should for the most part be read observantly, analytically, and thoughtfully. And practice argument frequently. Severe thinking on the preacher's own part is a necessity: let him think subjects through, working out processes of reasoning in his mind. Debate in conversation is very useful, and may be well managed. By all means let the disputant be cool and courteous. The good George Herbert truly says:

> Be calm in arguing; for fierceness makes
> Error a fault, and truth discourtesy.

(2) Let us also note a few suggestions as to the conduct of argument.

(*a*) Do not undertake to prove anything unless you are sure it is true and you are satisfied that you can prove it.

(*b*) Let your argument start from something which the persons addressed will fully acknowledge. This is obviously important, but is often neglected.

(*c*) Use arguments intelligible to your hearers and likely to make an impression on their minds. This must be the rule, though individual hearers may have so low a grade of intelligence that we cannot uniformly keep within their reach. The preacher, of all men, should study the common mind and seek fully to understand not only its forms of expression but, what is still more important, its ways of thinking. He should strive to put himself in the position of his hearers and consider how this or that argument will appear from their point of view.[42]

For this is the reason why uneducated men have more power of persuasion among the rabble than the educated have, just as the poets say [Euripides has such a saying] that the uneducated are in the estimation of the rabble finer speakers. For the one class say what is matter of common knowledge and of a general character; but the others speak from their own knowledge and say the things that lie close to their hearers.[43]

[42] In these respects much may be learned from the critical observation of able "stump-speakers" and jury-lawyers.

[43] Aristotle, *Rhet*. II., xxii. 2.

How true it is now of many able and learned preachers that they can speak only of generalities, belonging to the common stock of human knowledge, and know not how to fall in with the modes of thought which are familiar and agreeable to the masses. That this last can be done without the sacrifice of truly profound thought or the violation of refined taste has been shown by some ministers of every age and country, and most conspicuously by that Great Teacher of whom it was said—O exalted eulogium!—"the common people heard him gladly."

(*d*) In general, depend principally on Scripture arguments, and prefer those which are plain and unquestionable. When we engage in religious controversy before a popular audience, we shall usually do well to say but little concerning that great mass of learned matter about which the people cannot personally judge, and rely mainly on common-sense views of the plain teachings of Scripture. And apart from controversy, let us use chiefly arguments from Scripture. This is common ground between us and our hearers. In general, no other arguments can come so appropriately from us or be so effective with the people. And in the general principles, the many special precepts, and the immense number of living examples, good and evil, to be found in the Bible, we have a boundless store of material for argument.

(*e*) Do not try to say everything, but select a suitable number of the most available arguments. It is true that sometimes the judicious combination of many comparatively slight arguments may have a great effect. "Singly they are light," say Quintilian, "but taken together they do hurt, though not as by a thunderbolt, yet as by hail."[44] Still, it is a very common fault to multiply arguments to excess. With sore travail of the mind the preacher has brought all these into existence, and surveying them with parental affection, he thinks each of them too good to be abandoned. But how many thousand men did Gideon dismiss that he might conquer with three hundred? Where there are so many arguments, either the discourse must be excessively long, or they must be too hurriedly presented. Where it is really necessary to present many arguments, let them be skillfully grouped, and let the more obvious be briefly stated, in order to pause and dwell upon those which demand special attention.

(*f*) Avoid formality. Have the reality of argument, but as little as possible of its merely technical forms and phrases.

(*g*) As to the style of argument, the chief requisites are, of course,

[44] *Inst. Orat.* V. 12, 3.

clearness, precision, and force. But a simple elegance is usually compatible with these. And where the subject is exalted and inspiring, and the speaker's whole soul is on fire, some great thunderbolt of argument may blaze with an overpowering splendor.[45]

[45] Compare Quintilian, V. 14, 33.

CHAPTER III

ILLUSTRATION

STRICTLY speaking, one would not call illustration a distinct element of the sermon co-ordinate with explanation and argument, or with persuasion, which will be studied in the next chapter. Its function is solely auxiliary, coming to the support now of one and now of another of the principal elements. As a means of explaining, proving, or awakening emotion, it would fall under the heads of explanation, argument, and application; as a means of adornment, it would belong to elegance of style. But as the same illustration often subserves different ends, and as the proper handling of illustrations is a matter of great practical importance, it seems best to give the subject a separate discussion.

To "illustrate," according to etymology, is to throw light (or lustre) upon a subject,—a very necessary function of preaching. The preacher cannot rely upon his gift of lucidity and power in exposition, reasoning and persuading; he must make truth interesting and attractive by expressing it in transparent words and setting it in the light of revealing metaphor and story and picture. "The necessity of illuminating the sermon properly is found in the mental attitude of the people. Whether we like it or not, most of us preach to the 'moving picture mind.' It is the mind accustomed to images, pictures, scenes, rapidly moving. It certainly is not accustomed to deep thinking or long, sustained argument. Current magazines, billboards, novels, drama, rapid transit, all add to this popular method of visual thinking. We as ministers may not approve of the daily fare of the people; we may regret their inability to pursue abstract logic; we may wish them to prefer theoretical reasoning. But, whatever our wishes, we must recognize that they regard thinking which is not imaginary and concrete as dull and uninteresting."[1] Illustration is a psychological necessity.

---

[1] Bryan, *The Art of Illustrating Sermons*, p. 17. One of the many values of this book is that it shows the significant relation of illustration to every part of the sermon.

ILLUSTRATION   197

I. VARIOUS USES OF ILLUSTRATION

(1) Perhaps the principal use of illustrations is to explain. This they do either by presenting an example of the matter in hand, a case in point, or by presenting something similar or analogous to it which will make the matter plain.

(2) But illustrations are also very frequently employed to prove. This is done in some rare cases by presenting an example which warrants an induction; commonly, it is an argument from analogy. In Romans, chapters 6 and 7, the apostle introduces three illustrations, as showing the absurdity of supposing that justification by faith will encourage to sin: believers are dead to sin, and risen to another life; they have ceased to be the slaves of sin and become the slaves (so to speak) of holiness, of God; they have ceased to be married to the law and are married to a new husband, Christ, to whom they must now bear fruit. Each of these is not merely explanatory of the believer's position but involves an argument from analogy. So with the olive tree in chapter 11. We have heretofore seen that arguments from analogy are most frequently and most safely employed in refutation, and that, when used to establish positive truth, they demand very great care, lest we infer more than they actually prove.

The fact that an illustration may furnish proof at the same time that it serves for explanation, ornament, etc., calls for special attention. Some analogy may be so ornamental, so amusing, or pathetic, as to make us overlook the fact that it has of right an argumentative force also; and some comparison may be so beautiful an ornament as to be allowed force in the way of proof when in reality it is a mere simile founded on resemblance and presents no true analogy, and thus no argument.[2] We should look closely at illustrations employed for other purposes and see whether they also contain an argument.

(3) Illustrations are valuable as an ornament. To make truth attractive and pleasing is legitimate and desirable, but one must make sure that a beautiful illustration really adorns the truth that is preached and does not itself become the center of interest. In the Mammoth Cave of Kentucky the guide throws colorful flares upon ledges of rock, not to display the flares but to reveal the grandeur of that natural wonder. The use of illustration for this purpose, as to kind and amount, must be governed by the general principles

---

[2] Compare Whately, pp. 164-166.

which pertain to elegance of style.[3] Those who find themselves much inclined to the use of ornamental illustration should exercise a rigorous self-control, and so cultivate their taste that it will discard all but the genuinely beautiful. Those whose style is barren of such ornament should seek after it, not by tying on worn and faded artificial flowers but by encouraging the subject to blossom, if that be at all its nature.

(4) Illustrations are an excellent means for arousing the attention. Often they will happily serve this purpose in the introduction to the sermon, securing at the outset the interest of the audience. But perhaps they are in this respect even more serviceable in the progress of the discourse, particularly if the attention has been somewhat strained by argument or description and begins to flag. They thus, as Beecher says,[4] afford variety and rest to the mind; and this is very important.

(5) They also frequently serve to render a subject impressive, by exciting some kindred or preparatory emotion. Thus, in the parable of the Prodigal Son, the natural pathos of the story itself touches the heart and prepares it to be all the more impressed by the thought of God's readiness to welcome the returning sinner. Most preachers use illustrations very freely for this purpose. The story or description may have some value for explanation, proof, or ornament, but their chief object in employing it is to arouse the feelings. This is lawful and useful, provided the occasion be seized to plant in the softened soil the seeds of divine truth. But we sometimes hear stories told, and at great length, which purport to be illustrations of sacred truth and yet have no other effect, and to all appearance no other design, than to awaken a transient and aimless emotion.

(6) Finally, they greatly assist the memory of the hearer in retaining the lesson of the sermon. Good illustrations are far more easily remembered than bright sayings and trains of argument. It is a not uncommon experience with preachers to find that their finest sentences and profoundest observations easily slip the memory, while some apparently trivial anecdote or illustration remains. If these can be made so apt as necessarily to recall the argument or train of thought, so much the better.

The importance of illustration in preaching is beyond expression. In numerous cases it is our best means of explaining religious truth, and often to the popular mind our only means of proving it. Orna-

[3] Compare Brooks, p. 175.
[4] Yale Lectures, First Series, pp. 156, 160.

ILLUSTRATION 199

ment, too, has its legitimate place in preaching, and whatever will help us to move the hard hearts of men is unspeakably valuable. Besides, for whatever purpose illustration may be specially employed, it often causes the truth to be remembered. Sometimes, indeed, even where its force as an explanation of proof was not at first fully apprehended, the illustration, particularly if it be a narrative, is retained in the mind until subsequent instruction or experience brings out the meaning. Such was frequently the case with the first hearers of our Lord's parables. In preaching to children and to the great mass of adults illustration is simply indispensable, if we would either interest, instruct, or impress them, while good illustration is always acceptable and useful to hearers of the highest talent and culture. The example of our Lord decides the whole question; and the illustrations which so abound in the records of his preaching ought to be heedfully studied by every preacher, as to their source, their aim, their style, and their relation to the other elements of his teaching. Among the Christian preachers of different ages who have been most remarkable for affluence and felicity of illustration, there may be mentioned Chrysostom, Jeremy Taylor, Christmas Evans, Chalmers, Guthrie, Spurgeon, Richard Fuller, and Beecher.[5]

2. SOURCES OF ILLUSTRATION [6]

Illustration of religious truth may be drawn from the whole realm of existence and of conception. It might seem idle to make any classification of the sources, but there are two reasons for doing so. The preacher may thereby be stimulated to seek such materials in directions which he has comparatively neglected, and the attempt at classification will furnish the occasion for some useful suggestions in passing.

(1) *Observation.* It is pre-eminently important that the teacher of religion should be a close observer, partly that he may know how to adapt religious instruction to the real character of his hearers, and the actual conditions of their life, but also that he may be able to draw

---

[5] Of works discussing the subject of illustration, see Gowan, *Homiletics*, Chap. X; Bryan, *The Art of Illustrating Sermons*; C. R. Brown, *The Art of Preaching*, Chap. V.; Blackwood, *The Fine Art of Preaching,* Chap. VIII; Ozora S. Davis, *Principles of Preaching*, Chap. IX. Beecher has some excellent hints in the seventh lecture of his first series of Yale Lectures; and Spurgeon, in his third series of Lectures to my Students, on the Art of Illustration, discusses the whole subject in his own racy, commonsense fashion.

[6] Compare Beecher, p. 169; and Spurgeon, Lect. IV. p. 54 ff.

from that inexhaustible store of illustration which lies everywhere open to the man who has eyes to see and ears to hear.

Nature teems with analogies to moral truth; and we should not merely accept those which force themselves on our attention but should be constantly searching for them. Besides those analogies which are embodied in our familiar metaphors and those which belong to the common stock of illustration, there are others, almost without number, which every thoughtful observer may perceive for himself; and here, as elsewhere, what is even relatively original has thereby an augmented power. The writings of John Foster are particularly rich in such analogies, and his *Memoir* shows that he habitually sought for them and systematically recorded all that he found. Several of our Lord's most impressive illustrations are drawn from his own close observation of nature, as, for example, the lily, the mustard seed, the birds. And notice that although these are all so stated as to be very beautiful, he employs them for higher ends, for explanation or for argument. There is here an important lesson, for preachers who derive illustration from nature are too apt to follow the poets in making it chiefly ornamental.

A still richer field, if possible, is human life, with all its social relations and varied callings and pursuits, its business usages, mechanical processes, etc., and with all its changing experiences. Here a man's personal experience will blend with his observation of others. And he who really and thoughtfully observes life, spreading in its immense variety all around, and embracing, too, the world within us, can surely never be at a loss for illustration. Chrysostom, though somewhat ascetical in his views, and though a diligent student, overflows with allusions to real life, of which he had observed much while serving as deacon and presbyter in the great city of Antioch, before going to Constantinople. Beecher, who lived for years in the midst of a continent and a nation condensed within a few square miles, shows that he diligently carried out the lesson which he declares himself to have learned from Ruskin, to "keep his eyes and ears open." He watched the ships and the sailors, acquainted himself with the customs, good and bad, of commercial life, curiously inspected a great variety of mechanical processes, often visited his farm and closely observed agricultural operations and the various phases of rural life, was constantly seeing and hearing what occurred in his home and in other homes that he visited, supplemented his own observation by inquiring of others as to all the manifold good and evil of the

ILLUSTRATION 201

great world that surged around him, and everywhere and always was asking himself, till that became the fixed habit of his mind, What is this like? What will this illustrate? Hence the boundless variety and the sparkling freshness of his illustrations, and these formed a notable element of his power as a preacher. Spurgeon, though perhaps not equal to Beecher in this respect, was also a close observer in many and various directions; and he drew far more than Beecher from reading.

It should not be forgotten that much of the choicest illustration is derived from the commonest pursuits and the most familiar experiences of life, and a man may excel in this respect without living in New York or London. The great mass of our Lord's illustrations are drawn from ordinary human life. Of agricultural operations, we find reference to sowing wheat and various circumstances which help or hinder its growth, to harvesting, winnowing, and putting in barns, to the management of fig trees and vineyards, and to bottling the wine. In domestic affairs, he speaks of building houses, various duties of servants and stewards, leavening bread, baking, and borrowing loaves late at night, of dogs under the table, patching clothes and their exposure to moths, lighting lamps, and sweeping the house. As to trade, etc., he mentions the purchase of costly pearls, finding hidden treasure, money intrusted to servants as capital, lending on interest, creditors and debtors, imprisonment for debt, and tax-gatherers. Among social relations, he tells of feasts, weddings, and bridal processions, the judge and the widow who had been wronged, the rich man and the beggar, the good Samaritan. Of political affairs, he alludes to kings going to war; and the parable of the Ten Pounds (Luke 19:11ff.) corresponds in every particular to the history of Archelaus as enacted during our Lord's childhood. The Prodigal Son is a series of the most beautiful pictures of real life. And who can think without emotion of Jesus standing in some market place and watching children at their sports, from which he afterwards drew a striking illustration? All these form but a part of the illustrative material which, in our brief records of his teaching, we find him deriving from the observation of human life, and in nearly every case from matters familiar to all. The lesson is obvious, but it should be pondered long; and we should not fail to remark the sweet dignity with which these common things are clothed; not one of our Lord's illustrations is ludicrous.

The observation of children is particularly profitable to a religious teacher. They reveal much of human nature, and their words and ways are usually interesting to adults. But let us never repeat a child's striking sayings in its own presence or in any wise flatter children, as preachers sometimes do. The recollections of one's own childhood grow increasingly interesting as life advances; but we must be careful not to exaggerate and glorify those recollections in employing them, not to fall into egotism, not to imagine that these perhaps trifling matters will be sure to interest others as much as ourselves.

Narrations of actual experience of the religious life, whether our own or that of others known to us, are apt to be generally interesting, and will often, as cases in point, furnish admirable illustration. The great revival preachers usually have a multitude of such narratives, drawn from their observation at other places, and they often use them with great effect. This is one secret of the power possessed by some comparatively ignorant preachers in secluded districts. They tell their own experience freely and do not shrink from mentioning persons even in an adjoining neighborhood, whose cases they can make instructive.

(2) *Pure Invention.* It is perfectly lawful to invent an illustration, even in the form of a story, provided that it possesses verisimilitude and provided that we either show it to be imaginary or let nothing depend upon the idea that it is real. Some of our Lord's parables are in this sense fictitious. It is shown, in one case, by the very form of the expression, "The sower went forth to sow." When we use imagined illustration as affording an argument, great care must be taken to make it fair. It is very common for controversial speakers or writers to "suppose a case" and suppose it of such a kind as just to suit their purpose, without due regard to fairness. "If lions were the sculptors, the lion would be uppermost." Imagined illustrations for explanation or ornament are frequently too formal or elaborate. "As when some giant oak," etc., etc. "Suppose there were a man, . . . and suppose, . . . and suppose," etc. We all know how such things are done.

(3) *Science.* Besides what is derived from our own observation of nature and of human life, there is an immense fund of illustration in science, which collecting the results of a far wider observation, classifies and seeks to explain them. With the vast growth of physical science in our day and the extensive diffusion of some knowledge of its leading departments, it becomes increasingly appropriate that preachers should draw illustration from that source. In this way, too, they will most effectually counteract the efforts of some infidel men

ILLUSTRATION 203

of science, and some unwise teachers of religion, to bring Christianity and science into an appearance of hostility. It is much better, both for this purpose and for others, that a preacher should strive to be well acquainted with one or a few departments of physical science than that he should dip lightly into many.

Two especial difficulties beset the use of scientific illustration. It has been so common to make astronomy, geology, etc. the occasion for marvelous flights of would-be eloquence that many persons shrink from all allusion to such subjects as savoring of mere declamation. But one highly objectionable extreme should not drive us to the other. It is surely possible to use such illustrations in a direct and quiet fashion; and if now and then they really kindle the imagination and excite emotion, in such cases it will be natural and the effect will be good. The other difficulty is that much of the finest scientific illustration demands more knowledge of science than the great mass of hearers really possess. Now an illustration which would be particularly acceptable and profitable to a few may sometimes be employed, provided we introduce it with some quiet remark, not saying that most persons are unacquainted with this subject, but that such persons as happen to have paid attention to such or such a matter will remember, etc. Then no one will complain of our alluding to a topic of which he is ignorant. Or it may be proper to give the information necessary in order to appreciate the illustration, provided we can do so in few words and without anything that looks like display. It is certainly lawful to spend as much time upon describing a phenomenon or explaining a principle of nature which will afford good illustration as we should spend upon telling an anecdote for the same purpose, if only the description or explanation be made intelligible and interesting to all. Some sermons are but scientific lectures with a religious application. And it is of extreme importance that the preacher should use scientific illustrations intelligently. To betray his ignorance by employing some outmoded scientific theory or by misrepresenting scientific truth is disastrous.

Besides astronomy and geology, physics and chemistry, other branches of science are coming to be freely used. Antony of Padua, the most popular preacher of the Middle Ages, drew many illustrations from the habits of animals, real or reported. Whately was very fond of illustrations from zoölogy, and James Hamilton from botany. The various departments of medical science have always been thus employed. There is an obvious and always interesting analogy between bodily disease or healing and that of the soul; and Bacon has noticed that the figurative language of Scripture is drawn with especial frequency from agriculture and medicine. Psychology, in its several departments, is often itself the theme of pulpit discussion, but is also rich in illustration of distinctively religious themes. Social science will add much to what is furnished by our own observation of life; and the science of law is of great value, not only from its connection with the revealed law but as illustrating the doctrines of atonement and justification.

(4) *History*. Preachers have always made much use of illustration from history. The field is in itself boundless but is in practice greatly limited by the popular lack of extensive acquaintance with it. As in the case of science, we may sometimes skillfully introduce what is familiar to but a few and may often give, briefly, without ostentation and in an interesting manner, the requisite information. Great as is the value for our purposes of science and the attention now bestowed upon it, we must not forget that history, from its narrative and descriptive character and its human interest, has a peculiar and almost unrivaled charm. And in some respects this is especially true of biography, both general and religious. Here there is the interest which always attaches to a person, to an individual human life. And biographical facts can often be more readily stated than those of general history. Early English preachers drew nearly all their historical and biographical illustration from ancient history. Jeremy Taylor, for example, greatly abounds with this. In our day more modern sources are, of course, chiefly in request, and ancient writers are again comparatively a fresh field, particularly if one will take them at first hand and not simply borrow from other preachers or from recent works on ancient history. Thus Herodotus and Plutarch, even in a translation, may be used with great advantage; and so as to Josephus, whose works are now by most preachers unwisely neglected. Spurgeon often used illustrations from the lives of devout men; and Richard Fuller employed all manner of historical and biographical incident, both secular and religious, with rare felicity and power.

All preachers derive illustration from the news of the day. Some carry this too far, warranting the reproach that they "get the text from the Bible, and the sermon from the newspapers." But it is a grave mistake if any are thereby repelled into avoiding a source of illustration so fresh in its interest, and so much more generally familiar to the audience than either science or history. By judiciously alluding

ILLUSTRATION 205

to all suitable matters of recent occurrence, whether recorded in the newspapers or happening in our own community, we may render the sermon more interesting and may at the same time have opportunity to throw in useful practical remarks about many questions of right and wrong.[7] The danger is that we shall set the people's minds a-going upon the matters which occupy them every day to the neglect of our sacred theme. This may be avoided if, on the one hand, we take care not in intermingle an excessive amount of such allusion, and, on the other hand, to keep it strictly subordinate, in our own feelings and in the method of introduction, to the religious aim of the discourse. If not thus subordinate, then the most interesting allusion will be the worst illustration.

Anecdotes, literally things unpublished, originally denoted interesting matters, chiefly historical and biographical incidents, gathered from unpublished manuscripts of ancient authors and thrown into a miscellaneous collection. Though now more widely used, the term is still most properly applied to stories of particular or detached incidents or occurrences of an interesting nature, and especially of what one has himself observed or has drawn from oral sources. These are a valuable means of illustration, which some preachers employ excessively or in bad taste but which others ought to employ much more largely than they do. He who feels that his style would be degraded by introducing an anecdote, may profitably inquire whether his style be not too stilted or, at any rate, too monotonous in its sustained elevation for popular discourse. Let anecdotes be certainly true if we present them as true, and let them be told without exaggeration or "embellishment." Let them not be ludicrous,—though, a slight tinge of delicate humor is sometimes lawful,—not trivial, and especially not tedious. And as illustration is in general a subordinate thing in preaching, and that which is subordinate should rarely be allowed to become prominent, a preacher should avoid such a multiplication of anecdotes in the same sermon or in successive sermons as would attract very special attention. A greater freedom, both as to amount and kind, is admissible in platform-speaking than in those more grave discourses which are usually called sermons.

(5) *Literature and Art.* Even when science and history have been excluded, literature, ancient and modern, in prose and in verse, covers an immense field and offers a vast store of illustrative material. Sug-

---

[7] See Brooks' *Lectures*, p. 176. He says the illustration drawn from current events "brings in its own associations and prejudices. It is too alive."

gestive, pleasing, or impressive sentiments, and striking expressions may be quoted, and allusion made to well-known literary works and characters, whenever it will really help to render the discourse interesting and useful. Quotations of poetry, though made by some men in offensive excess, are employed by very many with admirable effect; and while a few need to check their exuberance in this respect, the great mass of ministers should stimulate themselves to observe and retain more largely and to use more freely any appropriate poetical quotations. No one can have failed to notice how often quotations from hymns, particularly when they are familiar, add greatly to the interest and impressiveness of a sermon. Spurgeon often uses these very effectively. The *Pilgrim's Progress*, with its strong sense and homely simplicity, its poetic charm and devotional sweetness, is so rich in the choicest illustration that every preacher ought to make himself thoroughly familiar with it and to refresh his knowledge again and again through life. Fables are so often alluded to in common conversation that we scarcely notice it, and the occasions are very numerous in which they might be usefully employed in preaching. An author of distinction and of wide attainments and experience of life remarked some years ago that, in his judgment, next to the Bible and Shakespeare, the most instructive book in the world was Æsop's *Fables*. Even nursery rhymes, though not often exactly appropriate in regular sermons, have been employed to good purpose in speaking to children.

Proverbs are a singularly valuable means of stating truth forcibly and impressively. True, they usually represent an imperfect generalization, and are one-sided so that almost any proverb can be matched by an opposite one. Yet in exhibiting particular aspects of truth, in impressing particular points, they have great power, especially with the popular mind. "Great preachers for the people, such as have found their way to the universal heart of their fellows, have been ever great employers of proverbs."[8] Our Lord once expressly employs a proverb and repeatedly uses expressions which appear to have been proverbial. This was one of the various ways in which he sought to strike the common mind, and impress the popular heart. The preacher should study the Proverbs of Solomon, and often quote them. The proverbs of our own country and language have, of course, peculiar force with us; but those of other countries will have freshness and, if readily

---

[8] See Trench on the *Lessons in Proverbs*. There is a good deal about both fables and parables in Spurgeon's *Art of Illustration*; and quite a collection in his *Salt Cellars*.

ILLUSTRATION 207

intelligible as well as striking, they may be very effective. All nations have numerous proverbs; and besides among peoples more nearly related to ourselves, they especially abound among the Hindus, the Chinese, and some African tribes. It would sometimes be profitable to read slowly over lists of proverbs, considering what religious truth this and this will illustrate, and collecting such or making reference to them on the margin, and associating them in our mind with the particular truths to which they relate. Proverbs are often humorous; and while the coarse or ridiculous should be avoided, we may remember that

a thousand beauties are snatched from the very verge of propriety,— while many humdrum commonplace men deserve the rebuke of Quintilian: "His excellence was that he had no fault, and his fault that he had no excellence." A sermon had better have too much salt in it than too little.

Besides proverbs proper, there are many sage maxims which are often repeated in conversation, and many striking sayings which may be quoted from the Fathers, the Old English divines, and others.

Illustration is also frequently drawn from works of art, especially from pictures. These are constantly used in books under the name of "illustrations" of the narrative or treatise and never fail, when good, to interest every class of readers; and in like manner the description of pictures and statues may be very effectively used in a sermon. Such a description should, of course, be brief and free from any appearance of display.

(6) *Scripture.* The Scriptures present materials of illustration suited to every legitimate subject of preaching and belonging to almost every one of the above-mentioned classes, especially history and biography, poetry and proverbs, and all manner of pointed sayings. Several causes combine to make this the best of all the sources of illustration. The material is to some extent familiar to all, and thus the illustration will be readily intelligible. Again, this material will be much more impressive than any other because of its sacredness and its known and felt relation to ourselves. Besides, the frequent use of Scripture illustration serves to revive and extend the knowledge of Scripture among the hearers.

Every preacher should most diligently draw from this source. And to this end, besides keeping on hand some book or other particular portion of the Bible for thorough study, preachers should continue through life the rapid but attentive reading of the whole Bible, that its facts and sayings may be kept fresh in their minds and readily present themselves for use.

3. CAUTIONS AS TO THE EMPLOYMENT OF ILLUSTRATION

(1) Do not use every illustration that occurs to you or seek after them for their own sake. The question is whether this or that will really conduce to the objects of the discourse, will really explain or prove what is under discussion or make it more interesting and impressive. Some men get a general notion that illustration is a good thing and that it is their duty to employ it, and they laboriously bring forward so-called "illustrations" which really effect nothing and are therefore but useless lumber. Others, who have a fertile fancy or a well-stocked memory, while wanting in genuine culture and good taste, will excessively multiply or expand their illustrations. They forget that command of illustration, like command of words, involves not only copious production but judicious selection and real adaptation.

(2) Seek for great variety of illustration, both in your preaching in general and in each sermon. Do not, for example, have too many anecdotes to the exclusion of the other kinds. Watch yourself as to this, and pay attention to the hints of good critics. The preachers who have greatly excelled in the use of illustration, as Guthrie, Spurgeon, Beecher, have not failed to observe this point.

(3) As a general rule, it is not well to talk about illustrating but just to illustrate. If you can throw the light vividly on your subject, it will seldom be necessary to give notice beforehand that you are about to do so.

(4) Carefully avoid turning attention away from the subject illustrated to the illustration itself. This is obviously a very grave fault, but it is often committed. Illustrations stated at great length, with high-wrought imagery and polished phrase, such as Guthrie frequently employs, will almost inevitably have this effect; but sometimes, as in the case of Chalmers, they may be so felicitous and applied with such passionate earnestness that we at last forget everything in the subject illustrated. So many hearers are caring mainly for entertainment that it is a sad thing if we divert their minds from some subject they ought to consider to the curious or admiring examination of the mere

ILLUSTRATION 209

apparatus by which we throw light on it.[9] It is said of a Spanish artist that in painting the Last Supper he put on the table some chased silver cups so beautiful that they were the first thing in the picture to attract admiring notice. Observing this, he took his brush and effaced them, that nothing might hinder the beholder from looking at Jesus.

From this whole discussion it will be evident that a preacher should be constantly accumulating the materials of illustration. Whether he had better jot down all that occur to him, keep a scrapbook, or rely mainly on his memory will depend on his mental constitution and habits; but neither method should be employed to the total neglect of the other.[10]

[9] This fault occurs very frequently in speaking to children. There is a mere succession of stories or pictures, which teach nothing, impress nothing, and, save as idle entertainment, are nothing.

[10] See Davis, *Principles of Preaching,* pp. 243-246. Davis lays down ten guiding principles for the use of illustrations which deserve careful study: (1) economy and restraint, (2) unity of central idea, (3) holding to one central theme, (4) subordination, (5) blending, (6) dignity and strength, (7) beauty, (8) freshness, (9) picturesqueness and vividness, and (10) accuracy.

CHAPTER IV

APPLICATION

THE application in a sermon is not merely an appendage to the discussion or a subordinate part of it, but is the main thing to be done. Spurgeon says, "Where the application begins, there the sermon begins." We are not to speak before the people but to them and must earnestly strive to make them take to themselves what we say. Daniel Webster once said and repeated it with emphasis, "When a man preaches to me, I want him to make it a personal matter, a personal matter, a personal matter!"

Preaching is essentially personal encounter, in which the preacher's will is making a claim through the truth upon the will of the hearer. If there is no summons, there is no sermon. Certainly this is true of evangelistic preaching. But, as Dr. H. H. Farmer says,

even in the instruction, edification, and confirming of the saints the note of claim and summons should not be absent, though it will make itself felt in a different way. Almost everything depends on the mood and intention of the preacher and on his whole conception of his task. If his message has been prepared in the right way, with a clear and serious perception of the "I-thou" relationship which must lie at its heart if it is to be real preaching, the note of summons is certain to get through, even though nothing is said about it in explicit terms. It must be realized that in this sphere of our life instruction without this note does not instruct, edification does not edify, confirmation does not confirm.[1]

In application this note of summons is made articulate.

In the chapter on Conclusion[2] application was discussed briefly as comprising a large part of the conclusion. But the two are not identical. Application may and often should appear in other parts also. As an end it properly involves every element of the sermon and dominates the whole process of preaching. As illustration is the servant of all, application is the master of all. The sermon is always moving within the purpose of making truth vitally effective. In many

[1] *The Servant of the Word*, p. 67.
[2] See p. 127.

sermons, especially when the discussion is a close-knit unity, the conclusion is the natural place for application. In such cases, let it be said in passing, too much formality should be avoided. In England two centuries ago, from the passion for logical analysis in preaching, it was common to make a great number of inferences in concluding, sometimes twelve, sometimes twenty, and sometimes fifty. These were called uses: (1) of information, (2) of instruction, (3) of examination, (4) of reproof, (5) of encouragement, (6) of comfort, (7) of exhortation, etc.[3]

The sermons of Jonathan Edwards, with all their power, show the evil of having always a regular "application," formally announced or indicated. Often a brief and informal application is best. Often, too, it is better not to reserve the application for the latter part of the discourse, but to apply each thought as it is presented, provided they all conspire towards a common result.

Application is not a perfect word for this element of the sermon. Some prefer the term "persuasion," but if "application" is too limited in one direction, "persuasion" is limited in another. It is perhaps better, therefore, to use the more familiar term and give it a technical connotation. As here employed, then, the application includes three distinct things: (1) application proper, in which we show the hearer how the truths of the sermon apply to him; (2) practical suggestions as to the best mode and means of performing the duty urged; and (3) persuasion in the sense of moral and spiritual appeal for right response. Or, more succinctly, it is (1) focalizing the claims of truth, (2) suggesting ways and means, and (3) persuading unto vital response.

I. FOCALIZING THE CLAIMS OF TRUTH

Application, in the strict sense, is that part, or those parts, of the discourse in which we show how the subject applies to the persons addressed, what practical instructions it offers them, what practical demands it makes upon them.

Such application may draw the meaning down only to certain areas of life, leaving more particular application to the individual. This was largely the practice of Dr. Alexander Maclaren, whose modesty and respect for men's right and ability to see and choose for themselves, as well as his belief that truth, understood and accepted,

[3] Robinson's edition of Claude, II, 457.

would speak for itself inwardly through conscience, restrained him from drawing too sharp a focus. That, however, is not for the ordinary people of this world. The finger must often be put on the very spot where ailment is. If truth is not focalized sharply enough to "spot light" some particular principle, or habit, or practice, or motive, or sentiment, or prejudice, or disposition, or need, it will not be very effective. And sometimes it must be made sharp enough to burn. Sometimes this is effected by means of what are called "remarks," that is, certain noticeable matters belonging to or connected with the subject, to which attention is now especially directed. These should always be of a very practical character, bearing down upon the feelings and the will. And the remarks must not diverge in various directions and become like the untwisted cracker of a whip but should have a common aim and make a combined impression. In sermons upon historical subjects, it is lawful to bring out several distinct lessons, but these had better be pretty closely related. It is obvious that while some subjects may be applied to the congregation as a whole, others will be applicable only to particular classes or will have to be applied to distinct classes separately, as converted and unconverted, old and young. But it is not necessary, as some preachers seem to imagine, always to make some kind of application to the unconverted, or some remark to them in conclusion. A sermon addressed throughout to pious people will often specially instruct and impress the unconverted. What men apply to themselves, without feeling that it was aimed at them, is apt to produce the greatest effect. It is never judicious to make an application to any particular individual, and very rarely to a small and well-defined class. What is popularly called "hitting at" some person or some few persons will almost always do more harm than good.

Application also frequently takes the form of inferences. This form of making application of the subject ought to be in two directions carefully limited. Nothing should be presented as an inference which does not logically and directly follow from the subject discussed. The other limit is that no inferences should be drawn in applying a subject which are not of practical importance. It is not a preacher's business to exhibit all the matters which may be inferred from his discussion, as if he were attempting an exercise in logic, but only to draw out those which will appeal to the feelings and the will of his hearers and move them to action. Of course, in other parts of the sermon than the application these merely logical inferences may be allowable and instructive.

Again, application is often best presented in the form of lessons. This term implies that the practical teachings of the subject are more thoroughly brought out and more fully applied than would be done in mere "remarks," while it does not restrict the application to those teachings which appear as logical "inferences" from the propositions established. This way of applying the truths of the discourse would seem, therefore, to have some advantages over the other methods. These "lessons" must, of course, be thoroughly practical, and must not be too formal or have a magisterial air. The preacher is not a dignitary, speaking ex cathedra to his inferiors. He had better speak, in general, of lessons which "we" may learn.

Of course, there are applications which it would not be proper to designate by any one of these terms, remarks, inferences, or lessons. Nor is it necessary, or even advisable always, to use these somewhat formal phrases, even where they are appropriate. The preacher must, in the mode of presenting applications, study naturalness, simplicity, and variety.

2. SUGGESTING WAYS AND MEANS

Another way of making application consists of suggestions as to the best means and methods of performing the duty or duties enjoined in the sermon. To give good practical suggestions is a task often calling for experience and the fruits of thoughtful observation, and sometimes demanding delicate tact, but is certainly, when well managed, a most important part of the preacher's work. When one has argued some general duty, as that of family or private prayer, of reading the Bible, or of relieving the needy and distressed, it is exceedingly useful to add hints as to the actual doing of the particular duty, so as to make it seem a practical and a practicable thing, so as to awaken hope of doing better, and thus stimulate effort. Many a Christian duty seems to most people impracticable for them; and the most effective application in such cases is to show that it is practicable. This should not often be done in the way of reproof, as if the preacher was wishing simply to take away excuses for neglect, but with a sympathizing recognition of real difficulties which are "common to man."

When the problem raised by truth involves conduct that reaches beyond person-to-person relations to social institutional relations, the preacher's task grows more problematical. We live not only in a world of persons but of powerful social organizations and institutions, which exert constant and relentless pressure upon the moral and spiritual life of individuals. The preacher cannot be indifferent to these wider and more complex areas. He must pass unflinching judgment upon the wrongs of society; he must voice the Christian principles of righteousness and justice and good will; he must stir the consciences of men to meet the conditions and practices of the social order with unselfish devotion to truth and honor and common humanity. This duty has already been emphasized in the discussion of ethical preaching. But what shall he propose in a practical way? Devise strategies and programs for labor or for capital? Write platforms for the political parties? Propose and advocate particular statutes for legislative bodies? Agitate for particular solutions of the race problems? Turn expert in international procedures? Obviously such things are beyond his ability and outside his function. He is not an expert social planner. He is a prophet, a seer, and critic, and voice of high conscience in the name of God. He should not be complacent in the belief that society is impersonal organization and natural process. Society is composed of men, women, and children. The forms of society are created and managed by persons. The human factor is determinative of many things, including principles and goods. Human responsibility for the social order is therefore real, and the preacher must not permit complacency in himself or in those who hear him. He must ask burning questions of persons: "Where is thy brother?" "What meaneth this bleating of the sheep?" But he must ask in knowledge, not ignorance, speaking out of an understanding of conditions and problems won by diligent study. With such understanding he will be able to affix blame where blame lies and to propose with boldness the ways and means that brotherhood, honesty, high motive, and reverence for God will suggest. Such is the preacher's function. It is within his province and responsibility to bring every kind of evil, individually and corporately upheld, to the light and judgment of Christ's moral principles, and then to insist that men put these principles to the test where they are, making adventure along paths which an enlightened conscience can choose.

3. PERSUASION UNTO VITAL RESPONSE

But the chief part of what we commonly call application is *persuasion*. It is not enough to convince men of truth, nor enough to make them see how it applies to themselves, and how it might be practicable for them to act it out,—but we must "persuade men." A distinguished minister once said that he could never exhort; he could explain and prove what was truth and duty, but then he must leave people to themselves. The apostle Paul, however, could not only argue, but could say, "We pray you, in Christ's stead, be ye reconciled to God." Do we not well know, from observation and from experience, that a man may see his duty and still neglect it? Have we not often been led by persuasion to do something, good or bad, from which we were shrinking? It is proper, then, to persuade, to exhort, even to entreat.

(1) Persuasion is not generally best accomplished by mere exhortation but by urging, in the first place, some motive or motives for acting, or determining to act, as we propose. This is not properly called a process of argument. The motive presented may require previous proof that it is something true, or right, or good, but this proving is distinct from the act of presenting it as a motive; and if when bringing a motive to bear we have to prove anything concerning it, the proof ought to have great brevity and directness, or it will delay and hinder the designed effect.

A preacher must of course appeal to none but worthy motives that are harmonious with Christian moral ideals. The principal motives he is at liberty to use may be classed under three heads, namely, happiness, holiness, love.

We may lawfully appeal to the desire for happiness, and its negative counterpart, the dread of unhappiness. Those philosophers who insist that man ought always to do right simply and only because it is right are no philosophers at all, for they are either grossly ignorant of human nature or else are indulging in mere fanciful speculation. No doubt some preachers err in that they treat happiness as the almost exclusive, at any rate, as the chief motive. In the beatitudes and elsewhere Jesus spoke of the blessedness of the poor in spirit, the meek, the pure in heart, the peacemakers, and indicated why they would be "blessed." Happiness was to be desired, but it was not something to be sought as an end. Experience testifies that when it is directly sought, it evades us; it overtakes us when we are absorbed in duty and service. Certainly this should always be subordinated to duty and affection; but when thus subordinated, it is a legitimate desire and a legitimate basis of appeal. The Scriptures appeal not only to our feelings of moral obligation, but to our hopes and fears, for time and for eternity. "It is profitable for thee" is a consideration which the Great Teacher repeatedly employs in encouraging to self-denial. A desire for the pleasures of piety in this life or even for the happiness of heaven would never, of itself alone, lead men to become Christians or strengthen them to live as such; but, combined with other motives, it does a great and useful work. And there is here included not only the pleasure to be derived from gratification of our common wants, but that of taste and of ambition.

There is in men a spark of desire, and often a deep longing for holiness or, as most would express it, "goodness." The most abandoned man sometimes wishes to be good, nay, persuades himself that in certain respects he is good; and the great mass of mankind fully intend, after indulging a little longer in sinful pleasure, to become thoroughly good before they die. This is to say that conscience is a reality. Man, however wicked he may be, has a sense of difference between right and wrong, and something in his nature, his better part, votes for the right.

Here, then, is a great motive to which the preacher may appeal. The thorough depravity of human nature should not make us forget that goodness can always touch at least a faintly responsive chord in the human breast. We ought to hold up before men the beauty of holiness, to educate the regenerate into doing right for its own sake and not merely for the sake of its rewards. We ought to stimulate and at the same time control that hatred of evil which is the natural and necessary counterpart to the love of holiness. And as regards the future life, we should habitually point men, not only to its happiness but still more earnestly to its purity, and strive by God's blessing to make them long after its freedom from all sin and from all fear of sinning. Such noble and ennobling aspirations it is the preacher's high duty and privilege to cherish in his hearers by the very fact of appealing to them.

And the mightiest of all motives is love. In the relations of the present life, love is the great antagonist of selfishness. They who "have none to love," by any natural ties, must always interest their hearts in the needy and the afflicted, or they will grow more and more narrow and selfish. Accordingly, we may constantly appeal to men's love of their fellow-men, as a motive for doing right. Parents may be urged to seek personal piety and higher degrees of it for the sake of their growing children; and so with the husband or wife, the brother or sister or friend. Now to this motive the gospel appeals in a very peculiar manner. We ought to love God supremely, and such supreme love would be our chief motive to do right and to do good. But sin has alienated us from God, so that we do not love Him. And Christ presents himself, the God-man, the Redeemer, to win our love to him and thus to God. "Whosoever shall lose his life for my sake" are words which reveal the new and mighty gospel motive, love to Christ. To this, above all other motives, the preacher should appeal. Far from excluding others, it intensifies while it subordinates them.[4]

Closely akin to love is admiration.

Even where there is not what can be properly called affection, because the knowledge may be inadequate and the intimacy not close enough, there may be admiration for greatness, wisdom, goodness, as embodied in the tale of achievement, experience, character. By study of Paul's letters it is quite conceivable that a man may today even reach a personal affection for the great apostle, for he seems so close to us, lays his heart so bare. But the Holy Scriptures, biography, and history present to us many personalities who gain admiration rather than win affection. If this admiration depends on what is from the Christian standpoint admirable, the preacher need not hesitate about seeking to awaken it by the way he presents these personalities in his sermon.[5]

(2) But our task is not merely the calm exhibition of motives, that men may coolly act according to them. Many truths of religion are eminently adapted to stir the feelings, and to speak of such truths without feeling and awakening emotion is unnatural and wrong. And so mighty is the opposition which the gospel encounters in human nature, so averse is the natural heart to the obedience of faith, so powerful are the temptations of life, that we must arouse men to intense earnestness and often to impassioned emotion if we would bring them to surmount all obstacles and to conquer the world, the flesh, and the devil. Who expects to make soldiers charge a battery or storm a fortress without excitement? Many persons shrink from

---

[4] On the subject of motives, see profound and suggestive remarks in Vinet, pp. 203-222. Compare Arist. *Rhet.*, I. 10, 7, ff.

[5] Garvie, *The Christian Preacher*, p. 412.

the idea of exciting the feelings. "It seems to be commonly taken for granted, that whenever the feelings are excited, they are over-excited."[6] But while ignorant people often value too highly, or rather too exclusively, the appeal to their feelings, cultivated people are apt to shrink from such appeals quite too much. It may be that this is partly the fault of preachers, and the shrinking is not so much objection to having the feelings moved as to the kind of feelings appealed to, the character of the motives applied, and the mode of manifesting feeling which is sought. Nevertheless, our feelings as to religion are habitually too cold,—who can deny it? And any genuine excitement is greatly to be desired. Inspired teachers have evidently acted on this principle. The prophets made the most impassioned appeals. Our Lord and the apostles manifestly strove not merely to convince their hearers but to incite them to earnest corresponding action, and their language is often surcharged with emotion.

Yet, we should never wish to excite feeling for its own sake but as a means of persuasion to the corresponding course of action. In this respect many preachers err; some from not clearly perceiving that emotion is of little worth unless it excites to action, and others, it is to be feared, from an excessive desire for popular applause. These last give their hearers the luxury of idle emotion, as a pathetic novel or a tragedy might do, and hearers and preacher go away well pleased with themselves and each other.[7] No wonder some preachers find that their pathetic descriptions and passionate appeals now make but little impression upon persons who were once powerfully affected by them. The emotion was treated as an end, not as a means, and was habitually allowed to subside without any effect upon the hearer's active habits; and a steady diminution of the emotion itself was the inevitable result. Surely that is not good preaching,—whatever the unthinking may suppose,—which excites a mere transient and unproductive emotion.

It is matter of universal observation that a speaker who would excite deep feeling must feel deeply himself. Demosthenes sometimes spoke with such passionate earnestness that his enemies said he was deranged. Cicero remarks that it is only passion that makes the orator

---

[6] Whately, p. 215.

[7] The remarks of Day on excitation (*Art of Discourse*, p. 171), insisting that it is distinct from persuasion and that "a considerable part of pulpit oratory" aims at excitation alone, are to be regretted, as tending to encourage a common error.

a king; that, though he himself had tried every means of moving men, yet his successes were due, not to talent or skill, but to a mighty fire in his soul so that he could not contain himself; and that the hearer would never be kindled unless the speech came to him burning. It is said of Ignatius Loyola, the founder of the Jesuits, that he preached

with such an unction and emotion, that even those amongst his audience who did not understand the language in which he spoke, were, nevertheless, moved to tears by the very tones of his voice—the earnestness and burning zeal which appeared in his every gesture and look.[8]

Alas! it is often our chief difficulty in preaching to feel ourselves as we ought to feel. And a genuine fervor cannot be produced to order by a direct effort of will. Nor is it possible to conceal from the audience the deficiency of real emotion by high and loud or tremulous tones of voice, wild gesticulation, etc. We must cultivate our religious sensibilities, must keep our souls habitually in contact with gospel truth, and maintain, by the union of abundant prayer and self-denying activity, that ardent love to God and that tender love to man which will give us, without an effort, true pathos and passion. The famous John Henry Newman, in his *University Preaching,* speaks as follows:

Talent, logic, learning, words, manner, voice, action, all are required for the perfection of a preacher; but 'one thing is necessary,'—an intense perception and appreciation of the end for which he preaches, and that is, to be the minister of some definite spiritual good to those who hear him. . . . I do not mean that a preacher must aim at earnestness but that he must aim at his object, which is to do some spiritual good to his hearers and which will at once make him earnest.[9]

When the preacher does feel very deeply, his mere exhortation will have some power to move, especially where he has personal influence as a devout man, or for any reason has the sympathies of his audience. There is, then, the inexplicable contagion of sympathy. But he must avoid getting clear away from the hearers in his passionate feeling, for then sympathy will give place to its opposite.

Apart from sympathy with our own emotion, we can excite emotion in others only by indirect means, not by urging them to feel, though we should urge with the greatest vehemence. We must hold

---

[d] Potter, *Sacred Eloquence,* p. 211. See Gardner, *Psychology and Preaching,* Chap. VI, for a good discussion of the means of arousing emotion.

[9] Quoted by Potter, p. 213.

up before the mind considerations suited to awaken emotion and let them do their work.[10] For this purpose the preacher may of course learn from the contemplation of the basic human emotions, those that originate in the instincts and are therefore most powerful in conduct. Among them are fear, disgust, wonder, anger, subjection, elation, and tender emotion. The preacher may study their nature and the best means of exciting them and using them for high spiritual ends. And we need not only to know human nature in general but in most cases also need to understand the peculiar circumstances, sentiments, prejudices, tastes, of those whom we address. This is plainly demanded in the case of a missionary to the heathen but is hardly less necessary at home. One reason why unlearned preachers often have such power with the masses is, that they understand and fully sympathize with, the persons whom they address, while learned men sometimes do not.

In order to excite any of the passions by speech, we have to operate chiefly through the imagination.

A passion is most strongly excited by sensation. The sight of danger, immediate or near, instantly rouseth fear; the feeling of an injury, and the presence of the injurer, in a moment kindle anger. Next to the influence of sense is that of memory, the effect of which upon passion, if the fact be recent, and remembered distinctly and circumstantially, is almost equal. Next to the influence of memory is that of imagination.[11]

In proportion as the hearer's imagination is kindled, he seems to see that which we present, and the effect upon his feelings approximates to the effect of sight.

In presenting an object so that it may awaken imagination and impress the feelings, we usually need to give well-chosen details. Without this, as we have before seen, it is impossible to make a narration or description impressive. But preachers sometimes so multiply details as to weary the hearer, offend his taste, or betray a lack of right feeling on their own part. It may be gravely doubted whether a man can carry through a minute description of the crucifixion, who is at the time cherishing an intense faith and love towards Christ. A few vivid details, presented very briefly and with genuine emotion, will usually make a far deeper impression. And so with elaborate descriptions of the day of judgment and the agonies of

---

[10] Compare Whately, pp. 216-219.
[11] Campbell, *Phil. of Rhet.*, p. 103.

perdition. One who truly realized the scene and tenderly loved his fellow-men could hardly endure to dwell so long on the most harrowing details, and the preacher who does this is apt to be for the time (though unconscious of it) mainly alive to the artistic interest in his picture.

Comparison is often very effective in awakening emotion. Thus we make men feel more deeply how shameful is ingratitude to God, by first presenting some affecting case of ingratitude to a human benefactor. The emotion excited by something as regards which men feel readily and deeply, is transferred to the object compared. For example, "Like as a father pitieth his children, so the Lord pitieth them that fear him." The effect of climax, gradually working the feelings up to the highest pitch, may also be very great, as everyone has observed.

We must not try to be highly impassioned on all subjects, on all occasions, or in all parts of a discourse. Appeals to the feelings will usually be made only at the conclusion, sometimes, after the discussion of each successive topic, but then we must be sure that the interest first excited can be renewed and gradually increased. It is a common fault with inexperienced preachers to make vehement appeals in the early part, even in the very beginning, of a sermon; in such cases there will almost inevitably be a reaction, and a decay of interest before the close. If several impassioned passages are to occur, those which come first should be comparatively brief and followed by something calm or familiar. It is also important to avoid exhausting our physical force before reaching that portion of the sermon which calls for the most passionate earnestness. He who is exhausted not only cannot speak forcibly but cannot feel deeply. And a concluding exhortation should never be prolonged beyond the point at which the preacher is still in full vigor, and the hearers feel a sustained interest.

Part IV

THE STYLE OF THE SERMON

CHAPTER I

GENERAL OBSERVATIONS ON STYLE

I. NATURE AND IMPORTANCE OF STYLE

WE frequently say of a writer, that he wields a ready, an elegant, or a caustic pen. In like manner the *stylus*, the pointed iron instrument with which the Romans wrote upon their tablets covered with wax, is often employed by Cicero to denote the manner of writing, the manner of expressing one's thoughts in writing, and at a later period was very naturally extended to speaking. In modern times the use has been still further extended by analogy, to the fine arts, to dress, and a great variety of matters. A man's style, then, is his characteristic manner of expressing his thoughts, whether in writing or in speech.

Everyone has his own handwriting if he writes at all easily and well. And so in the higher sense everyone has his own style. The most slavish imitation could not be perfect; the man's own character will sometimes, in spite of him, modify his style. No writer on the subject fails to quote the saying of Buffon, "The style is the man." This saying Buffon himself curiously illustrated, for his style is marked by a stately and elaborate elegance, and it is said that he could not write well unless he was in full dress. To the same effect Landor said, "Language is a part of a man's character";[1] and Lessing, "Every man should have his own style as he has his own nose."[2] But here, as everywhere else, that which is most characteristic in a man

[1] Hoppin, p. 585.
[2] Haven's *Rhet.*, p. 241.

may be disciplined and indefinitely improved without losing individuality.

It is not surprising that the term "style," as figuratively denoting one's manner of expressing his thoughts, should be used in different cases with a very different extent of meaning. It is sometimes taken to include arrangement, even that of an entire treatise or discourse; and there can certainly be no absolute distinction made between the arrangement of sentences and paragraphs and that of the discourse. Commonly, however, the general arrangement is not included in the term. On the other hand, style is sometimes distinguished from diction, the latter then denoting one's vocabulary, the character of the words and particular phrases which he employs, while the former would include everything else belonging to his mode of expressing thought. But it is best, according to the usual practice, to include diction as a part of style.

Thus understood, style is obviously a matter of very great importance. A man's style cannot be separated from his modes of thought, from his whole mental character. The natural and common image by which we call it the "dress" of thought is very apt to mislead; for style, as Wordsworth forcibly says, is not the mere dress, it is the incarnation of thought. We know another's thoughts only as thus revealed, thus incarnate.[3] Aristotle, it is true, speaks slightingly of style, as a subject recently introduced into treatises of rhetoric which it is to some little extent necessary to consider in every system of instruction, though the proof is the main thing.[4] His practice accords with this opinion, for his own style is not only careless and harsh but often vexatiously obscure. And yet there were already in his language many noble specimens of style, in poetry, history, oratory, which have never been surpassed; so true is it in rhetoric that just theory follows excellent practice.[5] It is only a few men whose matter is so surpassingly valuable as to be highly prized, like Aristotle's, notwithstanding great faults of style. The speakers and writers who have been widely and permanently influential have usually accomplished it by good thoughts, well expressed. Often, indeed, excellence of style has given a wide and lasting popularity to works which had little other merit. Goldsmith's *Histories* long held their place in many

[3] See also Day, p. 213.

[4] Arist., *Rhet.*, III. 1.

[5] Cicero says (*Orator*, 16) that "when one has found out what to say and in what order, there still remains by far the greatest thing, namely, how to say it"; but in this he includes style and delivery.

schools, because they were so charmingly written, though they were inaccurate and very poorly represented the historical attainments of their own age. The widespread, though short-lived popularity gained by Renan's fanciful *Life of Jesus* was due not merely to the sensational character of its contents but very largely also to the extreme beauty of the style, particularly in the original French. When a student at a Jesuit College, Renan paid great attention to the cultivation of his style and afterwards devoted himself mainly to the study of language and literature. In like manner science has in many cases gained a just appreciation only when recommended by a pleasing style. This was what Buffon did for natural history. The popularity of geology was immensely increased among the English-speaking peoples by Hugh Miller through his marvelous powers of description and the general freshness and animation of his style. And so it was later with Agassiz, and Huxley, and Tyndall. Such facts go to show that style is not a thing of mere ornament. Style is the glitter and polish of the warrior's sword but is also its keen edge. It can render mediocrity acceptable and even attractive, and power more powerful still. It can make error seductive, while truth may lie unnoticed for want of its aid. Shall religious teachers neglect so powerful a means of usefulness? True, Paul says, "My speech and my preaching were not with persuasive words of man's wisdom" (I Cor. 2:4). He refused to deal in the would-be philosophy and the sensational and meretricious rhetoric which were so popular in that rapidly growing commercial city; but his style is a model of passionate energy and rises upon occasion into an inartificial and exquisite beauty.[6]

Yet style is in this country much neglected. The French surpass all other modern nations, in respect of perspicuity, elegance, and animation, if not energy. The cultivated English come next to them in finish of style and surpass them in power. The English university training, with all its defects, has in this respect produced noble results, as may be seen not only in the great Parliamentary orators and the admirable newspaper writing which England boasts but also in preachers. The famous *Oxford Tracts* would not have been so influential but for their admirable style. The sermons of J. H. Newman, Robertson, Liddon, and Bishop Wilberforce are in this respect greatly to be admired. And in that tradition the public speakers of England, both in the pulpit and in Parliament, continue to maintain for the most part a high standard.

[6] Witness in this same epistle, chapters 13 and 15.

In America we have a growing number of writers and speakers, both secular and religious, who can be held up as models. But in general we fall seriously below the English. An extreme negligence and looseness of style is observable in many otherwise capable ministers. And the great American fault, in speaking and writing, is an excessive vehemence, a constant effort to be striking. Our style, as well as our delivery, too often lacks the calmness of conscious strength, the repose of sincerity, the quiet earnestness which only now and then becomes impassioned.

He will be an eloquent man who shall be able to speak of small matters in lowly phrase, of ordinary topics temperately, of great subjects with passion and power.[7]

One cause of this neglect of style among us, and to some extent in England also, is the failure to understand its inseparable connection with the thought conveyed and the dependence of shining truth upon the transparency of the manner in which it is expressed. The best style attracts least attention to itself, and none but the critical observer is apt to appreciate its excellence, most men giving credit solely to the matter and having no idea how much the manner has contributed to attract and impress them. The thought is certainly the main thing; but the style also is important.

The experience of all times, and the testimony of all teachers, present to us as inseparable, these two propositions: (1) That we must not flatter ourselves that we shall have a good style, without an interesting fund of ideas. (2) That even with an interesting and substantial supply of ideas, we must not flatter ourselves that style will come of itself.[8]

2. STYLES AND STYLE

To say that every writer or speaker has his own characteristic manner of expressing thought and feeling does not mean that every man is a law unto himself. In music Handel, Bach, Chopin, each had his own characteristic style, but their compositions were great music because in each case genius allied itself with, or, rather, found itself in, the basic laws of music. So in preaching, effective style is achieved by observing the fundamental requirements of language and the whole context of circumstance. Indeed, the nature of preaching makes

[7] Cicero, Orator, 29.
[8] Vinet, p. 353.

it doubly imperative that great care should be given to every factor and condition that might help or hinder the power of utterance, for preaching is more than art for art's sake, more than self-expression; it is speaking for God.

(1) Individual style, let us say then, moves properly within boundaries. First, it is under obligation to the laws of language. There are grammatical principles which ought to be observed for both moral and practical reasons.

Grammar discovers the facts of language, from which it formulates the laws of correct expression; and these laws rhetoric must observe, because correctness lies necessarily at the foundation of all intelligible utterance, rhetorical or other.[9]

Grammatical processes are the working-tools of rhetoric, too useful, too necessary, to be neglected. Again, style must have regard for "the times." It is not bound by tradition. We have noted that as Christianity moved out into the gentile world the style of preaching changed. It followed the customs and tastes of different peoples and different ages.[10] No age, no school furnished a "sacred rhetoric" which could ignore or transgress the best methods of public speech in current use. To be sure, Christian preaching, by its very excellence, has been an influential factor in creating standards of style; but its excellence has been its ability to sense the intellectual and emotional dispositions and tastes of a given age and relate itself to them effectively. Whenever preaching has failed to do this and become merely imitative of another age or some prophetic hero like Chrysostom, or Bernard, or Jeremy Taylor, or Liddon, or Beecher, or Spurgeon, it has lost in power. And history's road is strewn with the bones of ineffective imitators. Concerning the limitations set by our own day, Patton points out that

the tempo of our life is fast, not to say jerky. The entire religious service takes less time than the sermon used to have for itself. The shortness of the sermon reacts upon its vocabulary and style, as well as upon the mood of the listeners. People today will hardly have patience or know how to listen to a preacher whose leisurely, orotund, well-balanced periods suggest that he is in no hurry to get through.[11]

[9] Genung, *Practical Rhetoric*, pp. 108 f.
[10] See Dargan, *The Art of Preaching in the Light of Its History.*
[11] *Preparation and Delivery of Sermons*, p. 67.

Yet, again, style must bend to the occasion of the sermon, the character of the audience, and the nature of the subject. A street corner
and an old ladies' home call for quite different things; so do children's sermons, baccalaureate addresses, and revival sermons. As to
appropriate styles for different subjects and purposes, compare the
Sermon on the Mount with the twenty-third chapter of Matthew.

(2) There are certain qualities or properties of style that are indispensable, grammatical qualities which have to do with correctness
and purity of language, and rhetorical qualities which have to do
more particularly with the impression or effect of discourse. The latter may be classified as clearness, energy, and elegance.

Precise and perspicuous expression, being the staple, the backbone of
composition, is to be cultivated first and most conscientiously of all; but
the cases in which mere clearness is enough, without the aid of other qualities, belong to the comparatively elementary forms of literature, those
works in which the bare thought is all-sufficient to supply the interest.
But when the idea comes home more closely to reader and writer—when
on the one hand it must gain lodgment in dull minds or stimulate a lag-
gard attention, or when on the other its importance rouses the writer's
enthusiasm or stirs his deep convictions—there is or must be imported to
it greater life than its merely intelligible statement would demand. . . .
An idea (however) may be stated with perfect clearness, may make also
a strong impression on the reader's mind and heart; and yet many of
the details may be an offense to his taste; or a crude expression and harsh
combinations of sound may impair the desired effect by compelling attention to defective form. Any such disturbing element is a blemish in the
style. Nor is it an offense to the cultured reader alone. Everyone may be
aware that a style is crude, though he may not be able to locate or explain
the cause; and when an idea is expressed with supreme felicity, everyone
may appreciate it. There is needed, therefore, in every well-formed style,
an element of beauty to make the style a satisfaction to the reader's taste
as well as to his thought and conviction.[12]

What Genung here says concerning writing is equally true of preaching and of such importance that these qualities will be discussed at
length in subsequent chapters.

(3) It is necessary to warn against giving way wholly to one's
"natural bent" and thus falling into faulty styles. One's personal
dispositions must be under discipline, not smothered, but corrected
and supplemented. Among the faulty styles observable in preachers

[12] Genung, *Practical Rhetoric*, pp. 21 and 23.

are those that result from too exclusive attention to the fact that the sermon is something to be heard. There is an over-consciousness of sound. Among the kinds of style discussed by Dr. Oman,[13] four may be traced to this cause. First is the *spacious style*, in which grandeur is the goal, which is pursued by solemn, resonant, impressive tone and expanded statement. Oman gives this example:

'The sun never sets on the king's dominions' might seem to be spacious enough, but this style would expand it to: 'As I have had occasion to remark before, the celestial luminary is never at any time wholly below the horizon of the imperial dominions of our most gracious sovereign.'

A second variety is the *polished style* in which the conspicuous thing is that the sermon is well tailored and well kempt. Its best compliment is neatness and finesse. A third variety is the *fine style*, which "concerns itself with words and phrases for their own sake, and mostly for their mellifluousness." It specializes in prettiness of sound. There may be distinguished, also, the *flowery style*, which is highly ornamental, often hiding the truth in a bower of roses or making conviction of truth appear less important to the preacher than his oratory. It is speech over-dressed.

Other faults of style result from too exclusive attention to the fact that the sermon is concerned with truth. One of the dangers of theological and literary studies is that the materials and forms of the classroom will be carried bodily into the pulpit. It is very easy to introduce into one's sermons the style of the professor in the classroom and to write in the style of a paper on theology or ethics. An abstract, or an essay or lecture style, may be from the purely intellectual and literary standpoint excellent. But a sermon requires to be understood, to be interesting, to come to grips with life and its problems, to be moving. True preaching is not truth centered; it is truth, truth centered on life. The preacher must be always conscious that a sermon is prepared to be spoken. But, again, too exclusive attention to this fact may result in faulty style. Some preachers thus fall into a casual, not to say careless, conversational style. Properly defined the conversational style is highly appropriate in the pulpit. Preaching must be audience-conscious, person-to-person; it is something told; but there are levels of conversation, and the pulpit is not a park bench, nor is the subject the weather; moreover, the place is the house of God and the issue is critical. The sermon is properly conversational in its

[13] Oman, *Concerning the Ministry*, pp. 85-89.

personalness and directness and simplicity, but it is more; it is a prophet's evangel, it is august truth. Too exclusive attention to the persons addressed has the further danger of leading a preacher, according to his disposition, into a dogmatic or combative or else ingratiating style, in which language as well as manner will be either harsh or velvety beyond measure.

Be careful to observe that these faulty styles are such only as they are severally developed without regard for all the demands of a sermon. In combination and proper proportion they become the instruments of effectiveness. A sermon is something to be heard, it is concerned with truth, it is addressed to individuals; it needs not one but the three qualities of beauty and clearness and force.

3. MEANS OF IMPROVING STYLE

It follows from all this that every writer and speaker should pay great attention to the improvement of his style. High excellence in style is necessarily rare; for a discourse, a paragraph, even a sentence, is really a work of art, fashioned by constructive imagination—and artist-gifts of every kind are rare. But any man who will try, long enough and hard enough, can learn to say what he means, to say forcibly what he deeply feels, and to clothe his thoughts in a garb at least of homely neatness. Some of the best writers and speakers have had peculiar difficulty in acquiring a good style; and their success affords encouragement to us all. We are, therefore, to consider the means of improvement, not merely as regards that which is peculiar to oratory, but as regards style in general.

(1) The study of language, particularly of our own language, is in this respect exceedingly profitable. The science of language, which within this century has accomplished so much and which is now making such rapid progress, cannot be considered inferior, in point of interest and instructiveness, to any other of the sciences. But the study of the science as such, has only an indirect bearing on style; it is the practical acquisition of languages that is here the great source of benefit. This, when pursued with system and on sound principles, compels close attention to the nature of language in general, to the history, changes, and capacities of words, and the relation of syntactical construction to the different forms and processes of thought. It also attracts to the peculiarities of our own language a keener and more intelligent notice than most persons would otherwise bestow. These

benefits are more or less derived from the study of any language what soever. There is peculiar advantage in choosing French or German, because they correspond to the two great elements of which our own language is chiefly composed. But the time-honored study of Latin and Greek is more advantageous still. In their inflections, their syntax, their prose rhythm, these languages exhibit the full and instructive development of excellencies which English, French, German possess only in part.

But whether acquainted or not with other languages, a man must earnestly study his own. Apart from its incomparable practical importance to us, the English is in itself a worthy study, a most noble tongue. Foreigners naturally complain much of those irregularities in spelling and pronunciation which have been almost necessarily produced by the union of two diverse languages into one. Critics at home can easily point out its weakness and compare it unfavorably, in this or that respect, with some other idiom. It is not like Italian for music, nor like French for conversation, nor like German as to facility in forming new compounds, but taken all in all, for history, poetry, philosophy, oratory, for society, and for business, it is at present unequalled. A popular writer has recently called it "the grammarless tongue"; but English has a grammar, a very regular syntax, and one that is often and flagrantly violated, even by able and cultivated men. De Quincey declares:

> It makes us blush to add, that even grammar is so little of a perfect attainment amongst us, that with two or three exceptions, (one being Shakespeare, whom some affect to consider as belonging to a semi-barbarous age) we have never seen the writer, through a circuit of prodigious reading, who has not sometimes violated the accidence or the syntax of English grammar.[14]

Persons who have been carefully drilled in Greek and Latin, especially by written translations from English into those languages and from them into English, usually feel that they have no use for the common treatises on English grammar. It is true that books on grammar are not everything in acquiring command of the language or the main thing. There are men among us who have studied no such books, no other language, and yet who speak and write English with correctness and even with force and beauty. The great works of Greek poetry and history were written before any treatises on grammar

[14] De Quincey on Style, p. 105.

existed. These facts remind us that we must find elsewhere the principal means of improvement in style, but they by no means prove that grammars are useless. We have to learn the usage of the language, and grammars undertake to present this usage in a systematic and convenient form. They show us our faults and warn us where there is danger; they set us to observing language and reflecting upon it. The rules of grammar have most effectually done their work when conformity to them has become habitual, and we need the rules no longer,—yea, when we have so fully entered into the principles involved that upon occasion we may even violate a rule. Correct habits may be formed and right principles comprehended without books of grammar, but more rapidly and surely with them, provided we use them only as helps and aim to go deeper than they can carry us. As to this whole matter of studying English grammar, two practical errors widely prevail and greatly need to be corrected. Men who have been to college are apt to think they have no need to study their own language at all, and especially no need of consulting books on the subject,—the latter part of this opinion being a mistake, and the former a very great mistake. On the other hand, men who have had fewer educational advantages are in danger of supposing that without systematic instruction they can do nothing to improve their style, or else that after studying a book or two on English grammar, they have nothing more to do.

It may be remarked in general that a preacher ought to employ pure English, according to current use, not quickly catching up the novelties of the street or the daily paper, and not introducing those archaisms with which he is familiar from commerce with old books, but which his hearers would not readily understand. He should speak the English of general use, not employing local peculiarities of phrase except for special reason; but he should retain genuine English idiom, even where superficial critics attempt to displace it. The preacher must never invent words. Madame de Staël says, "There is in general no surer symptom of barrenness of ideas than the invention of words,"—a remark which may at least be set over against the notion that such invention is a symptom of originality. And he should not, save in very peculiar cases, employ words or phrases from foreign languages. It was once very common and thought to be very appropriate for a minister to quote much Latin and Greek in his sermons. Even Wesley's sermons abound in such quotations, though he preached mainly to the common people. It is a sign of improved taste that this is no longer the practice. A speaker must now use his knowledge of other languages only as giving him increased power over his own language. Even where one refers to the original Scriptures, it is very rarely proper to mention the Greek or Hebrew word.

(2) The study of literature perhaps contributes still more to the improvement of style than the direct study of language. From reading we gain much in the knowledge of language, especially as to richness of vocabulary, fullness of expression.[15] But more. It is chiefly by reading that we form our literary taste,—a matter of unspeakable importance. Cicero makes one of his characters say, referring to Greek literature:

As, when I walk in the sun, even though I walk for another reason, my complexion is yet colored, so, when I have read these books, I feel that my style of speaking is as it were colored by their influence.[16]

And what Shakespeare mournfully says is true in this better sense also:

My nature is subdued
To what it works in, like the dyer's hand.

To bathe our minds in choice literature till they become imbued with correct principles of style, to nourish them with good learning till our taste grows healthy, so as to discern quickly and surely between good and bad, is a process surpassingly profitable in its results and in itself delightful.

And not only do we need to cultivate good literature for its positive benefits but also to counteract certain evil influences of great power. Few among us have learned from childhood to speak graceful and forcible, or even correct, English. And as men grow up and go on in life, so large a part of what they read in newspapers and of what they hear in conversation and even in public speaking is in a vicious style, that they inevitably feel the effect. Besides the more obvious errors as to pronunciation and syntax, which are too often committed by cultivated speakers, there results from these influences a more subtle and more serious injury to taste, which only a continued application to the best literature can remedy and prevent. De Quincey points out that the immense multiplication of newspapers has injured our style of

---

[15] Kossuth derived his wonderful knowledge of English from the study of Shakespeare, while in prison.
[16] *De Orat.*, II. 15, 16.

conversation. Everybody reads them constantly, and their writers too often use the most bookish and inflated language in treating of common things, as well as the most undignified language in treating of serious things. But it would be idle to enumerate the many and grievous faults of our current newspaper dialect. One who wishes to form a good style would do well to select his newspapers, secular and religious, with reference to this as well as to other considerations. The style of preaching will always naturally and to a great extent properly share the peculiarities which mark the literature of the day. When this exhibits bad taste, as is so often true now of newspaper writing and public speaking, we must correct the evil by intimacy with the truly great authors of our own and of former times.

It is delightful to think how many good authors there are in English and in other languages. Our religious literature, both sermons and other works, presents noble specimens of style, in which one may at the same time nourish the intellect, warm the heart, and refine the taste, and among which he may select such as will exert the kind of influence he particularly needs. The important matter is that one should not read at haphazard; that taking account of his mental constitution, his previous training, and present stage of development, the particular tendencies as to thinking and style of which he is now conscious, he should select, according to the best accessible information, such works as will best meet his actual wants.

Preachers ought to derive very great benefit in point of style from their constant reading and minute study of the English Bible. The Scriptures embrace almost every species of style, and each with many varieties. And the current English translation, though some of its phrases have become nearly obsolete, presents the English language in its most admirable form. It dates from the golden age of English literature and deserves, in an eminent degree, the eulogy which Spenser passed upon Chaucer, as a "well of English undefyled."

Besides the common ground of general literature, which no one, of whatever special calling, can afford to neglect, preachers may learn much from the great secular orators, even as lawyers and statesmen often diligently study the great preachers. And this is true, not merely for the beginner but even more for the practiced speaker. To see the same principles carried out in material and for purposes quite different from his own will illustrate those principles afresh and will prevent his becoming formal in arrangement and monotonous in style.

But let not the young student submit himself to the authority of any writer as a perfect standard or be repelled from some of the greatest by their manifest blemishes.

There is no writer who has not some faults, and faults of taste are perhaps those the most common to the highest and the lowest order of writers. The taste of Shakespeare and Milton is not always unimpeachable. But it is to the greatest writers that Adam Smith's exclamation applies— 'How many great qualities must that writer possess who can thus render his very faults agreeable!' If we desire to find a writer without fault, we must not look for him among the greatest writers.[17]

Augustine had been in his youth a teacher of rhetoric. He knew the folly of that artificial instruction in style and delivery which there have always been teachers to recommend, and he knew that even a just rhetorical system is but a help to something higher. He says:

Moreover, I enjoin it upon him who would combine eloquence with wisdom, by which he will certainly become more effective, to read and listen to the eloquent, and imitate them in exercises, rather than apply to the teachers of the rhetorical art, provided those whom he hears and reads were, or are now, justly celebrated, not merely for their eloquence, but also for their wisdom.[18]

It will also be found very helpful as well as entertaining to read inspiring lives of literary men.

It should be added that conversation, especially that of intelligent women, may also furnish admirable and influential examples of clear, sprightly, varied, and in every way attractive style. So too with letters.

Would you desire at this day to read our noble language in its native beauty, picturesque from idiomatic propriety, racy in its phraseology, delicate yet sinewy in its composition—steal the mail-bags, and break open all the letters in female handwriting.[19]

Cicero's epistles are for most men far better examples of style than Cicero's orations. And if to an acquaintance with Bacon, Milton's prose, Barrow, and Burke, one should add a familiarity with some of the finest letters, he would see the English language in all its most

---

[17] Bulwer, on Style, *Caxtoniana*, I. 131.
[18] *De Doct. Christ.*, IV.
[19] De Quincey on Style, p. 77.

prodigal strength and splendor, and in all its most flexible grace and delicate beauty.[20]

(3) But the chief means of improvement in style is careful practice in writing and speaking,—not mere practice without care, for this will develop and confirm what is faulty as well as what is good.

In written composition, it is very unwise, although very common, to neglect details. If a man spells badly, he should set himself vigorously to correct the fault, which usually requires nothing but a little system and perseverance.[21] To take some pains in this direction is worth while, not only for the sake of removing a literary blemish, but because accuracy in detail is apt to react profitably upon our mental habits and also to increase our love for the work of composition. Someone has said that there never was a great sculptor who did not love to chip the marble. And if spelling be worth attention, so is punctuation, though this is still more commonly neglected. Punctuation indicates the relation of the parts of a sentence to each other. The only real difficulty in punctuating properly is the difficulty in determining the true relation of clauses, and he who does not mark the points is apt to neglect, more than he is aware, the structure of his sentences. It will be evident, too, that every man's punctuation must be to some extent his own, as it indicates his mode of constructing sentences. Of this, Chalmers is an example, in his infrequent use of the comma. The dash, which has of late become so common, is convenient to indicate a break in the sentence, whether an interruption, so as to insert something akin to a parenthesis, or an abrupt transition to something related to what precedes but not joined to it by strict grammatical connection. It is thus an affectation to abjure the dash altogether, as some propose to do, but it should be used only for a distinct and positive reason. In practical attention to punctuation, we must endeavor to master the principles involved, the fundamental

---

[20] Holcombe's Literature in Letters (New York, Appleton), is a delightful volume, containing a choice collection of English and American Letters, classified and with all necessary annotation.

[21] Let him have whatever he writes examined by some accurate speller and make lists of the words corrected, putting them down as they ought to be, and frequently running over the growing list, with the resolve, at every step, that this error, and this, shall occur no more; further, let him habitually consult a dictionary when doubtful as to the spelling of a word; and, moreover, he must begin to notice spelling in the books and periodicals he reads, and to take interest in disputed questions. We often find it harder to correct confirmed habits about trifles than about more important matters, because the former do not awaken an interested and watchful attention. The plan proposed will meet this difficulty.

significance which usage has assigned to the several points, and then use them according to our own meaning, and not according to the stiff and unbending rules which are so often laid down. And it should be noticed that although forbidden by many of the books, punctuation may be sometimes employed, apart from grammatical relations, to indicate the *rhythmical* movement of the successive parts of a sentence.

And so as to all the details of grammar. Campbell tells of a preacher who was consulted by a friend having a mind to publish, "Whether he thought it befitting a writer on religion to attend to such little matters as grammatical correctness?" and he answered, "By all means. It is much better to write so as to make a critic turn Christian, than so as to make a Christian turn critic."[22]

There can be no question that grammatical accuracy is an object worthy of earnest pursuit. The young preacher who finds himself particularly deficient in this respect, ought, besides such study of treatises on grammar as we have already urged, to go through some good work on composition, laboriously writing the exercises. If nothing else were gained, it is much to be relieved from all fear of committing blunders that would be ridiculed.

But while attentive to the details of composition, one must be chiefly occupied with the thought; and in order to this, composition as a mere exercise must more and more give place to writing with a real interest, with some practical aim. In all such writing, one should become possessed with the subject, and then write as rapidly as is consistent with perspicuous and forcible expression, leaving minute correction to be made afterward. But he must be sure to make the corrections. Thought once cast into a mold is apt to harden very soon, and any considerable alteration is then a difficult and laborious task. Sometimes a whole paragraph must be thrown back into the furnace of the mind and fused anew, in order to remove a single flaw in one sentence. Think of John Foster, toiling over a sentence for two hours, determined to have it right. Virgil wrote his *Georgics* sometimes at the rate of one line a day. He would dictate some verses, then spend the day in revising, correcting, and reducing them. He compared himself, as Aulus Gellius mentions, to a she-bear licking her offspring into shape. Tennyson wrote "Come into the garden, Maud" nearly fifty times before it suited him, spending nearly a month over it. He wrote "Locksley Hall" in two days,

22 On Pulpit Eloquence, Lect. III.

and then spent six weeks in altering and polishing it. Macaulay and George Eliot were diligent and careful in rewriting and correcting their work; and there are numerous other instances among the great masters in literature, ancient and modern, who spent hours, sometimes days, in revising and altering their writings.

A most valuable means of improvement in command of language and style in general is written translation into English from other languages. This tests and develops, in a peculiar manner, our knowledge of English. When attempting to express our own thoughts, we have the idea at first only in a dim, shifting, nebulous form; and in struggling to find the exact expression, we may unconsciously change the idea into something else for which fit expression presents itself. But in translating,—not merely putting word for word, like a schoolboy, but getting the exact idea conveyed by a sentence, and then seeking the exact expression for that idea in English,—no such substitution or shifting can take place. The thought stands fixed in the other language, with the peculiar shape and color which that language gives it, and we must find English to express it or must know that our effort to do so has failed. Thus careful translation is in one respect a better exercise than original composition. It is obvious that a similar benefit will be derived, though in a less degree, from oral translation. It is well known that William Pitt was carefully trained by his father to offhand translation from Greek and other languages, and that he believed himself to have derived immense advantage from it.

In addition to writing, one must studiously practice speaking, in order to form his speaking style. A man skilled in both, may closely imitate in writing the style of speaking, but the two are really distinct, and in some respects quite different. Let one speak much that has been carefully prepared, though not written, and speak sometimes, as in social meetings, upon the strong impulse of the moment. Let him always have a practical purpose, and throw himself into an effort, not to make a discourse but to accomplish his object. Let him closely observe his hearers and learn to perceive how far they understand and are impressed. He will thus become able to judge when to be diffuse, and when rapid, and will acquire the directness of address, the power of constant movement towards a fixed point, the passionate energy and unstudied grace, the flexibility and variety which characterize the speaking style. And he who aims at skill in extemporaneous speaking must give special attention to his style in conversation.

so that the difference between his more elevated and his more familiar style may be a difference in degree and not in kind.

After all that has been said or can be said as to style, no one should imagine that he need only seek to acquire power of expression and may give little attention to thought. Some young men fall into this error, and it is simply fatal. "Let there be care about words," says Quintilian, "but solicitude about things."

CHAPTER II

QUALITIES OF STYLE—CLEARNESS

THE most important property of style is clearness or perspicuity. Style is excellent when, like the atmosphere, it shows the thought, but itself is not seen. Yet, this comparison and the term "perspicuity," which was derived from it, are both inadequate; for good style is like stereoscopic glasses, which, transparent themselves, give form and body and distinct outline to that which they exhibit.

A certain grand-looking obscurity is often pleasing to some hearers and readers, who suppose that it shows vast learning, or great originality,[1] or immense profundity. To treat subjects in this fashion is no new thing. Quintilian says it was not new in his day, for that he found mention in Livy of a teacher who used to direct his pupils to "darken" the idea. He adds a witticism of someone whose hearers complained that they did not understand, and who replied, "So much the better; I did not even understand it myself,"[2] and elsewhere speaks of men who think themselves talented because it requires talent to understand them. M. Huc says that in the Lama Convents, where the Buddhist professors lecture to their pupils, the more obscure and unintelligible their sayings, the more sublime they are reckoned. Alas! that preachers of the gospel are not always proof against this pitiful temptation.

A preacher is more solemnly bound than any other person to make his language perspicuous. This is very important in wording a law, in writing a title-deed or a physician's prescription, but still more important in proclaiming the Word of God, words of eternal life.

It is also true that a preacher has greater difficulty than any other class of speakers in making his style perspicuous to all his hearers, for no others speak to so heterogeneous an audience, including persons of both sexes, of every age from early childhood, and of every grade of intellect and culture. But this difficulty, when most deeply felt, should but stimulate to diligent and painstaking effort. For what is the use of preaching unless we may hope to do good? And

[1] Compare on originality, Part I. chap. v. § 3.
[2] Quintilian, VIII. 2, 18.

what good can be done, save in proportion as we are understood? Pretentious obscurity may excite a poor admiration, unmeaning prettiness may give a certain pleasure, mere vociferation—like Bottom's part, "nothing but roaring,"—may affect some people's nerves, but only truth, and truth that is understood, can bring real benefit. Moreover, something worse may happen than the failure to do good; we may do harm. Some hearers are repelled and disgusted by obscurity. Others are misled. It is a mournful thing to think of, but one of not infrequent occurence, that men should so misunderstand us, as to take what we meant for medicine and convert it into poison. As we love men's souls we must strive to prevent so dreadful a result. One cannot expect, as Quintilian already remarks,

that the hearer will be so intent upon understanding as to cast upon the darkness of the speech a light from his own intelligence. What we say must be made so clear that it will pour into his mind as the sun pours into the eyes, even when they are not directed toward it. We must take care, not that it shall be possible for him to understand, but that it shall be utterly impossible for him not to understand.[3]

The German philosopher Fichte wrote a treatise with this title: "An account clear as the sun, of the real nature of my philosophy; an attempt to compel the reader to understand."[4] None but a very self-confident man would put forth such a title; but it indicates what every teacher of men ought to aim at, not arrogantly but resolutely, —to compel the reader or hearer to understand.

Two general remarks as to clearness may be here made. The style may be not lacking in clearness and yet the discourse may seem hard to comprehend because the subject is difficult or what is taught about it is unacceptable. For example, men speak of the Epistle to the Romans as obscure; how far is this opinion due to a desire to understand more upon some subjects than it teaches, or a reluctance to receive as true what it does teach? The more plainly a discourse presents the truths of the Epistle, the more obscure it will seem if we strive to make it mean something else. The other remark is that clearness of style is closely allied to clearness of thought. It is true, as Whately says,[5] that men sometimes speak obscurely on a subject for the simple reason that they are familiar with it, and forget that others are not so,—a practical mistake which preachers are in no small

---

[3] Quintilian, VIII. 2, 23.
[4] Quoted by Shedd, p. 72.
[5] *Rhetoric*, p. 307.

danger of making. If anyone should assert that clear ideas of a subject will always lead to clear statements, this common experience would set aside the assertion. The statement of clear ideas will be subjectively clear but is by no means sure to be objectively clear; it will be plain to him who makes it but may be very obscure to other people. But all this has nothing to do with that other proposition, that there can be no clearness of expression without clear thinking. The effort to gain a clear conception and to work out a perspicuous expression of it will usually go on together; and the habit of perspicuous expression reacts powerfully on habits of thought.

Sometimes we are required to speak of things which we cannot fully comprehend but can only apprehend, as the doctrines of the Trinity, the incarnation, the atonement; and oftener yet we must discuss matters which we cannot hope to make clear to all who hear us, though we must make sure of some. Yet, in all such cases we must be as clear as the subjects and circumstances allow.

Clearness of style depends mainly on three things, namely, the choice of terms, the construction of sentences and paragraphs, and the proper management of brevity and diffuseness.

(1) So far as clearness depends on the terms employed, it requires the combination of two elements.

(a) We must use, as far as possible, words and phrases that will be intelligible to our audience. Where the audience comprises many who are comparatively illiterate, we must strive to make the terms intelligible to them, for if the less cultured understand, there will be no question about the others. Dean Swift, in his famous Letter to a Young Clergyman, puts the matter as follows:

> I have been curious enough to take a list of several hundred words in a sermon of a new beginner, which not one of his hearers among a hundred could possibly understand; neither can I easily call to mind any clergyman of my own acquaintance who is wholly exempt from this error, although many of them agree with me in the dislike of the thing. But I am apt to put myself in the place of the vulgar and think many words difficult or obscure, which the preacher will not allow to be so, because these words are obvious to scholars.

Whether the preacher be what is called a linguist or not, he ought to know at least two languages,—the language of books and the language of common life. Wesley said that preachers may think with the learned, but must speak with the common people.[6] And Spurgeon,

---

[6] Quoted by Phelps, p. 152.

as someone has expressed it, mastered three languages, the language of John Bunyan, that of the King James Version of the Bible, and that of the man in the street. When one learns a thing in Latin or German and undertakes to state it to his people, he must of course translate. And so, what we study in learned works, using, as is there convenient and necessary, the technical language of science, we must in preaching translate into popular language, the language of common life. Many a young graduate, from college or theological seminary, errs not merely in treating subjects little suited to the popular mind but in using many terms which have grown familiar to him but which the people in general cannot at all understand. Most persons afterwards learn to correct this, at least in some measure; but occasionally we see a man of mature years and of great ability, who seems wholly unacquainted with popular modes of thought and forms of expression and wholly unaware that such is the case. The few who understand and sympathize with him speak with delight of his sermons, but for the many they might as well be delivered in German.[7] Even those technical terms in theology with which the people are very familiar do not always represent to them any distinct conception. Yet such terms as regeneration, depravity, etc., it is necessary to use in preaching, or much time will be lost in tedious circumlocutions. Besides taking frequent occasion distinctly to explain these terms, we may often prefix or add to them some words of a more popular character or may introduce them in such connections as will throw light on them.[8] That even the commonest words of Scripture may be employed in an utterly unscriptural sense is shown by the frequent use of them on the part of modern pantheistic infidels.

It is often remarked that Anglo-Saxon words are usually more perspicuous to the people at large than words of Latin origin. The latter are frequently more precise, being restricted in usage to a certain specific sense, while the Anglo-Saxon word is the general term. In fact, the Anglo-Saxon element of our language deserves great attention, for its terms are not only perspicuous to all but are apt to be singularly suggestive, through life-long association of ideas; besides the bulk of meaning contained, they carry with them an atmosphere of suggestion, often surpassingly attractive and stimulating. Those who have studied Latin and French ought to study Anglo-Saxon also;

[7] See a striking passage in Vinet, pp. 373, 374.

[8] As to Foster's objection to the use of such terms, compare below an Elegance, chap. iv.

and whether a student of language or not, every preacher should practically master the homely "household words" of our own English. Let it not be taken for granted that we know these already; for the discriminating use of them is by no means universal, even among educated men.[9]

(b) We must use words and phrases that exactly express our thought. Terms may be intelligible to the audience and yet not certainly represent to them our meaning. They may be ambiguous, so that while the hearer understands both senses of the word, he does not readily see which is here intended. Even the sacred writers, employing an easy, colloquial style, have sometimes left us ambiguous expressions. For example, the love of God, in Greek as in English, may denote our love to God or his love to us. Which it means in any case must be determined from the connection, or perhaps from the usage of the writer. John uses it in both senses, Paul almost invariably in the sense of God's love to us. A style absolutely free from such ambiguities would not be natural, and yet they ought of course to be avoided as far as possible. Or terms may be used in different senses in the same connection, and thus, although not in themselves ambiguous, may leave the meaning doubtful. Or they may be general terms and fail to indicate what specific idea was meant. Or they may be indefinite and leave it uncertain what extent of meaning was designed. In general, the terms ought to be precise, as it were cut down to fit the meaning, so that the expression and the idea exactly correspond, neither of them containing anything which the other does not contain. Such terms may almost always be found, and we should habitually constrain ourselves to seek for them. Besides the advantage of perspicuity to others, this habit will greatly benefit our own minds, for our thoughts attain a definite form and distinct outlines only in proportion as we find the precise terms to express them. It will also give freshness. No two men think exactly alike, even as all countenances are different; and he who thinks at all upon a subject and then says just what he thinks cannot fail of being to some extent original.

One important means of securing precision is accurate discrimina-

[9] Of course it would be folly to prefer an Anglo-Saxon word merely because it is such, when a word of Latin or other origin would be equally intelligible and more appropriate. But the effort to use the most perspicuous and expressive terms will be promoted by habitual attention to the Anglo-Saxon part of our language.

tion between so-called "synonyms." Even the English language, which in so many cases retains both an Anglo-Saxon and a Latin word of much the same original meaning, has, strictly speaking, no synonyms. Our usage has assigned to the words different departments of the field once common to both, or at least a different extent of application. The more cultivated a language becomes, as De Quincey has remarked, the more it distinguishes between apparent synonyms. To take a familiar example, the Greek word "sympathy," the Latin "compassion," and the compound of Anglo-Saxon "fellow-feeling," are in origin substantially the same; but how distinct they now are as English words. Yet, there are very many cases in which different words will coincide, to a greater or less extent, so that the careless observer would regard them as in all respects equivalent, and between these it is highly important to discriminate. Our own language, for the reason just indicated, greatly abounds in these synonyms, and the preacher cannot be too earnestly urged to give them his constant and painstaking attention.[10]

Skill in the choice of terms comes to no man as a matter of course. All who succeed in this respect, however gifted or however unlettered, have attained it by observation, reflection, practice. He who thinks words unimportant will never be perspicuous in expression or clear in thinking.[11]

(2) Perspicuity also depends on the construction of sentences and paragraphs. This important subject will not here be discussed at length, because it requires to be illustrated by numerous examples and can be thoroughly mastered only by means of written exercises.

It is obvious that a short sentence will be more perspicuous than a long one. Yet, a succession of very short sentences must not only be

---

[10] Whately's *Synonyms* is a good book, so far as it goes. The latest editions of all the great Dictionaries treat all the more important synonyms, and many of them in a very instructive manner. Roget's *Thesaurus of English Words* is also useful, for this and kindred purposes. Crabb's *Synonymes*, which became famous because we had nothing else, is deficient in clearness and often inaccurate. Smith's *Synonyms Discriminated* is probably the best book on the subject. Fallows' *One Hundred Thousand Synonyms and Antonyms* does not discuss the meanings but is a useful work.

[11] A talented and highly educated young man, who was made Professor of Natural Sciences in an American University, rarely met a particular friend of his without speaking of words. "What do you think is the difference between this word and this? It is so hard to find the precise word for describing physical forces and phenomena." A few years later a gentleman who had heard the Professor lecture said to the same friend, "He is thoroughly master of the subject, and he has an extraordinary readiness and felicity in the use of words. What a wonderful gift! He wants a word, and there it is." Fluency is a gift, but precision is the fruit of labor.

deficient in respect of harmony and of the energy which belongs to climax, but is really unfavorable to perspicuity. Sentences aggregate the thoughts which are to be comprehended and retained; and if these bundles, so to speak, are of considerable dimensions, the whole mass of thought will be more readily grasped and more easily borne with us. For variety, there should be a combination of short and long sentences. Even one that is very long may be quite perspicuous, provided the sense be not suspended till the close, as is done in periodic sentences. In general it is better that the qualifying clauses of a sentence should precede those qualified; in order that when we do reach a concrete conception, it may be the complete conception proposed, needing no subsequent addition or correction. But,

as carrying forward each qualifying clause costs some mental effort, ic follows that when the number of them and the time they are carried becomes great, we reach a limit beyond which more is lost than is gained.[12]

This limit is much sooner reached in what is to be heard than in what is to be read. And the difficulty is greater for uneducated minds than cultivated people can well imagine.

Aim at a certain simplicity in the structure of your sentences, avoiding long, intricate, and complex periods. Remember always that the bulk of the people are unused to reading and study. They lose sight of the connection in very long sentences, and they are quite bewildered when, for the sake of rounding a period, and suspending the sense till the concluding clause, you transgress the customary arrangement of the words. The nearer, therefore, your diction comes to the language of conversation, the more familiar will it be to them, and so the more easily apprehended. In this the style of Scripture is an excellent model.[13]

It may be added that sentences should be so framed as to leave no obscurity or ambiguity in respect to the relation of different clauses. Special care in this respect is needed in our language, because our pronouns present very imperfect means of distinction as to gender, number, and case. It is grievously common to find difficulty in perceiving to which of two preceding nouns some "it" or "that", some "they" or "those" is designed to refer.[14]

However great may be the practical difficulty of learning to construct sentences well, everyone can see that this is important. Inex-

[12] Herbert Spencer on Style, p. 24.
[13] Campbell on Pulpit Eloquence, Lect. III.
[14] See this matter well discussed in Campbell's *Phil. of Rhet.*, pp. 253-265.

perienced writers and speakers are seldom equally impressed with the importance of the paragraph. "The grouping of sentences into paragraphs is the true art of modern prose."[15] It is not uncommon to find a man of considerable ability writing an extended discourse or essay without any indication of paragraphs at all, though there will have been, in spite of his inattention, some natural connection of the thoughts, and a critic or compositor may succeed in breaking up the whole into rude blocks. Others do still worse, for they indicate paragraphs at haphazard, often separating matters which should be united. Now in some respects the proper construction of paragraphs is more important than that of sentences. If a sentence is badly arranged, the reader or hearer will at any rate have the matter of it before his mind and can usually perceive, with more or less effort, what relation of ideas was meant to be expressed. But when paragraphs are neglected, it requires a very broad view of the whole connection of discourse to supply the defect. In reading, there may be opportunity, if it is thought worth while, to look back and carefully scan the whole, so as to perceive the grouping of thoughts; and besides, in reading print, the compositor has helped us. But in hearing, we have no help and no time to study out the connection. It is thus plain that, especially in discourse which has to be heard, the proper management of paragraphs is indispensable to perspicuity.

The prime requisite in a paragraph is unity. Genung defines: "A paragraph is a connected series of sentences constituting the development of a single topic."[16] There must be some one thought, or group of related thoughts, occupying the whole. Digressions, when made at all, must constitute separate paragraphs. This one thought may commonly be presented in the opening sentence; or it may so present the first of a series or group of thoughts as to indicate the character and purpose common to them all. Sometimes, however, the opening sentence will be manifestly preparatory, perhaps repeating what has preceded, in order to facilitate the transition. Another requisite is that the successive sentences should so grow out of each other, or be so joined together by particles as to make the paragraph a whole. As to the length of paragraphs, there is, of course, no rule, and the main thing to be sought is an easy and natural variety.[17]

[15] Earle, *Eng. Prose,* p. 473.
[16] *Practical Rhetoric,* p. 193.
[17] The subject of paragraphs is treated at length, and with some good examples, by Bain, pp. 142-152, and by Genung, *Prac. Rhet.,* pp. 193 ff. Most treatises neglect it.

In the formation of paragraphs, and also of sentences, careful attention should be given to the conjunctions and other connectives. What grammarians call the particles, or little parts of speech, are not less important than the greater parts, for they establish a relation between these, converting crude matter into a structure, an operative organization—like the joints in a body. The felicitous choice of a preposition or conjunction, or the proper handling of a relative pronoun, will often contribute immensely to the perspicuity of a sentence or a paragraph.[18]

In unwritten composition, or what is called "extemporaneous speaking," it is practically better, though amounting to the same thing, to fix the mind on points rather than on paragraphs. Do not be thinking how you would distribute this on pages if you were writing, but arrange a succession of points to be treated. Then taking up each of these in order, remember the homely saying, and "stick to your point." One may thus gain the unity and consecutiveness which belong to a written paragraph. Yet there is probably no one particular in which a speaker so much needs the discipline of written composition as in respect to this matter of consecutiveness in developing a single thought. A man who never writes anything may sometimes learn to frame sentences well and to arrange discourses well. He may have distinct points, corresponding to paragraphs, and each constituting a unit. But to develop these points in an orderly manner, so that each sentence may grow out of the preceding or have a well-indicated connection with it, so that the developed unit may become a structure, an harmonious organization, this is what few men learn to achieve without practice in writing paragraphs. Nor does the hurried writing so common among those who write and read their sermons at all mend the matter. Nay, it requires careful writing, not hurried, even though sometimes rapid, and not put forth without critical revision, to give the kind of training which is needed. Such careful writing, though not necessarily of what he is about to speak, an extemporaneous preacher ought frequently to practice.

(3) Perspicuity depends not only on the choice of terms and the proper construction of sentences and paragraphs but also on the general brevity or diffuseness of the style.

It is a mistake to suppose that the briefest statement of an idea

---

[18] See, on the connectives, Campbell's *Phil. of Rhet.*, Part III, Chap. IV and V. See also Bain, as above.

is sure to be the clearest. If it be really made clear to the person addressed, then, of course, the briefer the better. But

extreme conciseness is ill-suited to hearers or readers whose intellec-tual powers and cultivation are but small. . . . It is remarked by anatomists that the nutritive quality is not the only requisite in food;—that a certain degree of distention of the stomach is required, to enable it to act with its full powers;—and that it is for this reason hay or straw must be given to horses, as well as corn, in order to supply the necessary bulk. Something analogous to this takes place with respect to the generality of minds, which are incapable of thoroughly digesting and assimilating what is presented to them, however clearly, in a very small compass. . . . It is necessary that the attention should be detained for a certain time on the subject; and persons of unphilosophical mind, though they can attend to what they read or hear, are unapt to dwell upon it in the way of sub-sequent meditation.

The usual expedient, however, of employing a prolix style by way of accommodation to such minds is seldom successful. Most of those who could have comprehended the meaning, if more briefly expressed, and many of those who could not do so are likely to be bewildered by tedious expansion; and being unable to maintain a steady attention to what is said, they forget part of what they have heard before the whole is com-pleted. Add to which, that the feebleness produced by excessive dilution (if such an expression may be allowed) will occasion the attention to languish; and what is imperfectly attended to, however clear in itself, will usually be but imperfectly understood. Let not an author, therefore, satisfy himself by finding that he has expressed his meaning so that if attended to, he cannot fail to be understood; he must consider also what attention is likely to be paid to it. If on the one hand much matter is expressed in very few words to an unreflecting audience, or if, on the other hand, there is a wearisome prolixity, the requisite attention may very probably not be bestowed.[19]

Prolixity, then, is worse than extreme conciseness. The latter, though imperfectly understood, may stimulate attention and reflec-tion and lead to subsequent examination of the subject. The former does but weary and disgust. It must be granted that prolixity is very common in the pulpit. Preachers often have to prepare and preach sermons when their minds are not in a creative mood. It seems their duty to say something, and custom requires that, however unfruitful the subject and however unfavorable their own state of mind, they shall continue for at least a certain number of minutes.[20] Under such

[19] Whately, pp. 301, 302.
[20] Compare Whately, p. 315.

circumstances a man's ideas are not clear, and in the feeble struggle to express them, he inevitably becomes prolix.

There are several means by which we may avoid too great conciseness without falling into prolixity. One of these is repetition. In some cases it is well to repeat the statement in the same words. More commonly, we may

repeat the same sentiment and argument in many different forms of expression, each in itself brief, but all together affording such an expansion of the sense to be conveyed, and so detaining the mind upon it, as the sense may require.

This repetition must of course not be a mere tautology. The thought must be presented in some other view or some new relation.

What has been expressed in appropriate terms may be repeated in metaphorical; the antecedent and consequent of an argument, or the parts of an antithesis may be transposed; or several different points that have been enumerated, presented in a varied order, etc.[21]

Another means is by varied illustration. After stating the thought as clearly as can be done within a moderate compass, we may present various illustrations of it or of its different aspects. These interest the hearer and detain his attention on the matter in hand, until he becomes perfectly familiar with it and yet not weary of it. There is no more remarkable example of this than Chalmers. His sermons often consist of a single idea, which is held up in different lights, turned over and over, and round and round, until we have seen every facet it possesses; and yet each of these aspects is made so bright with fresh illustration, so brilliant with hues of fancy, that we cannot grow weary.[22] In this, as in some other respects, Chalmers is one of the worst models to be imitated but one of the most profitable examples to be studied. A third means of gaining the requisite expansion without prolixity is division. The matter presented, however minute, may often be divided into several points, just as we divide larger topics; and these points being successively stated, the whole is clearly seen.

And here let us emphasize the fact, which the preacher cannot too carefully consider, that as in several other respects, so particularly in respect to expansion, the proper style of public speaking is widely different from that appropriate to an essay or to anything designed

---

[21] Whately, pp. 302, 303.

[22] Robert Hall said of Chalmers' sermons that their movement was on hinges, not on wheels.

to be deliberately read. This has been often stated and in the strongest terms, as by De Quincey in the following words:

That is good rhetoric for the hustings which is bad for a book. Even for the highest forms of popular eloquence, the laws of style vary much from the general standard. In the senate, and for the same reason in a newspaper, it is a virtue to reiterate your meaning: . . . variation of the words, with a substantial identity of the sense and dilution of the truth, is oftentimes a necessity. . . . It is the advantage of a book that you can return to the past page if anything in the present depends upon it. But return being impossible in the case of a spoken harangue, where each sentence perishes as it is born, both the speaker and the hearer become aware of a mutual interest in a much looser style. It is for the benefit of both that the weightier propositions should be detained before the eye a good deal longer than the chastity of taste or the austerity of logic would tolerate in a book.[23]

In conclusion, let us remember that efforts to be perspicuous may be carried too far. It is wretchedly tiresome to hear a man carefully explaining what everyone present understands beforehand, or continuing to repeat and open and illustrate what he has already made sufficiently plain. And the oratorical diffuseness just spoken of is a very different thing from that torrent of useless words which we are so often compelled to endure.

[23] De Quincey on Style, p. 69.

CHAPTER III

QUALITIES OF STYLE—ENERGY

THE term "energy" as applied to style, includes all that we mean by such separate terms as animation, force, and passion. Animation, or liveliness,[1] serves to stimulate attention; it is not enough for a speaker to say what the hearer may understand if he attends; the point is to arouse him, to put life into him, to make attention easy and pleasant, and inattention difficult. For this the freshness of the thought and the magnetic power of delivery are the chief agents; but much may also be accomplished by animation of style.[2] The term "force" is used especially with reference to arguments, and the kindred word "power" is applied both to arguments and to motives. Passion—which in its milder and more tender forms we call "pathos" and in its highest form the "sublime"—has its effect upon the feelings, often by means of the imagination; and both force and passion aim at last to influence the will. It is thus plain that the characteristic property of an eloquent style is energy. Perspicuity it needs in common with the philosophical or didactic style; elegance it may possess in common with the poetic style; but energy, that is, animation, force, or passion, is its characteristic.

The chief requisite to an energetic style is an energetic nature. There must be vigorous thinking, earnest if not passionate feeling, and the determined purpose to accomplish some object, or the man's style will have no true, exalted energy. It is in this sense emphatically true that an orator is born, not made. Without these qualities one may give valuable instruction; without them one might preach what silly admirers call "beautiful" sermons; but if a man has not force of character, a passionate soul, he will never be really eloquent. There are, however, timid and sensitive men who, when practice has given them confidence and occasion calls out their powers, exhibit far more

[1] Campbell's term, "vivacity," is now restricted to conversation and the lighter kinds of writing.

[2] There is a homely story of a preacher who suggested to a sleepy hearer that snuff might keep him awake and was asked in return, "Couldn't you put a little more snuff into your sermons?"

of this masterful nature than they had ever imagined themselves to possess. Phelps[3] well says:

Nothing else can take the place, or do the work, of this force of feeling. Energy and enthusiasm coexist in character: they must coexist in style.

He wisely adds, in another place,[4] that true energy is founded in self-possession. Extravagance and vehemence by going too far defeat the ends of a true eloquence. Their effect is far different from that produced by an energy intense yet restrained by self-mastery.

The next requisite is something to say and something regarded as exceedingly important. The mind must be full of thought, if there is to be forcible expression. That which is said must be what the speaker heartily believes to be true, deeply feels to be important, and earnestly desires to impress upon others. The preacher has peculiar advantages in respect of materials conducive to energy, if he has a familiar, profound, and ever-freshened acquaintance with the Bible. No temporal interests are so momentous as those of eternity. No other topics can impart to the mind such vigor and authority as truths which we personally know to be taught in God's Word.

Energy of style must be considered under four heads: the choice of terms, the construction of sentences, conciseness, and the use of figures.[5]

(1) As to the choice of terms, one point is that, so far as the subject may admit, we should prefer concrete to abstract terms and particular or specific to general terms. In philosophical discussion or in comprehensive statements, there is of course need for abstract or for general terms, but these are very unfavorable to energy of style.

The more general the terms are, the picture is the fainter; the more special they are, it is the brighter. The same sentiments may be expressed with equal justness, and even perspicuity, in the former way as in the latter; but as the coloring will in that case be more languid, it cannot give equal pleasure to the fancy, and by consequence will not contribute so much either to fix the attention or to impress the memory.

[3] *English Style in Pub. Disc.*, p. 208.
[4] P. 217 ff.
[5] Some figures, as metaphor and synecdoche, would of course fall under the head of choice of terms, but many others would not. The division made by Campbell (followed by Whately), namely, choice of words, number of words, and arrangement of words, is simple and pleasing but does not cover the ground. The divisions suggested above have the fault of not being mutually exclusive but are yet practically convenient.

Campbell proceeds to illustrate this by striking examples from Scripture.

In the song of Moses, occasioned by the miraculous passage of the Israelites through the Red Sea, the inspired poet, speaking of the Egyptians, says, 'They sank as lead in the mighty waters.' Make but a small alteration on the expression, and say, 'They fell as metal in the mighty waters,' and the difference in the effect will be quite astonishing. Yet, the sentiment will be equally just, and in either way the meaning of the author can hardly be mistaken.

And the difference is wholly due to the change from specific to general terms.

'Consider the lilies how they grow; they toil not, they spin not; and yet I say unto you that Solomon in all his glory was not arrayed like one of these. If, then, God so clothe the grass which today is in the field and tomorrow is cast into the oven, how much more will he clothe you.' Let us here adopt a little of the tasteless manner of modern paraphrasts, by the substitution of more general terms, . . . and observe the effect produced by this change. 'Consider the flowers how they gradually increase in their size; they do no manner of work, and yet I declare to you that no king whatever, in his most splendid habit, is dressed up like them. If, then, God in his providence doth so adorn the vegetable productions which continue but a little time on the land, and are afterward put into the fire, how much more will he provide clothing for you.' How spiritless is the same sentiment rendered by these small variations![6]

In order to give animation and passion to style, there must be an appeal to the imagination. Now we can form images only of individual objects, and the image of some individual belonging to a species, as a lily, will be far more easily formed and far more vivid than that of an individual belonging to a genus, as a flower.

Whately points out that we are seldom shut up by the nature of the subject but can usually choose between generic and specific terms. Thus the terms can be made more general than the subject requires, and this is appropriate

when we wish to avoid giving a vivid impression,—when our object is to soften what is offensive, disgusting or shocking; as when we speak of an 'execution,' for the infliction of the sentence of death on a criminal. . . . Many, especially unpracticed writers, fall into a feeble style by resorting

[6] Campbell, *Phil. of Rhet.,* pp. 307, 308. Compare pp. 309-315. See below in this chapter, under the head of Synecdoche.

unnecessarily to this substitution of the general for the specific, or of the specific for the singular; either because they imagine there is more appearance of refinement or of profundity in the employment of such terms as are in less common use among the vulgar, or, in some cases, with a view to give greater comprehensiveness to their reasonings and to increase the utility of what they say, by enlarging the field of its application. Inexperienced preachers frequently err in this way by dwelling on virtue and vice,—piety and irreligion,—in the abstract, without particularizing; forgetting that while they include much, they impress little or nothing.[7]

Epithets will seldom contribute to energy. An "epithet" is an adjective added to a noun or an adverb added to a verb, which does not add anything to the sense conveyed by the noun or verb, but simply brings into prominence something contained in it. Now as commonly managed by third-rate novelists, essayists, and orators, epithets never render the expression forcible. Even when really ornamental, they are appropriate only to poetry and poetical prose. If you cut a bough from an apple tree in spring to please your friends with its beauty, you would retain the twigs and leaves and blossoms; but if you wish to knock a man down with it, all these must be trimmed away.

The superfluous adjective is to your message what barnacles and seaweed are to the clean straight lines of a ship designed to cut through the water like the edge of a knife.[8]

Yet when properly introduced, epithets may add force. For instance, they may bring to notice properties of an object which would otherwise have escaped attention, or cause the mind to dwell on the characteristic thus brought out, until it gets the full impression. Or they may be

so many abridged arguments, the force of which is sufficiently conveyed by a mere hint; for example, if any one says, 'we ought to take warning from the *bloody* revolution of France,' the epithet suggests one of the reasons for our being warned, and that not less clearly, and more forcibly, than if the argument had been stated at length.[9]

It is, however, a matter with reference to which the young writer or speaker, particularly if he is highly imaginative, has more need to restrain than to encourage himself.

[7] Whately, pp. 221, 222.
[8] Farmer, *The Servant of the Word*, p. 61.
[9] Whately, pp. 332 ff.

Words in which the sound resembles the sense (*onomatopœia*) will sometimes promote energy, but in oratory they must come unsought, if used at all.

Unusual words and phrases may also be energetic, because they contrast with the common and homely, so as to awaken peculiar interest, like a visitor or a foreigner. Yet if the visitor be a reserved stranger or the foreigner be ridiculous, the effect is not good; and so the uncommon expressions must not be unintelligible or grotesque.

Anglo-Saxon words are not only clearer, as we have seen, but also often more forcible than the corresponding words of Latin origin. In some cases they are more specific, the Latin having furnished the general term. In other cases they have the power of association, having been connected in our minds from childhood with real objects and actions, while the Latin term represents only ideas. Others are more forcible because shorter, so as to strike a quicker blow, while, on the contrary, some long Latin words are energetic, because so ponderous and sonorous.[10]

(2) Much depends, as to energy, upon the construction of sentences.

The periodic structure of sentences requires special attention. The word "period" signifies a going round, a circuit, revolution, etc., and, strictly speaking, a sentence would be called a period when it returns at the close to the matter with which it began. It was very common in Greek and Latin, particularly the latter, to begin with a noun in the nominative case, then make a long sentence, consisting first of adjuncts to the noun and afterwards of adjuncts to the verb, and as the closing word to give the verb. This would be strictly a period; the sentence circles round, and the last word is in close grammatical connection with the first. In English we seldom give precisely this form to long sentences, except in the inverted style of blank verse.

> The blest in heaven, above the starry sphere,
> Their happy hours in joy and hymning spend.

But more generally, any sentence is called a period when the sense is so suspended as to be nowhere complete till we reach the last clause. Campbell gives an excellent example: "At last, after much fatigue, through deep roads, and bad weather, we came, with no small difficulty, to our journey's end." Contrast this with what is called the

---

[10] Compare Herbert Spencer on Style, pp. 12-14. His theory is inadequate, but the facts are well stated.

"loose" arrangement: "We came to our journey's *end* at *last,* with no small *difficulty,* after much *fatigue,* through deep *roads,* and bad weather."[11] Here the sense would be complete and the sentence might end at any one of the five points indicated by italicized words, —a procedure which, with its repeated revision of the completed mental picture, exhausts rather than sustains the attention.

Periods, or sentences nearly approaching to periods, have certainly, when other things are equal, the advantage in point of energy. An unexpected continuation of a sentence which the reader had supposed to be concluded, especially if, in reading aloud, he had under that supposition dropped his voice, is apt to produce a sensation in the mind of being disagreeably balked: analogous to the unpleasant jar which is felt, when in ascending or descending stairs, we meet with a step more than we had expected; and if this be often repeated, as in a very loose sentence, a kind of weary impatience results from the uncertainty when the sentence is to close.[12]

In speaking,

the periodic style is much less necessary and therefore much less suitable than in skillful compositions designed for the closet. The speaker may, in most instances, by the skillful suspension of his voice, give to a loose sentence the effect of a period; and though in both species of composition the display of art is to be guarded against, a more unstudied air is looked for in such as are spoken.[13]

In fact, very long periodic sentences are, in speaking, to be avoided. The hearer must retain the whole period in mind and cannot fully understand any part of it until he reaches the end; and undisciplined minds will find this very difficult. A period concentrates its whole force into one blow; but we must not gain this energy by the sacrifice either of perspicuity or of naturalness and ease. It is sometimes advantageous to make a long sentence partly loose and partly periodical.

The emphatic arrangement of sentences is confined to much narrower limits in English than in many other languages. In the familiar sentence, "Will you ride to town today?" the sense will be different according as the emphasis is laid on "will," or on "you," or on "ride," etc. Now in Greek or Latin, where the order of words in a sentence

[11] *Phil. of Rhet.,* p. 389. See Herbert Spencer on Style, pp. 26, 27.
[12] Whately, p. 365.
[13] *Ibid.,* p. 371.

can be very freely varied, the emphatic word in each of these cases might be indicated by its position. But English idiom does not permit this; and the emphasis has to be determined from the connection or must be marked by italic letters. So far as our idiom does allow inversion, we ought to employ it and dispense with italics. In speaking, one will indicate the emphasis by the manner of utterance; but much is gained if it can at the same time be indicated by the position of the words.

The most prominent position in a sentence is the beginning, and next to this, the end. If now a word which, according to the common grammatical order, would come elsewhere be placed at the beginning or the end, it will attract special attention; it will become one of the important, the emphatic words of the sentence. And in general, to put a word out of its ordinary place will cause it to be specially noticed. Such inversions of order, by giving particular prominence to the most important word or clause, will often render a sentence far more energetic. Compare "Great is Diana of the Ephesians" and "Diana of the Ephesians is great." In the saying of Peter, "Silver and gold have I none, but such as I have, give I thee," take the common grammatical order, "I have no gold and silver," etc., and how feeble! Observe, too, that here our version increases the energy by separating the adjective "none" from its substantives and putting it at the end of the clause, the other most emphatic position.[14] And not only may the predicate thus come first, for emphasis, but many other inversions are possible. "Not every one that saith unto me, Lord Lord, shall enter into the kingdom of heaven." "Now is the accepted time."

Sometimes an emphatic word or phrase is put first, though it must afterwards be represented in its proper grammatical place by a pronoun. "Your fathers, where are they? and the prophets, do they live forever?" How cold and languid, compared with this, would be, "Where are your fathers? and do the prophets live forever?"[15] So also, "To be or not to be, that is the question." In other cases, an emphatic word which could not stand at the head of a sentence is introduced by some pronominal phrase. We could not say, "Came forth two bears out of the wood," but we can say, "There came forth," etc., (II Kings 2:24).

The word 'it' is frequently very serviceable in enabling us to alter the arrangement: thus, the sentence, 'Cicero praised Cæsar,' which admits of

14 Campbell, p. 378.
15 Most of these examples are from Campbell, pp. 381-383.

at least two modifications of sense, may be altered so as to express either of them by thus varying the order: 'It was Cicero that praised Cæsar,' or, 'It was Cæsar that Cicero praised.'[16]

There are also numerous cases in which a convenient inversion may be effected by changing from the active to the passive construction. Thus: "There is a yet more signal instance of ingratitude. One of his chosen twelve disciples denied Jesus Christ, and another betrayed him." Here "Jesus Christ" is most emphatic and ought to come first. This could be managed, but with some awkwardness, as follows: "Jesus Christ, one of his chosen twelve disciples denied, and another betrayed." All becomes easy as well as forcible by making it passive: "There is a yet more signal instance of ingratitude. Jesus Christ was denied by one of his chosen twelve disciples, and by another he was betrayed."

No sentence ought to end in a large number of unaccented syllables, as "comparable," "exquisitely," "agreeableness." It is best to end with a word which accents the last syllable or at any rate to have the accent only one syllable from the end. In like manner, we must not close the sentence with a large number of unemphatic words. Thus: "I will give my own attention to the matter," is much feebler than "I will give the matter my own attention."

Antithesis often adds greatly to energy. For example, "The Sabbath was made for man, not man for the Sabbath." "Thou art anxious and troubled about many things: but one thing is needful." "The memory of the just is blessed: but the name of the wicked shall rot." Such antithetical expressions abound in the Scriptures, as they do in the literature of all nations, their terseness and force contributing to give them popularity. How vigorous is the saying quoted by Quintilian: "I do not live to eat, I eat to live." In all such cases, each of the two contrasted clauses throws light upon the other, so that without losing perspicuity the expressions may be made very brief and thus more pointed and forcible, while at the same time the contrast makes the whole statement more striking. So much does antithesis contribute to energy and brilliancy of style that many writers and speakers employ it in great excess. This disfigures the style of Macaulay, which is in many respects so admirable. In preaching, a manifest and especially a frequent effort to strike is particularly unbecoming. And besides the violation of taste in the excessive use of antithesis, there is danger, in any single case, of violating truth. In order strikingly

[16] Whately, p. 364.

to contrast two things, we may unconsciously exaggerate the difference. The danger of such exaggeration is very great, and it is a sad
thing to gain force at the expense of truth.

One who speaks under the influence of strong feeling is very apt
sometimes to use broken constructions. He will be so absorbed as not
to notice the syntax, or after beginning the sentence in one way, a
sudden impulse will cause him to break off and end it in a different
way. The most impassioned speakers and writers naturally employ
such expressions most frequently; for example, they are very common
in the writings of the apostle Paul. Whenever actually prompted by
real feeling, broken constructions are admissible and forcible. But
they must never be used from calculation and must not be allowed,
even when perfectly natural, to recur too often.

Akin to this is what grammarians call "aposiopesis," where part
of a sentence is suppressed through emotion. For example, Luke 19:42,
"If even thou hadst known . . . the things that belong to thy peace!"
How much better would have been her destiny, it is left for silence
to suggest. Luke 22:42, "Father, if thou art willing to remove this
cup from me!" He does not go on to ask that it be removed; but,
after a pause, he adds, "Yet, not my will but thine be done." Acts 23:9,
"We find no evil in this man; but if a spirit spoke to him, or an
angel—?" How expressive was this silence, from a Pharisee speaking
in the Sanhedrim, in presence of the Sadducees! The words, "let us
not fight against God," were added by some critic or copyist who
understood grammar better than rhetoric.

As regards the whole matter of energy in the construction of sentences, one may find great benefit in the exercise of recasting sentences.
This would also conduce, it is obvious, to perspicuity and to elegance,
but it is still more important as to energy.

(3) Energy is greatly promoted by conciseness.

It may be established as a maxim that admits no exception, that the
fewer the words are, provided neither propriety nor perspicuity be
violated, the expression is always the more vivid. 'Brevity,' says Shakespeare, 'is the soul of wit.' Thus much is certain, that if whatever kind
the sentiment be, witty, humorous, grave, animated, or sublime, the more
briefly it is expressed, the energy is the greater, or the sentiment is the
more enlivened. . . . As when the rays of the sun are collected into the
focus of a burning-glass, the smaller the spot is which receives them,
compared with the surface of the glass, the greater is the splendor.[17]

[17] Campbell, *Phil. of Rhet.*, p. 353.

There is no more remarkable example of energetic conciseness than the famous saying of Cæsar, *Veni, vidi, vici,* "I came, saw, conquered." The studied brevity of Lacedæmonian speech has given us the word "laconic." The orators among the American Indians have often been remarkable for brief, pithy, pointed sayings. All men, cultivated and uncultivated, appreciate brevity.

Opposed to conciseness are tautology, pleonasm, and verbosity. Sheer tautology, saying the same thing over, even if in different words; is perhaps not a very common fault. Pleonasm, the use of words or phrases which add nothing to the sense, is quite common, and often greatly detracts from energy, though sometimes it promotes energy. And verbosity, the multiplication of words which add something, but nothing of any real importance, is surpassingly frequent and hurtful.

A certain high-sounding verbosity is apt to be greatly admired by very ignorant or half-educated people. But this admiration does not argue any real benefit to them or any real power in the speaker.

It is not uncommon to hear a writer or speaker of this class mentioned as having 'a very fine command of language,' when perhaps it might be said with more correctness that 'his language has a command of him'; that is, that he follows a train of words rather than of thought, and strings together all the striking expressions that occur to him on the subject, instead of first forming a clear notion of the sense he wishes to convey and then seeking for the most appropriate vehicle in which to convey it. He has but the same 'command of language' that the rider has of a horse which runs away with him.[18]

The Hebrew narrative style is peculiarly diffuse and circumstantial; and the parallelism of Hebrew poetry leads to much repetition. As used in the Bible, these are not blemishes but positive excellences; but in our own speaking and writing we must remember that in these respects modern taste, for the most part, demands a different style, and that in such matters the taste of our hearers ought to be consulted.

Tautology and pleonasm may be corrected by merely striking out the superfluous words; and this should be carefully and vigorously done. To correct verbosity it is often necessary to recast sentences, and substitute other terms.

It is to be remembered that in seeking conciseness we must not

[18] Whately, p. 347.

sacrifice perspicuity. Sometimes a terse, pointed phrase that would not be readily intelligible to all may yet be employed by prefixing some more diffuse statement.

The hearers will be struck by the forcibleness of the sentence which they will have been prepared to comprehend; they will understand the longer expression, and remember the shorter.[19]

Interesting examples of this may be seen in our Lord's teaching, and in the Epistle of James.[20] In other cases a brief statement may be of such a nature as to suggest more than is expressed; either the intellect is set to pursuing a train of thought, or the imagination is stimulated to fill up an outline. Such exercise of the intellect and imagination, if not made too difficult, is highly agreeable to all; and the mind, being thus aroused to grasp the subject actively, will hold it much more firmly than if it had been passively received. It is the highest type of style to be terse and suggestive.

The great majority of young speakers and writers need with especial care to cultivate conciseness. Most of those who feel moved to write or speak are naturally fluent. They find volubility and verbosity to be easy to themselves and acceptable to many of their hearers. An excessive luxuriance of style is much more promising than extreme barrenness; but, as Cicero remarked, it needs, like an overgrowth of grain in spring, to be pastured down with the pen. The task often requires rigorous self-control. The lad who is thinning corn longs to leave three stalks yonder in one hill because they all seem so large and fine. But he must remember that three will make no more than two, nay, will make less. Some persons, on the other hand, should stimulate themselves to greater fertility in respect to style, which may be effected by improving the imagination, by familiarity with good writers whose style tends to luxuriance, and by endeavoring to speak and write under the influence of a more stirring passion, or a more tender sentiment.

And it must not be forgotten that, while diffuseness is unfavorable to energy, there may be a profuseness, as in Cicero, Barrow, Chalmers, De Quincey, Gladstone, which is highly energetic. The former spreads sluggishly over a wide expanse; the latter pours onward in a rushing torrent. Longinus compares the impassioned style of

[19] Whately, p. 351.
[20] For example, see Matt. 19:30; 20:16; 22:14; 23:12. Also, Jas., 1:12,17, 27; 2:13, 26; 3:18; 4:17; 5:6.

Demosthenes to a storm or a thunderbolt, that of Cicero to a conflagration, wide-spreading, all-devouring, long-continuing. Even repetition, which is often necessary in order to perspicuity, and which many preachers make distressingly feeble and tedious, may be so managed by a man deeply in earnest as to be but strong blows in quick succession.

(4) Perhaps the chief element of energy in style is the use of figures of speech.[21] Passionate feeling, whether anger, fear, love, or the emotion of the sublime, naturally expresses itself by means of bold imagery,—bold, though never elaborate or far-fetched.

Figures are sometimes to be considered as belonging rather to the materials of discourse than to the style. Thus, apart from the expression of an idea, some comparison may be introduced by way of proof or elucidation. Usually, however, figures are employed as a means of expressing the thought,—although they may add something to the expression,—and they are thus properly regarded as a part of style. Figures usually contribute to elegance of style, and some of them—comparison especially—to perspicuity; but their most considerable aid is in the matter of energy. Those which are of particular importance to a forcible style of preaching will be briefly discussed, the student being referred to the works on rhetoric for fuller treatment of the subject as a whole.

Metaphor is more conducive to energy than comparison. The latter is useful in order for perspicuity or elegance but is apt to be avoided in impassioned or otherwise energetic discourse. It has been often remarked that in Demosthenes' great oration On the Crown, where he had so much at stake and speaks with such directness and force and vehemence, there is but a single comparison, and that couched in two words. Yet, comparisons may sometimes, from the nature of the subject matter, be exceedingly impressive. "His eyes were as a flame of fire, and his voice as the sound of many waters." "As the lightning cometh out of the east, and shineth even unto the west, so shall the coming of the Son of man be." "The ungodly . . . are like the chaff which the wind driveth away."

The metaphor, instead of comparing one thing with another, identifies the two by taking the name or assuming the attributes of

---

[21] Usage has not made a well-established distinction between the terms "figure" and "trope", but the latter is commonly applied only to certain figures, particularly metaphor, metonymy. and synecdoche.

the one for the other.[22] Jesus often spoke in metaphorical terms, such as "I am the door," "This is my body." Where a metaphor would not be readily intelligible, it may be combined with a comparison or made plain by some additional term. A great multitude of metaphors have become so familiar that they no longer possess any special force; but in the many that never wear out and in the unlimited range of new invention and combination, metaphors present to the orator an inexhaustible source of energetic expression. It is imagination that must produce them and good taste that must regulate their use. Inexperienced speakers often employ metaphors that are incongruous in themselves or carried out into ridiculous or wearisome detail. But much will depend on subject, occasion, and feeling. Even Shakespeare's often condemned example of a mixed metaphor,—

To take arms against a sea of troubles,

is allowable and natural in Hamlet, when frenzied and meditating suicide, and speaking to himself alone.

The synecdoche is also favorable to energy. When a part of a thing is taken for the whole, or the species for the genus, the expression is apt to be more animated and suggestive; just as we have already seen that particular or specific terms are more energetic than general terms. "They shall beat their swords into ploughshares, and their spears into pruning hooks" is immensely more forcible than to say in general that they will convert their weapons of war into implements of agriculture.

Hyperbole, or saying more than is meant, is very natural to a person so absorbed in the contemplation of a particular object or subject as to exaggerate its comparative importance, or to one so intensely excited that all ordinary expression seems to him tame. It is also allowable in any case where one knows that the exaggerated language need not be misunderstood and desires to make a deep impression as to an important fact. "And there are also many other things which Jesus did, the which, if they should be written every one, I suppose that even the world itself could not contain the books that should be written" (John 21:25). Such expressions are particularly natural to the fervid Oriental mind, and they have great power with the masses of men. The apostle Paul is remarkable for hyperboles and for strong language of every kind. His impassioned expression, "I could wish that myself were accursed from Christ for my brethren" (Rom. 9:3) is best understood as an instance of hyperbolical language and can be

[22] Genung, *Practical Rhetoric*, p. 90.

appreciated only in proportion as we sympathize with his patriotic and pious ardor and devotion. Our Lord's teaching has a singular and very striking peculiarity in the use of extreme cases to set forth a principle. "Whosoever shall smite thee on thy right cheek, turn to him the other also." When he himself was smitten on the cheek, we do not read that he turned the other. It was an extreme, hyperbolical way of stating the injunction not to strike back; and though sometimes misunderstood and misrepresented, the statement is one which no man ever forgets. Compare the expressions, "Let not thy left hand know what thy right hand doeth," "If any man come to me, and hate not his father and mother," etc. (Matt. 6:3; Luke 14:26). As a teacher of men, our Lord used a great variety of expedients for stimulating their languid attention, for compelling them to remember and reflect. Many a phrase of his fails to be understood unless we bear this in mind; and his example shows that such efforts may be made in a spirit and tone wholly unlike that of "sensation" preachers.

Personification, representing or addressing an inanimate object as if it had life, sometimes imparts to discourse great animation and beauty, and even passionate energy. Examples of it abound in the Scriptures, as well as in all poetry and oratory. The personification of wisdom in the Proverbs of Solomon is very striking. Personifications of the church are often carried further in preaching than is wise. Our language presents unusual facilities for this figure, from its unique peculiarity of treating all names of things as of the neuter gender, so that to call an inanimate object "he" or "she" will at once make a personification. We must be careful not to abuse this advantage. All high-wrought imagery must be sparingly employed.

Apostrophe, which is sometimes confounded with personification, consists in "turning away" from our audience and addressing some person or thing, usually one of which we had been speaking. If it be a thing that is thus addressed, there is also a personification. "It cannot be that a prophet perish out of Jerusalem. O Jerusalem, Jerusalem, which killest the prophets," etc. (Luke 13:33). But there may be apostrophe to a real person, and there is often personification when we only speak of the object personified without addressing it. Apostrophe properly belongs to the language of passion, and, even as such, it must not occur too frequently or be too long continued. A preacher, standing with upturned eyes, and addressing some Scripture character, departed friend, or personified virtue, can not go on through many sentences.

Exclamation is sometimes akin to apostrophe but properly distinct. Impassioned preachers are somewhat apt to use it too freely. Some say oh! ah! or alas! so often that it loses all power. Others indulge too much in such exclamations as: How grand! Momentous issue! Fearful thought! and the like. On the other hand, we must not be overfastidious in avoiding exclamation where it is naturally prompted by actual feeling. But to use the same exclamation habitually makes it ineffective.

Interrogation is with all orators a frequent means of giving animation to discourse. Not only may an antagonist, real or imaginary, be questioned in such a manner as to awaken lively interest on the part of the hearers, but questions are constantly addressed to the hearers themselves. Their minds are thus aroused somewhat as if called on actually to answer. It should be observed that one is liable sometimes to fall as it were into an interrogative mood, and throw so much of his discourse into the form of questions as to produce the most disagreeable species of monotony. It is important to be on our guard against this and, when upon any occasion conscious of it, to break away by a resolute effort.

Dramatism gives to discourse a life and vigor and charm that can in scarcely any other way be equalled. To personate some character and speak his sentiments, to introduce an objector stating his objections, and answer them point by point, to sustain a dialogue between two supposed persons, to reproduce some scene by dramatic description, are methods which all effective speakers more or less employ and examples of which abound in Demosthenes, Chrysostom, Spurgeon. In the pulpit, dramatism must usually be kept within somewhat narrow limits, and must always be regulated by good taste and sobriety of feeling. Especially do limitations of action and tone require to be carefully guarded, lest they become ridiculous or at any rate unsuitable to devout discourse.[23]

As to the whole matter of energy of style, grave mistakes are often committed. Some speakers imagine that they must be energetic in style and manner even when it does not suit the subject or does not accord with their actual feelings. Now it is only strong feeling that prompts impassioned or in any wise energetic expression. To gain the latter we must cultivate our sensibilities and must keep the mind in contact with the subject to be treated until the corresponding emotions are excited. If little or no emotion really exists, the language

[23] Compare Vinet, pp. 459-465.

of passion produces no effect, or even a contrary effect to that desired. It is one of the most important lessons a preacher can learn, not to assume earnestness of style or delivery when he has not earnestness of feeling.

Another serious and very common mistake is in the effort to main-tain uniform energy throughout a discourse.

An author should guard against the vain ambition of expressing every-thing in an equally high-wrought, brilliant, and forcible style. The neglect of this caution often occasions the imitation of the best models to prove detrimental. When the admiration of some fine and animated passages leads a young writer to take these passages for his general model and to endeavor to make every sentence he composes equally fine, he will, on the contrary, give a flatness to the whole and destroy the effect of those portions which would have been forcible if they had been allowed to stand prominent. To brighten the dark parts of a picture produces much the same result as if one had darkened the bright parts; in either case there is a want of relief and contrast; and Composition, as well as paint-ing, has its lights and shades, which must be distributed with no less skill if we would produce the desired effect.[24]

In highly passionate speaking there must be variety, alternation. In any intense physical exertion, one needs frequent change of posture, so as to bring different muscles into play and let them relieve each other. The same thing is true as to mental excitement.[25] Neither the hearers nor even the speaker himself can keep up a very high excite-ment for more than a brief period, certainly not in a natural and healthy way. Now the most complete alternation here would be from pathos or passion to humor. The humorous writers and speakers almost always introduce pathetic passages merely for relief, and, vice versa, the principle applies equally well. But the preacher cannot relieve the minds of his hearers by any but rare and delicate touches of humor.[26] He may, however, again and again descend from the impassioned to the quiet and easy, may cause passion to swell by successive waves, receding in order to advance farther; and he must in other ways vary the emotions excited, just so far as will be compatible with his specific design.

And great mistakes are also made as to what constitutes energy of

[24] Whately, p. 334
[25] Compare Spencer on Style, p. 36.
[26] See C. R. Brown, *The Art of Preaching*, pp. 135 ff., for the place of humor in preaching.

style. There is a jerky, convulsive energy, like that of Carlyle, which is by no means worthy of imitation. There is an over-wrought, exaggerated energy, which Longinus describes as "not sublime, but sky-scraping," and a turgid, inflated, would-be energy, which is nothing but bombast. And in this stirring age, especially among our American people, there is a tendency to be prodigiously excited upon small occasion, to use superlatives, exaggerated epithets, and impassioned imagery where they are unnecessary, and therefore inappropriate.

CHAPTER IV

QUALITIES OF STYLE—ELEGANCE

ELEGANCE of style is the product of imagination, alone or in combination with passion, and operating under the control of good taste. Any exercise of taste comprises an emotion and a judgment. The emotion excited by beauty or by its opposite is involuntary; but the judgment that a certain object, idea, or expression is beautiful or the contrary can be controlled and corrected, and the internal standard by which we judge admits of indefinite improvement. He who would attain elegance of style, then, must on the one hand cultivate imagination and sensibility and on the other must seek, by thoughtful contemplation of the truly beautiful, to improve his taste.

Elegance, in speaking, is less important than perspicuity or energy, but it greatly contributes to the objects of even the most serious discourse. Real elegance will, of course, be widely modified by subject, occasion, and design; and thus modified, it is free from all just objection and worthy of very earnest pursuit.

Aristotle remarks:

The first style of rhetoric was formed on that of poetry; witness the style of Gorgias; and even at the present time the majority of ignorant people fancy that such orators speak most delightfully; this however is not the case, but the style of poetry and that of prose is distinct.

For the poet, beauty is the most important element of style; for the orator, it is thoroughly subordinate to perspicuity and force. There is a similar though not equal difference between a history and a romance. In holiday speeches, and all set orations, to please becomes a more prominent object, and here the style of poetry is more nearly approached.

This important difference between oratory and poetry is strikingly illustrated by Adam Smith,[1] who contrasts dancing with walking, and singing with speaking. To walk as if dancing or speak as if sing-ing would be ridiculous affectation. But in a dance, graceful and

---

[1] Quoted by Whately, p. 286.

measured movement in order to please is "the proper purpose of the action," and so in a song, the rhythmical modulation of the voice. But in a speech the case is different.

In speaking, as in every other ordinary action, we expect and require that the speaker should attend to the proper purpose of the action,—the clear and distinct expression of what he has to say. In singing, on the contrary, everyone professes the intention to please by the tone and cadence of his voice; and he not only appears to be guilty of no disagreeable affectation in doing so, but we expect and require that he should do so.

So in poetry the "proper purpose" is to give pleasure; and we simply require that it be skillfully adapted to that purpose. The same thing is true of novels, and all other prose writings belonging to what is called "light literature." But in oratory, as we have seen, the proper purpose is very different, and entertainment, the gratification of taste, has place only as subsidiary to conviction and persuasion. Especially is this true of the preacher, who ought to have everywhere a practical and thoroughly serious, if not a uniformly solemn, purpose. And to preaching beyond almost every other variety of public speaking applies the following instructive quotation from Henry Rogers:— "If a speaker is in earnest, he never employs his imagination as the poet does, merely to delight us, or indeed to delight us at all— except as appropriate imagery, though used for another object, necessarily imparts pleasure. For this reason, illustrations are selected always with reference to their force rather than their beauty; and are very generally marked more by their homely propriety than by their grace and elegance. . . . Everything marks the man intent upon serious business, whose sole anxiety it to convey his meaning with as much precision and energy as possible to the minds of his auditors."[2] We can thus easily understand why some preachers care too much for embellishment. They take a wrong view of their office or at any rate are influenced by a wrong motive. They aim too much at entertaining, at gratifying the audience. They do not feel the seriousness of their work, the solemnity of their position. While perhaps really desiring to do good, they dwell too much on the necessity of pleasing the people in order to profit them. And aware that many hearers care only, or chiefly, to be entertained, aware that they talk in going home not of the truth but of the performance and the performer, such preachers too readily yield to this apparent demand and make it a

[2] On Sacred Eloquence, in *Reason and Faith and Other Essays*, p. 213.

distinct if not a principal object to please their hearers. But if the earnest desire to do men good quite swallows up the wish to please them, if the sense of responsibility to God rises superior to concern for men's criticism, then the preacher's style will have only such modest beauty as is easily kept in its proper place. And when he is tempted to yield to the false taste of many, it may help him to remember that the desire to please is very apt to defeat itself. His elaborate prettinesses will not only grieve the devout and disgust the really intelligent, but will soon pall upon the taste of those whom he seeks to win, who will have all the while in their hearts a vague feeling that this sort of thing is unworthy of him and will presently begin to find it rather tiresome to themselves.[3]

On the other hand, some preachers very unwisely take pains to avoid the beautiful. There are thoughts which naturally incline to blossom into beauty; why sternly repress them? There are grand conceptions which spontaneously clothe themselves in robes of majesty and march forth in a stately but native dignity. And besides subjects that naturally shine and blaze, there are many very commonplace topics which the preacher must be constantly bringing to view, and which will gain a much more interested attention from even the most devout hearers if delicately touched with some hues of fancy. It is a noble thing thus to take important truths which have grown dull by use and give them new brightness. This must not go so far that the attention of the speaker, and so that of the hearers, is drawn to the beauteous garb rather than to the truth itself. Far better leave the truth unadorned, to win such notice as it can. But this excess will be readily avoided, if one has good taste and a serious purpose. Vinet has well said that the really beautiful excludes the pretty.

They who are so afraid of elegance, forget that a native beauty, and even some ornament of style, is not of necessity unfavorable to perspicuity.[4] They forget that the beautiful and the useful are in nature often closely connected; that the blossoms of the apple tree, and the silks of the corn are remarkable for their rich and varied but delicate beauty. The fanciful style of some preachers is as little appropriate as if one who was called to build the family a home should build a garden bower; but a family mansion may be thoroughly suited to convenience and comfort and yet have a pleasing form and even a certain moderate ornamentation.

[3] Compare Vinet, p. 349.
[4] Compare Whately, p. 305.

True energy of style also is often at the same time elegant. Impas-sioned feeling often cannot express itself otherwise than by bold images, and these, though chosen for their strength, may also have an unstudied beauty.

It should be added that quotations, whether of verse or prose, which are made merely or even chiefly for their beauty, can never be appro-priate in preaching. The flowers suitable in serious discourse are never artificial flowers. Especially unbecoming is the introduction of orna-mental passages from poets well known to be grossly irreligious. Some preachers make themselves worse than ridiculous by "spouting" Byron.

Elegance of style depends especially upon terms, arrangement, and imagery; and there is much true elegance in that simplicity of style which is, on every account, so much to be desired.

(1) The most energetic terms are often at the same time the most elegant; so that we gain the latter excellence while seeking the former.[5] But this is not always the case. Some highly forcible expres-sions have to be avoided because they are indecent or vulgar. And if ever slang phrases are employed by a preacher, it ought to be under very peculiar circumstances. Ideas which are too painful must not be expressed in the most forcible terms but softened. The use of words too grand for the subject is a very common offense against elegance. Whether an energetic expression shall be rejected because inelegant is a question on which no general rule can be given; each case must be decided on its own merits. Many of the most effective speakers have been accused by fastidious persons of vulgarisms,—for example, Cicero, Burke, Patrick Henry, Webster, Luther, Whitefield, and others. But words which really weaken the expression or do not at all strengthen it must scarcely ever be employed because of their supposed elegance.

John Foster, in one of his celebrated essays, urges very earnestly that one reason for the aversion of men of taste to evangelical religion is the too frequent employment in preaching of the technical terms of theology and the language of Scripture. He himself took great pains to avoid both. No doubt there is sometimes an excessive multiplica-tion of such terms, giving the sermon a dialect quite different from the language of ordinary life, and this error good taste must correct. But "the aversion of men of taste to evangelical religion" is much more

---

[5] Compare the discussion of energetic terms in the foregoing chapter.

largely the cause than the effect of this dislike to theological and scriptural terms.

(2) As to the arrangement of words,[6] we must of course avoid harsh or disagreeable combinations, unless they are necessary for energy. The English language is specially liable to the frequent recurrence of hissing sounds, *s, z, sh, ch,* etc.[7] Thus the phrase, "in Jesus's name," has an unpleasant sound.

It is also of some importance to avoid the too frequent repetition of a word in the same sentence or paragraph. Modern taste is more fastidious about this than was that of the ancients. We must not, through mere desire for variety, sacrifice anything important to the sense, a fault into which our common English version has very often fallen. Thus in Romans, chapter 4, the word "reckon" occurs very often, being the leading term of the argument; but our version renders by three different words, "count," "reckon," and "impute," thus seriously obscuring the verbal connection, with no gain but that of variety. Where, however, the connection of our discourse does not really require the repetition of the same word, it should be suitably varied. There is in English special danger that certain pronouns, particularly "it," "that," and "which," and the preposition "of," will be too often repeated in quick succession.

Antithesis will frequently contribute to elegance, as well as to energy;[8] but if used too freely, it tends to stiffness or to monotony.

Alliteration was a leading peculiarity of Anglo-Saxon poetry and is still somewhere frequently employed in poetry and even in prose. Chalmers was very fond of it. In prose, especially in preaching, it should be used but rarely, and in an easy, unstudied fashion.

Sentences are, of course, most elegant when smooth and flowing. But better harsh strength than smooth weakness. "You may break grammar if you break hearts." And a constant succession of smooth and graceful sentences will inevitably become monotonous. Gibbon wearies by his uniform stateliness. Even Prescott's style would be improved by the occasional introduction of sentences quite different in pattern.

The parts of a sentence are often so proportioned as to give it a rhythmical movement. Excited feeling naturally tends to rhythmical

---

[6] The number of words is here a matter of subordinate importance; there may be an elegant conciseness or an elegant diffuseness, though the former is best for energy and often best for perspicuity.

[7] Foreigners sometimes call it the "snake language."

[8] Compare in the preceding chapter.

expression, as is sometimes seen even in voice and gesture. The meter of poetry is one species of rhythm. The perfectly regular recurrence of the same movements is, however, too labored and deliberate a thing to be natural in speaking. Accordingly, as Aristotle remarks, the rhythm of oratory must never become meter. The only exception, if there be one, is in eulogistic orations and the like, where there is high-wrought but somewhat artificial feeling, and where, as in poetry, the principal object is to please.[9] It is not proper, just for rhythm in prose, to throw in clauses simply for that purpose, as is often done by Johnson and his imitators;[10] but the expressions may be so chosen and so co-ordinated as to give the whole a rhythmical movement. This had best be spontaneous but need by no means be unconscious; one may lawfully give, even in extemporaneous speech, a certain occasional and subordinate attention to the proportion of clauses, the harmonious flow of the sentence. It is obvious that the cadence, or concluding strain of a sentence, is in this respect most important. Here, as was seen with regard to energy, we must avoid ending with a number of unemphatic words or unaccented syllables. This requires special care in English. We have not only a great number of such terminations as "-osity," "-ility," etc., but many words like occupancy, profitableness, in which, according to the Gothic tendency, the accent remains on the first or leading syllable, no matter how many syllables may be added which are exceedingly ill-suited to close a sentence. Moreover, it does not sound well if a sentence containing one or more long clauses should end with a short one. Many points of this sort might be noted; but after all, rhythm in prose scarcely requires particular rules, being sufficiently regulated by the ear, if once a man has learned to give it some attention in his own speaking and writing and in the books he most carefully reads. It is highly important that the rhythm of successive sentences should frequently vary, as is eminently the case in Burke. A smoothly flowing style or the majestic movement of a grand style would have more power with a miscellaneous audience if now and then a sentence were in its ending more abrupt—some quick, sharp saying that would crack like a whip.

(3) Most of the figures which give energy to style will also impart elegance. Those which especially conduce to elegance are simile,

---

[9] In some pathetic passages of Dickens, a whole paragraph might be cut up into blank verse without changing a word. But this would be intolerable in an appeal to a jury or in a sermon.

[10] Compare Whately. pp. 353-355.

metaphor, and personification. A comparison, or simile, which has any considerable value in the way of elucidation or proof, becomes much more valuable if also beautiful, because then it gains a pleased and sympathizing attention. That which does not contribute to perspicuity or force must never be introduced merely as an ornament, for this, as we have seen, belongs to poetry but not to practical and serious discourse. Everyone is familiar with the use of comparisons and metaphors to elevate or to degrade. No better example can be found than that often quoted from Aristotle.[11] The poet Simonides was requested by the victor in a mule-race to write a triumphal ode, and, offended at the small present offered, said he would not write about "half-asses," which was the common Greek name for mules. But a larger present being offered, he addressed them in an ode as "daughters of storm-footed steeds." It is much to know which side of a subject to select.

(4) No quality of style is more frequently urged as an object of pursuit than simplicity. Everyone feels that simplicity is a great excellence. But when we attempt to analyze simplicity and show how it may be attained, we are apt to find unexpected difficulty. The opposite of a simple style would seem to be one that is involved or that is too elaborate or that is overloaded with ornament. In the first case we might say that a simple style does not roll up an idea in manifold clauses and sentences, which we must painfully unroll in order to perceive it, but spreads out the idea at once to our view; that it is direct, and easy to understand. Then usage extends the term to denote a style that is not excessively labored or in any respect artificial, that does not appear to be produced with great effort. And in a particular variety of this use we mean by it a style that has no elaborate ornamentation. "In manner simplicity is the opposite, not of art, but of artifice; and in motive it is the opposite of conceit, vanity, ambition."[12]

A simple style, then, as it unfolds the thought at once, will be perspicuous, though there may be a certain kind of perspicuity where, strictly speaking, there is not simplicity. You may make an idea plain by repeated and varied statement and illustration; a simple style makes it plain at once. In this respect simplicity demands both of the conditions of perspicuity which we have heretofore noticed; the language must be such as the hearers will easily understand, and it

[11] *Rhet.*, III. 2.
[12] Dabney, *Sacred Rhet.*, p. 291,—a good discussion.

must exactly express the idea. A man is not certainly "simplifying" a thought when he is hammering it by prolonged and tedious explanation. Archbishop Usher said, "We need all our learning to make things plain." The speaker must find the least complicated, the most direct and readily intelligible expression, which at the same time exactly hits his meaning. Men often use familiar words but do not so choose and connect them as to make their style simple. The famous critic, Lord Jeffrey, is credited with the saying, "Simplicity is the last attainment of progressive literature."

In the other case a simple style means a style which is not labored or artificial, which flows freely and seems to be natural. If it is at the same time really perspicuous, this easy, inelaborate style is always the result of careful self-discipline and the expression of ideas patiently reflected on and clearly conceived. There are peculiarities of natural tendency in this as in all respects, but it is a great mistake to regard true simplicity of style as a mere gift of nature. One must habitually think his thoughts into clearness and must acquire wide and easy command of the best resources of language, if he would be able to speak simply and yet really say something.

And when by simplicity we mean the absence of excessive ornamentation, let us beware of going to the opposite extreme. South has sharply satirized his great contemporary, Jeremy Taylor, by extracting from his writings some specimens of over-wrought, fanciful ornament.

'I speak the words of soberness,' said St. Paul, and I preach the gospel not with the 'enticing words of man's wisdom.' This was the way of the apostle's discoursing of things sacred. Nothing here of 'the fringes of the north star'; nothing of 'nature's becoming unnatural'; nothing of 'the down of angels' wings, or the beautiful locks of cherubims'; no starched similitudes introduced with a 'Thus have I seen a cloud rolling in its airy mansion,' and the like. No,—these were sublimities above the rise of the apostolic spirit. For the apostles, poor mortals, were content to take lower steps, and to tell the world in plain terms that he who believed should be saved, and that he who believed not should be damned. And this was the dialect which pierced the conscience and made the hearers cry out, Men and brethren, what shall we do? . . . In a word, the apostles' preaching was therefore mighty and successful, because plain, natural, and familiar, and by no means above the capacity of their hearers; nothing being more preposterous than for those who were professedly aiming at men's hearts to miss the mark by shooting over their heads.[13]

[13] Quoted by Henry Rogers, p. 219.

The expressions quoted by South are, at least as they here stand, supremely ridiculous for a sermon; and unfortunately they are sometimes paralleled in our own day. But simplicity by no means excludes all ornament in all cases. Many a thought, no doubt, is "when unadorned, adorned the most," because, like a statue without drapery, its own form is beautiful. But, as we have heretofore observed, there are thoughts which naturally so stimulate the imagination that of its own accord it clothes them in a garb of beauty. And there is many a truth which must have some touches of fancy, or it is not fairly presented. The maiden on a summer evening, arrayed in simplest white, yet knows how, by the bit of ribbon skillfully placed, or the rosebud in her hair, to give the whole a modest charm. Shall the simple garb of truth be denied a like advantage? Wherever simplicity is to have its full attractiveness and to exert its true power, it must not be bald simplicity; there is sure to be now and then some little quaintness of phrase or delicate tinge of fancy, some slight felicity of expression, which lifts it above the vulgar or the commonplace. In using colloquial phrases, those homely English idioms which have such power, it is curious to observe how Bunyan or Spurgeon will divest them of vulgarity and give them an air almost of refinement by this light play of fancy.

Two things ought here to be borne in mind: (*a*) The worst of all affectations in style is the affectation of simplicity. It is like affected modesty in an immodest woman. And (*b*) a style may have real beauty and real power that is not simple. The processional pomp of Milton's grand sentences, the revolving splendors of Chalmers, the lightnings and auroras of Chrysostom and Jeremy Taylor may remind us that simplicity is not everything. These men, however, are often simple; they have too much good taste and natural feeling to employ inflated diction when speaking of common things. And so those who seek to be habitually simple must let their style vary according to subject and feeling. While usually confining themselves to those medium tones which suit the common thought and experience of mankind, let them be willing and be able to range the whole gamut of expression, to rise and fall as occasion demands or passion prompts.[14]

"The constant employment of one species of phraseology, which all have now to strive against, implies an undeveloped faculty of language.

[14] Choice examples of a simple style, which is at the same time forcible and elegant, may be found in Bunyan, Spurgeon, and Maclaren, and in the writings of Washington Irving and Charles Lamb.

To have a specific style is to be poor in speech. . . . As in a fine nature, the play of the features, the tones of the voice and its cadences vary in harmony with every thought uttered, so, in one possessed of a fully-developed power of speech, the mold in which each combination of words is cast will simply vary with and be appropriate to the sentiment. . . . The perfect writer will express himself as Junius, when in the Junius frame of mind; when he feels as Lamb felt, will use a like familiar speech; and will fall into the ruggedness of Carlyle when in a Carlylean mood. Now he will be rhythmical and now irregular; here his language will be plain and there ornate; sometimes his sentences will be balanced and at other times unsymmetrical; for a while there will be considerable sameness and then again great variety."[15]

From all this it will appear that true simplicity of style, which is at once intelligible, which has an easy movement, a natural beauty, and a natural variety, requires patient thought, disciplined imagination, and thorough mastery of language.

[15] Spencer, *Essay on Style*, p. 46.

CHAPTER V

IMAGINATION IN PREACHING

THE foregoing chapters of this study have dealt with the sermon in respect of its basic materials, its forms, functions, and style. The concluding chapters will be on methods of preparation and delivery. This chapter on Imagination lies in between as an essential consideration, for without imagination the principles of preaching cannot be utilized in effective practice. The invention of materials, the construction of discourse, the style of expression in language and delivery are equally dependent upon it. Joseph Addison ranked a sound imagination with correct judgment and a good conscience as life's three best endowments.[1] And Henry Ward Beecher[2] regarded it as "the most important of all the factors which go to make the preacher," that is, to make the minister, in whom genuine faith, character, and consecration are taken for granted, an effective interpreter and herald. Apart from the insight and lift and power of a consecrated imagination the highest intellectual and moral attainments are insufficient. It is highly necessary, therefore, for the preacher to give particular attention to the nature of imagination, its service in preaching, and the means of its cultivation.

I. THE NATURE OF IMAGINATION

Imagination is the imaging function of the mind. It is thinking by seeing, as contrasted with reasoning.

The imagination sees. Out of the material stored in the mind it creates a living world. By its forces the Parthenon is no longer a ruin, and all the Greeks yet live. The imagination gives atmosphere and stimulates individual ideas. Mere facts may make a wrong impression, but imagination clothes facts with living scenes and situations and presents the hidden truth. Imagination is the basis of all figurative language. It compares object with object, identifies the unknown and the known, and creates a new whole.[3]

[1] Cited by Cadman, *Imagination and Religion*, p. 18.
[2] *Yale Lectures*, p. 109.
[3] S. S. Curry, *Foundations of Expression*, p. 145.

The popular conception of imagination connects it with the unreal, as seeing what is not there, its product being imaginary rather than an imaginative representation of reality. In this conception it is indulgence in exaggeration and caricature and assists the orator only in the way of producing high-wrought imagery, in letting off such fireworks of fancy as sophomores affect and half-educated people admire. But modern psychology assigns it a high position and varied domain. It is recognized as giving indispensable aid in scientific research and philosophical abstraction, in the formation of geometrical and ethical as well as artistic ideals, in the varied tasks of practical invention, and even in the comprehension and conduct of practical life.

In an excellent chapter on imagination Woodworth distinguishes it from such other mental processes as attention, perception, and reasoning. These are explorative; they seek to discover facts; their concern is simply to find out what is there. Imagination, on the other hand, is manipulative; it uses facts that have already been discovered. It begins with the accumulated elements of experience, observation, and intellection. They are the materials of imagination. The first step in the imaginative process is the recall to consciousness of material from the mental store. It has thus an element of "remembering," but it has more. Whereas memory only seeks simple and literal reproduction, comparable to taking old photographs out of a drawer to look at, imagination proceeds to compare the recollected facts, to observe their relations, and to set them in new relationships. To quote Woodworth directly,

Sometimes it has been said that imagination consists in putting together material from different sources, but this leaves the matter in mid-air; recall can bring together facts from different sources and so afford the stimulus for an imaginative response, but the response goes beyond the mere togetherness of the stimuli. Thinking of a man and also of a horse is not inventing a centaur; there is a big jump from the juxtaposition of the data to the specific arrangement that imagination gives them. The man plus the horse may give no response at all or may give many other responses besides that of a centaur, for example, the picture of the man and the horse politely bowing to each other. The particular manipulation, or imaginative response, that is made varies widely; sometimes it consists in taking things apart rather than putting them together, as when you imagine how a house would look with the evergreen tree beside it cut down; always it consists in putting the data into new relationships.[4]

4 *Psychology*, p. 520.

In this respect imagination also differs from reasoning, although they are closely parallel. The first stage of each is getting data together—premises, facts. The final responses are alike reaction,

but imagination is freer and more variable. Reason is governed by a very precise aim, to see the actual meaning of the combined premises, that is, it is exploratory; while imagination, though it is usually more or less steered either by a definite aim, or by some bias in the direction of agreeable results, has after all much more latitude. It is seeking not a relationship that is there but one that can be put there.[5]

In this high meaning imagination is thus closely bound to reality.

It is creative in that it originates meritorious ideas, embodying them in poetry, prose, the material works of inventive genius, and the numberless hypotheses of science. There are, however, limitations to the creative activity of this type of imagination. The man who would visualize anything both new and valuable must bind his supposed novelty to reality by bonds which cannot break. The region of reality may itself be whatever one pleases to select, ranging from the Dismal Swamp in Virginia to the Sistine Madonna. Once adopted, far-reaching variations may be imposed upon it. But no imaginative strength can overcome those fixed barriers which inhere in the nature of things as they are; a new combination of colors may be imagined, but not a new color.[6]

Imagination, that is to say, is under the control of reality. Mental manipulation, however, always moves at this high level. It is sometimes free and at play, as, for example, when a child plays with its toys, and in daydreams (including reverie and worry) and dreams.[7] In these there is no control, either by objective fact or intelligent criticism and purpose. The mind simply plays along in the instinctive desire for mastery over circumstance or some other gratification and so fabricates all sorts of fanciful and absurd mental pictures. For this ungoverned, unprincipled process is reserved the term "fancy." Ruskin and others have made a sharp distinction between fancy and imagination as representing two distinct mental "faculties." But the proper distinction is not between faculties, but between principles of operation in the mental process. The one is free; the other is controlled.

Fancy is the inventive power of the mind working without reference to fact and eliciting from it more than it yields to observation. The artists

5 *Ibid.*
6 S. Parkes Cadman, *Imagination and Religion*, pp. 33 f.
7 See Woodworth, pp. 485-509, for a good discussion.

are always careful to make and to keep this distinction. An artist may endow a sunrise or a sunset with the light that never was on land or sea. But he may not make his sun rise in the west and set in the east.[8]

We call mental manipulation "fancy" when playing on the mere surface of things, "imagination" when penetrating to the heart, the essence; fancy when sportive or cold, imagination when passionate, or at least serious; fancy when it is careless of facts and ends, imagination when it gives facts a new radiance and vital significance.

With Woodworth, then, we may think of imagination not simply as the imaging function of the mind, but that function controlled by facts, with the end result of placing facts in new combinations and relationships. Dr. Cadman calls it " the power to evoke the prophetically new from material which is familiarly old."[9] It is at once reproductive or descriptive, constructive or synthesizing, and creative or analogical. For example, it sees the familiar picture, often repeated in experience, of a farmer sowing in a field; it constructs in kaleidoscopic fashion a whole series of pictures portraying the drama of the field from seedtime to harvest, making a fresh synthesis of facts; and then it proceeds to show the analogy between that drama and the experience of the evangelist and teacher in the field of life. Or in the worshipful mood of the poet it contemplates a sunset, and sings:

> Hills, wrapped in gray, standing along the west;
> Clouds, dimly lighted, gathering slowly;
> The star of peace at watch above the crest—
> Oh, holy, holy, holy!
>
> We know, O Lord, so little what is best;
> Wingless, we move so lowly;
> But in thy calm all-knowledge let us rest—
> Oh, holy, holy, holy![10]

2. THE ROLE OF IMAGINATION IN PREACHING

(1) Beginning at the point of technique it may be said that imagination is of indispensable value in the construction of discourse. To give familiar materials any fresh interest, they must be brought into new combinations; and to form a discourse at all, the materials must be

---

[8] Willard A. Sperry, *We Prophesy in Part*, p. 147.
[9] *Imagination and Religion*, p. 66.
[10] John Charles McNeill, quoted in Jerome Stockard's *A Study in Southern Poetry*.

made into a complete and symmetrical structure. Piles of bricks and lumber and sand are as much a house as the mere piling up of thoughts will constitute a discourse. The builder, of palace or of cabin, works by constructive imagination; and it is the same faculty that builds a speech. In fact imagination, the wonder-worker, does much more than this. It is only a lower imagination that takes fragments of material and builds them, each fragment preserving its individuality, into a new structure; high, intense imagination fuses the materials, reduces them to their natural elements, and forms of them a structure possessing complete unity. The one process is a new composition of fragments; the other, a new organization of elements. The one cements the materials together, or at best welds them together; the other makes them grow together by furnishing a principle of vitality which takes up the analyzed material and organizes it according to new laws. Imagination does not create thought in the primary sense; but it organizes thought into forms as new as the equestrian statue of bronze is unlike the metallic ores when they lay in the mine. This constructing, fashioning, organizing function of the imagination is exercised in forming a poem or a story but still more in forming a discourse, where there is far greater need of unity, symmetry, and adaptation to a specific design.

And not only is it needed in constructing discourses, but every paragraph, yea, every sentence, is properly a work of imagination, a work of art. The painter, sculptor, or architect does not fashion merely the general outline of his work and leave the details to chance. The whole is but the parts taken together. Each part must have a certain completeness in itself and yet must be in itself incomplete, being but a fragment of one whole. So must it be in the construction of discourse.

What are the precise functions of imagination in the invention of thought, students of psychology have not yet settled. There can be no doubt that it does somehow aid us in penetrating to the heart of a subject, and developing it from within; that it thus assists the work of original analysis, as well as that of exposition; though Ruskin's theory of "the penetrative imagination" is, as he virtually confesses, uncertain and obscure.[11]

(2) Imagination also enables the preacher to clothe ideas in familiar and revealing imagery. It thus gives thought a definite shape, concrete expression. This excites the imagination of another and thus affects his feelings. Objects of sense affect the feelings most power-

[11] *Modern Painters*, Vol. II. pp. 160 ff.

fully, and images more closely resemble objects of sense than do mere ideas. Thus if, instead of dwelling upon the idea of benevolence, we bring forward the image of a benevolent man or a benevolent action, it is much more affecting. And a picture of reality is often more convincing than an argument.

The poets, the dramatists, the prophets move us more strongly than the logicians, because they bring facts, situations, problems alive for us as our own concern.[12]

And whether the particular idea can or cannot be converted into an image, we may associate with it, may group around it, by resemblance or analogy, or by contrast, some other idea or ideas which can be formed into images and which will reflect their light and splendor upon the thought in hand. This is illustration, with all its power not only to gratify the taste but to assist comprehension, to carry conviction, and to awaken emotion.

It is thus mainly through imagination that we touch the feelings and thereby bring truth powerfully to bear upon the will, which is the end and the very essence of eloquence. And, on the other hand, emotion kindles imagination. Love, for instance, will cause the dullest mind to give forth some sparks of imagination. Anger, overwhelming grief, passionate supplication, will often struggle to express itself by means of the boldest images. Thus imagination and feeling continually act and react, causing the one to glow more brightly and the other to grow fiercer in its blaze.

(3) Another use of imagination, though not wholly distinct from the last, is in realizing and depicting what the Scriptures reveal. We have already noticed how much of the Bible consists of narrative, and how important it is that the preacher should be able vividly to describe its scenes and events.

One can only make history real by an imaginative revival in his own mind of the scenes, persons, and events of the past, by thinking oneself back into a period, or bringing it forward to our own time, and mentally observing and participating in what transpires. This is true, for example, of the life of our Lord himself, as C. R. Brown so well says:

The bare events even of that matchless life which has come to be the light of the world have little power to change and to move the hearts of men until they are interpreted and related to the immediate interests

---

[12] Sperry, *Effective Preaching*, p. 76.

of these lives of ours. It is for us, every man in his own order and according to the grace given him, to repeat and realize in our own experiences the majestic truths suggested by the incarnation, the transfiguration, the crucifixion, the resurrection. We are set not only to revere, but according to the measure of our ability to reproduce the life which was in him. And the minds of men can only be inspired to these high endeavors as the sacred, significant events which lie in the remote past are made to live before their eyes.[13]

"Historical imagination," in reproducing the past, is one of the most powerful allies of preaching. In the exercise of it great care must be taken that it shall be directed and controlled by thorough knowledge of the times reproduced, and true sympathy with their spirit, or we shall carry back our own experiences and our modern conceptions and make, as historical description often has done, an utterly erroneous representation. But with this caution, historical imagination may be declared indispensable, not only to description of biblical history but to the just comprehension of the whole system of doctrine and duty, for all rests upon a basis of fact. Controversialists, for example, often greatly err, from failing to realize the circumstances of the primitive age and thus misconceiving the precise aim of many a lesson or observance, and likewise from failing to understand the real views and sentiments of those whom they oppose.

And not only as to the past is imagination needed; it is requisite if we are justly to conceive and vividly to realize the Scripture revelations concerning the unseen world and the eternal future. Faith believes these revelations, and imagination, aroused by faith and called into its service, makes the things unseen and eternal a definite reality to the mind, so that they affect the feelings almost like objects of sense and become a power in our earthly life. It may also to some extent fill out the Bible pictures of the unseen world by following the analogies of this world; but there is here demanded a moderation and reserve, a care in distinguishing between the revealed and the supposed, which in some books and many sermons are sadly wanting.

(4) Of equal value is what may be called "sympathetic imagination." It has been said of George Eliot that

she had the secret not only of reading the diverse hearts of men but of creeping into their skins, watching the world with their eyes, feeling the latent background of conviction, discerning theory and habit.[14]

[13] *The Art of Preaching*, p. 147.
[14] Lord Acton, quoted by James Reid, *In Quest of Reality*, p. 181.

It is that sympathetic visualization of the experiences and problems of others that makes any writer or preacher interesting and challenging. Imaginative participation in the fortunes and feelings of his people enables the preacher, as nothing else can, to make the healing and guiding connections between life and truth which alone make his preaching worth while. Ezekiel set an example for prophets of all time. Said he in a critical time, "I sat where they sat; and I remained there astonished among them seven days." He put himself in their place. He contemplated the whole situation until their doom became his own sorrow. The preacher who sits where young people are until he knows their hearts, their motives, and temptations and aspirations, until he is young with them, will be heard by them. The same is true in respect to all persons and classes and groups.

Sympathetic imagination lends appropriateness to preaching. To put ourselves in the place of others will give to their needs a new importance and urgency, compelling us to speak, not of some pet interest of our own, but of the living issues that press upon our hearers. It thereby goes far toward solving the problems of freshness and of holding attention. When anyone touches my problem, my interest, shows knowledge and just appreciation of my point of view, feels my difficulties, speaks in my language, he will not need to ask for my attention or catch me by subtle artistry. Such a preacher speaks to me with authority. He has the secret of power. On the other hand if the preacher is mentally lazy or selfish and will not take time and trouble to get into the life of people, if he chooses to live in a world pleasant to himself and is content to generalize about truth, he will inevitably be academic, conventional, and dull—and futile. George Fox's prayer is properly every preacher's prayer: "I have prayed to be baptized into a sense of all conditions, that I might be able to know the needs and feel the sorrows of all."

3. MEANS OF CULTIVATING THE IMAGINATION

In some degree all men possess the power of imagination. Like all mental processes its qualities rest upon native endowments and cultural development. Some people seem to have what we may call imaginative genius. Poets, we say, are born not made. But even poets, artists, and inventive geniuses have to cultivate their native gifts. And average men, subjecting themselves to an equal discipline with a Shakespeare, a Michelangelo, an Edison, always find an open road of progress. Imagination, whatever its original promise, depends upon and responds to cultivation.

How it may be cultivated becomes apparent when we recall the nature of imagination, namely, that it is the mental process by which we bring together facts of experience, set them in their true or actual relations to one another, and rearrange them in new combinations and relationships. Facts, reality, recollection, discrimination, inventive manipulation,—these are the elements of a sound imagination. It follows that imagination suffers in quality when it lacks facts, and its possibilities increase with the acquisition of facts. But facts are so much lumber if there is no architect, no artist, in the soul. The principles of reproductive, constructive, creative imagination must be learned under the tutelage of men of imaginative genius. It should be observed, also, that the practical value to others of our imaginative power depends upon the imagery by which we express what we see. An unfamiliar picture may mean as little as an abstract idea and be even more misleading. Many a preacher wonders why his vision of truth, which stirs him so profoundly, falls flat, not realizing that his words gave no familiar pictures. His hearers were farmers, per-haps, while his pictures were of city life, problems, scenery. It is, accordingly, necessary to the cultivation of effective imagination for the preacher to see with his people's eyes and imagery. Still further, in preaching it is the task of imagination to relate the seen to the unseen, the actual to the ideal, the present to the future, the transient to the eternal. That suggests the need of something beyond rhetoric and logic; it calls for what Isaiah did in the year that King Uzziah died, and what the psalmist did when by reasoning he could find no harmony between human fortune and human character,—it calls for worship, prayer, spiritual meditation. Jesus had his wilderness and lonely mount, Paul had his Arabia, and every man has his closet.

As practical disciplines of the imagination, then, the following may be suggested:

(1) Study nature and art in order to gain a rich factual knowledge of our world, together with its treasure of aesthetic and spiritual values. A certain indefinable sympathy exists, by a law of our being, between external nature and ourselves. Its forms and hues have a meaning for us more subtle than language conveys, and excite in us strange longings and kindlings of soul, till we idealize all we behold. And our thoughtful observation of nature may be quickened and exalted by science. The systematic study of minerals,

vegetables, animals, reveals to us new and wonderful things, teaches us to read, where we had not seen it before, the handwriting of our God. Geology acquaints us with earth's mighty past, Astronomy introduces us to the ever widening and brightening glories of the wonder-crowded universe, till the "music of the spheres" attains for us a sublime, orchestral grandeur, an unearthly sweetness, a wealth of precious meaning, which the wise Greek never knew. We need not now to people all natural objects with unseen, half-human creatures, nor need we lose ourselves in the vagueness of pantheism; our personality may everywhere indulge its longing for communion with a person, for we may find in all nature the personal God.—But words are here vain. If we wish for power of imagination, let us observe, contemplate, commune with nature.

Nature, however, is by most of us very imperfectly understood and appreciated till interpreted to us by the artist. Perhaps we grew up amid glorious mountains or beside the many-sounding sea and yet little knew their meaning, little felt their inspiration, till some high-priest of nature had taught us how to behold and comprehend and sympathize.

Sculpture, painting, architecture, music, have a strange power to develop the imagination in general and sometimes to stimulate it for particular efforts, and they can be devoid of interest to none who possess this faculty in even a moderate degree. When Andrew Fuller stopped suddenly amid the architectural glories of Cambridge and proposed to his guide to go home and discuss with him the doctrine of justification, he betrayed that deficiency of imagination which is conspicuous in the structure and the style of his otherwise admirable sermons. There is many a preacher who could tell how some picture, perhaps casually looked at, has helped him in making a sermon: there is many a one utterly unable to tell how much the general study of works of art has contributed to develop his imagination.

(2) Study imaginative literature (drama, poetry, fiction) in order to learn not only what men of imagination are able to see, but where they see it and how they portray their vision in vivid scenes and gripping imagery.

To be sure, all literature is the servant of imagination in the degree that it makes knowledge more accurate, leads us into wider ranges of truth, and sets facts in their organic relations. But poetry and drama and certain types of fiction express truth in picturesque and emotional language, in moving scenes and episodes that challenge the reader's imagination more than his reason, and so kindle his own powers of pictorial realization and inventiveness. The poets are accessible to all, and they are here our chief teachers. They see the analogies of external nature to moral and religious truth as most of us cannot; and they open up to us unknown depths in our own nature. From them we may learn how to observe and compare, how to depict and interpret, though we must not forget that they aim mainly to please, while we must subordinate everything to spiritual profit, and that such difference of aim should lead to great difference of method. And it is not of necessity those poets who seem to the general reader to show most imagination but those who most kindle our imagination that will in this respect be most useful. Thus the poems of Wordsworth and the Brownings are much more profitable than those of Moore and Scott. We must seek by effort of our own imagination to conceive the poet's image if we are to have not mere entertainment but improvement; and he is for us the best poet who awakens our imagination, gives it general direction, stimulates it by some of the most suggestive details, and leaves it to do all the rest for itself. That is to say, in order to the benefit here proposed, we must study poetry.

There is much highly imaginative prose which has a similar value. Fiction would, if properly managed, be to some preachers exceedingly profitable in respect to imagination and literary taste. As a rule, one should read only the very best works of the very best novelists; and he should never read two novels in succession but always put between them several works of a very different kind. The danger in reading fiction, as McComb points out, is that it may leave the reader too passive, giving him passive enjoyment without rousing him, as the poet does, to exercise his own imagination in order to see and utilize in full measure what is said. This, however, is a matter of lassitude or alertness and purpose in the reader.

Become at home in this imaginary world (of the fiction-writer); know it as if you were an observer on the scene; become a member of its population, willing to befriend its characters and able to participate in its happenings by sympathetic insight, as you would do in the actions and sufferings of a friend. If you can do this, the elements of fiction will cease to be so many isolated pawns moved about mechanically on a chessboard. You will have found the connections which vitalize them into the members of a living society.[15]

[15] Mortimer J. Adler, *How to Read a Book*, p. 310.

It is well to notice, also, that writers such as Goethe, Edgar Poe, and many others have given us imaginative writings not properly called tales, which may in like manner be profitable. Some of the historians powerfully appeal to and exercise the imagination of their readers, for example, Macaulay and Motley. And the great orators and preachers present to us imagination operating in precisely those methods with which we are most concerned. If one wishes to stimulate in himself the desire for affluence of imaginative thought and diction, let him read Plato, Cicero, Chrysostom, Jeremy Taylor, Milton, Burke, Chalmers; if he wishes to chasten himself into a more sober and regulated use of imagination, so that it shall be duly subordinated to other faculties, let him read Demosthenes, Tacitus, Daniel Webster, Robert Hall. In general it must be remembered that here, as elsewhere, appetite is not always a sure guide.

(3) Keep close to the people of your time, particularly the people of your congregation. Sympathetic imagination is not possible otherwise. In his chapters on mental imagery and mental systems Dr. C. S. Gardner shows the importance of intimate fellowship with and close observation of men and their ways of life.

There is laid upon the preacher the necessity of entering, as far as is humanly possible, into the mental systems of his hearers and of limiting himself as closely as practicable to the use of meanings that are common to his own and the various minds of his auditors. Before him are represented mental divergences arising from organic differences, differences of occupation, various types and stages of culture, and usually also divergences arising from various mental environments in which the hearers have lived. . . . And his disadvantage is increased by the fact that he has usually had special training in an order of ideas and terms which in recent times seem to be becoming less and less familiar to the people. This does not mean that he should quit studying theology, but that he needs more and more to study the daily life of the people as well. It is obvious to one who closely studies preaching today how comparatively few preachers realize the extent to which they are not understood or are positively misunderstood, in their solemn deliverances. They simply do not know how seriously they are insulated mentally from the masses of the people.[16]

This insulation can be broken by pastoral interest and association that will supply the factual and emotional materials of a sympathetic imagination. If the preacher would know how to interest his people and make those connections between the actual and the ideal in terms

[16] *Psychology and Preaching*, p. 57.

that catch and grip them and come home to their hearts with unclouded meaning, let him go among them and learn their attitudes, their words and meanings, their work and play, their morals and religion, and give himself to the unselfish task of finding in God's eternal truth a definite word for definite need.

(4) Keep close to the eternal source of spiritual vision. Imagination finds its inspiration and power in the "upper room" today as on that wonderful day of Pentecost; expectant waiting, continuing prayer, reflection upon the Word of the gospel, faith, these were the background. And what happened? Tongues of fire and a rushing sound were its open symbols and the coming of the Holy Spirit the explanation of it. By the power of the Spirit these things happened: A great realization, an overwhelming spiritual energy, and power of utterance. The eyes of their faith were opened and they saw Reality as they had never seen before. The invisible spiritual world became more real than the upper room; it was no longer remote or future. They were even now under the ruling authority of God more than under Caesar or the Sanhedrin. Henceforth their imaginations—power to see and to relate facts—were given unclouded vision, their wills the strength of a rushing wind, and their speech the glow and energy of fire. Thus the spirit of God ever responds to the open heart. We leave out the appeal to God and faith in his continuing power at the peril of our souls. Rhetoric, logic, psychology are the channels and instruments of preaching; the spirit of God is the source of power, as his word is the message of life.

(5) To these should be added exercise as a constant practical necessity. We must begin where we are and do always the best we can, undeterred by what others do.

The excessive display of second-rate imagination which some men make so offensive, drives other men to the opposite extreme, so that they shrink from illustration and imagery where they are really needful, and never stop to consider how numerous and varied and surpassingly important are the functions of this much-abused faculty. Let a man freely exercise imagination, in constructing and inventing, in picturing and illustrating, in reproducing the past and giving vivid reality to the unseen world; but let him everywhere exercise it under the control of sound judgment and good taste, and above all of devout feeling and a solemn sense of responsibility to God. The imaginative reproduction of scenes witnessed, read, or heard of, and the imaginative construction of new scenes may be helpful or harmful to the moral nature according as these scenes are good or bad, elevating or degrading. It is impossible to estimate what a profound influence a man's imagination has upon his moral and spiritual life; and thus through these channels, as well as more directly, it has for the preacher a momentous importance in his preaching.

Part V

METHODS OF PREPARATION AND DELIVERY OF SERMONS

◇◇

Chapter I

PREPARATION OF SERMONS

THOSE who have had no experience in preaching often ask how much time is required for the preparation of a sermon. No definite answer is possible, for all of a minister's past study, all of his reading, meditation, prayer, all pastoral ministration, all open-eyed contacts with the world of men and things contribute something to the groundwork and superstructure of every sermon. Experience warrants only the general statement that the time required in immediate preparation is in inverse ratio to the time spent in general preparation. The sermons that require least time in immediate preparation are frequently better than sermons laboriously wrought out through long hours only because they have drawn copiously upon materials accumulated in the mind through months and years, and now by favorable circumstance, subjective and objective, are lifted happily into consciousness. To both kinds of preparation, therefore, the preacher must give serious attention.

I. GENERAL PREPARATION

More than once in previous chapters it has been pointed out that preaching requires constant study. Obviously, the values of that study will be greatly increased if it is projected purposefully in view of the preacher's sacred mission and the demands of that mission. Otherwise, one may spend lots of time on little nothings, or read in fields restricted to suit one's private interest and pleasure, or read so widely as to grasp nothing in its deepest significance. Young men who have enjoyed but limited opportunities of culture and have never looked out with eager eyes upon the great world of books sometimes need to be urged to read more widely; but in the immense majority of cases very different advice is required. He who would become really a man must abandon as early as possible the childish dream of reading everything. Except for what is done for recreation—and excessive recreation is destruction—he must have a limited field of study and must cultivate that field with the utmost possible thoroughness. And upon every subject studied he must find out the best books and restrict himself almost entirely to those. If the men of true scholarship and real power were called on to give one counsel to young students in this age of multiplied books, they would probably all unite in saying, Read only the best works of the great authors, and so read these as to make them thoroughly and permanently your own.[1]

The study of the Scriptures must come first. For those who are preparing to preach, no argument should be needed on this point. There is a danger, however, that it may be taken for granted that Bible courses in college and seminary are enough of serious study except as texts or portions are to be used in the preparation of sermons. No more crippling mistake could be made. To use the Bible as a repository of texts is to cut oneself off from the broad perspectives of the biblical writers and miss those unexpected springs of inspiration, the fresh light on divine truth, which only persistent and ordered study discovers. To master the Bible is the work of a lifetime, and no haphazard study will ever accomplish it. Let every preacher be always engaged in the serious study of some one of the sixty-six books, with the best obtainable helps at his side, such as the Hebrew or Greek texts if he can use them, the modern translations, the best critical and exegetical commentaries, expositions, etc. The study of two (sometimes three) books of the Bible a year in this fashion will bring the preacher to the end of twenty-five years with a freshness and plenitude of knowledge that will make his later ministry his crowning work. This, however, is not all of Bible study. It has been suggested that every preacher should have in addition two other ways of studying the Bible: for its religious and theological ideas as they are developed throughout; and devotionally, for personal spiritual enrichment. There is no dead-line in the ministry of the man who thus progressively masters the Bible and lets its truth master him.

[1] Compare Shedd, *Hom.*, pp. 121-124.

Quite naturally the right kind of Bible study will create new interests, discover new outreaches of its truth, raise problems that will lead into various other fields of study. It will inspire men to tap the many auxiliary sources of preaching: history, science, literature, philosophy and contemporary life. Modern social backgrounds, approaches to knowledge, philosophies, literature's report on life, all have marked differences from those of biblical times. And the preacher's business being to make truth plain and convincing unto eternal life, it is necessary for him to get a comprehensive view of these backgrounds of modern living. General preparation here is essential. Out of these cultural studies come sympathetic understanding, richness of reference and illustration that multiplies contacts between truth and life, and the kind of originality that makes truth striking. Freshness and force are not matters of technique but of vital connection of eternal truth with the thought and life and needs of men. It should be in the preacher's plan, therefore, to be constantly storing up in his mind and heart an understanding of his world.

It is important also to find some way, fitted to one's own genius and disposition, of conserving the fruits of his studies. Some men are able to use elaborate filing systems in which everything finds a place. Others use notebooks for special studies and general notebooks for texts, subjects, illustrations, quotations, observations, etc., and depend on memory to keep track of things. Others read without pencil in hand (a practice called by some a form of self-indulgence), depending wholly on memory or being content with a general effect.

Whether it is better to make extracts, summaries, and references in a commonplace book, or to rely mainly on memory in reading, will depend on a man's turn of mind and general habits and on the kind of reading in question. Even a man of extraordinary memory can hardly dispense with memoranda in reading books of information, while books of thought, though they may be profitably analyzed in writing, should be thought over, thought through and through; and then all that is cognate to our own thinking will be without difficulty retained. As regards whatever is not matter of pure thought, an important part of the benefit derived from reading is this, that one will always know where to look for what he wants; and this can be best accomplished by a system of references, unless the power of local memory is found, upon fair trial, to suffice for the purpose. Whichever method one adopts, he must strive to make the best of it, guarding carefully against its disadvantages and dangers.

2. SPECIAL PREPARATION

No matter how widely read and full of general knowledge and thought a preacher may be, he must yet make special accumulation of materials for each sermon. Many a preacher, particularly after he has had long years of experience and has accumulated a considerable amount of sermon stock, has failed right here. He depends on general instead of special preparation. No man can keep fresh who does not put fresh material in every sermon—something which particularly belongs to that sermon and occasion and fits no others so well. It is imperative, therefore, that the preacher should also give his very careful thought not only to his general stock but to what may be called "materials provided at the time."

These embrace the interpretation of the text and the choice of a subject, which we have already considered. The precise mode of stating a subject can in many cases not be fixed until after we have wrought out much of the general materials for the treatment of it. Besides interpreting the text, in the strict sense of the phrase, much may be derived from reflecting on it and on its connection. If the treatment be textual or expository, a large part of the materials will be derived from this study of the text; if it be a subject-sermon, still the text and its context may furnish much that will be useful in the discussion of the topic. Then in fixing the mind upon the subject or in succession upon the several related subjects furnished by the textual or expository method, the preacher must attempt the complete analysis and copious development of the matters involved and the collection of all associated matters which are likely to be useful. Yet, it is plain that this provision of material for immediate use will often really be very largely selection from the general stock of previously acquired knowledge and thought. It will be a combination of two things: deliberate choice and selection from the storehouse of memory and reflection, and the spontaneous coming of thoughts by the law of association of ideas. Awaken a memory, get a thought, and others will come to keep them company. So there will be a delightful mingling of old and new. The well instructed scribe, as the Master has said, will be bringing out of his treasury things new and old.

Probably no two preachers have exactly the same method of procedure in immediate preparation. But a review of the self-reported habits of outstanding preachers reveals several constants. Dr. George

A. Buttrick,[2] out of his own practice, suggests the following: (1) Choose your subject and text. The order of choice will vary. (2) Study the text in its context until you get its meaning and its mood. (3) Study the text in commentaries. (4) Pass the text through your own experience, jotting down any ideas that occur, any reminders of relevant happenings, quotations, passages in books. Often in a day or two an amorphous mass of material, more than can be used, will be at hand. (5) Brood over the material in mind. "Let the sun go down a day or two upon a sermon: the subconscious mind must do its part." (6) "Let the imagination have large liberty." (7) Then write the sermon,—not as an essay is written, with only the subject in mind, but as a sermon,—with the eyes of the congregation looking at the writer over his desk. "Let the sermon be written. If not written on paper, it must be written just as scrupulously on the tablet of the mind." The procedure of Dr. Henry Sloane Coffin is as follows: (1) Decide upon a pressing need of the congregation. (2) Select the aspect of the gospel which meets that need. (3) Look for a text that embodies the message. (4) Study the text for its full meaning. (5) Make an outline with a few notes as to illustrations. (6) Write it out whether it is to be read or delivered extemporaneously. (7) Correct and polish it. Dr. S. Parkes Cadman's practice was (1) to choose a suitable theme and a text that fits; (2) to assemble all the literature available on the subject; (3) to con over it; (4) to write the sermon; (5) to revise it carefully; (6) to make an abstract for pulpit use. Dr. H. A. Prichard[3] begins with a theme, "suggested usually by some conversation that has been held in the recent past, by some episode or observation or experience or sentence in a book." He then finds a text, preferably one that lends itself to illustration and elaboration. His next step is "to think of all references, historical, biographical, scientific, theological, personal, that may bear on it, with a view to weaving these somewhere into the fabric of the sermon. Gradually, by a process of mental digestion, this matter begins to assume a systematic shape." On Friday, he notes down the main sequence of thought, with illustrations, and on Saturday evening writes down on a small sheet of paper the essential points for pulpit use. "No thought is given to any verbal form of expression."

In that inspiring volume, *The Preacher: His Life and Work*, Dr.

[2] *Jesus Came Preaching*, pp. 152-162.
[3] *The Minister, the Method, and the Message*, p. 181. The reports on Dr. Coffin and Dr. Cadman and others also are given in Dr. Prichard's book, pp. 147-183.

J. H. Jowett[4] emphasizes several things as having great value to himself. (1) Men ought to prepare and preach their own sermons. "You will find that the freshness of your own originality will give new flavor and zest to the feast which you set before your people." (2) One ought not to preach on a theme too soon after it occurs to him. "I think it frequently happens that we go into the pulpit with truth that is undigested and with messages that are immature. Our minds have not done their work thoroughly, and, when we present our work to the public, there is a good deal of floating sediment in our thought, and a consequent cloudiness about our words. It is a good thing to put a subject away to mature and clarify." (3) "Let the preacher bind himself to the pursuit of clear conceptions, and let him aid his pursuit by demanding that every sermon he preaches shall express its theme and purpose in a sentence as lucid as his powers can command." It was Dr. Jowett's conviction that "no sermon is ready for preaching, ready for writing out, until we can express it in a short, pregnant sentence as clear as a crystal." (4) Very suggestive is Dr. Jowett's habit of imagining how other preachers might deal with his theme. "I ask,—how would Newman regard this subject? How would Spurgeon approach it? How would Dale deal with it? By what road would Bushnell come up to it? Where would Maclaren take his stand to look at it? Where would Alexander Whyte lay hold of it? . . . I have looked at the theme through many windows, and some things appear which I should never have seen had I confined myself to the windows of my own heart and mind." (5) Another practice of his was to hold in mind at least a dozen men and women whom he knew as he sat down to prepare his exposition and to ask constantly how he might help one or another: "What relation has this teaching to that barrister? How can the truth be related to that doctor? What have I here for that keenly nervous man with the artistic temperament? And there is that poor body upon whom the floods of sorrow have been rolling their billows for many years— what about her?" So he kept his touch with life and sought to relate truth to actual experience. (6) Dr. Jowett wrote his sermons, taking great care to make his expression fresh and free from the much-worn phraseology that has lost its significance. His counsel on this point is, "Do not foolishly attach value to carelessness and disorder. Pay sacred heed to the ministry of style. When you have discovered a jewel give it the most appropriate setting." (7) Finally, he put great

---

[4] This paragraph is gathered from Chap. 4, The Preacher in His Study.

emphasis upon the prayer attitude of the preacher as he seeks to interpret the Scriptures. "Unless our study is also our oratory, we shall have no visions . . . Even hard work is fruitless unless we have 'the fellowship of the Spirit.'"

Every preacher must find the procedure that suits him best. But there is no easy way. Self-discipline is necessary, and method must be improved until the product represents one's best effort and can stand the essential tests of good preaching. The student preacher needs to be warned against the peril of falling into slipshod and unworthy habits of sermon-making. Occupied principally with his theological studies, it is easy for him to take other men's outlines or entire sermons and otherwise to deal superficially and even immorally with his subjects. Let him remember that it is easier to form a habit than to break one. At the cost of time and great difficulty, therefore, he should find and incorporate in his early methods what will not need to be abandoned later. It would be of immense value to the young preacher to examine critically the habits of others and mark out for himself a procedure to which he can give himself whole-heartedly.

3. ADVANTAGES AND DISADVANTAGES OF WRITING SERMONS

Most of the practices noted above will commend themselves as worthy of emulation. The habit of writing out the sermon will probably raise more questions than any other. Many preachers never write a sermon; few write all their sermons. The matter should be settled by the individual, not according to his general inclination but on the basis of values.

(1) Let us consider the advantages of writing sermons:

(a) Writing greatly assists the work of preparation by rendering it easier to fix the mind upon the subject. Mental application is facilitated by any appropriate bodily action; and men who do not write often find it necessary to walk the floor or in general to assume some constrained posture or perform some regularly recurring act.[5] Now writing involves a high degree of that control of body which so contributes to control of the mind and has at the same time the advantage of possessing a closer natural relation to thought than any

---

[5] It was the habit of Schleiermacher to lean out of a window for hours while composing his sermons.

other act except speaking itself. Indeed, everyone knows how greatly writing helps to keep the thoughts from wandering.

(b) Besides, writing a sermon compels to greater completeness of preparation. He who prepares without writing may, and as a rule ought to, follow out all the developments and expansions of his thoughts as far as the discourse is to carry them; but he who writes must do this, is compelled to it.

(c) Still further, writing serves to secure, in several respects, greater excellence of style. As a general thing, unwritten speech cannot equal that which is written, in grammatical correctness, in precision, conciseness, smoothness, and rhetorical finish. These are highly important properties of style, and particularly with respect to the demands of some audiences, occasions, or subjects. Thus, if one is discussing a controverted point of doctrine, in the presence of persons ready to misunderstand or misrepresent him, it is even more than usually desirable that his language should be precise and unmistakable, an achievement greatly facilitated by having written it out beforehand. Some hearers are very fastidious as to the preacher's finish of style. His language, as well as his manner of delivery and his dress, must be *comme il faut,* or they will have nothing to do with him. Such fastidiousness may not deserve any high respect, but, of course, it should not be needlessly disregarded. And sermons on an occasion of academic or other specially literary interest are commonly and naturally expected to possess an unusual degree of flowing smoothness and elegant finish. The preacher himself, too, especially the young preacher of fine literary cultivation, is apt to be sensitive as to minute faults of style; and writing enables him better to meet the demands of his own taste.

(d) Besides, writing sermons tends to promote the preacher's usefulness in several other respects. The written discourse can be used on subsequent occasions without the necessity of renewed preparation and thus frequently saves a good deal of time and labor. The sermons remain for publication, if ever that should be desirable. Many a truly great preacher, and widely useful in his day, has left but a fading, vanishing name, while some contemporary of perhaps no greater ability, but who wrote his discourses, is still known and still useful. For example, compare Fénelon with Bourdaloue. And then the practice gives facility in writing, which in our day is a highly important means of usefulness. The successful preacher has now many opportunities to publish, and it is apt to become a sort of reproach to him, diminishing his influence, if he is not sometimes heard from through the press.

(2) To write has thus a number of advantages, some of them decidedly important. What, now, are its disadvantages?

(*a*) If writing aids in thinking, it is apt to render one largely dependent on such assistance. Especially objectionable is the fact that this practice accustoms the preacher to think connectedly only as fast as he can write, when it is more natural and more convenient that a man should think as fast as he can talk.

(*b*) And if writing compels the preacher to go over the ground more completely, it is not always done more thoroughly. The thinking is more extensive but may be less intensive. Being obliged to run over the surface everywhere, the preacher may go beneath it nowhere. If many sermons are spoken with very superficial preparation, so with very superficial preparation are many sermons written, particularly if they are not to be read or published. There is an immense amount of strictly extemporaneous writing.

(*c*) Akin to this last is the disadvantage of consuming so much time in the merely mechanical effort of writing,—time which might often be more profitably spent upon the thoughts of the discourse or upon the preacher's general improvement. True, the extemporaneous speaker, in his earlier efforts, needs to spend no less time but rather more in preparation; but if this is laborious at the outset, his power of working out the details will rapidly increase, and the time necessary for this become much less, while the writer must as long as he lives spend a number of hours in the task of writing. Now the pastors of large churches in this country are often, indeed commonly, expected to do the work of several different men. Their pastoral and social work, the various demands of their position as leaders of thought and benevolent activity, the calls for general denominational service, and the imperative need of constant self-improvement in order to keep fresh and growing, all press very heavily upon our overburdened pastors. In such a state of things it becomes a very serious matter that a preacher should condemn himself, for life, to spend every week six, eight, twelve hours in merely writing out each of two sermons, when by far the most important and difficult portion of his preparation—the selection of text and subject, interpretation, invention of materials, and arrangement of the discourse—ought to have been completed before he begins to write.

The wise conclusion for the pastor would seem to be that he

should not attempt to write all sermons, but that he should compel himself to write often, perhaps at least one sermon a week. And the written sermon should not always be the morning sermon. In this twofold method the preacher will incline to center on one or the other. Let him remember that although "a man cannot serve two masters," he can use two servants and make both profitable if he uses them wisely, if he gives to his written sermons and unwritten sermons equally careful and thorough preparation. Because of the neglect of writing among American preachers we should make ourselves write until we have claimed all its rich advantages.

CHAPTER II

PREPARATION OF SPECIAL TYPES OF SERMONS

IT IS convenient to offer at this point a few suggestions as to sermons on particular occasions, or addressed to particular classes. For it will often happen that in the choice and treatment of his subjects the preacher must be decisively influenced by the demands of some special occasion, or by the peculiar character of the audience or a part of the audience which he is to address. It will be desirable, therefore, briefly to discuss in this connection some matters pertaining to the style and management of these special sermons.

I. FUNERAL SERMONS

In some places, especially though not exclusively in the cities, the current demand for brevity in religious services, with perhaps other causes also, has induced some decline in the practice of preaching set funeral sermons. People often prefer a simple religious service with sometimes a brief memorial address, or several addresses in cases of special interest. Yet, there is still in many quarters a powerful sentiment sustained by long usage in favor of special funeral sermons; and the preacher should know how to meet this demand. Besides, much that needs to be said about funeral sermons will apply as well to the short personal address as to the more elaborate and formal discourse.

Those who clearly see and vehemently condemn the faults which disfigure many funeral discourses are very apt, when themselves bereaved, to find their hearts demanding such a service and will not unfrequently prefer the very preacher whose course had often seemed to them most objectionable. Sorrowing and softened, we feel then a special need of God's mercy and grace, and the preacher should gladly seize the opportunity to recommend the gospel of consolation and to impress the need of personal piety, that we may be ready to live and ready to die. And not only will some habitual hearers be then better prepared to receive the word, but persons will be present who seldom attend the place of worship. It is highly important, therefore, that funeral sermons should clearly point out the way of life and tenderly invite to the Saviour. Moreover, in the freshness of our grief we instinctively desire to utter, or at least to hear, some eulogy upon the departed; and all nations have had some method, by speech or song or broken lament, of indulging the desire. That among us Christian ministers are expected to perform this function, while it sometimes places them in a difficult position, is yet a sign of their influence and a means of using that influence to good purpose. Yet the preacher must remember that he is not a mere eulogist of the dead but only adds this task to his work of preaching the gospel. Accordingly, his utterances as to the departed must be only a part of what he says, usually but a small part, and must be scrupulously true, though not necessarily all the truth, for this would often be superfluous and sometimes painful. No promptings of his own sorrow or regard for the feelings of others, must lead him to the exaggerated praises which are so natural. When the departed was a Christian, he should speak chiefly of that fact, bringing out anything in the character or course of life which he knows and which others will recognize to be worthy of imitation. When the departed was not a Christian, he may sometimes lawfully speak a few soothing words as to anything which specially endeared the deceased to his friends. But this must be done, if done at all, without exaggeration, and it is a solemn duty to avoid saying one word which suggests that these good points of character afford any ground of hope for eternity. Some preachers will on such occasions give the lie to all their ordinary preaching by leaving room to suppose that without being born again, a very excellent person may perhaps see the Kingdom of God. "He did not make any profession of religion, *but* he was this or that, and we leave him to the mercy of God." Or "he had never professed to be a Christian, but he was perfectly willing to die"—as if that proved anything. Nay, if the deceased did not give evidence of being regenerate, a believer in Christ, let us say nothing about his eternal future, nothing whatever. Any such suggestions encourage the ignorant or unthinking in false hopes and to right-minded mourners are but a mockery of their woe. Pains should be taken not to make much of deathbed conversions, which are proverbially uncertain and the hope of which, as a last resort, is so often taken by the living as an encouragement to delay. In general, the preacher ought to exercise reserve in what he says of the departed; and in the case of wicked people, it is frequently in the best taste and shows the most real kindness to say nothing. Young preachers sometimes allow themselves, in their first sermons of this sort, to indulge in copious eulogies with no great foundation, and then afterwards seem compelled to do likewise in cases where they feel it to be a great trial and know that they are liable to do serious harm to the cause of truth. It will save much embarrassment to begin right.

The services on such occasions, and especially the sermon, are often made too long.

A prevailing fault of funeral discourses is the occupation of too much time with generalities or truths that have no special application to the existing circumstances. It is far better to confine such discourses to narrower limits and to that particular range of thought which all will recognize to be pertinent.[1]

The tendency to ostentatious parade in funerals, which is in some communities a great evil, ought in every judicious way to be discouraged.

2. ACADEMIC AND ANNIVERSARY SERMONS

Sermons at institutions of learning or on occasions of literary interest are often managed in a very mistaken fashion. The preacher imagines that he must not give a regular gospel sermon but must betake himself to matters highly erudite or metaphysical. It is really desirable on such occasions to preach upon eminently evangelical topics, the very heart of the gospel. Science and erudition are the everyday work of these professors and students; from you, today, they had much rather hear something else. Even those who care nothing for religion will feel, as persons of taste, that it is congruous, becoming, for a preacher to preach the gospel; while the truly pious, yearning over their unconverted associates, will long to have the preacher urge saving truth upon them in the most practical way, and with whole-souled earnestness. Of course, the sermon should have point, force, freshness; and the associations of the occasion may sometimes suggest slight peculiarities of allusion, illustration, and style; but it ought to be a sermon full of Christ, full of prayerful zeal to save souls. Ah! as one looks over those hundreds of intelligent young faces, and his heart goes out to them in sympathy and love, as he thinks what a power they will be in the world for good or for evil, and how they are all there present before God, to hear his message, he must surely feel an unwonted emotion, a solemn sense of privilege

---

[1] Kidder's *Hom.*, p. 280, where there are other good remarks.

and responsibility; and if never before, there ought to be true of him then, those words of Baxter:

> I preached as never sure to preach again,
> And as a dying man to dying men.

Preachers are often called on to deliver sermons at various kinds of anniversaries. In general, such sermons are never so acceptable to devout hearts and never so helpful to the objects sought on these occasions, as when they are filled with the very essence of the gospel. For example, the "annual sermon" before an association, convention, or other religious body should not be soaring, philosophic, ambitious, but should seek by earnest, direct, and moving presentation of gospel truths and motives to arouse a deep religious feeling. He is a wise man who prayerfully avoids making a show on such occasions but sincerely endeavors to bring his brethren with himself nearer to his Master. Even where some particular doctrine or topic, historical, memorial, or other, is assigned him, the preacher should strive so to present his theme as to awaken and encourage devout sentiments.

And the same principles hold in regard to other anniversary sermons. It sometimes occurs that a Society, religious or benevolent, celebrates its anniversary by having a sermon preached. Besides the sermon, it may be remarked in passing, the minister should look well to the other services of the occasion and see that they are not only suitable and impressive but solemn and spiritually profitable. Occasions of this kind often give the preacher an opportunity to reach people who seldom go to church, or to his church, and whom he may never meet again. Well will it be for him and for them if by skillful and deeply earnest handling of his theme and his opportunity he may be able to win and edify the souls of his hearers. The preacher cannot afford to be merely the head man of the parade at such time; he must be the devout and inspiring soul of the occasion.

3. REVIVAL SERMONS

The phrase "revival sermons" is not altogether a felicitous or suitable one; yet, it is readily understood to mean those sermons which are especially appropriate in revival meetings where the principal object is to arouse those who are not Christians and win converts. Now it is obvious that in their general conduct and treatment discourses for these occasions should not materially differ from other sermons; and yet in the choice of topics for successive presentation, and in many of the details of treatment, there are some points of special interest which make these discourses somewhat peculiar and warrant particular discussion. Sometimes the pastor may have to conduct his own revival services, and this is an exceedingly desirable thing for him to do. At other times he may be called on to aid a brother pastor in a series of meetings, preaching always once and very frequently twice a day. Thus the selection, order, and treatment of his subjects are matters of moment and sometimes of difficulty. So varied are these occasions of revival, and so different their demands, that it would be impossible to make rules to cover all cases; and yet a few practical suggestions as to the general character and management of revival sermons may be useful, especially to the inexperienced preacher.

(1) *They should be short.* The people are wearied by coming often to successive meetings; and there are other things besides the sermon that need to be interspersed, such as the appeals, the songs, the prayers; so that it is a mistake to make the sermon as long as it usually is. Many otherwise successful revivalists have erred in this point.

(2) *They should be greatly varied in character and contents.* Monotony is injurious to the best effects. In the congregations which usually gather for these special services there is every variety of people with every variety of sentiment, and at no time is the preacher more solemnly bound to be all things to all men that he may by all means save some. This variety of adaptation will be necessary both in the selection and the treatment of the topics of discourse. Sometimes the sermon must edify, comfort, and encourage the saints and faithful workers; at others it must rebuke the lax and cold church members whose worldliness and inconsistencies are a hindrance to the success of the gospel; now it must proclaim in no uncertain voice the fearfulness of the Lord's judgment upon sin; and again, it must gently win and urge the hesitating by presenting the inestimable love and mercy of God. With some the preacher must argue, to some he must dogmatize, others he must touch with tender anecdote and pathetic appeal; some he must rebuke with sharp attack upon the conscience, others he must encourage, with patient persuasion, to venture now upon the Lord's promises. Yet, with all this variety another thing is important in these revival discourses.

(3) *They should generally follow some law of sequence.* What that order shall be will depend upon such a variety of circumstances

that it would be impossible to make any general rule cover all cases; the exceptions would be likely to be more important than the rule. Not even the same order of topics should be pursued in different places or in the same place at different times. Yet, partly for the sake of the preacher's own mind in its logical, and therefore more efficient, working and partly for the sake of continuity of effect upon the minds of others, some orderly arrangement in the series of discourses is usually desirable in revival preaching. A general sequence like the following is often found useful: First address the church, seeking to arouse a more active spiritual life, to recall the worldly and quicken the pious, awakening in all the spirit of prayer and of intense concern for the salvation of others; then present for several meetings the terrors of the law, searching the conscience, arousing concern for sin, the fear of judgment, and the consequent imperative need of a Saviour; then set forth the mercy and love of God as displayed in the gospel of his Son, the certainty and completeness of the divine forgiveness of sin upon repentance and faith; and finally urge immediate decision and acceptance of the gospel terms, with public confession of Christ. Whatever order may be observed, none of these topics can be safely omitted from a series of revival sermons. Several of them may be combined in the same discourse, they may be often repeated in various connections, and very often the earnest presentation of one will incidentally and powerfully enforce another. Grave mistakes are often made by insisting too exclusively upon one or another of these parts of the gospel message. Especially is this true in regard to the last—the duty of immediate confession of Christ. Some take this up at once and insist upon it all through the meetings to the slighting of the topics which naturally and logically precede it; and it is to be feared that many superficial persons are thus induced to make a public confession of religion who have had no true conviction of sin, no real sense of their utter need of the Saviour, and consequently no sound scriptural conversion. This brings us to notice another requisite in revival sermons:—

(4) *They should pre-eminently exemplify a sound, thoroughgoing and complete gospel preaching.* There is much so-called revival preaching which sadly lacks this character. Mere claptrap and sensationalism, tirades of cheap wit and vulgar denunciation, extreme and one-sided statements, half-truths and specious errors—all these infect as a deadly poison a large proportion of that which is called evangelistic preaching. An earnest and loving, but at the same time faithful

and strong, presentation of pure Bible truth on the great matters of sin, judgment, atonement, salvation, regeneration, grace, repentance, and faith is the distinctive and emphatic need of the revival preaching of our age.

4. SERMONS TO CHILDREN

Work for the children and young people is one of the characteristic movements of our age; and it is well for us to give particular attention to the subject of preaching to children. Suggestions on this subject will also bear upon the less formal addresses to children in the Sunday school, on anniversary and festal occasions, and the like. There is apt to be too broad a difference in style and tone between "sermons" to children and "speeches" to them. If the sermons could be a little more familiar, and the speeches a good deal more serious, than is commonly the case, then suggestions for the one could, without any appearance of incongruity, apply to the other.

Everyone notices how few persons succeed decidedly well in speaking to children. But many preachers possess greater power in this respect than they have ever exercised, because they have never devoted to the subject much either of reflection, observation, or heedful practice. Examples may be found of men who for years considered that they had no talent for speaking to children, and whose attempts were always comparative failures, and yet who afterwards became very popular and useful in this important department of preaching. There are others, however, who have had great success with sermons to children. In modern times the first to be noticed is the celebrated French Catholic preacher, Massillon, who addressed to Louis XV, when a child of nine years, a series of sermons which have obtained the name of "Le Petit Carême," The Little Lent. Dr. Thomas Arnold, the famous teacher of Rugby School in England, preached to his boys with good effect. In later times many English preachers have given special and successful attention to this work. Here in America not a few of our pastors and evangelists have done good service in this department.

It has been frequently remarked that in the young child imagination is predominant; in the child of ten or twelve years, memory; and not until they are nearly grown, do the powers of abstraction and reasoning become active. It is to the two former classes that we commonly speak, whatever is aimed at older people being also addressed to the children. We see at once that it is necessary to avoid abstract terms and formal processes of reasoning. Many preachers find this difficult because they are too much accustomed, even for the wants of the ordinary adult mind, to discourse upon gospel doctrine in an abstract and purely argumentative way; and learning how to preach to children may make them better preachers in general. Merely to refrain from using long words is not the thing needed. Children understand polysyllables just as well as monosyllables, when they represent concrete and familiar or easily intelligible conceptions. Besides, those of a dozen years are not pleased at the appearance of excessive effort to use short words to them, as if they had no sense. Eschew, then, all abstract terms. And instead of argumentation, give them facts and truths, confidently stated, with the quiet air of authority to which children naturally bow. Let these facts and truths be so stated, described, or illustrated as to awaken the imagination. The illustrations should generally be in the form of narrative (as the Great Teacher's were), and the stories and descriptions should be pictorial—not minutely finished pictures, for children weary of those, but with broad outlines, prominent features, and vivid touches of suggestive detail. Thus telling them what they will receive as interesting facts or important truth, and in such a way as to charm the imagination, we are able to reach the child's affections and conscience. Only through what appeals to the imagination can this be readily done.

In general, in preaching to children the three principal things to do are to interest, to instruct, to impress. We shall speak in vain unless we interest them. Grown people may pay a becoming attention to what does not deeply interest them, but children do not, perhaps they cannot. In order to interest them there must be clearness both in plan and style; they must comprehend. Now two favorite words with children are "pretty" and "funny"; these are to them two radiating centers of thought, the terms being extended to many things which only in some respects are pretty or funny. It is well, therefore, in seeking to interest children, to employ freely the beautiful and the humorous; yet, neither must be overdone. In all sermons to children there should be instruction by such illustrations as will appeal to the childish mind; it may be as regards the fundamental verities of religion, sin, atonement, repentance, faith, or as to moral virtues, such as courage, honesty, purity, unselfishness, industry, reverence. In impressing children with religious truth care should be taken to appeal commonly to their affections rather than to their fears. We should not frighten but win them. Yet, we must not forget to speak in a proper way of wrath and judgment.

The children must feel that they are learning something and must see that we are trying to do them good. However thoughtless, changeable, passionate, a child may be, its conscience is active. Every child quickly recognizes the propriety of our seeking to win it to love and serve the Lord, and feels that something is lacking where this is not the case. However great the external attractions of a Sunday school, it will soon grow dull to the little ones if they do not learn, especially learn the Bible, and breathe there an atmosphere of genuine piety. The spasmodic efforts to keep up the interest which are sometimes observed in Sunday school officers and speakers must only become more and more vehement and extravagant if they are neglecting religious instruction and devotional impressiveness.

In dealing with such restless beings, variety is, of course, indispensable. If the same man speaks to them long, he must have great variety of matter, feeling, and utterance. Nothing pathetic or even solemn can long engage their attention, save under extraordinary circumstances; and it is therefore proper to make free use of the natural reaction between pathos and humor. The childish mind readily passes "from grave to gay" and almost as readily back again to what is grave. Few men can succeed well in speeches or sermons to children unless they are able to employ at least a few touches of humor. But if some speakers through uniform gravity fail to maintain the interest, a still greater number at the present day indulge in such an excess and predominance of humor, as to fail of doing real good and by degrees to lose the power even of holding the children's attention. The humor employed had best be delicate; it may be broad and grotesque, but never coarse or silly. It must be manifestly subordinate to a serious purpose. Children feel that you have no business seeking on that occasion merely to amuse them; and the funniest story, the oddest saying, the wittiest allusion must by analogy or by contrast give impressiveness to something useful and serious, or else it is out of place and ought to have been omitted. And a perpetual succession of merely funny things will soon utterly pall upon the children's taste. The little ones that hear much speaking grow to be keen critics; and it were well if some speakers could often hear their talk at home.[2]

Speak, then, of interesting and instructive facts and truths, in concrete and familiar terms, without formal argument, analytical processes, or abstract ideas. Speak to the child's imagination, heart, and conscience. Speak with a prevailing seriousness, with an earnest desire to do them good. And if you would learn their range of ideas and their vocabulary, would find the door to their hearts, talk much with children and allure them into talking freely to you.

The remark may be added, as of great importance, that children are not to be addressed as pious, but as needing to become so; and that they have to become Christians in essentially the same way as adults—by repentance and faith, through the renewing of the Holy Ghost. Great mischief results from the fact that so many who speak to children seem not to perceive clearly, or to keep distinctly in mind, this unquestionable truth.

It may be well to say a few words as to the occasions or services in connection with which it will be proper to preach to the children. Naturally there is considerable diversity of practice in regard to this. It was a custom of Whitefield to address himself to the children sometimes in the midst of his sermons to the general congregation. This is an excellent method and should be often pursued in our regular ministry; but it is scarcely sufficient. The children should sometimes have a whole sermon to themselves. Others have had a brief address to the children before or after the regular sermon to grown people. This might be well sometimes, but it would hardly be suitable or desirable on many occasions. Children are tired at the close of the sermon, to say nothing of the grown people whose interest might then be dissipated. And at the beginning there would be other disadvantages. Some preachers take the Sunday-school hour for an occasional sermon to the children. Short addresses are generally better on these occasions, better both for the children and the preacher. Sometimes the method has been tried of having a separate service for the children at the same hour as the stated service for the congre-

---

[2] "He kept trying to make us laugh all the time, and I got mighty tired of that." "He told us about a little boy, and wound up like they always do, you know, 'And, children, that little boy is here to-day.'" "He tried very hard to be funny, but I didn't feel like laughing." "O pa, do you think anybody ought to be saying so many foolish things, when he's talking about our Saviour?" "O me, I used to think that story was right funny, but I've heard it so often." Parents sometimes have difficulty in correcting the evil effects which are indicated by such sayings.

gation; but as this renders it necessary to have different preachers and rooms, it is usually inconvenient. In large churches where there are several pastors, or assistants, and suitable auditoriums this might do very well. Another method is that of having stated or occasional services for the children in the afternoon in addition to the regular services. This plan works very well and is generally perhaps better than any that have been mentioned. But the best way of all seems to be to give, either at regular intervals (as fifth Sundays, or once a month), or by special appointment, some morning service to the children. Let the whole service be theirs. Make it shorter than usual, and let them feel that it is their special occasion. The grown people—mostly parents or others interested in children—will commonly gladly acquiesce in this arrangement. In fact, some have been known rather to prefer the children's sermon to their own because they understood it better!

5. SERMONS FOR OTHER SPECIAL CLASSES

For various reasons the preacher may find it desirable, and sometimes even necessary, to preach to other special classes besides the children. Sometimes this may be in connection with an anniversary, or stated occasion, or celebration, when the class interested will be specially concerned; sometimes it may be by request, formal or private, of societies or individuals representing the classes to be addressed; sometimes it may be by his own choice along the course of his regular work, either with a view to variety or for some particular reason. Thus, for example, the pastor may sometimes wish to preach especially to the aged, to the bereaved, to young men or women, to mothers or fathers, to merchants, lawyers, doctors, teachers, workingmen of various trades, and the like. It is easy to see how occasion for this kind of preaching will frequently arise. It will be the pastor's privilege and duty to make the best of such opportunities.

It is not necessary to take up each of these classes of hearers and discuss the best ways of preaching to them, as was done in the case of children; but a few general suggestions, applicable more or less in all cases, may be offered: (1) Be careful in the selection of text and subject. Try to have those which will be fresh, striking, and appropriate; but avoid straining after effect, and particularly eschew what is forced and farfetched in the application of subject to occasion. (2) Do not be too pointed and personal in address and application.

The occasion itself will do much in applying what you say to the particular class of people before you. There is danger of repelling the very persons you wish to reach, if you single them out too pointedly for direct address. Yet, delicate personal appeal is natural and may be highly effective. (3) Be sure to treat the theme and use the occasion in such a way as to interest and profit the general congregation. The special class addressed may be small in comparison with the rest of the audience, and, even if they were in the majority, there would still be reason for having something useful and helpful to all. (4) As always—preach the gospel. Do not be betrayed or inveigled into mere sensationalism. These occasions easily degenerate, in the hands of worldly preachers, into means of airing themselves before the community and in the newspapers. Shun this as you would sin, for it is sin. Let the grand truths of the Bible find clear and unmistakable expression and earnest, prayerful application.

Chapter III

THREE METHODS OF DELIVERY

READING, reciting, extemporaneous speaking—which is the best method of preaching? Though so often discussed, this question constantly recurs, not merely for the young preachers whom every year brings forward but for many of maturer age, who are not satisfied that they have been pursuing the wisest course. It is a question affecting not only one's manner of delivery, but all his habits of thought and expression. While not so indispensable a condition of usefulness as that a man shall hold the truth, or that he shall love his work, or that he shall be a born speaker, it is surely a matter of very great importance to one whose best energies through life are devoted to preaching that he should speak in the most effective way.

I. READING

Reading to a congregation a sermon which has been more or less carelessly written out beforehand is one method, which has been and is still often practiced, though it is scarcely so common in this country as it was a generation or so ago.

The practice of reading sermons, as a frequent thing, is generally believed to have originated in the reign of Henry VIII.

Those who were licensed to preach [says Burnet, in his *History of the Reformation*] being often accused for their sermons, and complaints being made to the King by hot men on both sides, they came generally to write and read their sermons, and thence the reading of sermons grew into a practice in this church; in which if there was not that heat of fire which the friars had shown in their declamations, so that the passions of the hearers were not so much wrought on by it, yet it has produced the greatest treasure of weighty, grave, and solid sermons that ever the Church of God had; which does in a great measure compensate that seeming flatness to vulgar ears, that is in the delivery of them.[1]

The practice increased in consequence of the civil wars, especially through strong dislike to the impassioned preaching of the Inde-

[1] Quoted by Gresley on Preaching, p. 391.

pendents. The impression long prevailed in England that extemporaneous preaching was the invention of the Puritans. A curate was once driven from a London pulpit because he was accustomed to raise his eyes from his manuscript while preaching![2] Charles II, not accustomed, on the Continent, to this tamer method, vainly attempted to correct it, as shown by the following curious letter, extracted by Gresley from the statute-book of the University of Cambridge:—

VICE-CHANCELLOR AND GENTLEMEN: Whereas his Majesty is informed that the practice of reading sermons is generally taken up by the preachers before the university, and therefore continues even before himself; his Majesty hath commanded me to signify to you his pleasure, that the said practice, which took its beginning from the disorders of the late times, be wholly laid aside, and that the said preachers deliver their sermons, both in Latin and English, by memory, without books; as being a way of preaching which his Majesty judgeth most agreeable to the use of foreign churches, to the custom of the university heretofore, and to the nature of that holy exercise: and that his Majesty's command in these premises be duly regarded and observed, his further pleasure is, that the names of all such ecclesiastical persons as shall continue the present supine and slothful way of preaching be, from time to time, signified to him by the Vice-Chancellor for the time being, on pain of his Majesty's displeasure.

MONMOUTH.

Oct. 8th, 1674.

The effort failed, and reading was frequently practiced in the Church of England. To this day, however, it is quite rare on the Continent and among Romanists everywhere and is common only among certain Protestants of Great Britain and America. The growing number of Episcopal ministers in this country who extemporize are very popular, even among their own brethren, if they manage it effectively. Many leading Presbyterian ministers, and some of their ecclesiastical authorities, have discouraged reading and even vehemently condemned it.

Most of the eminent examples of reading admit of some explanation. Jonathan Edwards, late in life, regretted the practice and believed that it was better to preach memoriter for the most part, sometimes extemporizing.[3] Dr. Chalmers, so often adduced, as if the example of a very peculiar man could establish a rule, declared himself unable to extemporize. But look at his style. He was extremely, in fact, exces-

[2] *Ibid.,* Mediaeval Preaching.
[3] Hoppin, p. 494.

sively fond of long sentences, formed of nicely balanced clauses, with the corresponding terms in each clause often indicated by alliteration, and he had an exceeding desire to achieve quaint felicities of phraseology. His images are frequently drawn on a grand and elaborate scale, and he was fastidious as to their color and finish. These well-known peculiarities go far to account for his persuasion that he could not extemporize. It would be almost as difficult to improvise a choral ode, as some of those elaborate passages in which he delighted. And, after all, Dr. Wayland states:[4]

A gentleman who was in the habit of hearing him, has assured me that his extempore discourses, delivered to operatives in the outskirts of Glasgow, were far more effective and more truly eloquent than the sermons which he delivered with so much applause in the Tron church of that city;

—and there is other testimony to the same effect.

As regards the delivery of the sermon, this method has the advantage of placing the preacher more at his ease, both before and during the delivery. Having the sermon written, he will be preserved, and knows that he will be, from any utter and mortifying failure. It is a great relief to escape the tremulous and often distressing anxiety which one is apt otherwise to feel. The preacher who means to read has a far better chance to sleep soundly on Saturday night. It is also an advantage to be collected and confident while delivering the sermon, rather than oppressed by nervous solicitude or driven wild by uncontrollable excitement. Some preachers find that reading saves them from an excessive volubility or an extreme vehemence which otherwise they find hard to control; and very many fear that without the manuscript they would be utterly crushed by the dread of breaking down.

On the other hand, reading the sermon has several disadvantages. (1) It deprives the preacher's thinking of the benefit of all that mental quickening which is produced by the presence of the congregation. As to thoughts which are then for the first time struck out, it is true that men of rare flexibility, tact, and grace can often introduce them effectively in connection with their reading. But such men establish no general rule, and the great mass of those who read have to lose such thoughts altogether or to introduce them awkwardly

---

[4] *Ministry of Gospel*, p. 126. See also the account of Chalmers' speeches in the General Assembly, in Hanna's Memoir, Vol. IV, 114, 199, 438.

and with comparatively poor effect. And besides the distinct thoughts which occur only in the act of delivery, there is something much more important in the warmer color which the now kindled and glowing mind would give to the whole body of thought, in those differences of hue and tone which change the mass of prepared material into living, breathing, burning speech. Yonder stand the autumn trees, with their many colors all dull and tame beneath the ashen sky; but presently the evening sun bursts through the clouds, and lights up the forest with an almost unearthly glory. Not less great is the difference between preparation and speech for everyone who was born to be a speaker. Now whatever of this concerns the mere mode of utterance, the reader may to some extent achieve. But all that belongs to the transfigured conception, to the changed color and heightened tone of expression, which in free speaking would show itself with ease and completeness, all this he can but partially feel and is powerless to manifest. It is true, as we are sometimes told, that by an effort of imagination when composing, one may to some extent bring before his mind the congregation and feel by anticipation the quickening of its presence; but there are few respects in which imagination falls so far below the actual experience.

(2) Reading is of necessity less effective, and in most cases immensely less effective, for all the great purposes of oratory than speaking. Greater coldness of manner is almost inevitable. If one attempts to be very animated or pathetic, it will look unnatural. The tones of voice are monotonous or have a forced variety. The gestures are nearly always unnatural, because it is not natural to gesticulate much in reading; and they scarcely ever raise us higher than to feel that really this man reads almost like speaking. The mere turning of the pages, however skillfully done, breaks the continuity of delivery. In the midst, perhaps, of some impassioned passage, while the preacher's face glows, his action has become varied and passionate, and he has wrought us up to a high degree of sympathy with him, presently his right hand descends and flings over a leaf, and the spell is broken; we are made to remember what we are doing, are reminded that, after all, this is not living speech but only splendid reading,—that we are not, as a moment ago we seemed to feel, in immediate and fully sympathizing contact with the burning soul of the speaker, but "that paper there" is between us. Consider, too, that the most potent element in the delivery of a real orator is often the expressiveness of the eye. No man can describe this; he cannot

fully recall it afterwards, and at the moment he is too completely under its influence to think of analyzing and explaining it. But every man has felt it,—the marvelous, magical, at times almost super-human power of an orator's eye. That look, how it pierces our inmost soul, now kindling us to passion, now melting us into tenderness. And all the better that it is not felt as a thing apart from speech but blends with it more thoroughly than gesture can, more completely than music blends with poetry, and reinforces, with all its mysterious potency, the power of thought and sentiment and sound. Now in reading, this wonderful expressiveness of the eye is interrupted, grievously diminished in power, reduced to be nothing better than occasional sunbeams, breaking out for a moment among wintry clouds.

In a word, reading is an essentially different thing from speaking. When well executed, reading has a power of its own, but it is unnatural to substitute it for speaking, and it can at best only approximate, never fully attain, the same effect.

(3) It should be added that reading is more injurious to the voice. Anyone who is so unfortunate as to have become subject to laryngitis will soon find that he can speak with much less fatigue than he can read. This shows a natural difference, though persons whose vocal organs are not diseased may not notice it. There are several causes which combine to produce the "minister's sore-throat," which is so common. The practice of reading sermons is by no means the principal one, but there can be no doubt that it has some effect.

(4) That the habit of reading should make one afraid to attempt speaking without a manuscript is not a necessary consequence. Every enlightened defender of reading would urge that the preacher ought to practice himself in unwritten speech also and thus be able to speak when suddenly called on; and certainly there are men who habitually read and yet upon occasion can extemporize very effectively. Yet, the manifest tendency, and the common result of habitual reading, is to make one dependent and timid; and such preachers often miss opportunities of doing good and are sometimes made ridiculous by their inability to preach from not having "brought along any ser-mons." Such a slavish and helpless dependence upon manuscript is almost universally felt to be painful, if not pitiful. For this and other reasons, uniform reading is very seldom advocated, though still often practiced in some quarters.

The advantages and disadvantages of reading sermons having been considered, a few suggestions may now be offered to those who adopt this method.

If you read, do not try to disguise the fact. Coquerel remarks that all the artifices practiced for this purpose

have bad grace and little success. If one reads in the pulpit, it is better to read openly and boldly, taking no other pains than to have a manuscript easily legible and properly smoothed down on the front of the pulpit; then, to turn the leaves without affecting a disguise, which is useless and unbecoming. We may be certain that the hearers are not deceived in this respect; they always know when an orator is reading.[5]

But more. Do not attempt to convert the reading into speaking. The two are, as already said, essentially different. Is it possible for a man to speak as if he were reading? Let it be tried, and he who comes nearest to success will most effectually spoil his speaking. But on the other hand, is it really possible to read as if you were speaking? Schoolmasters often tell their boys, "Read it just as if you were talking"; and the effort to do this may help to cure the schoolboy singsong, by making the reading more like talking. But in fact, no one can read precisely as he talks, and no one ought to. In private reading and private conversation, probably no considerate person will deny this essential difference. Is it not similarly and equally true as regards public reading and public speaking? Reading before a large audience will, of course, differ from quiet reading to a few persons; and where the matter read is preceptive or hortatory, something which we personally desire to impress upon the hearers, this also will give a peculiar character to the reading. But still it is reading. The attempt to convert it into speaking is against nature, must fail, and ought to fail.

It seems to us that when a preacher, for whatever reason, reads his sermon, then, instead of wishing to produce the appearance of free speaking, which is always in some measure an attempt at deception, he should make it his aim to read well; somewhat as when one with warmth and interest reads to his family a printed discourse.

To this view of the German writer, Palmer, we should say, Yes, somewhat; but with the difference naturally produced by the fact that you are reading to a large assembly, and reading what intensely interests yourself. Palmer proceeds:

[5] Coquerel, p. 177.

To hear a good thing well read is always a pleasure. But instead of this, one man gives himself no trouble with his reading but drawls out the contents of his manuscript with monotonous indifference and tedious-ness. This is revolting. But another falls into the opposite extreme. Feeling that reading is a fault, he wishes to make amends by disclaiming his sermon with a powerful pathos. This makes a contrary impression, for the more exaggerated the declamation and action in the case, the more glaring the contrast produced by the extremely prosaic act of looking into the manuscript. He who is so terribly in earnest with what he is saying ought also, people think, to know what he wants to say; his zeal ought, as is everywhere else the case, to put words into his mouth. A modest, quiet, but expressive reading would be more appropriate.[6]

We add again that the reading may sometimes become very earnest, even if not impassioned, but it must still be reading. Let not the reader try to assume postures, gestures, or looks, such as he thinks would be appropriate to one speaking these words. To do so is not natural; it is to be an actor; and acting, however skillful and however much admired, is in the pulpit a crime,—and, as the diplomatists say, not only a crime, but worse, a blunder. Nay, let the reader know that he is reading; let him mean to read and mean to have everybody understand that he is reading; and then let him try to read well, so as to impress the truth upon his hearers and do them good.[7] The observance of this distinction may also solve the much discussed question, whether it is well for one who reads to interpolate unwrit-ten passages. If he attempts to do this without having the difference observed, it will fail. But if his reading does not profess nor attempt to be speaking but simply reading, then he may, wherever there is occasion, introduce something unwritten, either in the familiar tone appropriate to some additional illustration or remark or even in the outburst of some impassioned appeal. It will be distinct from the reading, but this may give variety; and the reading need not seem flat when he returns to it, because it did not profess to be speaking. This is in fact the practice of many skillful readers of sermons, though it may not be their theory; nature often triumphs over wrong theory and leads men to read simply as earnest reading and then to diverge, when they see proper, into speaking as a distinct thing. If those who read sermons would settle it well in their minds that reading is not speaking and cannot be converted into it, and would give nature free play in their reading, the advantages of this method would remain

[6] Palmer, *Hom.*, ss. 526, 527.
[7] Pittenger (*Extempore Speech*, p. 29) forcibly defends this same view.

intact, and its disadvantages would be considerably diminished. Whether, even then, reading can be made as impressive, in general, as well-prepared speaking, is another question. The remark may be added, that where defective vision or bad light or a low pulpit makes the reading difficult, it would be better just quietly to hold up the manuscript so that it can be seen. If the pages are separate and not too large, this can be done without awkwardness; and if the people see that the preacher does not pretend to be speaking but reads with a straightforward simplicity, they will rather like his openness and at any rate will in a few minutes grow used to what at first looked odd. If anyone objects to all this and insists that it is necessary, whether from the nature of the case or from the notions and feelings of the people, to keep the manuscript out of sight and make the reading look as much as possible like speaking, then he is in fact saying what has not been said in this discussion, that a preacher ought never to read sermons at all.

2. RECITATION

Recitation, or repeating from memory what has been written and learned, is a method of preaching which not a few distinguished men have followed. It has been defended by even so acute and sensible a writer as Coquerel.[8] On the other hand, Phillips Brooks speaks of it as "a method which some men practice, but which I hope nobody commends."[9] It has had more general use in Europe than in our country; but a few things concerning it should be said.

(1) This has all the advantages of the first method, as regards more complete and finished preparation, practice in writing, and possession of the sermon for subsequent use and for publication. There is here, however, no preservation from utter failure and from the dread of failure, but quite the contrary. It has two advantages which the former method does not possess. To recite one's own composition is really one kind of speaking,—and we have seen that reading is not. To recite is speaking under difficulties and disadvantages, but it is speaking. It is not against nature to treat it as such or impossible to make it approximate somewhat closely to the excellence and power of well-prepared free speech. The other advantage is, that recitation cultivates the memory. Any real improvement of the memory is

---

[8] *Obs. Prat. sur la Préd.*, pp. 181 ff.
[9] *Lecture on Preaching.* p. 171.

certainly a matter of great value; men who habitually recite must always gain benefit in this respect, and with some the results are remarkable. It must not be forgotten, however, that while recitation is in this superior to reading, it is not superior to extemporaneous speaking; for the power of verbal memorizing is really less valuable than the ability to retain ideas with only such of the words as are essential to their precise expression.

(2) As to disadvantages, recitation labors under many of those which attend upon reading. There is here still less opportunity for correcting errors observed at the moment of delivery, for interpolating thoughts which then for the first time occur, or for giving new shape and color to the thoughts and new force to the expressions, under the excitement of actual speaking. The mind is apt to be all in shackles, having little use for any of its faculties except memory. In the exercise of this, there is often a confusion of local with what might be called "logical memory"; the recollection of what comes next on the page and that of the connection of thought, though sometimes aiding each other, will at other times become confused and distracting. There is also with this method a still greater consumption of time in preparation. He who adopts it has not only to prepare the materials and form the plan of the discourse, as must be done upon any method, and not only to spend many hours in writing it out in full, as the reader also must do, but to give other hours, and with most men not a few, to the task of memorizing. For one who preaches two or three times a week to write and memorize all his sermons is, if not impossible, certainly incompatible with patient and profound thinking in preparation, with wide general improvement, and with the proper performance of a pastor's other duties. The painful dread of failure is also a very serious objection to recitation, a dread from which the preacher can for no moment be free till the delivery begins, and which is then only heightened. For the extemporaneous speaker, anxiety as to failure may cause a helpful excitement; but to him who recites it brings no benefit but only distress. We are told that Bourdaloue would often keep his eyes shut throughout the sermon; and upon being asked the reason, he explained that he was afraid he might see some occurrence which would distract his attention and cause him to forget. In so great a man this is lamentable, pitiable; of course, it is an extreme case. Furthermore, the delivery of what is recited must always be more or less artificial. Whatever may be done with occasional brief passages, such as Lord Brougham boasted his ability

to introduce into an extemporaneous discourse without its being possible for the auditor to distinguish between them, we question whether any man could so recite an entire and extended discourse— verbatim recitation,—as to prevent the audience from detecting, especially from feeling, the difference. Certainly very few can do it, and we are discussing general questions. It is all very well to say that art must conceal art. We ask earnestly, can art conceal art? Who ever heard Edward Everett in one of his orations, without uneasily feeling that it was a splendid unreality,—only the finished declamation of a magnificent composition. This was all well enough in a great oration, such as that on Washington, because then one expects a work of art and is satisfied and delighted if the art be consummate. We readily yielded ourselves to the spell and were deeply moved, as we might be by a drama. But when a man is pleading for the life of his client or the salvation of his country, and still more when as an ambassador on behalf of Christ he prays men to be reconciled to God, we feel that all conscious art is out of place.

This method, then, may answer very well, if skillfully managed, for college addresses, for public lectures, for extraordinary orations, for any speaking in which art properly forms an important element. It is to be noticed, moreover, that to make the delivery as free and unconstrained as is possible for recitation, a man needs—unless he be one of the few who possess a wonderful memory—to have ample time for becoming thoroughly familiar with the discourse. Now the great French and German preachers who adopted this method usually preached much less frequently than an America pastor does and could afford to spend all necessary time in making perfectly sure that they had memorized their sermons. Besides, the preachers at Louis XIV's court were expected to make their discourses works of art, so that artificiality was not objectionable; and later in the case of a fervent evangelical preacher, like Adolphe Monod, it was seldom a real recitation but again and again would become free speech from written preparation. Wherever preacher and hearers are satisfied with the habitual practice of verbatim recitation, it may be questioned whether either party deeply feels the reality of preaching. Sydney Smith's inquiry, "What can be more ludicrous than an orator delivering stale indignation, and fervor of a week old?" is not only a keen sarcasm but contains an unanswerable argument.[10] He who recites

---

[10] See the whole passage in *Ad Clerum*, p. 38, and Pittenger, p. 29. Hervey (*Christian Rhetoric*, p. 555) makes as good a reply as could be made. See also W. M. Taylor, *Ministry of the Word*, p. 150.

must either be devoid of indignation and fervor, or else the delivery of these must be more or less artificial; and we repeat that conscious art cannot be tolerated by a preacher or manifest art by a congregation, if they justly appreciate and deeply feel the reality of preaching and hearing. Of course, there may be so much of genuine earnestness in a really great preacher, as in spite of the inevitable artificiality of manner to make a deep impression; yet, even then, the mode of delivery is a drawback, a serious one, and most serious precisely where the discourse ought to be most impressive.

(3) But may not a man write out his sermon and then speak freely from this written preparation? Certainly. Some eminent preachers do this and with the most admirable effect; but this is not recitation. Some of these men tell us that they do not memorize the discourse at all, in the sense of making a distinct effort to remember the words, and yet that they reproduce all the thoughts, and to a great extent in the same words that they had written down. And as already remarked, some of those who memorize learn by degrees to break away from recitation and express substantially the same thought in very different language. Now this is a wholly distinct thing from recitation. When one makes no effort to remember the words and recalls them at all only by their association with the ideas he is seeking to express, the process lacks the essential character of recitation. What then is it? The answer must be that free speaking from written preparation is only one of the varieties of what we call extemporaneous speaking. When one endeavors to repeat the words used in preparation, that is reciting, whether he wrote them down or did not; and when there is no effort to repeat the words, that is extemporizing, whether the preparation was partial or complete, purely mental, or written in full. Some men have such good memories that if they prepare beforehand at all, the delivery will be virtual recitation. It is said of Rufus Choate that he could write out a speech, rise from his desk immediately, leaving it there, and speak it as written. Alexander Hamilton wrote out his greatest speech, then tore it up (in order to be free) and next day spoke it with overwhelming power.

3. EXTEMPORANEOUS OR FREE SPEAKING

The technical meaning of this expression requires to be defined. Primarily, of course, it denotes speaking without preparation, simply from the promptings of the moment. The colloquial expression for this is speaking "off hand," the image being that of shooting without a rest; and the Germans have a corresponding phrase, speaking "from the stirrup," as when one shoots on horseback, without dismounting. This popular phraseology is suggestive. By a natural extension, the phrase "extemporaneous speaking" is applied to cases in which there has been preparation of the thought, however thorough, but the language is left to be suggested at the moment. Still further, when notes are made, as a help to preparation, when the plan of the discourse is drawn out on paper, and all the principal points are stated or suggested, we call it extemporaneous speaking, because all this is regarded only as a means of arranging and recalling the thoughts, and the language is extemporized. If one to any great extent relies on these notes for his language, then it is so far a recitation, where the notes are left at home, and reading, where they are kept before him in the pulpit; as a general thing, however, this is not true, and preaching from notes is fairly called extemporaneous. And one step further we go, when, as already stated, we insist that free speaking, after the discourse has been written in full as preparation, but without any effort to repeat the language of the manuscript, shall be called extemporaneous speaking. We think it has been satisfactorily shown that this last extension of the phrase is proper and necessary. And if so, then many eminent men, for example, Whitefield, who have usually been spoken of as reciting, were really, in part or in whole, extemporaneous preachers; and Whitefield in later life seldom wrote at all.[11]

No intelligent man would now propose that preachers should habitually speak extempore, as regards the matter. It is true that occasions not unfrequently arise which make it important that they should be able to speak without any special immediate preparation; but this will be done most fitly and effectively by those whose habit it is to do so otherwise. In truth, the fanatical or slothful men who say that they never make any preparation deceive themselves. Most of what they say has been prepared by saying it many times before, and in many cases its substance was originally borrowed, whether from books, or from the preaching of others and from conversation. Except as to single thoughts suggested at the moment, their minds are led by association of ideas, even though it be unconsciously, into what they have previously worked out. Really to extemporize the matter

---

[11] *Ad Clerum*, pp. 44, 45.

of preaching is as impracticable as it is improper. And it is utterly unfair to represent the advocates of extemporaneous preaching as meaning that men shall preach without preparation.

In presenting the advantages and disadvantages of this method, there must be some repetition of ideas already advanced. This is obviously necessary to completeness, and such matters will now be regarded from a different point of view.

(1) Consider then, the advantages.

(a) This method accustoms one to think more rapidly, and with less dependence on external helps, than if he habitually depended on a manuscript.

(b) Again, this method saves time for general improvement and for other pastoral work. Not at first, to be sure, for the inexperienced preacher often needs more time to make thorough preparation for preaching extempore than he would use in writing; but after he has gained facility and self-reliance, much time may be saved. Beecher and Spurgeon could never have done as much other work as they did, and at the same time have preached so well, if they had taken time to write out their sermons fully beforehand.

(c) In the act of delivery, the extemporaneous speaker has immense advantages. With far greater ease and effectiveness than if reading or reciting, he can turn to account ideas which occur at the time. Southey says:

The salient points of Whitefield's oratory were not prepared passages; they were bursts of passion, like the jets of a geyser when the spring is in full play.[12]

Any man who possesses, even in an humble degree, the fervid oratorical nature, will find that after careful preparation, some of the noblest and most inspiring thoughts he ever gains will come while he is engaged in speaking. If, full of his theme and impressed with its importance, he presently secures the interested and sympathizing attention of even a few good listeners, and the fire of his eyes comes reflected back from theirs, till electric flashes pass to and fro between them and his very soul glows and blazes and flames,—he cannot fail sometimes to strike out thoughts more splendid and more precious than ever visit his mind in solitary musing.

---

[12] Quoted by Skinner, p. 146.

If the audience be antagonistic rather than sympathetic, the orator is put upon his mettle—chooses his ground, watches his opportunity, closes in and triumphs.[13]

(d) And, as we have before seen, there is a more important gain than the new thoughts elicited. The whole mass of prepared material becomes brightened, warmed, sometimes transfigured, by this inspiration of delivery. The preacher's language rises, without conscious effort, to suit the heightened grandeur and beauty of his conceptions; and, as Everett has expressed it in speaking of Webster, "the discourse instinctively transposes itself into a higher key." This exaltation of soul, rising at times to rapture, can never be fitly described; but the speaker who does not in some measure know what it means was not born to be a speaker. And great stress should be laid upon the fact that besides the thoughts which then first occur to the mind,—a matter constantly remarked,—there is this effect of far greater importance produced by delivery, in changing the form and color, and incalculably augmenting the power of the thoughts previously prepared.

(e) Moreover, the preacher can watch the effect as he proceeds, and purposely alter the forms of expression, as well as the manner of delivery, according to his own feeling, and that of the audience. Especially in the hortatory parts of a sermon, which are often the most important parts, will this adaptation be desirable. If preacher and hearers have been wrought up to intense excitement, then it will be proper to use strong figures, impassioned exclamations, and in general to speak the language of passion. Nothing else would then be natural, and if in such a case one's language be unfigurative and quiet, it is felt by the disappointed hearers to be flat and tame, and no vehemence of mere delivery can supply the deficiency. Still worse is the effect if feeling has not risen high, and the preacher comes to language previously prepared which is figurative and passionate. If now his manner accords, as it ought always to do, with the actual feeling of himself and his hearers, there will be a painful incongruity between the delivery and the style; if he strives to rise to his prepared language, any partial success in so doing will but put him out of harmony with the feelings of the audience. Surely no one can question that this consideration is one of immense importance. What preacher has not often found, in repeating a sermon to another audience, that there was a difference and sometimes a very great

[13] W. M. Taylor.—Review article.

difference in the feeling with which he and his hearers approached the closing exhortation? A few sentences then, which in conception, style, and delivery strike precisely the right key, will wonderfully enhance the effect of the whole discourse.[14] What that right key will be, no man of oratorical nature can always foretell. Here, then, the reader or reciter must inevitably fail, while the cultivated extemporaneous speaker easily and naturally rises or falls to suit the feeling of the moment. But someone might reply, "I do not aim at high oratorical effects. I am content with more modest efforts." That of which we speak is constantly practiced by some humble men in prayer-meeting addresses. It is the simple rhetoric of nature.

(*f*) As to the delivery itself, it is only in extemporaneous speaking, of one or another variety, that this can ever be perfectly natural and achieve the highest effect. The ideal of speaking, it has been justly said, cannot be reached in any other way. Only thus will the voice, the action, the eye, be just what nature dictates and attain their full power. And while painstaking culture vainly strives to read or recite precisely like speaking, the extemporaneous speaker may with comparative ease rise to the best delivery of which he is capable. In this way, too, as before remarked, we most readily gain the sympathy of our hearers; they are sympathizing with a man, not a composition, —a man all alive with thoughts he is now thinking and fervors he is now feeling, and not simply reviving, as far as possible, the thought and feeling of some former time. If one preaches an unwritten sermon many times till it becomes a mere recitation, then it loses power. If he cannot somehow interest his mind in the subject, so as to be expressing living thought, he should lay the sermon aside and not use it for a long time.

(*g*) It is also an advantage of this method that it gives facility in speaking without immediate preparation. The preacher who cannot do this upon occasion misses many opportunities of usefulness and loses influence with the people by an incapacity which they consider a reproach.

(*h*) This leads to what is really among the most important advantages of extemporaneous preaching. With the masses of the people, it is the popular method. Where principle is involved, one ought to withstand the notions of the people; but when it is a mere

---

[14] Matthews (*Oratory and Orators*, p. 29) tells of a preacher who electrified his people by an extempore discourse during a thunderstorm; and on being asked to print it, replied that he would if they would print the thunderstorm along with it!

question of expediency—and the present question is nothing more—then a general and very decided popular preference is an exceedingly important consideration. It does not mend the matter to sneer at the folly of the masses in so often preferring ignorant preachers who thoroughly sympathize with them and speak in the way they like. There is real and grave danger that we shall "educate away from the people." Here, now, is one respect in which educated preachers have it in their power to suit the popular taste and gain the popular sympathy. If some obstacles to such sympathy can be but partially removed, there need be no difficulty with this obstacle. Those denominations, in particular, whose strength has always been with the masses ought to make almost everything bend to retain their hold upon the people. No doubt some congregations have been educated into a toleration of reading, but it is almost always an unwilling acquiescence, or a high regard for some man's preaching in spite of the fact that he reads. Instead of striving to educate the people into enduring what they will never like and what can never so deeply move them, let the preacher educate himself into preaching in such a way that he can reach and hold the masses and leave the fastidious few to think what they please.

(2) But we must turn to the disadvantages of extemporaneous speaking, some of which require not only careful consideration in argument but very watchful attention in practice. Some of these do not apply, so far as preparation is concerned, to free speaking after writing in full; but they may as well be discussed together.

(a) Perhaps the gravest of them all consists in the tendency to neglect of preparation, after one has gained facility in unaided thinking and extemporized expression. Men are prone to abuse all their privileges; but is it a superficial philosophy which thence concludes that privileges should be avoided. And if many extemporizers grow indolent and rely too much upon the suggestions of the moment, at least they must at the moment have some mental activity; whereas the same indolent men, if accustomed to read or recite, would repeat sermons long ago prepared, with their minds no longer active or their hearts truly warm. This tendency to neglect of preparation is real and powerful, but it may be resisted, and many extemporizers do resist it, continuing through life to prepare their sermons with care; and as just intimated, it is only many readers, and by no means all, that do likewise.

(b) There is difficulty in fixing the mind upon the work of preparation without writing in full. This may be removed by practice. At the outset, it can be overcome either by making copious notes or by speaking the subject over in private.

(c) Still another, and a serious disadvantage of this method, is in its tendency to prevent one's forming the habit of writing. As fluency increases, the contrast between winged, glorious speech and slow, toilsome writing becomes to many men too great for their patience, and there grows upon them what someone felicitously calls a "calamophobia," a dread of the pen. And not only does this cut them off from many important means of usefulness—especially in our day, the era of the printing press—but it reacts disastrously upon their power of speaking. Both the beginner in oratory and the experienced, ready speaker must constrain themselves to write, much and carefully. Not, indeed, to write out what they are about to speak, unless they belong to the class who can speak freely after fully written preparation, but to write for other purposes—essays and exegeses, by way of thoroughly studying a passage or subject, articles for publication, sermons after preaching them, and the like. Writing promotes accuracy of thought as well as exactness of statement; the thought becomes objective and can thus be more carefully scrutinized. Thus our habits of writing and of speaking will maintain an equilibrium in our methods of thinking and style of expression, while yet each is practiced according to its own essential and distinctive character.

(d) If the sermon is to be used again, and has not been written out in full, it requires some renewed preparation. But this, too, is rather a gain than a loss; for thus the discourse can be more easily and exactly adapted to the new circumstances. A sermon precisely suited to one audience and occasion would usually be, at least in many of its details, quite unsuited to any other; and it is only the extemporaneous speaker that can readily make the requisite changes, which are often slight and delicate but surpassingly important to the practical result. Besides, while the times change, we are changing in them. A sermon prepared years ago will often need no little modification in order to suit the altered opinions, tastes, and feelings of the preacher himself. And then the necessity for reworking the preparation makes it all fresh to the preacher's mind and warm again to his heart. So the extemporaneous method does make the repeated use of the same sermon more laborious, but it also serves to make it much more effective.

(e) The extemporizer cannot quote so largely as the reader, from Scripture, or from the writings of others. But he is likely to quote only what is really important to the subject and thus easily remembered. Facility of quotation is not an unmitigated blessing. Those who read often quote long passages which do not increase, which some‹ times positively diminish, the interest and impressiveness of the sermon. What fits exactly, we repeat, can be easily remembered. Besides, it is often much better to borrow (with some sort of acknowl‹ edgment) the ideas of others but to state them in our own language. People are almost always more interested in this than in extended quotations. Where the quotation of the language itself is really important, and the passage long, one may read it from his Bible, or if from some other source, may write it off and read it, expressly as an important quotation. Perhaps a man who commonly speaks in an easy and familiar manner might carry with him the *Pilgrim's Progress, Paradise Lost,* or a volume of Spurgeon, and just take it up as the lawyers do and read an extract. Something like this is frequently done in controversial sermons and public discussions.

(*f*) The style of an extemporaneous sermon is apt to be less con‹ densed and less finished than if it were written out and read or recited. But this is not necessarily a fault. The style may be all the better adapted to speaking, as distinguished from the essay-style. That there is a real and broad difference between these has been strongly asserted by such masters of effective speaking as Fox and Pitt and Brougham. Copiousness, amplification, even the frequent repetition of a thought under new forms or with other illustrations are often absolutely neces‹ sary in addressing a popular audience, even if it be as cultivated as the House of Commons. Paragraphs of this sort may be preceded or fol‹ lowed by terse, pithy statements, such as those which occur so strik‹ ingly in the Epistle of James. Now we learn the writing style by writing, and we must form the speaking style in the process of actual speaking. In the case of definitions or other brief passages in which the language becomes especially important, one may fix beforehand, whether with or without writing, the precise terms to be employed. While, however, a condensed and highly finished style is not generally to be sought after in speaking which aims to make any practical impression, there is danger of a wearisome repetition, of "linked dullness long drawn out," especially of what someone calls "conclusions which never conclude." This danger can be obviated by care in preparation and in speaking, and by the constant practice of careful writing.

(*g*) A similar and more serious disadvantage is the danger of making blunders in statement. In the ardor of the moment the extemporaneous speaker is likely to say some things that are irrelevant, ill-considered, improper, and sometimes, alas! even untrue. Some men more than others run this risk, but all are more or less liable to the danger. Some hints may be given as safeguards: Make thorough preparation and thus greatly diminish the danger. Keep a cool head, no matter how warm the heart becomes, while preaching. If the slip is serious, correct it on the spot and go on; if very serious, and not observed at the time, correct it on another occasion. But for the most part leave these mistakes alone. If you have real merits and enjoy the confidence of the people, it will be one of your most blessed privileges to live down many blunders.

(h) The success of an extemporaneous sermon is largely dependent upon the preacher's feelings at the time of delivery and upon the circumstances, so that he is liable to decided failure. It is by this, more than anything else, that many men are restrained from attempting to extemporize. And yet this is a condition by which preachers will much oftener gain than lose. Many of the greatest orators have suffered from a nervous timidity in beginning their speeches and sermons. E. P. Hood[15] speaks in a striking way of "the power of nervousness as an element in successful oratory; that throbbing, thrilling nervousness of emotion united to the perfect command over the subject, and interest in it." Macaulay once wrote of one whom he describes as "the most ready and fluent debater almost ever known," as follows:

Tierney used to say that he never rose in the House without feeling his knees tremble under him; and I am sure that no man who has not some of that feeling will ever succeed there.[16]

A man not capable of failing can never be eloquent. If he has not so excitable a nature, so sensitive a sympathy with his surroundings, as to be greatly depressed by very unfavorable circumstances, then the most favorable conditions will not greatly exalt and inspire him. In like manner a method of preaching which renders failure impossible also renders the greatest impressiveness impossible. Preserved from falling below a certain level, the preacher will also be hindered from soaring as high above it as would otherwise be in his power. Nay, let a man commit himself to the occasion and the subject,—let him take heart and strike out boldly, sink or swim.

[15] *Vocation of the Preacher*, p. 245.
[16] *Life*, by Trevelyan, Vol. I. pp. 188. 220.

(*i*) The reaction and nervous depression following extemporaneous preaching are apt to be greater than in the other cases. This is perhaps inevitable but is compensated for by the greater impressiveness and effect of free delivery.

Let it now be carefully observed that all the disadvantages of extemporaneous speaking are such as can be completely obviated by resolute and judicious effort, while reading and recitation have many inherent disadvantages, which may, of course, be more or less diminished but can never be removed. The born speaker will be able to overcome the difficulties of extemporaneous speaking and will find here, and here alone, free play for his powers. We are not referring merely to the few great orators, but to all who have really a native talent for speaking, including some in whom this long remains undeveloped, through lack of exercise or because of wrong methods. Some men, not born speakers, but anxious to do good, and zealous pastors, may be able to write and read tolerably instructive and acceptable discourses, while they could never preach extemporaneously. But certainly what is best for them is not thereby shown to be best in general. Methods of speaking ought to be chosen according to the wants and the powers of those who have some gift as speakers. Very few, if any others, ought to make speaking their business.

Public speaking is one of the noblest exercises of the human powers; preaching is its highest form; and if extemporaneous speaking be the best method of preaching, it is surely worth labor to attain excellence in this—diligent and faithful self-cultivation, resolute determination always to do our best, as long as we live.

CHAPTER IV

ON DELIVERY, AS REGARDS VOICE

I. GENERAL REMARKS ON DELIVERY

IT can never be necessary to urge the importance of delivery upon persons who correctly understand its nature and who appreciate the objects of public speaking.

The famous saying of Demosthenes, repeatedly mentioned by Cicero, is sometimes utterly misrepresented. He did not say that the first thing, second thing, third thing in oratory is "action," in the present English sense of that term, but "delivery," for this, as is well known, is what the Latin *actio* signifies. And delivery does not consist merely, or even chiefly, in vocalization and gesticulation, but it implies that one is possessed with the subject, that he is completely in sympathy with it and fully alive to its importance, that he is not repeating remembered words but setting free the thoughts shut up in his mind. Even acting is good only in proportion as the actor identifies himself with the person represented—really thinks and really feels what he is saying. In the speaker this ought to be perfect; he is not undertaking to represent another person, to appropriate another's thoughts and feelings, but aims, or should aim, simply to be himself, to utter what his own mind has produced.

Why then do speakers so often and so sadly fail in respect to this chief element of delivery? Partly because many of the thoughts they present are borrowed, and have never been digested by reflection and incorporated into the substance of their own thinking. Partly because they so frequently say not what they really feel, but what they think they ought to feel, and are, it may be earnestly but yet unsuccessfully, trying to feel. And still more because they are uttering the product of a former mental activity, namely, at the time of preparation; and even if the thought and feeling were then perfectly real and genuine, yet, the mental states which produced them do now but imperfectly return. In each of these respects it is seen that the speaker is likely to be to some extent an actor; and we can easily understand how a gifted and laborious actor may become much more thoroughly possessed with thought and sentiment which are wholly another's, than a speaker wanting in gifts and labor, with such as are at the moment not wholly his own. Besides, we do not expect of the actor perfect success in this respect, and we wonder and admire that he sometimes so nearly approaches perfection; while of the speaker we naturally do expect perfection and are offended that he obviously comes short of it. For a speaker, then, and above all for a preacher, it is a matter of the highest importance that he should resist the tendency to become in part an actor, should strive most earnestly to say nothing but what he now really thinks and now truly feels. It may sometimes be that while a preacher is chagrined at having forgotten a choice expression or a treasured thought, the omission of what his mind's present activity failed to produce may, in fact, have been a gain, for it would have come in only as a dead thing, detracting from the vitality and retarding the movement of the discourse as a whole. At any rate, it seems to be clear that a preacher should seek to form mental habits quite different from those of an actor. And while men who wish to be orators are found expecting to profit by taking lessons from actors, it is all the while true that the actor is but attempting to imitate the orator. It is surely better to strike at the heart of the matter and try to be the real thing one is called to be, than to copy an imperfect copy—better to practice ourselves in saying what we really do think and feel than to learn from an actor how to say what we do not, almost as if we did.

These views receive confirmation from the strong words of one who has rarely been equalled in his appreciation and his mastery of true art.

> *Wagner.* I've often heard them boast, a preacher
> Might profit with a player for his teacher.

> *Faust.* Yes, when the preacher is a player, granted:
> As often happens in our modern ways.

> *Wagner.* Ah! when one with such love of study's haunted,
> And scarcely sees the world on holidays,
> And takes a spyglass, as it were, to read it,
> How can one by persuasion hope to lead it?

> *Faust.* What you don't feel, you'll never catch by hunting.
> It must gush out spontaneous from the soul,
> And, with a fresh delight enchanting,
> The hearts of all that hear control.

Sit there forever! Thaw your glue-pot,—
Blow up your ash-heap to a flame, and brew.
With a dull fire, in your stew-pot,
Of other men's leaving a ragout!
Children and apes will gaze delighted,
If their critiques can pleasure impart;
But never a heart will be ignited,
Comes not the spark from the speaker's heart.

Wagner. Delivery makes the orator's success;
Though I'm still far behindhand, I confess.

Faust. Seek honest gains, without pretence!
Be not a cymbal-tinkling fool!
Sound understanding and good sense
Speak out with little art or rule;
And when you've something earnest to utter,
Why hunt for words in such a flutter?
Yes, your discourses, that are so refined,
In which humanity's poor shreds you frizzle,
Are unrefreshing as the mist and wind
That through the withered leaves of autumn whistle.[1]

A speech, in the strict sense of the term, exists only in the act of speaking. All that precedes is preparation for a speech; all that remains afterwards is report of what was spoken. Whatever may be necessary for convenience in our rhetorical treatises, it is yet exceedingly important not to think of the speech and the delivery as things existing apart. Whatever be our method of preparing, we should habitually regard all as but preparation; it must be cherished and kept alive in the mind, must be vitally a part of itself, and then as living, breathing thought it will be delivered.

And as the preparation is not a speech till it is spoken, so the mere manner of speaking should not at the time receive separate attention. It should be the spontaneous product of the speaker's peculiar constitution, as acted on by the subject which now fills his mind and heart. The idea of becoming eloquent merely by the study of voice and gesture, though sometimes entertained, is essentially absurd. No one would expect to become agreeable in conversation by such means. The Athenians set a far greater value than we do upon what has been called "the statuary and the music of oratory." They listened to political and

[1] Goethe's *Faust*, tr. by Brooks.

judicial speeches with much of the same critical spirit with which we hear a professional musician or a literary lecture. Yet, they were very far from giving their chief attention to the mere use of voice and gesture. And even taking delivery in its broadest sense, we find that Demosthenes by no means treated delivery as the great thing. He took it for granted that an orator would be careful about materials, arrangement, style, and his orations show that he himself was thus careful in the very highest degree. But delivery, peculiarly important in Athens, had been for him a peculiarly difficult task. Hence his striking, hyperbolical statement—delivery is everything.

The things requisite to effective delivery may be briefly stated as follows:

Have something to say which you are confident is worth saying; scarcely anything will contribute so much as this confidence, to give dignity, directness, ease, and power to delivery. Have the treatment well arranged, not after the fashion of an essay, but with the orderly and rapid movement proper to a discourse. Be thoroughly familiar with all that you propose to say, so that you may feel no uneasiness; for the dread of failure sadly interrupts the flow of thought and feeling. Think it all over within a short time of the hour for speaking, so that you may be sure of the ground, and so that your feelings may be brought into lively sympathy with the subject; it is, however, best immediately before speaking to have the mind free from active thought, maintaining only a quiet, devotional frame. Let the physical condition be as vigorous as possible. In order for this, seek good health in general; take abundant sleep the night before speaking; at the meal before speaking eat moderately, of food easily digested, and if you are to speak immediately, eat very little; and do not, if it can possibly be avoided, exhaust your vitality during the day by exciting conversation. A healthy condition of the nervous system is surpassingly important, not a morbid excitability, such as is produced by studying very late the night before, but a healthy condition, so that feeling may quickly respond to thought, so that there may be sympathetic emotion, and at the same time complete self-control.

Above all, be yourself. Speak out with freedom and earnestness what you think and feel. Better a thousand faults than through dread of faults to be tame. Some of the most useful preachers, men in a true and high sense eloquent, have had grave defects of manner. Habitually correct faults as far as possible, but whether the voice and

the action be good or bad, if there is something in you to say, speak
it out. And by all means let there be no affectation or even artificiality.

> In man or woman, but far most in man,
> And most of all in man that ministers
> And serves the altar, in my soul I loathe
> All affectation. 'T is my perfect scorn;
> Object of my implacable disgust.
> What! will a man play tricks, will he indulge
> A silly fond conceit of his fair form
> And just proportion, fashionable mien,
> And pretty face, in presence of his God?
> Or will he seek to dazzle me with tropes
> As with the diamond on his lily hand,
> And play his brilliant parts before my eyes
> When I am hungry for the bread of life?
> He mocks his Maker, prostitutes and shames
> His noble office, and, instead of truth,
> Displaying his own beauty, starves his flock!
> Therefore, avaunt all attitude, and stare,
> And start theatric, practised at the glass![2]

2. THE VOICE—ITS DISTINCT POWERS

The voice is the speaker's great instrument. Nothing else in a man's
physical constitution is nearly so important. "For an effective and
admirable delivery," says Cicero, "the voice, beyond doubt, holds
the highest place."[3] Not every eminent orator has possessed a commanding person, but every one of great eminence has had an effective
voice. The faults which come from natural organization, such as
drawling, fineness, feebleness, defective articulation, may often be
partially remedied by judicious and patient effort; witness Demosthenes. And a voice extremely faulty in some respects may yet in
other respects have great power and be precisely suited to the mental
character of the man; witness John Randolph. Mr. Gladstone says that
Sheil had a voice like a tin kettle battered this way and that. Newman's voice was thin and weak, and Chalmers had a harsh Scotch
accent; yet, in each case the voice was in such perfect keeping with the
entire delivery and the entire man that you would not have had it
otherwise. It is said of Burke that

[2] Cowper.
[3] *De Oratore*, III. 60.

his voice, which he never attempted to discipline, was harsh when he was calm, and when he was excited he often became so hoarse as to be hardly intelligible.

This, along with the essay-style of his otherwise magnificent speeches, will account for the fact that he was commonly listened to with weariness; yet, on some occasions, when expressing certain varieties of thought and feeling, his delivery was very forcible.[4] Robert Hall had a comparatively weak voice; but he gave it effect by rapidity of utterance, and when he was excited it would swell into power. The vocal gifts of Chrysostom, Whitefield, Spurgeon are well known. From all this it appears that while one cannot be an orator of the highest class without unusual powers of voice, he may yet be a highly effective speaker notwithstanding grave defects; so that everyone should be encouraged to make the best of such vocal powers as he possesses.

A minute acquaintance with the anatomy and physiology of the organs of speech is not necessary to the orator. Even a general knowledge of them is more useful in the way of avoiding disease than of positively improving delivery.

But there are certain powers of voice which, with reference to public speaking, it is important to distinguish.

(1) Compass, the range of pitch over which the voice extends. The difference between voices in this respect is very obvious in the case of singers, but it is not less real in speaking and is a matter of great consequence in expressing the immense variety of sentiments which a speaker will feel, even in the progress of the same discourse.

(2) Volume, the quantity of sound produced, is entirely distinct from pitch, though frequently confounded with it in the popular use of such terms as "loud" and "strong." Ample volume, properly regulated will render the voice audible to a greater distance, and will make it more commanding.

(3) Penetrating power. The distance to which one can be heard, does not depend simply on volume and pitch or on distinct articulation; there is a difference between voices as to their power of penetration. A similar difference exists in the case of many other sounds, natural and artificial. The philosophy of it has not been satisfactorily explained, and the fact is scarcely noticed in treatises on elocution, but a very little observation will convince one that the difference is real.

[4] See Bulwer on Style, in *Caxtoniana*.

Indeed, penetrating power is sometimes clearly hereditary, which proves that it is a natural property of voice.

(4) Melody. This depends on both sweetness and flexibility of voice. The single sounds must be sweet, and the constant transitions in pitch, required by variations of sentiment, must be made with promptness, precision, and smoothness. A voice is not melodious if in either respect deficient.

3. GENERAL IMPROVEMENT OF THE VOICE

Cicero tells us that Caius Gracchus, when speaking, kept a servant near him and out of sight, having a flute, the note of which would now and then bring up the orator's voice when flagging or recall it when overstrained; and he judiciously adds that it were better to leave the flute-player at home and carry to the forum the habit acquired.[5] This holds good as to all vocal improvement, in fact as to all that pertains to delivery. We must seek by general exercise and care to form such habits of speech and of bearing that there may be little need to give them attention when actually engaged in public speaking.

Whatever improves the general health will improve the voice, especially muscular exercise, and particularly such as develops the chest and promotes an easy erectness of position. Singing cultivates the voice in almost every respect and probably to a greater extent than anything else except actual speaking. It is on many other accounts also very desirable that a minister should be able to sing and to sing by note; and young ministers and those preparing for the ministry should take much pains to learn to sing. If it should acquire as much time and effort to gain the power of singing church music at sight as to learn a modern language or a branch of science, it would be fully as profitable, and almost any man who is still young can learn to sing moderately well by judicious and persevering effort. Reading aloud is also of good service in cultivating the voice. It is, however, more laborious than speaking and should be promptly suspended when it becomes decidedly fatiguing. A proper management of the voice in all ordinary conversation, is a matter of the very highest importance. As in politeness and as in style, so in the use of the voice (and also in action), it is impossible for one to do really well on special occasions who is habitually careless and slovenly. We have already urged this as

[5] *De Oratore,* III. 60 f.

regards style and extemporaneous preaching, but it deserves to be repeated and reiterated. Take care that your utterance in conversation shall always be audible, agreeable, and at the same time easy and natural; and then in public speaking your utterance will almost take care of itself. Vocal exercises may be quite useful for certain purposes and to some extent. If excessive or of an improper character, they may seriously injure the organs; and there is still greater danger that they will produce artificiality. When conducted in private, under the direction of a really judicious teacher of elocution, they might be of great service in correcting special faults; but many teachers of elocution, even intelligent ones, appear singularly prone to attempt too much, to be dissatisfied with the humble task of correcting faults; they undertake to superinduce some positive and, of necessity, artificial excellence. After all, practice in actual speaking is, next to care in conversation, the main thing. But it must be heedful practice, with observation of the faults developed and effort afterwards to avoid them, or it will but confirm and render incurable one's natural or accidental defects. Someone has said: "Practice makes perfect; and bad practice makes perfectly bad."

Care must constantly be taken not to destroy individuality of voice. A man's voice is a part of himself, a part of his power; he must keep it essentially unaltered, while improved as far as possible.

A few points may be noticed, as to the means of improving particular powers of voice.

(1) Compass will be improved by nothing so much as by singing. Something may be gained by taking a short sentence and repeating it (in the open air) on a key successively elevated or lowered, to the full limit of our range of voice, taking care that the utterance shall at every pitch be speaking and shall not become half singing. In such exercises it is necessary to remember that on a low key it is best to speak slowly, and swiftly on a high key. The difference is clearly seen in comparing the lower and upper tones of a piano or violin, and the human voice is also a stringed instrument. In actual speaking, nature at once prompts the swifter or slower utterance, if only we let nature have liberty.

(2) As to volume, we gain mainly by such habitual carriage and such physical exercise as may expand and strengthen the lungs. Riding horseback, cutting wood, and in a remarkable degree certain gymnastical exercises will have this effect, as soon appears from increased breadth of chest. Taking a series of long breaths every morning before

breakfast or at any time of day when the stomach is not full will act upon the lungs and, if regularly practiced, accomplish much more than might be supposed. The habit of talking with the mouth well opened, so as to give full and free utterance (of course, without mouthing), is here quite important. Occasional loud singing (not on a high pitch) will be of service, and actual speaking, unless very badly managed, will steadily augment the volume of one's voice through all his earlier years.

(3) Penetrating power may be increased by giving the matter distinct attention in vocal exercises and sometimes in speaking. The effort should be to project the voice, to make it reach farther, without elevating the pitch or increasing the quantity of sound. By calling to a friend on an opposite hill or by fixing the eye on a distant person in a large audience and endeavoring to make him hear, we naturally develop this power; but great care must be taken not to substitute an alteration of pitch or tone. It is found by physical experiments of different kinds that pure tones, those not mixed with irregular noises, tones full, clear, steady, are heard at a greater distance than others; and this is even a more important reason for cultivating purity of tone than its effect in the way of melody.

Purity of tone applies chiefly to the utterance of vowel sounds. But penetrating power of voice is also greatly assisted by the distinct articulation of consonants. Nothing is more common than in approaching a speaker to hear sound, even loud sound, before we hear words. This is chiefly due to the fact that the speaker swells his vowel sounds but does not bring out the consonants. Yet, it is mainly these that determine the word in speech as well as in stenography.

Now as to distinctness of articulation, great faults are very common, and there is ample room for cultivation, by simple means. In conversation, reading, speaking, especially in singing (because there it is most difficult), let pains be constantly taken to articulate every letter according to its true sound, and particularly every consonant. Special exercises may be used, containing consonants often neglected, such as the strong r and the nasal sound of ing, or difficult combinations of two or three consonants, as "shrink," "expects," "fifth and sixth verses." It is on various accounts important that preachers should learn to utter with ease the forms of the second person singular of verbs, such as wouldst, blessedst, etc., which constantly occur in prayer and sometimes in exhortation. Where a consonant or combination of consonants ends one word and begins the next, there is often special difficulty. For example, "take care," "sit down." Not one in five of educated ministers will correctly articulate the words, "in the evening it is cut down and withereth." An excellent example is the saying, "It is the first step that costs."

Distinctness of articulation is everywhere much neglected by the masses of men; it is especially so in this country and particularly at the South. American English is feebler in sound than the language in England; and at the South there is already to some extent seen the general tendency of people living in a warm climate to prolong and make musical the vowel sounds, but to drop, alter, or slur over the strong combinations of consonants. This is a grave fault in public speaking. Italian is admirable for music, but for oratory, genuine English is far better. At the same time let us beware of extremes. The rolling Scotch *r*, for instance, is contrary to the established usage of America and should not be imitated. And in general, we must not show an effort at distinctness; even mumbling is hardly so bad as this. A man need not speak—a German writer suggests—like one who is teaching the deaf and dumb to talk. When one who grew up with careless habits as to articulation first attempts to correct them, he will for a while betray the effort; but this can be soon overcome, by practicing exercises in private and especially by care in conversation.

He who wishes to be heard at a great distance must speak rather slowly. There is thus a clear interval between the sound waves, and even when they have come a long way and are growing faint, they will still be distinct.

This penetrating power of voice, with the distinct articulation which aids it, is believed to deserve the special attention of all public speakers.

(4) As regards melody, we have seen that it depends on sweetness and flexibility of voice. The former is chiefly a natural quality, but it may be improved by singing; also in conversation by attention to purity of tone, avoiding huskiness, and all mingling of mere noise with the vocal utterance; and in general, by keeping the organs of speech in a healthy condition. The vowel sounds are here most important, the prolongation of these making the sweet tones. The consonants, while distinctly articulated for other purposes, must in order for melody be uttered with smoothness and ease. There is a marked tendency in this country, particularly at the North, to omit or disguise many unaccented vowel sounds, thereby greatly impairing the melody of the words and sometimes making them indistinct.

Take, for example, the shortened utterance we so often hear, of "absolute," "tolerable," "immensity."[6] This tendency ought to be studiously avoided by all who desire to speak agreeably and should be resisted and corrected by all who wish well to our language. But not a few preachers go to the opposite extreme and exhibit an affected precision. Thus in "difficult" the vowel of the second syllable should have its proper sound (though vulgarly sounded like short *u*), but in "audible," "sensible," this would be an affectation, for the disguised sound is established by the best usage.

Flexibility is necessary for the exact expression of varying sentiment as well as for melody. It will improve by practice, if one speaks with earnest feeling, and it may be cultivated by any exercises involving quick transitions from one pitch to a much higher or lower one.

Probably the best exercise is that of reading aloud . . . dialogues, in which the reader represents alternately a number of interlocutors. The animation which is characteristic of this species of discourse, and the frequent and rapid changes of the voice which are requisite to maintain the distinction of persons and characters, afford the most effective aids to the development of this power. Humorous selections also are good for this purpose.[7]

Melody is exceedingly desirable, but without possessing it in a high degree a speaker's voice may be, on other accounts, very effective. And it is a grave fault to "play tunes" on the voice, to give a sort of musical accompaniment, distinct from the sentiments uttered, as appears to be quite common in England and is sometimes seen in America, in the pulpit tone of even educated men.

4. MANAGEMENT OF THE VOICE WHEN PREACHING

A few simple hints may be profitably borne in mind.

(1) Do not begin on too high a key. One is particularly apt to do this in the open air, or in a large and unfamiliar church, or when much excited. It is wonderful how difficult a speaker finds it to lower the main key on which he has once fairly started. He may become aware of it in three minutes and make repeated efforts to correct the mistake, but in most cases he will fail; and when impassioned passages come, in which the voice must rise, it will rise to a scream. Everyone has often

---

[6] Compare Dabney's *Sacred Rhetoric*, p. 305.

[7] McIlvaine, p. 320. His chapters on the qualities and powers of the voice, and their improvement, pp. 294-320, contain a good deal that is useful.

witnessed this process. It is, of course, not impossible to change the key, and this should be carefully attempted when necessary. But the great matter is to avoid beginning wrong. Tenor voices, it is obvious, are especially apt to begin too high.

If one becomes impassioned in the early part of the discourse, he ought not then to let out his voice in its full force but reserve its highest power for some later and culminating point, as is done with the more powerful instruments in an oratorio. In fact, the voice should very rarely go to its highest pitch or to its fullest volume; there ought always to be a reserve force, unless it be in some moment of the most exalted passion. Long passages of bawling, relieved only by occasional bursts into a harrowing scream, are in every sense hurtful to all concerned.

It was speaking long on a high key in the open air, with unrestrained passion, that led many of the early Baptist preachers of this country into that singsong, or "holy whine," which is still heard in some parts of the country. The voice, strained and fatigued, instinctively sought relief in a rhythmical rise and fall, as is also the case in the loud cries of street peddlers. They were commonly zealous and sometimes great men who fell into this fault, and it was often imitated by those who followed them, after the usual superficial fashion of imitators, mistaking the obvious fault for the hidden power. To some of the ignorant people, this peculiar whine is connected by a lifelong association with the most impressive truths and the most solemn occasions; and so it touches their feelings, independently of what is said, and sometimes when the preacher's words are not heard—like the revival tunes or those familiar to us from childhood.

We must not begin on a high key, and yet the text should be distinctly heard. The difficulty thus arising when the audience is large may be overcome by stating the text slowly, distinctly, and, if necessary, a second time, and by projecting the voice, instead of elevating it.

(2) Do not suffer the voice to drop in the last words of a sentence. Though it must often sink, returning to the general pitch of the discourse, yet, it must not fall too suddenly or too low. It is not uncommon for the last words to be quite inaudible.

(3) Never fail to take breath before the lungs are entirely exhausted; and usually keep them well filled. This will generally be done without effort in extemporaneous speaking; but in recitation and reading it requires special attention. Monod says: "For this purpose, it is

necessary to breathe quite often, and to take advantage of little rests in the delivery."[8] A speaker must not gasp in his breath through the mouth but breathe through the nostrils, regularly and steadily. He must keep the head and neck in an upright posture for the sake of breathing freely as well as for other reasons; and there must be nothing tight around his throat.

(4) Look frequently at the remotest hearers, and see to it that they hear you. If particular persons anywhere in the room have grown inattentive, they may often be aroused by quietly aiming the voice at them for a moment.

(5) Let there be variety—of pitch, of force, and of speed. Monotony is utterly destructive of eloquence. But variety of utterance must be gained, not by assuming it from without, but by taking care to have a real and marked variety of sentiment, and then simply uttering each particular sentiment in the most natural manner. Emphasis requires much attention. In speaking, a correct emphasis will be spontaneous whenever one is fully in sympathy with his subject.

For the rest, let rules alone, and think not about your voice but your subject and those on whom you wish to impress it. Except that when some marked fault has attracted attention or been pointed out by a friend, care must be taken to avoid it hereafter.

NOTE.—There is a peculiar disease, produced by excessive or ill-managed use of the organs of speech, which occurs so often with preachers as to be called "minister's sore-throat." The causes of this laryngitis are apparently several: (1) Feeble health in general, especially of the alimentary system. (2) Speaking much when under the influence of depressing emotions, which tend to contract the throat. (3) Speaking when hoarse. (4) Singing when the organs are already fatigued from speaking. (5) Speaking from an elevation, and so looking down, which causes a bending and contraction of the vocal tube just at the point where this disease arises. (6) It may be added that reading is much more injurious to the throat than speaking, and preachers, even when they do not read their sermons, have much public reading to do.

Thus it appears that preachers are peculiarly liable to throat-trouble, but most of the causes can be removed or counteracted. The symptom which especially demands care is a feeling of fatigue and feebleness in the organs, so that speaking, even before becoming painful, seems burdensome and laborious. At any time, and particularly when the general health is feeble, this symptom imperatively calls for rest. But even if laryngitis has actually occurred, the matter, while serious, is not hopeless. Good medical attention, rest, bodily exercise, travel, and increased attention to the laws of health will often work a cure in a few weeks.

It is very apt to injure even a healthy voice if it be much strained in very cold or very hot air. When one has grown quite warm in preaching and goes out into cold air, it is extremely important to guard against taking cold, not so much by wrapping the throat as by protecting the whole body. Neglect of this often produces worse diseases than laryngitis.

[8] *On the Delivery of Sermons*, p. 402.

CHAPTER V

ON DELIVERY, AS REGARDS ACTION[1]

THE term "action" is now commonly restricted to what Cicero calls the *sermo corporis*, or speech of the body, including expression of countenance, posture, and gesture, but not including the use of the voice.

The freedom and variety of action exhibited by children when talking to each other shows that it is perfectly natural. Its wonderful expressiveness, even apart from language, is sometimes displayed by the deaf and dumb and by others skilled in pantomime. There is a familiar story of a dispute between Cicero and Roscius, an actor famous for pantomime, as to which could express a thought more eloquently, the one by words, or the other by signs. It many cases a gesture is much more expressive than any number of words.

How truly language must be regarded as a hindrance to thought, though the necessary instrument of it, we shall clearly perceive on remembering the comparative force with which simple ideas are communicated by signs. To say, 'Leave the room,' is less expressive than to point to the door. Placing a finger on the lips is more forcible than whispering, 'Do not speak.' A beck of the hand is better than 'Come here.' No phrase can convey the idea of surprise so vividly as opening the eyes and raising the eyebrows. A shrug of the shoulders would lose much by translation into words.[2]

He who is master of this sign-language has, indeed, an almost magic power. When the orator can combine it with the spoken language, he acquires thereby exceeding vivacity of expression. Not only his mouth but his eyes, his features, his fingers speak. The hearers read the coming sentiment upon his countenance and limbs almost before his voice reaches their ears: they are both spectators and listeners; every sense is absorbed in charmed attention.[3]

It was said of Cicero that there was eloquence even in the tips of

---

[1] On this subject profitable use has been made of the notes of lectures by the author's esteemed colleague, Rev. B. Manly, Jr., D.D.

[2] Herbert Spencer on Style, p. 11. Quintilian (XI. 3) compares also the impression made on us by pictures.

[3] Dabney's *Sacred Rhetoric*, p. 323.

his fingers, and of Garrick that by merely moving his elbow he could produce an effect that no words could achieve.[4]

How happens it that the man has so often lost this wonderful power which the child possessed? In some cases he has been hardened, even in early manhood, by the too fierce struggle of life and has lost the fresh and lively feeling of childhood. In most cases he has become constrained and self-conscious, no longer forgetting himself, as the child did, in the subject he speaks of, and whether he be timid or vain, his manner is of necessity unnatural and awkward. Thiers was at first, in his speaking in the French Assembly, vehement, oratorical—and laughed at. Talleyrand said, "Why don't you speak in the tribune as you do in the *salon*?" Thiers took the hint, adopted an easy, colloquial manner, and became a great power in debate. Action is true only when it is spontaneous and for the moment almost unconscious. Even the child becomes constrained as soon as it is aware of being observed; and, on the other hand, the shyest or most conceited man, if his whole soul be absorbed in his subject and himself for the time forgotten, again grows free and expressive in action,—so far, at least, as bad habits will now permit. And besides all this, there has sometimes been the influence of wrong notions about action, learned from unwise teachers or from casual talk.

How then shall the preacher, in this respect also, "be as the little children"? He must cultivate his religious sensibilities and a realizing faith. He must prayerfully seek to care more for his sacred themes and less for himself—to keep the thought of self habitually and thoroughly subordinate to the thought of saving souls and glorifying the Redeemer. He must remember that he himself, as the Creator made him, is called to preach the gospel, and that, with his individuality unimpaired, while faculties are developed and faults corrected, he is to do the work to him appointed. Then, thoroughly possessed with his subject, lifted above the fear of man and kindled into zeal for usefulness, let him speak out what he thinks and feels. No doubt he will make some blunders; but what of that? A child can never learn to walk without sometimes falling. But the child will not keep on falling the same way; and so the speaker's blunders may teach him something. Though probably not aware of them at the time because too busy with higher things, he may recall afterwards his faults of action or may be told of them by some kindly or perhaps some unkind critic, and next time he will notice a little, and correct or avoid them.

[4] W. G. Blaikie, *For the Work of the Ministry*, p. 234.

Some men have naturally much more action than others. And so with races and men of the same race in different regions. The more excitable nations, as the French, gesticulate almost constantly, the English comparatively little. On this subject English writers should not be heeded by us;[5] for Americans are naturally more ardent and excitable, more inclined to free and varied gesture, than the English. And the same man will have more or less action, according to his physical condition and the mood he is in, as well as according to the subject and the circumstances. Trust, then, to spontaneous impulse. Do not repress nature save where particular faults present themselves. And never force nature; for action is not indispensable, while unnatural action would be injurious. Robert Hall had usually not much gesture, though his expression of countenance was remarkable. Spurgeon had nothing very striking in his action but an extraordinary voice. On the other hand, "there is an oaken desk shown at Eisenach, which Luther broke with his fist in preaching";[6] and the apostle Paul appears to have had a peculiar and impressive manner of stretching forth his hand. Do, then, what is natural with you, and at the time. Have much or little action of this sort or of that. And always remember that you are not engaged in a tournament, but in a battle—that your great concern is not to keep within rules but to conquer.

It has been remarked above that action, the "speech of the body," includes several distinct things.

(1) Expression of countenance has great power.

But especially dominant is the countenance. With this we supplicate, threaten, or soothe, with this we are sad or joyous, elated or dejected; on this the people hang, this they look at and study, even before we speak , . . this is often superior to all words.[7]

With the exception, however, of one feature, expression of countenance is almost involuntary, and little can be done in the way of improvement beyond the correction of faults. When a man is possessed with his subject and thoroughly subordinates all thought of self, his countenance will spontaneously assume every appropriate expression.

But the exception is notable. Cicero says:

[5] For example, Whately, p. 443, says: "Action is hardly to be reckoned as any part of the orator's art."
[6] Hoppin, p. 667.
[7] Quintilian XI. iii. 72.

In delivery, next to the voice in effectiveness is the countenance; and this is ruled over by the eyes.[8]

The expressive power of the human eye is so great that it determines, in a manner, the expression of the whole countenance. It is almost impossible to disguise it. It is said that gamblers rely more upon the study of the eye, to discover the state of their opponents' game, than upon any other means. Even animals are susceptible of its power. The dog watches the eyes of his master and discovers from them, before a word is spoken, whether he is to expect a caress, or apprehend chastisement. It is said that the lion cannot attack a man so long as the man looks him steadily in the eyes. . . . All the passions and emotions of the human heart, in all their degrees and interworkings with each other, express themselves, with the utmost fullness and power, in the eyes.[9]

Now the eyes we can in some respects control. We cannot by a volition make them blaze, or glisten, or melt; but we can always look at the hearers. And the importance of this it would be difficult to overstate. Besides the direct power which the speaker's eye has over the audience, penetrating their very soul with its glance, it is by looking that he catches their expression of countenance and enters into living sympathy with them.[10] He who does not feel helped by this and does not greatly miss it when wanting was not born to be a public speaker, or has strangely perverted his nature by wrong notions and mad methods. And in addition to the involuntary effect upon the speaker of seeing the countenances of his hearers, he can watch the effect produced and purposely adapt his thoughts, style, and manner to their condition at the moment.

If a man feels as he should, his look at the outset will be respectful without timidity, independent without defiance or conceit, and solemn without sanctimoniousness, and then will spontaneously change its character with every variation of feeling.

(2) Posture also is important. In walking, standing, sitting, riding, one should take pains to acquire habitual uprightness and ease; and then in public speaking there will be little danger of his assuming any other than an appropriate posture. But there are various faults which, through lack of such habits or from mistaken views of oratory or wrong feelings at the time of speaking, many persons exhibit.

[8] *De Or.* III. 59.
[9] McIlvaine, p. 409.
[10] McIlvaine, p. 103 ff., states very strongly the value of sympathy in public speaking.

Quintilian and later writers give warning as to these and some of them ought to be mentioned.

Among the commonest faults of preachers is leaning on the pulpit. All inexperienced speakers are apt, feeling ill at ease, to have a tottering equilibrium and to look for something with which they may prop themselves. The pulpit is so convenient for this purpose that we need not wonder if a habit of leaning on it is often formed. When a young preacher finds himself inclined to this, he should not only resist the tendency while in the pulpit but should take pains in social meetings, Sunday-school speaking, etc., to stand out with nothing before him. A few early experiences will rapidly form a habit, good or bad.

The body should be simply erect. A slight inclination of the head at the opening is with most men a natural expression of deference for the audience, but it must be very slight and will disappear as the preacher grows more animated. An habitual stoop is a grave fault, both because unsightly and because hurtful to the organs of speech, and should be corrected if possible; with a few men it is natural and invincible. To "rear back," as some do, suggests, though it be unjustly, the idea of arrogance or conceit.

The arms should at first hang quietly by the side. To fold them on the breast is a gesture expressive of peculiar sentiments and to be rarely used. To place the hands on the hips, if with the fingers forward, seems to indicate a sort of pert defiance; if with the fingers backward, it suggests weakness in the back. To clasp the hands over the abdomen is offensive, and to clasp the hands behind the back, though not offensive, is scarcely graceful. To put them in the coat pockets is inelegant, and in the trousers' pockets is vulgar. To stand, as many do, with one hand in the bosom, or to occupy one hand in playing with a watch-key or guard or with coat-buttons, etc. (Andrew Fuller's practice), is in a greater or less degree undesirable. It is natural that the arms should at first hang easily by the side (with the palm towards the body), until there is occasion to move one or both in gesticulation, and that after any gesture they should tend back to the same position, though in many cases they remain for a while in some intermediate position of comparative repose.

The feet should neither be far apart, like a sailor's, nor in immediate contact. Their precise position will be determined by the man's form and habits, and rules laying down one particular posture should be rejected. The Roman orator commonly stood with the left foot forward because he bore up the toga on his left arm, and the ancient soldier advanced the left foot because his left arm carried the shield. No similar causes now exist for regularly advancing the left foot. The only ground of choice would seem to be that, if one hand is at any time actively used in gesticulating, it seems natural and easier to have the corresponding foot thrown somewhat forward. How often a speaker is to change posture will depend on his temperament and his excitement at the time; one need scarcely give himself any concern on that point, unless he happens to be inclined to a restless, fidgety movement, which is of course to be avoided. We must beware of "striking an attitude."

He who finds himself inclined to any of these faults ought resolutely to correct them, carefully to guard against them. The only real difficulty about correcting such comparatively trifling faults is that men will not think them worth the trouble. But nothing that at all affects a preacher's usefulness is really trifling. The young need have but little trouble in curing these bad habits; and for those of middle age it is still entirely possible. Resolute determination, with perseverance, and especially care to form counter habits when out of the pulpit, will commonly triumph. If such defects really cannot be remedied, one must try not to be worried about them but to do his best notwithstanding.

(3) Gesture—when we have excluded posture—denotes movement, whether of the whole person, the feet, the body, the head, or the hands. It is not natural for a speaker, if at all animated, to stand perfectly still, and it is important not to fidget about or to walk the platform like a tiger in his cage. Between these extremes, a man will change place more or less freely according to temperament, circumstances, and taste. To stamp with the foot may sometimes naturally express indignation or certain other vehement feelings, but it is apt to suggest an impotent rage; and, at any rate, it is scarcely ever becoming in a preacher. Movements of the body, such as rocking to and fro or swaying from side to side, are almost always to be avoided, and bending far forward is very rarely proper. The head has a variety of appropriate and expressive movements, but one must beware of awkwardness, extreme vehemence, and monotony.

The arms and hands have to be considered together, because in public speaking there can be scarcely any gesture with the hand that is not naturally accompanied by some movement of the arm. Thus either may be taken as representing both. The Greeks comprehended the whole art of elocution under the term "chironomy," or management of the hands. Certainly the hands and arms are in gesture of unequalled importance. Quintilian says:

> As to the hands, without which delivery would be mutilated and feeble, it can scarcely be said how many movements they have, when they almost equal the number of words. For other parts of the person help the speaker; these, I might almost say, speak themselves.[11]

But many speakers are greatly at a loss what to do with their hands, and a similar difficulty is often betrayed in the parlor and on the street. Gresley here points out an advantage of reading sermons:

> The extemporaneous preacher . . . must find employment for his hands. But when you have your sermon written before you, your hands are occasionally used in turning over the leaves of the manuscript,[12]

and so the reader, fortunate man, is not compelled to gesticulate.

It would be tedious to catalogue the faults which may be observed in gesture with the hand and arm. Among the commonest are a fluttering of the hands, which with some persons becomes a marked habit; a shoving motion, which is appropriate to express abhorrence, or any repulsion, but not otherwise; and a sort of boxing movement. Some work the arm up and down, like a pump handle, and others flap the forearm only, like a penguin's wings, instead of moving the arm from the shoulder, with the free action which public speaking naturally prompts. Angular movements are appropriate to certain sentiments but, as habitual, are very awkward. The palm of the hand, as its most expressive part, should in general be turned towards the audience and somewhat expanded.

Yet how often we see the hand of the speaker held out flat and close, like a piece of board, or edgewise, like a chopping knife, or feebly hollowed, like that of a beggar, receiving alms. Sometimes, on the contrary, we see it clinched in a style which calls up the associations of smiting with the fist of wickedness.

The clenched hand, the pointed forefinger, etc., are very effective when their peculiar meaning is wanted, and otherwise are proportionally inappropriate and damaging. It is also a common fault to bring down the hand with a slap on the thigh, a movement necessarily ungraceful, or to slap the hands frequently together, which is very rarely appropriate; and some preachers have quite a trick of banging the Bible.

[11] Quintilian, VI. iii. 85.
[12] Gresley on Preaching, p. 282.

In all the employments and circumstances of life, let the speaker see to it that his bearing shall be free, unconstrained, and not ungraceful. Then in speaking he will have little occasion to think of posture or gesture and may follow, without fear, the promptings of nature. In general, one should never repress a movement to which he is inclined because afraid it may not be graceful. After all, life and power are far more important than grace; and, in fact, timid self-repression destroys grace itself. On the other hand, never make any gesture from calculation. It must be the spontaneous product of present feeling, or it is unnatural and has but a galvanized life. He who declaims or even thinks over his address beforehand, and arranges that here or there he will make such or such a gesture will inevitably mar his delivery at that point by a fault, were he Edward Everett himself. It is inexpressibly foolish, though actually done by some teachers of elocution, to be determining how many sentences may be uttered before the first gesture. It is utterly unwise to begin gesticulating at any point from the notion that it is now time to begin. The time to begin is when one feels like beginning, neither sooner nor later. A sermon or other speech ought usually to open quietly, and therefore there will usually be no gestures just at the outset.

(4) A few simple rules may be added, with regard to action of every kind.

(*a*) Action should be suggestive rather than imitative. Closely imitative gestures, except in the case of certain dignified actions, are unsuitable to grave discourse and belong rather to comedy. In saying, "he stabbed him to the heart," one will make some vehement movement of the hand, suggestive of the mortal blow; a movement imitating it would be ridiculous, comic. A really good man, in preaching at a university, once said: "You shut your eyes to the beauty of piety; you stop your ears to the calls of the gospel; you turn your back," etc., and in saying it, shut his eyes, stopped his ears with his fingers, and whirled his broad back into view. Alas! for the good done to the students by his well-meant sermon. In "suiting the action to the word," he "o'erstepped the modesty of nature." Even lifting the eyes toward heaven or pointing the finger toward it, or pressing the hand upon the heart, etc., though allowable, are sometimes carried too far or too often repeated.

(*b*) Gesture must never follow, and commonly must slightly precede, the emphatic word of the sentence.[13] It seems to be natural

---

[13] Whateley, p. 445.

that excited feeling should find a more prompt expression in the instinctive movement than in speech, which is the product of reflection. In argumentative speaking, the gesture will naturally come with the emphatic word.

(c) Action must not be excessive, in frequency or in vehemence. To some subjects, occasions, or states of feeling in the speaker, it is natural that the action should be rare and slight. Too frequent gesture, like italics in writing and emphasis in speaking, gradually weakens its own effect. Extreme vehemence produces a revulsion of feeling in the hearer, a tendency to just the opposite of what the speaker desires. Hamlet says to the players:

> Do not saw the air too much with your hand thus, but use all gently: for in the very torrent, tempest, and (as I may say) whirlwind of your passion, you must acquire and beget a temperance that may give it smoothness.

(d) Avoid monotony. A certain unvarying round of postures and gestures, again and again repeated, is a somewhat common and most grievous fault. Akin to it, though not yet so offensive, is the use from mere habit of some favorite gesture, when the emotion felt would be better expressed by some other. The noticeably frequent recurrence of a word, a tone, or a gesture, is always a fault and, as soon as one becomes aware of it, should be carefully avoided.

In conclusion, it is proper to repeat that at all hazards there must be life, freedom, power. Do not repress nature, though it must be governed; and do not force nature. Aim not at positive improvement in action, but negative—the correction of faults as they appear. Look out for such faults. Now and then ask some true and very judicious friend to apprise you of such as may have struck him; and no one can be in this respect so helpful as an intelligent wife. Speak out freely and boldly what you feel. A man can never learn to perform any movement gracefully save by performing it frequently and with great freedom. The vine must grow, or you cannot prune it. And let us not forget that even some of a man's faults, in action and in voice, may be a part of himself. Correct them wherever possible; but better let them remain than be succeeded either by artificiality or by tameness.

CHAPTER VI

CONDUCT OF PUBLIC WORSHIP[1]

TWO tendencies are to be observed in modern evangelical churches with respect to preaching and worship. One would make preaching primary and the other parts of the church service secondary, at best, nothing more than preparatory to the sermon. The other would give small consideration to the importance of the sermon, magnifying the other parts, which by way of distinction are called "elements of worship." Nonritualistic groups have failed properly to appreciate the spiritual values of orderly worship, of dignity and solemnity of movement, and of congregational participation in responses and otherwise. The service of worship has too often become a "preaching service" in which other elements are no more than an emotional barrage to soften up the congregation for the preacher's attack. On the other hand, the ritualists have tended to discount the sermon. The minister thinks of himself as priest only, not a prophet or an evangelist. As the time allotted to the service of worship has been shortened, the subtraction has come from the sermon, and there remains only the possibility of a rather sketchy lecture on some point of theology or morals. This is the tendency not only of those churches commonly called "ritualistic," but of Baptists, Disciples, Presbyterians, and others.

These tendencies will remain where there is no proper evaluation of the various elements of worship. It needs to be said that the sermon itself is an act of worship and ought to be thought of as an organic part of the service of worship, not something different or as having a greater or less importance than other parts. The following paragraph from Morgan Phelps Noyes' *Yale Lectures* is to the point:

On any theory, the sermon should be for the congregation a creative experience in which they know themselves to be in the presence of God. Therefore, the sermon cannot arrive at God at the end of an argument, or at the end of a meandering process not to be dignified by the name of argument, nor can references to God be arbitrarily thrust into the con-

[1] The close relation between the sermon, both in its preparation and delivery, and the entire service of worship makes it highly appropriate that a treatise on homiletics should end with a consideration of that service.

cluding paragraph of a sermon where they seem ill at ease and out of place, but the whole sermon must be lived in the presence of God whether the references to Him be explicit or implicit. Some continuity of thought between the service of worship and the sermon helps to band the two together into one bundle of life. This continuity should not be so pronounced as to become monotony. Worship moves through a variety of moods, and if every hymn and every prayer center too directly in the same thought, the service as a whole loses a richness which it may rightfully claim. And yet if the sermon deals with a large theme the worship of the hour will naturally voice aspirations, thanksgivings, and confessions which come within the same orbit. . . . If the sermon links the worshiper with his Christian heritage in the Bible and the church, if it keeps constantly in touch with 'the timely and the timeless,' if it lays hold on the worshiper so that as he listens he makes his response not to the preacher but to God whose Word finds the worshiper through the sermon, then legitimately it may be said that the sermon is not distinct from the church's act of worship but is a living part of that worship.[2]

The evaluation of the sermon as an act of worship will accentuate at the same time the worship value of song and prayer and reading. The need is not more of one and less of the other but of fusing all into a harmonious worshipful whole. This does not mean that the freedom, spontaneity, simplicity, spirituality, of New Testament worship should be abandoned. The failure of many worship services to satisfy the souls of men is not because they are too simple or too free. The dissatisfaction is often caused, at least in part, by the coldness, lack of animation, want of connection, and general slovenliness which in so many cases mark our worship. We must pay far more attention to this than is common, both in the way of general cultivation and of preparation for each particular occasion. This is less necessary for those who have only to go through a form of service prepared by others than for him who, on every separate occasion, is required to produce a service, for himself and for the congregation. Thoroughly simple in form, so as not to encourage the people to rest in externals, but full of interest, animation, devoutness, solemn sweetness, and with a specific but inelaborate adaptation to the occasion—such should be our worship. That which is not interesting and impressive cannot be the full expression of warm devotion, and then the expression, by a general law, reacts upon the feeling. Externals, however they may appeal to æsthetic sentiment, can never create devotion; but animated

[2] Preaching the Word of God, pp. 178 f.

and earnest expression will strengthen devotion, and this may be achieved while carefully avoiding the danger of formalism.

It is therefore deemed important to speak of the preacher's part in the conduct of public worship. This can only be done very briefly here, though the subject deserves minute discussion and, in fact, a separate treatise.

I. READING THE SCRIPTURES

(1) In selecting the portion or portions of Scripture to be read, we should prefer such as are in a high degree devotional; for example, many of the Psalms, passages from the Pentateuch, from Isaiah and other prophets, from the Gospels, Epistles, and Revelation. These will not only instruct but will awaken devout feeling. The reading of them will naturally precede the principal prayer, whether immediately or with the intervention of a hymn. The particular kind of devotional passages selected, and the general tone of the sermon should harmonize. To read a mournful passage and afterward preach a joyful sermon, or vice versa, would be inappropriate. Still, a general harmony is sufficient; great effort to find an exact correspondence is unnecessary if not unbecoming.

But there are many cases in which the preacher wishes to read the connection of his text. If this connection is highly devotional in tone, it may be read at the usual point, as a part of the worship. If not, it should be read after the principal prayer, either before the second hymn or when announcing the text. In this case it is often well to read before the prayer some brief devotional passage, as a few verses from a psalm. Sometimes two different passages may be read in immediate succession. In all these details there is large liberty, and one need be no more bound by custom than by rubric. Good taste and devout feeling should govern, and there may be an interesting variety, without seeking after novelty. A good effect is sometimes produced by reading the connection of the text when just closing the sermon. In very many cases it is best not to read the connection at all but to make a summary statement of it in opening the discourse.

The passages selected need not begin or end with a chapter. Some preachers seem to feel bound to read a whole chapter, however long, and only a chapter, however short. We have heretofore seen that the current division into chapters is awkwardly made, often uniting matters which are wholly distinct and dividing where there is a close connection. By quietly disregarding them whenever the sense requires, a preacher will help the effect of the service and will accustom his hearers to look out for the real connection, in their own reading.

If the passage proposed contains expressions which now and to us seem indelicate, it may be either exchanged for another, or the portions in question omitted, where that can be done without attracting attention and without material loss. In general, such expressions should be read, and if so, then without the slightest hesitation, reserve, or manifestation of feeling. The beautiful air of unconsciousness seen in a refined woman, when she is led to hear or see something indelicate, is in all such cases the best model.

(2) To read well is a rare accomplishment. It is much more common to excel in singing or in public speaking. Good preachers are numerous compared with good readers. The requisites to good reading are several. First, one must have great quickness of apprehension, seizing the meaning of whole sentences at a glance; for one of the commonest faults is to begin reading a sentence with an expression which does not accord with its close; and, in fact, the reader must throughout keep clearly in mind the entire connection and read every sentence as part of a greater whole. This also shows the need of a familiar acquaintance with what is read, and, if not with the language of the passage, at any rate with its subject matter. A second requisite is sensibility, so as not only to understand but promptly and thoroughly to sympathize with the sentiment. Probably this is oftener wanting than the former. There must also be great flexibility of voice, so as at once and exactly to express every varying shade of feeling. And finally, it requires ample and careful practice. He who reads well must of course be a master of correct pronunciation, and must have acquired a distinct and easy articulation. Beyond these, everything is included in what we call "expression"; and power of expression, so far as it is not a natural gift, must be acquired by well-ordered practice. The practice ought usually to be in reading that with which one is well acquainted and in full sympathy. Besides such reading for practice, he should embrace every fit occasion of reading for the pleasure and profit of those who hear—selecting something full of interest, so that he may forget himself in the sentiment. And preachers inclined to be lugubrious ought by all means to read in private some humorous selections in order to maintain the equilibrium.

Among the different elements of expression in reading, two or three must be briefly mentioned. The first thing thought of is apt to be emphasis; and the first result of effort in this direction is usually a great amount of false emphasis. Besides the obvious fault of placing it on the wrong word, there is a subtler and very serious fault, which consists in failing properly to distribute the emphasis. Many men of ability and cultivation will throw the whole weight of emphasis upon a single word of the sentence or clause, when it ought to be divided, in different proportions, between two, or three, or several words. This point deserves special attention and practice, with mutual criticism on the part of friends. After all, the real difficulty about emphasis is in thoroughly comprehending the thought, and feeling the sentiment of what we read, as is shown by the fact that we very rarely hear false emphasis in unrestrained conversation. It may be remarked that the Book of Proverbs presents numerous admirable examples for exercise in emphasis. Very many persons read all interrogative sentences with the peculiar expression at the close which is appropriate to questions expecting the answer yes or no. Thus: Did he say he would come? But there is a second class of questions which expect an answer but not in the form of yes or no. Thus: Who said he would come? And in a third class no answer is expected, as, Will anyone ever come and help me? The distinction is here very obvious and never overlooked in conversation but frequently in reading. There should very rarely be any gesture in reading beyond some natural movement of the head, together with expression of countenance. The injunction often given by teachers, to "read precisely as if you were talking," is not strictly correct. A sort of oratorical reading is strongly to be condemned, and it may be convenient to say, "Read more as if you were talking," but the essential distinction between talking and reading should not, and in fact cannot, be destroyed.

It is particularly important that the Scriptures should be well read. A comparatively small and rapidly diminishing number of people in our congregations are now necessarily dependent on public reading for their entire knowledge of Scripture, as was so common at first, when it was said, "Blessed is he that readeth, and they that hear, the words of this prophecy" (Rev. 1:3). But as a matter of fact, many persons do not read the Bible themselves, and their minds are brought in direct contact with it only by the public reading; and others read it in a mechanical fashion without proper comprehension or impression. On the other hand, those who read the Bible most frequently and profitably at home are often most pleased to hear it read in public worship. And in general, whatever reasons there are for reading anything well, apply pre-eminently to the book of all books, the Word of God. Good reading has an exegetical value, helping to make plain the sense. It also brings out the full interest and impressiveness of the passage read. There are passages which have had a new meaning for us and an added sweetness, ever since we once heard them read, it may be long ago, by a good reader.

But to read the Bible really well is a difficult task. The common mode of printing the verses often seriously obscures the connection. The proper names require attention, that we may pronounce them readily, correctly, and yet without pedantry.[3] Far more important is the lack of full intellectual and spiritual sympathy with Scripture, which so often prevents our entering fully into the sense. There is a common tendency to be subdued by mistaken reverence into a uniform tone, devoid of real expression. The Bible should never be read precisely as we read other books. It is all sacred, and in reading even its less strikingly devotional parts there should be a prevailing solemnity; but this solemnity does not forbid a rich variety of expression, as many readers appear to imagine.

Different parts of the Bible also differ very widely in subject and style, and there must be a corresponding difference in the reading. There are narrative portions, varying from simple stories through many grades to the surpassingly pathetic or impassioned; didactic portions, of many kinds, as seen in our Lord's various discourses, in the precepts which everywhere abound, and in the elaborate and often passionate arguments of certain Epistles of Paul; and poetical portions, comprising the elevated imagery of prophetic description, both in the Old and in the New Testament, the poetical argument of Job and precepts of Proverbs, and the immense variety of lyrical passages, in the Psalms and elsewhere, presenting many phases of feeling, and often passing, in the same brief psalm, from penitence to rejoicing and praise.[4] In fact, the Bible is not so much a single book as a library, containing almost every species of composition and requiring to be read in almost every variety of manner.

One ought never to read a passage in public worship without being thoroughly acquainted with it, and this will usually require that it be carefully gone over but a short time before. Some preachers

---

[3] Never depart from the pronunciation of them which is common among educated people, unless there is something real to be gained by it.

[4] Russell, *Pulpit Elocution*, p. 295, has a partially similar classification, with some remarks upon the several classes and some good specimens of each variety.

in the course of their preparation will frequently memorize the passage; nevertheless, let it be read rather than recited. The latter tends to call attention (with admiration) to the preacher's memory and not to the meaning of what is read.

(3) It was once a very common practice, and is still wisely retained in some quarters, to make, in connection with the reading, explanatory and other remarks. These should not be so numerous or extensive as to usurp the attention due the passage itself. They should aim to explain it, to awaken interest in it, occasionally to indicate some of its practical bearings, and especially to give it effect in exciting devotional feeling. Spurgeon did this remarkably well, but many of his imitators have fallen far below the standard set by him. If there has been thorough study of the passage, and if the preacher has taken pains to acquire skill in this respect, there may be brief, lively, and yet devout remarks that will make this part of our public worship far more interesting and profitable. But random remarks, made without study and without skill, do but interrupt the reading and are sometimes a sore drag upon its movement.

2. HYMNS

(1) It is strange that some ministers should care so little for the proper selection of hymns. They surely do not consider the blessed power of sacred song or the fact that inappropriate and unimpressive hymns not only fail of doing good but are positively chilling and painful. Some take their hymns at the first opening of the book, with no care to make them suit the general tone of the service. Others are solicitous that every hymn shall be upon precisely the subject discussed in the sermon, forgetting that hymns are designed not specially to instruct, but to express and quicken devotional feeling.

To succeed well in selecting and also in reading hymns one must understand the nature and sympathize with the spirit of lyrical poetry —that is, of poetry suitable to be sung. Some men are so constituted as to do this with ease, but all will be benefited by making, as they may find opportunity, special study of the chief poets, such as Pindar and Horace, Goethe and Béranger, Burns, and the old English ballads, as well as good lyrics from many other sources. This will develop and refine not only the general taste for poetry, but the special taste for lyrics, which, besides their importance for our purpose, are among the highest and most potent forms that poetry can assume.

The devout study of the Psalms, while pursued chiefly for higher purposes, will also give one a better comprehension of the spirit of Scripture poetry. And Christian hymns, of different ages and nations, exist in rich abundance, suited to advance personal piety and at the same time to improve the critical appreciation of sacred lyrics, so that we may become able to select wisely. The most valuable of these are the patristic and medieval Latin hymns, the German and the English hymns. The first are often disfigured by more or less of unsound teaching, many of them being addressed to the Virgin Mary or the Saints; yet even these have much that is of great value, while others, including some of the very finest, are almost entirely free from objec-tionable matter and full of the noblest poetical and devout inspiration, The German hymns began to be composed at an earlier period, and many of them are unsurpassed for rhythmical movement and devo-tional sweetness. English hymns were very few before the time of Dr. Watts, early in the last century; but to the great number produced by him, and afterwards by Charles Wesley copious additions have ever since continued to be made, till now we have a goodly heritage. Most of the recent hymnbooks of the various denominations are rich with beautiful and blessed hymns, though usually containing some that could be spared. Songbooks privately edited and published for financial profit are often of inferior quality. The minister ought, by all means, whatever time and pains it may require, to make himself thoroughly familiar with his hymnbook, in order to prepare him for prompt and judicious selection, to make him ready in that timely quotation from hymns, which adds more in preaching than quotation from any other source except the Bible, and to increase his personal piety. A delightful hour may sometimes be spent by friends in discuss-ing the hymnbook, comparing favorite hymns, reading specimens, and thus gaining critical knowledge, at the same time with devotional enjoyment and profit. It is also important to examine other collections than our own, to search out the original form of hymns from the older writers which have been altered, and others which modern works omit, as seen in Watts and Rippon, in the complete *Poetical Works* of Charles Wesley, and in many of the recent and valuable books on hymnology. And there are in inferior collections homely pieces which would be at once rejected by the critics, but which have such power with the people as to provoke inquiry and often to reward it. One may also find it interesting to classify the principal writers of English hymns, according to the number and excellence of the hymns they have left us. The first class would doubtless contain Watts and Charles Wesley; the second, probably Cowper, Montgomery, and Miss Steele; the third, John Newton, Doddridge, and Beddome; and then there would be a numerous class of those who have written one or a few hymns of the highest excellence. The circumstances connected with the original production of a hymn are sometimes very interesting, and while it is seldom desirable to mention them when the hymn is about to be sung, they may occasionally be stated, with good effect, when it is quoted in a sermon.

The properties of a good hymn may be briefly stated as follows: (*a*) Correct in sentiment. Its general doctrine should be sound—which is not quite true of too many popular hymns and songs and choruses—and all its particular sentiments should be just. (*b*) Devotional in its spirit. Some, even of Beddome's hymns, are purely didactic, and not warm or moving. A good many hymns as to affliction, and as to heaven, present morbid or merely fanciful sentiment, altogether wanting in true devotional feeling. (*c*) Poetical in imagery and diction. Many hymns are only metrical prose without any touch of genuine imagination, and sometimes employing words that are alien to the very genius of poetry. But a song which is not really poetical lacks a vital element of power. Even when we chant unmetrical sentences, they must always be poetical in sentiment, the language of imagination and passion. (*d*) Rhythmical, being correct as to meter, animated and varied in movement, and yet not rugged or halting, but truly melodious. (*e*) Symmetrical, the verses exhibiting a regular progress in thought and forming a complete and harmonious whole. In a thoroughly good hymn it would not be possible to omit any verse without destroying the sense. Still, there are many useful and even delightful hymns in which this is not the case, and when the exigencies of our worship require the omission of some verse or verses, much greater care should be taken than is sometimes observed, so to manage the omission as to leave the hymn still coherent and harmonious.

It is better that the first hymn sung should not relate to the precise subject of the sermon but be emphatically a hymn of worship. Especially when the sermon is to the unconverted, must it be out of place to begin the solemn worship of God by a mere metrical exhortation to impenitent men. Of course, this opening hymn, as well as every other part of the worship, should have a general harmony of tone with all that is to follow. The hymn immediately preceding the sermon will naturally be preparatory. The last hymn will apply the sermon, or express the sentiments which the subject presented ought to excite, or form a general conclusion to the services. And it should be constantly borne in mind that specific appropriateness to the subject of the sermon is far less important in a hymn than that it should be a truly good hymn, eminently pleasing, impressive, warm. As in the case of texts, it is very unwise to avoid the familiar hymns, for they have become familiar because they are singularly good.

(2) Why should we read hymns at all, when they are about to be sung? Not only because many present, particularly in some parts of the country, will have no hymnbook, but because the previous reading brings the mind into a certain sympathy with the sentiment, so that we enter into it more fully when it is sung,—somewhat for the same reason that makes us so apt to ask that a good song may be repeated.[5] It follows that the reading ought to be animated and sympathetic. If a man cannot or will not read otherwise than in a dull, languid, monotonous fashion, he had probably better omit the reading altogether. True, the overdone, oratorical manner of reading hymns is extremely objectionable. There should be no effort, nothing but natural feeling. But then if the hymn is a good one, worthy to be read and sung at all, and if the man knows it well, from general acquaintance or from thoughtful reading not long before, it will not be natural to read it otherwise than with life and warmth. To read, in a calm and perfectly quiet manner, the words

> Jesus! I love thy charming name,
> 'T is music to mine ear,

would be, for a truly devout man, well-nigh impossible. In fact, as to all expression of feeling, cultivated people are more apt fastidiously to shrink back than to transcend the limits of propriety.

Similar considerations will show that the rhythm of hymns must never be disregarded. The singsong fashion of reading verse, often observed in ignorant men, and the monotonous inflections, regularly reproduced at the end of the first, second, third, and fourth lines by many educated men, are one evil; but it is going grievously to the other extreme if a man attempts, as some actually avow, to read

---

[5] Sometimes, particularly in informal meetings, say a word about a hymn before reading it,—as to its origin, its tone, its associations for us,—anything that will really awaken interest in it.

verse as if it were prose. The sense is predominant; but to neglect the rhythm is both to lose part of the beauty and impressiveness of the hymn and to offend by the conspicuous absence of what is naturally expected and demanded. Especially must we observe the rhythmical pause at the end of every line, not letting the voice drop or take the falling inflection, unless the sense so requires; but even where the sense goes right on, we should make a slight pause, with the voice suspended, in recognition of the rhythmical close. In all lines of any considerable length, there is also an equally important pause somewhere about the middle of the line, the varied position of which greatly contributes to the rhythmical effect. Those who have not studied the classic caesura, may, without embarrassing themselves with technicalities, easily learn to perceive the position of this pause, by privately reading many lines with a view to it, especially by exaggerating, at first, the rhythmical movement, making even a singsong. Sometimes there are two such pauses, one near the beginning, the other towards the end, of the line. These rhythmical pauses are too often neglected, though a man of good ear for music will frequently observe them unconsciously. And yet they may be mastered with comparative ease.

Not a little may also be gained from the study of English meters, particularly those common in hymns. A man's ear may for the most part carry him through, but it must often fail. There are exceedingly few persons who read verse without frequent faults, unless they have attended to its metrical structure. The task of learning the meters of our hymns is not difficult, and to classify them into the somewhat numerous varieties of iambic, trochaic (with combinations of the two), anapaestic, and (in a few specimens) dactylic verse will be to some persons a pleasant amusement, by no means devoid of profit. In reading anapaestic hymns, many of which are extremely beautiful, faults are most frequently observed.

It will, of course, greatly increase a man's skill in reading hymns and will especially serve to correct a tendency to be dolorous or monotonous if he will often real aloud from secular verse. Many a preacher would be helped with his common meter hymns by reading now and then to some friends, with full life and spirit, Cowper's "John Gilpin."

(3) With reference to the music of hymns, it is proper here to make only a brief remark. The superiority of congregational singing is beyond question. Yet, it seems generally necessary to have a choir,

whose proper function is to lead the singing of the congregation but whose well-known tendency is to usurp the whole. Hence result great evils, sadly familiar to us all. Now the preacher is the proper mediator between choir and congregation. If a lover of music, especially if able to sing well by note, he may keep the sympathies of the choir and may induce them, not by public but private requests, to sing for the most part familiar tunes; and then an occasional public and private exhortation to the people to take part in the singing will effect the best arrangement that is usually practicable. Friendly conference with the leader of the singing might also secure a better adaptation of tune to hymn than is often observed.

3. PUBLIC PRAYER

The prayers form the most important part of public worship. He who leads a great congregation in prayer, who undertakes to express what they feel, or ought to feel, before God, to give utterance to their adoration, confession, supplication, assumes a very heavy responsibility. We all readily agree, and sometimes partially realize, that it is a solemn thing to speak to the people for God; is it less so when we speak to God for the people? Whatever preparation is possible for performing this duty ought surely to be most carefully made. And yet, while very few now question the propriety of preparation, both general and special, for the work of preaching, it is feared the great majority still utterly neglect to prepare themselves for the conduct of public prayer.

The general preparation for leading in public prayer consists chiefly in the following things: (a) Fervent piety. This will include the habit of praying in private and in social meetings. If it be true that "the only way to learn to preach is to preach," it is still more emphatically true that the only way to learn to pray is to pray. And while some do tolerate preaching for practice, all will utterly condemn praying for practice. It is thus plain that no one will regularly pray well in public who does not pray much and devoutly in private. Along with this it may be observed that in every attempt to pray, under whatever circumstances, one should earnestly endeavor to realize what he is doing. (b) Familiarity with Scripture, both as furnishing topics of prayer, and supplying the most appropriate and affecting language of prayer. The minister should be constantly storing in his memory the more directly devotional expressions found everywhere in the Bible, and especially in the Psalms and Prophets, the Gospels, Epistles, and Revelation. Perhaps a few men err, in making their prayers consist of an almost uninterrupted succession of long quotations; but this is uncommon, and most of us greatly need in our prayers a larger and more varied infusion of Scripture language. (c) Study of instructive specimens of prayer. In the Bible there are found, besides the numerous single devotional expressions, various striking examples of connected and complete prayers, and very many instances in which the substance of a prayer is given though not the form. These ought to be carefully studied, for instruction in the matter and the manner of praying. Some of the long-established liturgies are also very instructive. However earnestly we may oppose the imposition of any form of prayer, there is certainly much to be learned from studying forms prepared with the greatest care and in most cases by very able and very devout men. More modern works, as collections of prayers and those recorded in diaries, will also repay occasional examination. In all such study of prayers, great pains must be taken not to lose the devotional in the merely critical spirit. The study of devotional works will also be found helpful.

The special preparation which ought to be made for prayer on any given occasion may be best understood by considering public prayer as to its matter, arrangement, language, and utterance.

(1) As to the matter, prayers will be very general and comprehensive, or very specific, according to circumstances. The simple and wonderfully comprehensive prayer given by our Lord as a model in the Sermon on the Mount and afterwards repeated in a much shortened form,[6] which is commonly called the Lord's Prayer, is a specimen of the former kind, while to the latter belongs the prayer in the seventeenth chapter of John. In both directions we often witness grave errors. Some prayers are so general as to include almost everything and thus to have no point. A prayer ought never to be indefinite and straggling but should always have certain well-defined topics; and these should, when practicable, be determined beforehand. Some who lead in prayer enter into such minute details as to be inconsistent

---

[6] See any of the recently revised texts, in Greek or English. The omission of several important clauses on this second occasion (Luke 9:2-4) and the alteration of some expressions prove conclusively that this was not meant by our Lord as a form of prayer, for on that supposition we should have him failing to repeat the form correctly. Notice how much is omitted in the corrected text of Luke.

with the character of a prayer suited to a whole assembly, and sometimes to be indecorous.[7]

Too many persons wholly omit, in public prayer, or mention only in a few conventional phrases before closing, those great subjects of supplication which lie apart from their own immediate concerns. Yet, in the Lord's Prayer these subjects occupy half the space and the first half. Prayer for missions, at home and abroad, for the increase of laborers, for Sunday schools, and other such objects ought frequently to occur—sometimes one of them being dwelt on, and sometimes another.

It is often and justly urged that we must not, in praying, undertake to instruct God. Yet, this idea must not be carried too far. Our Lord, in the prayer of John 17 states what he has been doing and explains how eternal life is attained. It is therefore proper sometimes to recite occurrences or make statements, provided they become the occasion of thanksgiving or petition. Again, prayer must not be used as a medium for exhorting the people, as is often half unconsciously done. Nor must it contain complimentary allusions. To pray with elaborate compliment for another minister present is a sadly frequent and grossly improper practice. Robert Hall erred in praying too often for distinguished persons in the audience. So with allusions to "this large and intelligent congregation." Of course, there may be prayer for particular classes of persons and sometimes for individuals, but no compliments. Allusions to political questions or any matters which are occasioning strife in the community can be justified only by peculiar circumstances and mode of handling.

Special pains should be taken to give to public prayer the requisite variety—in topics, as well as in order. Many preachers pray uniformly for the same objects, and where they also follow a fixed order and use many stereotyped phrases, it becomes virtually a form of prayer, without the advantage of having been eminently well prepared. Much may be done towards securing variety by inquiring beforehand what petitions would be suggested by the occasion or by the subject of the sermon or by the passage of Scripture just read or the hymn which has been sung. Of the topics which must of necessity be frequently introduced, some may be elaborated on one occasion, and some on another. In these, and many such ways, variety may be gained. Of

---

[7] Parker says that some of these prayers are "nothing better than catalogues of church institutions and advertisements of church work." *Ad Clerum.* p. 104, with examples.

course, there should be no straining after it, no elaborateness in the prayer, of whatsoever kind.

Any attempt to catalogue or classify the materials of prayer would be here inappropriate.

(2) The arrangement of prayer must not be formal, but there should always be a real order. It is not necessary, if desirable, that this should descend to details. The leading topics must not only be chosen, as we have seen, but arranged in the mind beforehand. All the arguments we have urged in favor of arrangement in preaching, apply, more or less, to order in prayer.

The order which seems to be usually thought most appropriate, may be stated as follows: (a) Invocation, adoration, thanksgiving. (b) Confession, and prayer for forgiveness. (c) Renewed dedication and prayer for help. (d) Intercession, for all general or special objects. Beginning with the thought of God's character and mercies, we are naturally led to think next of our own sins; and hence the order named. But adoration may also naturally be followed by prayer that God may be known and adored over all the earth (see the Lord's Prayer), and reference to ourselves, whether thanksgiving or supplication, be introduced afterwards. Or the very first words, after addressing God, may be a confession of sin and a cry for mercy. Moreover, something peculiar in the occasion, something known to be pressing upon the hearts of the worshipers, may demand a great departure from the usual order, as well as the usual selection, of topics. We must avoid the two extremes, of wandering hither and thither, and of stiff, formal, unchangeable order. Within these limits one may be guided by judgment and taste, by feeling and the occasion.

(3) The language of prayer must, of course, be grammatical, and free from all vulgarisms and oddities. It should be thoroughly simple, —not low and coarse but not learned or inflated. We must avoid elaborateness, and prettiness, which is extremely offensive to good taste and painful to truly devout feeling, but must not avoid, when deeply affected, the natural language of emotion, which is apt to be figurative and sometimes very highly figurative. Where this is really natural, it will never strike one as finery. It is one of the poorest compliments that can be paid a man to say that he made an "eloquent" prayer; earnest, fervent, solemn, deeply impressive, spiritually helpful—such are the terms to be desired, if indeed a prayer is commended at all.

Almost all who lead in prayer come to have pet phrases, whether they were originally imitated, or have only grown habitual. It is very well that the prayer of another should suggest to us topics or sentiments we had never introduced, but to borrow phrases in prayer is in wretched taste, and even unconscious borrowing should by every possible means be avoided. Yet, one hears certain favorite phrases all over the country which must have been adopted by imitation. Sometimes they involve an image, as "Stop them in their mad career"; or an alliteration, as "Choose all our changes for us," "Touch and tender their hearts" (which is bad English); or a big word, instead of homely Saxon, as "And ultimately save us," where "at last" would be simpler and better. Examples could, but need not, be multiplied, though the evil is extremely common and very hurtful. The use of such phrases seems to show that the mind is occupied with the mere externals of prayer, instead of being engrossed with devout feeling. Even where expressions are not borrowed but have merely become habitual, their too frequent recurrence is still more objectionable in prayer than in preaching.

Many are constantly repreating Oh! and Ah! or "O Lord!" or "We pray thee," "We beseech thee," and the like. Familiar language, such as the mystics use, "my Jesus," "sweet Lord," had better be avoided. The phrases used in addressing God will naturally be chosen with some reference to the connection. Thus our Lord says, "I thank thee, O Father, Lord of heaven and earth, that thou hast hid these things," etc. It is an act of sovereignty. "Shall not the Judge of all the earth do right?" is natural, rather than, "Shall not the Almighty [the All-wise, or the merciful God] do right?"

In employing the language of Scripture, as already recommended, it is quite important to quote correctly; and it is curious to observe the incorrect quotations which are heard in widely distant places, showing that they have been learned by oral tradition. "Where two or three . . . there am I in the midst of them, *and that to bless them.*" The words in italics are an addition. "Thou canst not look upon sin *with the least degree of allowance,*" spoils a forcible and beautiful image.[8] "That the word of the Lord may have free course, *run,* and be glorified," adds from the margin the word "run," there suggested as a possible substitute for "have free course." "The Lamb of God, that taketh away the sins of the world" is a curious change from "sin"

---

[8] See Hab. 1:13, where the language is, "Thou art of purer eyes than to behold evil, and canst not look on iniquity."

but is found in the Book of Common Prayer and in a Greek hymn probably as early as the third century.

(4) The utterance of prayer

should be softer, more level, . . . less vehement, more subdued. Every tone should breathe tenderness and supplication. . . . It is difficult to say which is most unsuitable to this sacred exercise—a hurried, perfunctory utterance, as of one who reads some tiresome or trivial matter, a violent and declamatory manner, as though one had ventured upon objurgation of his Maker, or a headlong and confused enunciation.[9]

The utterance must by all means be distinct—not boisterous, but perfectly audible throughout the room. To this end one should keep his head upright, not bowing forward or covering his face with his hands. It is very painful, and somewhat common, to be unable to hear. As to the precise tones to be employed, let one strive to realize what he is doing, and then speak simply as he feels, unless he becomes conscious of special faults. Some men are given to the use of a lugubrious tone, which does not belong to the natural language of penitence and love, and is sometimes ridiculous. The tone should, of course, be solemn and reverential rather than familiar, but that does not require it to be "mournful."

We must also avoid contortions of countenance and tricks of posture and gesture, which there will always be some persons to notice.

4. LENGTH OF THE SERVICES

The proper length will depend very much upon circumstances. Two centuries ago it was not uncommon, both in the Church of England and among Dissenters, to occupy from three to six hours. At present there is in many quarters a great impatience of long services, which should be neither yielded to nor disregarded. In the country, where people ride or walk some distance and have but one service a day, it may be much longer than in town. When some particular occasion demands unusual length and will make the services interesting throughout, they may be prolonged beyond the usual time. In general, while the customs of the place and the known preferences of the congregation are to be consulted, we must not allow them to bind us with iron fetters. There should be freedom and some variety so as to withstand the perpetual tendency to gravitate into formalism. Many

[9] Dabney, *Sacred Rhetoric*, p. 358.

persons regard custom as a sort of common law, more binding than an authoritative form of worship. Against this the minister may practically protest by such occasional variations as seem appropriate, taking care not to shock by abrupt or singular changes. There can be little of free, spontaneous life where it is cramped by unvarying forms, whether they be fixed by statute or by custom. But innovation merely for the sake of novelty is worse than useless.

As to the length of a sermon, it would be well for a pastor to get it understood that he may sometimes make the sermon very short, and sometimes quite long. There are subjects which can be made very interesting and instructive for twenty minutes, but to occupy thirty or forty minutes it would be necessary to introduce matter really foreign and such as will lessen the effect, or so to hammer out the style as will make it less impressive. Many a preacher has thought of subjects or texts of precisely this description and has been compelled either to abandon them or to spoil them in one of the ways indicated. Why not occasionally preach a very short sermon of twenty or even of fifteen minutes? In that case, if circumstances warrant, the other services might, without remark, be made longer than usual, pains being taken to render them interesting and impressive. On the other hand, there are subjects which imperatively demand an extended treatment and cannot well be divided. Within these limits, the proper average in towns will probably be from twenty-five to thirty-five minutes, the former being best where the habitual mode of treating a subject is condensed and concentrated, the latter where it is more discursive and varied. It is obvious that much depends on the mode of treatment. A long sermon may seem short, a short one may he "tedi-ous-brief," like the scene of Pyramus and Thisbe.

The prayers are very commonly made too long. The people cannot avoid becoming weary. It would be better to have a greater number of prayers during the service and have them shorter. In general, there may be three prayers but varying in length according to circumstances. The invocation, which opens the services—following the voluntary anthem from the choir or voluntary hymn from the congregation— is usually and properly short but might sometimes be made longer upon occasion. The principal prayer is especially likely to become too long. If there is a prayer after the sermon, it ought to vary widely in length. If the preacher, or some other who is called on, feels deeply moved, and if the services have not been unusually long, this prayer may be considerably extended. If not, it should be short, sometimes very short. Even where the sermon has made a great impression, the particular character of that impression and of the subject must determine whether it had better be followed by a prayer, or a hymn, or a closing benediction. Whitefield once rebuked a man who prayed too long by saying, "Sir, you prayed me into a good frame, and then you prayed me out of it."[10] It is sometimes well to let a hymn follow the sermon. In many churches it is customary to follow every sermon with an "invitation" hymn, during which any who desire to make a public profession of faith or to become members of the church are invited to present themselves by coming to the front. The benediction, which is nothing but a short prayer, may be preceded by a few sentences of other prayer, appropriate to the subject which has been presented.

In general, as has been intimated, the different parts of the service, reading Scripture, singing, preaching, prayer, should vary in length according to circumstances, one part being made longer when another is shorter, with no straining after sensational novelty, but with the variety which unrestricted feeling naturally prompts. The whole service should not often go much beyond the usual time of closing.

5. PULPIT DECORUM

Much harm is sometimes done by trifling acts of indecorum in the pulpit. The mode of entering the church or the pulpit should be neither bold nor affectedly humble, neither careless nor sanctimonious; the preacher should be thinking of God's truth, of really worshiping God, and be full of a desire to edify and save souls. If the preacher, especially a young man, is seen arranging his hair or his necktie, it will utterly prejudice some persons against his sermon. If his dress is slovenly or showy, it will have a similar effect. If he is seen or heard taking a glass of water or consulting his watch, while another prays after his sermon, or hunting up hymns while another prays before it, we can hardly wonder that people are offended. Two ministers should not talk together during the singing, unless there is peculiar occasion for it. In case of any special services, such as ordinations, funerals, dedications, when several ministers are to take part, the details should be carefully arranged and thoroughly understood beforehand, so as to prevent awkwardness and unnecessary conference during the service. To look about carelessly before beginning the services

---

[10] Quoted in *Ad Clerum*, p. 113.

betokens a mind little occupied with sacred things. Yet, it is far from desirable to substitute an elaborate solemnity of air. And the practice of kneeling upon entering the pulpit is of very doubtful propriety. The preacher ought to pray before beginning his solemn duties, but had he not better offer his prayer in private than in public? The following picture has become famous:

> Would I describe a preacher, such as Paul,
> Were he on earth, would hear, approve, and own—
> Paul should himself direct me. I would trace
> His master strokes, and draw from his design.
> I would express him simple, grave, sincere:
> In doctrine uncorrupt: in language plain,
> And plain in manner; decent, solemn, chaste,
> And natural in gesture; much impressed
> Himself, as conscious of his awful charge,
> And anxious mainly that the flock he feeds
> May feel it too: affectionate in look
> And tender in address, as well becomes
> A messenger of grace to guilty men.
> Behold the picture. Is it like? Like whom?
> The things that mount the rostrum with a skip
> And then skip down again; pronounce a text;
> Cry—hem; and reading what they never wrote,
> Just fifteen minutes, huddle up their work,
> And with a well-bred whisper close the scene![11]

A preacher should never exhibit irritation at inattention, or even at misconduct, in the audience. When it is really necessary to rebuke and to rebuke sharply, it ought to be manifest that he is not resenting a personal slight but affected by higher motives. And in the great majority of cases, public rebukes are better omitted. They often give offence, and the good they do might usually be reached in some other way. A kind but decided word in private is commonly much better. Few preachers have ever had occasion to regret that they had been silent when moved to public rebuke; many have regretted that they spoke.

There should be nothing self-important, or formal in the preacher's manner. It is generally better to say "I" than to use the royal "we," the plural of majesty. There may be more egotism in the latter case than the former. To avoid the too frequent recurrence of the first

---

[11] Cowper on Pulpit Proprieties.

person singular, the preacher may often associate himself with the hearers and then say "we."

After great excitement, in the pulpit or elsewhere, there is apt to be a corresponding reaction. But many persons fail to understand how a man who was so solemn during the sermon is now so light. Men of excitable nature should avoid exhibiting the effect of this reaction. Howsoever foolish people may be in criticizing trifles, we must not leave them, as to such minor matters, an excuse for finding fault.

6. CONCLUDING REMARKS

After all our preparation, general and special, for the conduct of public worship and for preaching, our dependence for real success is on the Spirit of God. And where one preaches the gospel, in reliance on God's blessing, he never preaches in vain. The sermon meant for the unconverted may greatly benefit believers, and vice versa. Without the slightest manifest result at present, a sermon may be heard from long afterwards, perhaps only in eternity. And the most wretched failure, seeming utterly useless, may benefit the preacher himself, and through him, all who afterwards hear him. Thus we partially see how it is that God's Word always does good, always prospers in the thing whereto he sent it.

Nor must we ever forget the power of character and life to reinforce speech. What a preacher is, goes far to determine the effect of what he says. There is a saying of Augustine, *Cujus vita fulgor, ejus verba tonitrua,*—if a man's life be lightning, his words are thunders.

BIBLIOGRAPHY

Revised by CHARLES S. GARDNER, D.D., *Prof. of Homiletics in the Southern Baptist Theological Seminary* (1907-1929)

No attempt is here made to give a complete list of books on homiletics and its related subjects; yet, it is supposed that the names and a brief critical account of a number of the more important works will be found helpful to the student. The books mentioned have all been tested by use or personal examination. It will be proper to mention: (1) Books upon general rhetoric. (2) Those which are particularly devoted to homiletics. (3) Those upon some subjects related to homiletics.

I. WORKS ON GENERAL RHETORIC

1. *Ancient Works.*—Some of the ancient works are especially deserving of mention. Aristotle's *Rhetoric* ought by all means to be studied in a translation, as that of Bohn's Library, if it cannot be read in original.

Longinus *On the Sublime* is celebrated and interesting.

Cicero's treatises on oratory, *De Oratore, Orator,* and *Brutus,* are quite unsystematic and incomplete but are full of striking thoughts and useful suggestions.

Quintilian's *Instruction of the Orator* ought by all means to be read by anyone who wishes to go to the bottom of the subject.

2. *Modern Works.*—Campbell's *Philosophy of Rhetoric,* though somewhat dry and difficult, is a remarkably able work and will repay careful study.

Among newer works, the following may be mentioned as especially valuable: *Vital Elements of Preaching* by Prof. Arthur S. Hoyt is a very sensible volume for effective preaching. Day's *Art of Discourse* is a thoroughly good book, perhaps a little too stiff in form, but analytical, clear, and sensible. Prof. J. H. Gillmore's *Art of Expression* is a condensed but lucid and helpful little work. Bain's *Composition and Rhetoric* has been a very useful treatise. The *Practical Rhetoric* and the *Hand-Book of Rhetorical Analysis,* by Prof. John F. Genung, are very sensible and useful discussions. Prof. A. S. Hill has two treatises, both of high order, namely, *The Foundations of Rhetoric,* and *The Principles of Rhetoric,* the latter being for more advanced students. *The Science of Rhetoric,* by D. J. Hill, is, as its name indicates, a treatise on the principles of rhetoric for advanced classes, and contains much that is valuable. One of the best recent books is *English Composition,* by Prof. Barrett Wendell of Harvard. It eschews the severe analytic form of most textbooks, and has a right to be esteemed for its own literary merits. The same may be said of the delightful volume of the late Austin Phelps on *English Style in Public Discourse.*

II. WORKS ON HOMILETICS

1. *Ancient.*—Chrysostom on the *Priesthood* is a charming little work and contains several excellent passages on preaching. The original may be had in a separate volume, and it has been newly translated into English by B. H. Cowper. Augustine was a teacher of rhetoric before his conversion, and in his treatise *De Doctrina Christiana* (On Christian Teaching), he devotes Book IV to instruction in the setting forth of Christian truth, giving many interesting and useful thoughts.

2. *German.*—Palmer's *Homiletik* is by a popular Lutheran writer and has decided merits. Otto's *Evangelische Praktische Theologie* is unusually full on this subject and on several branches of it is decidedly able. More recent is the *Geschichte und Theorie der Predigt* of Th. Harnack. It has the excellences and faults of the German method and point of view but is a suggestive and valuable treatise.

3. *French.*—Fénelon's *Diologues on Eloquence* are very readable, and excellent on some points. They may be found in the good collection entitled *The Preacher and Pastor.* Claude's *Essay on the Composition of a Sermon* is quite valuable and has exerted a wide influence. There are a number of English editions of this. Vinet's *Homiletics* (translated by Skinner) was published from his notes and those of some of his students after his death and, notwithstanding this defect, is on many subjects very valuable and interesting. Adolphe Monod's *Lecture on the Delivery of Sermons* is singularly good. It is published as an appendix in Fish's *Select Discourses* translated from the French and German.

4. *English.*—Campbell's *Lectures on Pulpit Eloquence* are judicious and useful, while quite brief. *Ad Clerum,* by the famous London preacher, Joseph Parker, is a lively and interesting little book, though not always judicious. The Rev. E. Paxton Hood has two entertaining and helpful volumes on preaching, *The Throne of Eloquence* and *The Vocation of the Preacher.* Spurgeon's three series of *Lectures to My Students* discuss miscellaneous topics relating to preaching and are full of striking suggestions and expressions and of devout earnestness. The second series attends especially to delivery, and the third to the art of illustration. *For the Work of the Ministry,* by Prof. W. G. Blaikie of Edinburgh, treats of both preaching and pastoral work. It is brief but full of good sense.

Among more recent works several should be mentioned. Highly useful in many ways is *The Christian Preacher* by Alfred E. Garvie; but the author seeks to cover too much ground in a single volume. After an elaborate introduction, he discusses the history of preaching, the credentials, qualifications and functions of the preacher, and the preparation and production of the sermon. Bull's *Preaching and Sermon Construction* also deals with the general problems of preaching as well as with the preparation of sermons. The work is elaborate and too prolix but is suggestive and helpful to the thoughtful student. Pattison's *The Making of a Sermon* is always good. *The Art of Preaching* by David Smith combines a sketch of the history of Jewish prophecy, Greek rhetoric and apostolic preaching with the preparation and delivery of sermons. It is well written and thoughtful but too sketchy. *The Preacher and His Sermon,* by Patterson Smyth, is a stimulating little volume.

5. *American.*—Our country has produced a large number of excellent books on homiletics. Among them may be mentioned the following: *Homiletics,* by D. P. Kidder is very complete in its range of topics and contains much that is good; but it is very unequal in its discussions, and the views presented on some subjects are regarded as objectionable. Alexander's *Thoughts on Preaching,* though fragmentary, is a capital book, stimulating and full of good things. *Christian Rhetoric,* by Rev. G. W. Hervey, is a noteworthy, and, for discriminating students valuable work. He attempts to reconstruct rhetoric for the pulpit entirely by biblical examples. He makes, therefore, a wide distinction between homiletics and rhetoric.

Of a somewhat similar character is *The Oratory and Poetry of the Bible* by F. S. Schenk, who, in the form of letters written by imaginary hearers of the prophets and of the preachers of the New Testament, seeks to help the reader to realize the individual qualities and power of those great messengers from God.

Shedd's *Homiletics and Pastoral Duties* is an excellent work. It discusses certain topics with the author's well-known power of analysis and vigor of statement. It is an admirable book to be read by those who are acquainted with the subject in general or to be studied in connection with some systematic treatise.

Homiletics, by Prof. James M. Hoppin, is a revised and enlarged edition of the homiletical matter contained in the earlier work on *Preaching and the Pastoral Office.* The sketch of the history of preaching is quite copious but altogether fragmentary. The arrangement is somewhat faulty and inconvenient; but the particular topics are discussed with marked ability and sound judgment and show a good acquaintance with the literature of the subject.

There are three very valuable works on the general subject of homiletics by the late Prof. Austin Phelps of Andover. The first of these is the *Theory of Preaching.* It is the fruit of long-continued instruction in the Andover Seminary. The work was made on the principle of answering questions that had at one time or another been raised by the students. The result is a unique volume, crowded with good thoughts and valuable hints, but it is not a complete or well-organized treatise. The style is clear, vivid, and strong. *Men and Books* treats of some subjects omitted in the *Theory of Preaching*, giving valuable suggestions as to the study of human nature and of literature. It is a very excellent treatise for the young preacher and pastor. *English Style in Public Discourse* treats of style with especial reference to the pulpit and is a book of great merit.

Sacred Rhetoric, by Dr. R. L. Dabney (Presbyterian), is a valuable and suggestive treatise on the theory of preaching and contains many judicious observations and sound principles.

Manual of Preaching, by Prof. Franklin W. Fisk of Chicago (Congregational) Theological Seminary, is an able textbook, clear, sensible, and just.

To the foregoing should be added Herrick Johnson's *The Ideal Ministry*, and Hoyt's *The Work of Preaching*, both well-balanced, sensible, and complete treatises.

There have appeared in recent years a number of volumes, which, while not dealing with the technique of preparation and delivery of sermons, are very suggestive and illuminating discussions of various aspects of the work of preaching. Only the titles of these volumes with their authors' names can be given; but although of unequal merit, every one of them is worthy of a place in every minister's library—*A Vital Ministry*, by W. J. McGlothlin; *Making Good in The Ministry*, by A. T. Robertson; *Ambassadors of God*, by S. Parkes Cadman; *The Highest Office*, by Jeff D. Ray; *The Minister and His Ministry*, by John M. English.

6. *The Yale Lectures on Preaching.*—In 1871 a lectureship on preaching was founded in connection with Yale Divinity School by Mr. Henry W. Sage of Brooklyn, a member of Henry Ward Beecher's Plymouth Church. In honor of Mr. Beecher's distinguished father, it was named the Lyman Beecher Lectureship on Preaching. Every year since that time some distinguished minister of America or from abroad has delivered a series of lectures on this foundation. Many of them have been published, and they constitute a valuable series of lectures upon the various aspects of preaching. Only a few of the more notable ones will be singled out for special mention.

First in order of time are the three series by Henry Ward Beecher, who delivered the lectures for the first three years. The first series related to preaching, the second to pastoral work, and the third to subjects of preaching. The first and second volumes are of great value, fresh, often very striking and everywhere suggestive. The works, however, are characterized by Mr. Beecher's fondness for half-truths, and they need to be read with discrimination.

The most valuable of the Yale course are the *Lectures on Preaching*, by

Phillips Brooks. The great preacher's noble characteristics appear in this volume. It is full of sound sense, deep spirituality, and eminently helpful suggestion. The style is very agreeable and striking.

The *Nine Lectures on Preaching,* by the late R. W. Dale of England, while very unequal in their treatment, contain much that is interesting and useful. The style is somewhat diffuse.

The volumes by Dr. Wm. M. Taylor, Bishop Matthew Simpson, Dr. John Hall, Dr. E. G. Robinson are all of considerable practical value and interest.

The *Lectures,* by Dr. Nathaniel J. Burton, delivered in 1884, to which have been added some other lectures and writings, is a unique book. The author was a very original and powerful man, and while one would dissent from many of his statements, his book is a suggestive and highly stimulating work.

The lectures of more recent years pay attention rather to the subjects of preaching, and the adaptation of preaching to the times. Among these should be mentioned *The Gospel for an Age of Doubt,* by Dr. Henry Van Dyke. It is written in admirable style and contains very useful suggestions as to the sort of preaching needed for the times. *The Cure of Souls* by Dr. John Watson, better known by his literary name of Ian Maclaren, is a genial, agreeably written, and suggestive book, but is marred by some serious errors.

Verbum Dei, the series for 1893, by the Rev. Robert F. Horton of England, is noteworthy, as having inculcated the opinion that preachers of today have a right to expect and should seek a real inspiration of God as much as the prophets and the apostles. There is much in the book that is good and striking, but this unscriptural and misleading position is a serious objection.

The Educational Ideal in the Ministry, by W. H. P. Faunce is marked by a broad conception of the minister's work and stresses with great power his need for a rounded, up-to-date culture to fit him for preaching in this age. Gunsaulus' *The Minister and the Spiritual Life* shows clear insight into the minister's personal problems. George Adam Smith's *Modern Criticism and the Preaching of the Old Testament* undertakes in an admirable style to help preachers to maintain positive faith and proclaim a positive message while accepting modern views of the Bible. Forsyth's *Positive Preaching and the Modern Mind* is very helpful also in fortifying the heart of the preacher in a positive faith while keeping an open mind toward scientific conceptions of the world. Jowett's *The Preacher: His Life and Work* treats the modern preacher's problems with rare insight and experienced sympathy. *The Romance of Preaching,* by Sylvester Horne discusses some of the great preachers of history in a style quite in keeping with the title of his lectures. Henry Sloane Coffin discusses with excellent judgment the minister's function of social leadership in a series entitled

In a Day of Social Rebuilding. In *A Voice from the Crowd* Mr. George Wharton Pepper, a layman, now United States Senator from Pennsylvania, tells us in a very interesting way how the preacher and preaching appear to the modern man in the pew. William Pierson Merrill discusses with much vigor a very live problem in *The Freedom of the Preacher.* The *Art of Preaching* by Charles Reynolds Brown is limited to a discussion of the sermon, but the method is not technical and his volume abounds in good sense and spiritual insight.

III. WORKS ON SUBJECTS RELATED TO HOMILETICS

1. *History of Preaching.*—Some works on this subject should be mentioned. The treatment of the history in Hoppin's *Homiletics* has already been noticed and is valuable. Moule's *Christian Oratory During the First Five Centuries* is an excellent little volume. Neale's *Mediæval Preachers and Preaching* is interesting but not very profound. Broadus' *Lectures on the History of Preaching* were delivered at Newton Theological Institution in 1876 and published soon afterwards. *Lectures on the History of Preaching,* by Prof. John Ker of Scotland, were published after his death. These lectures are somewhat fragmentary, but are well written and full of useful information on the topics and times of which they treat. The great and elaborate work of E. C. Dargan, *The History of Preaching,* transcends all other contributions to this subject. It is painstaking in attention to details and broadly comprehensive in its scope, leaving little to be done in this field. His more recent little book is called *The Art of Preaching in the Light of Its History.*

2. *On Oratory.*—*Oratory and Orators,* by Prof. William Matthews, contains much that is interesting and suggestive. *The History of Oratory,* by Prof. Lorenzo Sears of Brown University, is a very valuable and comprehensive, though brief discussion of the subject. *The Attic Orators,* by Prof. R. C. Jebb, is the most learned work upon the particular epoch indicated and is a book of permanent value. Goodrich's *British Eloquence* is an admirable collection of speeches, with introductions and notes, enabling one to understand them and very useful to the student of eloquence.

3. *Psychology.*—There have been some recent attempts to make an application of psychology to preaching. The forerunner in this field was Kennard's *Psychic Power in Preaching.* It is suggestive and helpful but does not approach the subject from the point of view of the more recent developments in psychology and is lacking in thoroughness of treatment. C. S. Gardner's *Psychology and Preaching* takes the functional point of view in psychology and undertakes a service for preachers similar to that done for teachers in the application of psychology to their work.

Adams' *Exposition and Illustration in Teaching* should be mentioned in this connection. Though intended for teachers, it is of almost equal value to preachers and is exceedingly rich in suggestion.

4. *Logic.*—The two great works for the English student on logic are the *Lectures* of Sir William Hamilton for deductive logic, and the *System of Logic*, by John Stuart Mill, for inductive logic. *The Theory of Thought*, by Prof. Noah K. Davis of the University of Virginia, is a profound discussion of the Aristotelian and Hamiltonian systems of deductive logic, with the addition of much that is of value by the author himself. *The Principles of Science*, by W. Stanley Jevons, is that author's most complete treatise on the general subject of inductive logic and contains much of value. Sidgwick on *Fallacies,* though written in the interest of the evolutionary theory, is a very thoughtful treatment of that particular subject.

All these are books for the more advanced students. Of the more elementary works, the following may be mentioned. For the beginner, the treatises by Prof. N. K. Davis on inductive and deductive logic, respectively, are useful. These two little volumes contain the very cream of the author's thinking and teaching upon this subject. They are admirable books.

The more recent works on this subject usually deal with the psychology of the thinking process. Of great value is Dewey's *How We Think,* a brief but very satisfactory work. Perhaps equally valuable, though more extended, are *The Psychology of Thinking* by Miller, and *The Psychology of Reasoning* by Pillsbury.

5. *English and Style.*—There is such a multitude of textbooks on this subject that the bare mention even of the best would itself fill a volume. Only a few among the best, therefore, will be noticed.

Of English grammars the great works are two German books, both of which have been translated. One is by Maetzner and the other by Koch. These are very thoroughgoing and scientific treatises upon the subject of English grammar. There is also a very useful and interesting work by Prof. Samuel Ramsey, *English Language and English Grammar.* To these may be added Whitney's *Essentials of English Grammar,* Bain's *Higher English Grammar,* and Morris's *Elements of Historical Grammar.*

There are works which treat of errors and the proper writing of English, many of which deserve notice. *Vulgarisms and Other Errors of Speech,* published by Claxton, Philadelphia, is a good help. Meredith's *Every Day Errors of Speech* is good. *English Lessons for English People,* by Seeley and Abbott, and *How to Parse,* by E. A. Abbott, are also helpful in securing accuracy in writing English.

A few special treatises on the English language should be noticed: Marsh's *Lectures on the English Language,* in the new edition; A. S. Hill, *Our English,* in the Chautauqua series; Oliphant's *Standard English,* and the several volumes of Richard Grant White. *English Prose,* by Prof. John

Earle of the University of Oxford, is a great book, treating of the subjects, elements, history, and usage of English prose. The book will repay earnest study. On English philology, the *Etymological Dictionary* of W. W. Skeat is very valuable. Professor Earle has also a valuable book on *English Philology.* In general studies Smith's *Synonyms Discriminated* is perhaps the best on that subject. Roget's *Thesaurus* (in the latest edition) is still a work of value. Likewise the little books of Archbishop Trench, though somewhat out of date, are still worth reading,—on *Words and Their Uses,* and on *English Past and Present.* Bishop Fallows has a useful compendium of *Synonyms and Antonyms,* with some other matters added. There is also a recent book of *Synonyms* by James C. Fernald, published by Funk and Wagnalls. Mention should also be made of Soule's *Synonyms.*

6. *Delivery and Elocution.*—*The Art of Extempore Speaking,* by Bautain, contains some valuable suggestions; also *The Spoken Word,* by Thomas J. Potter, is good. *Pulpit Elocution,* by William Russell, contains many useful and practical suggestions; and *Vocal Culture,* re-edited by the Rev. Francis T. Russell, is a useful and practical treatise. *Extempore Speech,* by Pittenger, is useful. *Extempore Preaching,* by Wilder Smith, has much good sense and is valuable. *Preaching Without Notes,* lectures by Dr. R. S. Storrs, is also very useful on extemporaneous preaching.

SUPPLEMENTARY BOOK LIST

I. *Homiletics*

Allen, Arthur, *The Art of Preaching* (1943).
Blackwood, A. W., *The Fine Art of Preaching* (1937).
Bryan, D. C., *The Art of Illustrating Sermons* (1938).
Bull, P. B., *Preaching and Sermon Construction* (1922).
Davis, Ozora S., *The Principles of Preaching* (1924).
Gowan, Joseph, *Homiletics,* or *The Theory of Preaching* (1922).
McComb, Samuel, *Preaching in Theory and Practice* (1926).
Patton, C. S., *Preparation and Delivery of Sermons* (1938).
Prichard, H. A., *The Preacher, the Method and the Message* Part II, (1932).
Reu, M., *Homiletics* (1922).

II. *Public Speaking*

Anderson, V. A., *Training the Speaking Voice.*
Borden, R. C., *Public Speaking as Listeners Like It.*
Brigance and Immel, *Speechmaking: Principles and Practice.*
Eisenson, Jon, *Psychology of Speech.*
Murray, Elwood, *Speech Personality.*
Woolbert and Nelson, *The Art of Interpretative Speech.*
Woolbert and Smith, *Fundamentals of Speech.*

III. *Preachers and Preaching*

Atkins, G. G., *Preaching and the Mind of Today.*
Bailey, A. M., *Stand Up and Preach.*
Black, J. M., *The Mystery of Preaching.*
Blackwood, A. W., *Preaching from the Bible.*
     " , " , *Planning a Year's Pulpit Work.*
Booth, J. N., *The Quest of Preaching Power.*
Buttrick, G. A., *Jesus Came Preaching.*
     " , " , (and others), *Preaching in These Times.*
Cairns, F., *The Prophet in the Heart.*
Christman, L. H., *The Message of the Christian Pulpit.*
Christie, D., *The Service of Christ.*
Coffin, H. S., *What to Preach.*
Crocker, L. G., *Henry Ward Beecher's Speaking Art.*
Day, A. E., *Jesus and Human Personality.*
Dodd, C. H., *The Apostolic Preaching and Its Developments.*
Farmer, H. H., *The Servant of the Word.*
Garvie, A. E., *The Preachers of the Church.*
Fosdick, H. E., *The Modern Use of the Bible.*
Hughes, T. H., *The Psychology of Preaching and Pastoral Work.*
Hutton, J. A., *That the Ministry Be Not Blamed.*
Jones, E. D., *American Preachers Today.*
Kerr, H. T., *Preaching in the Early Church.*
Luccock, H. E., *Preaching Values in New Testament Translations.*
McConnell, F. J., *The Prophetic Ministry.*
Meyer, F. B., *Expository Preaching: Plans and Methods.*
Montgomery, R. A., *Expository Preaching.*
Morgan, G. C., *Preaching.*
Newton, J. F., *The New Preaching.*
M. P. Noyes, *Preaching the Word of God.*
Miller, H. C., *The New Psychology and Preaching.*
Oman, J., *Concerning the Ministry.*
Oxnam, G. B., (editor), *Creative Preaching,*
                                 Contemporary Preaching,
                                 Effective Preaching,
                                 Varieties of Present-Day Preaching.
Patton, C. S., *The Use of the Bible in Preaching.*
Park, J. E., *The Miracle of Preaching.*
Poteat, E. M., Jr., *Rev. John Doe, D. D.*
Ray, J. D., *Expository Preaching.*
Reid, J., *In Quest of Reality.*
Roberts, R., *The Preacher as a Man of Letters.*
Sockman, R. W., *The Highway of God.*

Sperry, W. L., *We Prophesy in Part.*
Stidger, W. L., *Symphonic Sermons.*
Thompson, E. T., *Changing Emphases in American Preaching.*
Vance, J. I., *Being a Preacher.*

INDEX